D1351878

Journeying
With
The Lord

Reflections for Every Day

CARLO MARIA MARTINI
CARDINAL ARCHBISHOP OF MILAN

JOURNEYING WITH THE LORD

Reflections for Every Day

ALBA · HOUSE   NEW · YORK

SOCIETY OF ST. PAUL, 2187 VICTORY BLVD., STATEN ISLAND, NEW YORK 10314

Translated from the original Italian edition, *Sulle Strade del Signore* (Piemme-Ancora), by Rev. Thomas Fogarty, S.S.P. and James Provenzano.

© 1987 by the Society of St. Paul
With Ecclesiastical Approval
ISBN: 0-8189-0508-5

Printed in Italy

**Help us, O Lord,
not to remain sequestered
within the Cenacle walls.**

Foreword

We thank you, Lord, because this Word, spoken two thousand years ago, is alive and efficacious in our midst today.

We recognize our impotence and incapacity to understand it and to allow it to live within us. It is more powerful, more potent than our weakness, more efficacious than our frailty, more penetrating than our resistance.

For this reason, we ask you to illuminate this Word for us in order that we might take it seriously. Open our hope to that which you want to manifest to us. Give us confidence in our life and grant that this Word might operate in us according to the richness of its power.

Mother of Jesus, to whom He entrusted Himself without reserve, asking that He might come unto you according to the Word which He spoke to you, give us a spirit of availability that we might discover the truth about ourselves. Give us the grace to help others to find the truth of God about Himself. Grant that the world and the society in which we find ourselves and which we wish to serve might likewise find it.

We ask this, Father, through Jesus Christ, Your Word Incarnate, through His death and Resurrection and through the Holy Spirit who continuously renews in us the strength of this Word, now and forever. Amen.

Carlo Maria Martini

TABLE OF CONTENTS

MARCH

APRIL

MAY

AUGUST

SEPTEMBER

OCTOBER

NOVEMBER

DECEMBER

Introduction

1. Does the Lord provide many different "ways" or "journeys" or "pilgrimages," as it were, for us? The title in fact recalls a trip with the Lord that harkens back to an historical period of travail for ancient Israel: the great Babylonian exile.

The bard who sings about the topography of this divine journey is Second Isaiah: "See I am doing something new! Now it springs forth; do you not perceive it? In the desert I make a way, in the wasteland, rivers" (Is 43:19). "They shall not hunger or thirst, nor shall the scorching wind or the sun strike them: For he who pities them leads them and guides them beside springs of water. I will cut a road through all my mountains, and make my highways level" (Is 49:10-11).

Isaiah also puts us on guard against the confusion we easily fall into trying to choose between the ways of man and the pathways of God: "Seek the Lord while He may be found; call Him while He is near. Let the scoundrel forsake his way, and the wicked man his thoughts; Let him turn to the Lord for mercy; to our God, Who is generous in forgiving. For My thoughts are not your thoughts, nor are your ways My ways, says the Lord" (Is 55:6-8).

The history of salvation, of our journey with God, begins with an invitation to migrate (Gn 12:1-5): Abraham is the man *par excellence* of the journey with God.

The exodus is another highly symbolic journey for believers of every generation.

And in her prayer, Israel confesses her own faith and asks help in order to be able to know and to follow the ways of the Lord: "All the paths of the Lord are kindness and constancy toward those who keep His covenant and His decrees" (Ps 25:10). "Happy are you who fear the Lord and walk in His ways" (Ps 128:1). "Just is the Lord in all His ways, holy in all His works" (Ps 145:17).

It is in the meeting with Jesus of Nazareth that we are finally able to recognize how all these "ways" of man can become God's "ways," or "journeys with the Lord" when they are made together with Jesus who is *the* "Way" (Jn 14:6). Christianity itself is referred to in the Acts of the Apostles as the "way" (Ac 9:2; 18:25; 24:25).

It is, therefore, important to be able to put into practice the recommendations of Paul, if our life is to have sense: "Walk, therefore, in the Lord Jesus Christ Whom you have received . . ." (Col 2:6).

It is revealing to realize that the "ways" or "paths" are "of the Lord," not so much because they bring us closer to Him but because they are traveled by Him or by us but in His company, "with the Lord" — He working in us. We exist in the primacy of the "economy" of God's grace, more than in the primacy of our own abilities, strength or personal merit.

2. Here is how the new Archbishop of Milan, on the day of his taking office, expressed himself: "I come among you, therefore, as one sent by the Lord by means of the mandate conferred on me by Pope John Paul II: and I come in order to bring you a message, that of which St. Paul speaks to the Corinthians. It is the 'good news which you have received, in which you stand firm and from which you will also receive your salvation: that is

Jesus Christ, dead and risen,' the Redeemer of mankind, of each man and of each woman who comes into this world. Jesus Christ Who died for us; Jesus Christ Who is living and Who loves us as only God knows how to love. Jesus proclaimed in our preaching and in our catechesis, glorified in the liturgy. Jesus our justice, our food, our life, our pardon, our hope, our guileless and transparent friend. Jesus must increase in each one of us and in each of our communities just as love grows. Jesus, Son of God, manifestation of the goodness of God Who places Himself at our service on behalf of all the men and women of our time, and especially of the sick, the oppressed, the afflicted, the desperate. This is the sole object of my message, the only thing which I will have at heart to say and to repeat to you with gestures and words, in public and in private, to all of you and with all of you, and especially to the clergy, as long as the Lord gives me life and breath.''

3. These words are at the beginning of this volume: they are the reason behind it and the inspiration which motivated it.

In our study of religious and theological literature we were often reminded of the importance of having a theme, a thought for our meditation each day. There are those who know how to meditate by following a method; there are those who can place themselves in front of a written passage and be moved by the desire to speak to the Lord; and there are those who simply need a short reminder to enable them to recall a word or a resolution they have made during the course of the day.

4. The Office of Readings in the Liturgy of the Hours and in general the liturgical readings of the Word of God during the Mass; the short readings of the orations at Morning or Evening Prayer during the liturgical year are

like little crumbs of bread from the Word, day after day, which give us an appetite for a very precise need which, however you may want to call it, is born of the living dynamism of our faith and simply must be fed.

5. The problem lies always in how to promote and satisfy this desire to pause, to linger purposefully for awhile over an inspiration, a bit of encouragement to live willingly and with joy the duties of the day.

Perhaps it would be better to ask ourselves, in language more specifically Christian, how we can nourish ourselves from those pages which help us to recognize the presence of the Lord at work in our history? What pages should we go to in order to begin a new day with the will to love, to do good, notwithstanding everything, with the strength that comes to us from the love of the Spirit?

6. The words of Scripture are our first nourishment. Then how many pages from the Fathers of the Church like Augustine, Hilary, Ambrose, Clement of Alexandria, Cyril of Jerusalem, Basil, Leo the Great, Gregory the Great, are a gold mine of extraordinary inspiration!

It may not be easy, however, for all to draw near to the Scriptures in an authorized translation as has been proposed. And it isn't always easy to understand how to enjoy the works of the great masters of the faith who in the early centuries, in a cultural context very different from our own, interpreted the Word and educated the faith of their communities.

7. There is a service of the Word — and hence of the Presence of the Lord, our Intercessor — which is put into effect for us through the ministry of the pope and the bishops. It is important to read once again their teachings and in an organized and fruitful way, to be guided by their wisdom to open ourselves to the gift of the Lord and to the

meaning of life thanks to their writings.

8. This book — with simplicity, but not without depth and richness — brings us close to the teachings of over fifteen years by now of the Archbishop of Milan, Cardinal Carlo Maria Martini, S.J.

It is not given to everyone to read all that the Archbishop of Milan has written or preached in his Cathedral to those who want to approach the Word of the Lord. It is a matter then of being able at least to approach a few selected pages, to become a disciple of a master who interprets and helps us to discover the riches of the Word of God in the diverse conditions of our life which a bishop, just like every believer, assumes and experiences, offering to the Lord that which makes him suffer and that which makes him glad.

9. The use of this book is hinted at in the articulation of the theme. While following the succession of months one after another, the various passages lead us on a ''Journey with the Lord'' through the Christian life and seek to throw light on our pathway by promoting a recognition and acceptance of the gifts of God.

Both eye and heart are attentive to the liturgical year. And, while keeping in mind the general dates of the movable major solemnities of the year, the individual months are colored, therefore, by the mood and salvific significance of these feasts.

January opens with a series of reflections on *peace* and proceeds taking into consideration our *life as Christians*, the gift of the *four Gospels*, the divine reality of our *communion* with God and with one another which constitutes the *historic community* that we call the Church.

February becomes the month which prepares us for and introduces us into the season of *Lent*. Here we pause to ponder, more than the specific topics of *conversion* and *repentance*, a whole series of approaches to the practice of *virtue* which figure so importantly into our way of being Christian, thanks especially to the sacrament of *Baptism*.

March takes us on a pedagogical journey through the subjects of the *gift*, the *education* and the *growth* of *faith*, united to the acknowledgment and embrace of the *cross* in our lives.

April affords us an opportunity to confess our faith in the *presence* of the Lord who is in us and in our midst, *Risen* and *Alive*.

In **May** we contemplate the wonderful themes of *work*, of openness in a spirit of confidentiality and trust to *Mary*, and finally the theme of the first gift of Jesus to the believer, that of His *Holy Spirit*.

June is the month in which we meditate above all on the active presence of Jesus in the *Eucharist*. The community is built up principally around the eucharistic mystery. It continues to be founded on the apostles, among whom Sts. *Peter and Paul* especially stand out.

In **July,** vacation time, we reflect on the ethical and social demands of our faith and we recommit ourselves to being *witnesses* of the Risen Lord as we take stock of our daily walk with Him and the road which still lies ahead.

August gives us an occasion for an extraordinary pilgrimage through the *land of Jesus* to reconfirm us in the *works of faith*.

In **September** it is fitting that we take up our journey again at home, placing ourselves in the *school of the Word*.

In **October** God's design for the history of the world is announced. It is a plan of reconciliation which will permit even the spiritually disinherited to witness to their *faith in life*.

November opens us up to friendship with the *saints*, to an affectionate and familial *remembrance* in prayer of our *deceased* brothers and sisters, and to a reopening of the discourse on the subject of *interpersonal rapport*.

Finally, **December**, time of *Advent* and *Christmas*, gets us off to a rediscovery of the *wait*, the *search*, and the *hope* for His coming as we are offered a series of models by which we can come to recognize the face of God as it is revealed to us in Jesus.

An explicit word of thanks goes to the Little Daughters of the Sacred Heart in Milan who contributed in a decisive way to the collection and organization of these meditations under specific themes and to their editorial work in unifying the whole.

Luciano Pacomio
Rector, Capranica College - Rome

Journeying
With
The Lord

Reflections for Every Day

JANUARY

January 1
Peace is Born from a New Heart

What is the new heart from which peace is born?

The biblical texts can help give us a concrete idea of this new heart. In Saint Luke's Gospel we are told that "Mary kept all these things, pondering them in her heart" (Lk 2:19). In his turn, Paul writes in the Letter to the Galatians: "Because you are sons, God has sent the Spirit of His Son into our hearts, crying 'Abba! Father!' " (Gal 4:6).

Three reflections will help us to understand the significance of the heart according to these biblical texts.

First, the heart is not only the center of feelings and sentiments, but it is also that profound place where our *persona* takes consciousness of itself, reflects on happenings, meditates on the sense of reality, assumes responsible attitudes on the facts of life and the mystery of God.

Secondly, I wish to underline the decisive importance of the heart in the order of salvation. In the Letter to the Galatians, Paul tells us: "When the time had fully come, God sent forth His Son, born of a woman, born under the law, so that we might receive adoption as sons" (Gal 4:4-5). Jesus, then, is present in history as Savior, Redeemer, Liberator. But the divine salvific action becomes realistically effective in human history only through our hearts which, by the strength of the Holy

Spirit, become new hearts, animated by filial love towards God. We see, too, in Saint Luke's Gospel that the mere presence of Jesus among men does not bring about salvation: there are the self-righteous who ignore Jesus, who reject Him. Jesus' presence becomes a source of salvation, however, when His heart is in the hearts of the shepherds, in the heart of Mary who keeps, ponders, and applies to her life all that God communicates through the birth of Jesus.

Finally, there is a third point concerning the particular fullness of life that the heart finds in itself when, going out from itself, so to speak, it meets the new absolute of the love of God, which is given to us in Jesus.

If these are the characteristics of the human heart, we aren't surprised that it could intervene in a relevant way in the problems of peace.

January 2
The Challenge of Peace

Peace is a challenge to the whim that is in us to be braver and stronger, to show others. It's a challenge to that pins-and-needles of the hands and heart that would want to end quickly with those who think differently from us.

Peace is the challenge of the Beatitudes, of dialogue, of not putting first those things that generate violence.

Peace is the *beatitude of poverty* which does not put wealth, profit and earnings first.

Peace is the *beatitude of meekness* which does not put power and supremacy first. It's necessary, therefore, to know how to carry out courageous gestures of peace, disarmament and dialogue.

Peace is the *beatitude of hunger and thirst for justice* which does not put self-satisfaction and self-tranquility first, but submits itself to work for the defense of life, for the defense of the dignity of our brothers and sisters on the margins of life.

Peace is the *beatitude of being derided or persecuted for justice' sake* which does not put common consent or approval above all else, but humbly faces up to the cross, with the grace of the Holy Spirit, to actualize the reign of God, the reign of justice and fraternity.

January 3
Dialogue Without Bounds

Through the Beatitudes we must become such workers for peace. For this, we must accept dialogue as an instrument and way to peace.

Dialogue without boundaries — across races, with men of different color, different religions, different backgrounds and cultures.

Dialogue between persons who differ because of nature, because of sex, because of age, because of health, because of handicap, because of drugs.

Dialogue with persons who differ because of social position — with preferential treatment of those who are weak, unemployed, excluded, menaced.

Dialogue as an expression of our acceptance of others with an attitude of awareness, esteem, help, and service.

Dialogue as a protest against the abuses of the powerful, the violent, the oppressor.

The Christian, if he or she wants to be like Jesus,

must be like the God of Jesus — the God Who speaks to Isaiah, the God Who is with the oppressed, the humiliated, with the afflicted. This "being with" is valid for individuals as well as for social categories and for nations; all the more because at the root of this oppression, affliction and humiliation, there is sin. As the apostle James reminds us, it is necessary to overcome bitter fanaticism, attachment to our own things, ideas, privileges and "rights," which create suspicion and bitterness towards others.

This kind of talk strikes us as being hard. Are we capable of such coherence? Are we able to take the necessary steps to advance with concrete and progressive gestures on the way to peace — each one in the place where he or she is, each one responding to his or her own vocation?

January 4
Christian Existence

Christian existence is an itinerary which finds in the Gospels its "pastoral guide" or manual of initiation. The fundamental step is "Baptismal conversion," renewing us above all during the time in which we prepare for Easter and during spiritual exercises.

Then follows the period dedicated to the "conscious and convinced insertion into the Church," understood in all its dimensions and richness: Word of God, sacraments, prayer, moral choices, fraternity, mutual forgiveness, hierarchy and authority, etc.

Without that living experience of community which brings joy in being a part of the Body of Christ, a "testimony for the world," which makes up the successive stages of Christian experience, cannot be possible. Evangelization, as pastoral action, is the "art of arts." It must be learned, made the object of continual examination and reflection to better achieve it. It fortifies itself through contact with a community rich in faith and prayer. At the end of the Christian journey there then comes "contemplative maturity." The community lives, above all, in the Eucharist in which it contemplates and celebrates the mystery of salvation under simple signs.

January 5
The First Christian Community

I would like to refer first of all to the experience of the early Church as it is described in the New Testament. From it, we can understand the present journey of the Christian community and the place of the priestly ministry within it.

We mean, then, to describe the situation of the Christian community as the Word of God itself presents it. It is not a static, immobile situation which we could explain with a snap-shot. It is an itinerant situation that ever moves forward.

The image of this going forward or journey recurs over and over in the New Testament, and in particular, in the Acts of the Apostles — the book which describes the beginnings of the early Christian community.

Christian life is a journey, and so it is important to catch its point of departure, its direction and its successive stages. For this reason, I wish to focus on how the early

Church, the Church from which the written Gospels came, conceived itself as this itinerant Church.

What were the stages of this journey? How was the community able to know how to progress from one stage to another?

If we read the pages of the New Testament, we see that the community was aware of the various stages of its journey. This is apparent from the various names with which the community designated its different groups of Christians: There were *catechumens* who prepared for Baptism; the *enlightened ones* who received Baptismal enlightenment; the *disciples* or apprentices who were learning the faith more deeply; and the mature or perfected *Christians* who had in some way reached their goal.

So, the early Christian community was clearly guided along this progressive journey by the Gospels. In the early Church it was clear from the beginning that being a Christian is not a static point (before you're not one, and then you are and that's it), but rather, it's a line: you begin, you continue, you progress.

January 6
Mark: The Gospel of the Catechumen

Why this title? Mark is the oldest Gospel — the one the early Church put together first in order to better respond to its fundamental needs in preparing people for Baptism. It is the briefest of the Gospels; the one which contains the essential facts about Jesus. It was composed for pagans, probably Roman, and sets forth the teachings of Peter. It contains all that a pagan must assimilate (not just know) and live in order to be ready for the great step called Baptism, to make the leap of conversion.

We can better characterize Mark's Gospel by one of its typical phrases: "The secret of the kingdom of God is given to you, but to those who are outside everything comes in parables" (4:11). This is the journey Mark wants us to make. The catechumen is on the outside, and he sees the Christian rites, their prayers, their way of living, and it all seems so enigmatic. He doesn't understand why: why do they pray like that? Why aren't they like others? Why do they live the way they do — so full of charity, simplicity, fraternity? From the outside, the catechumen contemplates the mystery of Christ and wants to enter in. He wants to arrive at the moment when the mystery is awakened in him. He wants to move from being a catechumen to being a convert. Mark's Gospel offers a complete guide to this person. He gradually leaves behind his pagan religiosity with its excesses and magic, and moves towards his success in God.

The pagan catechumen must abandon his superstitious and possessive religiosity in order to achieve that attitude which Jesus on the cross showed to the Father. He must come to understand that the God of Jesus Christ is not the God that he knew up to that moment — that is, a god that he can possess and extort divine favors from with well-contrived and well-calculated magical conjurations. God is the God Who comes to meet us, the God to Whom Jesus abandoned Himself and by that action, revealed the power of God. In Jesus, the call resounds in every one of us to go forth from self-security and abandon ourselves to and to welcome the Word of Another, superior to us, Who saves us.

Matthew: The Gospel of the Catechist

At this point of the Christian's formation, Matthew's Gospel intervenes. Matthew reports many of Jesus' sayings, ordered and put together in five great discourses: The Sermon on the Mount (5-7), The Sermon on Mission (10), The Sermon in Parables (13), The Sermon on the Church (18), and The Eschatological Sermon (25).

What does the Gospel offer to the neo-Baptized? Matthew offers a guide for placement within the community. The neo-Baptized must recognize that through Baptism he not only said "yes" to God and to Jesus, but that he also said "yes" to a concrete community, to find in it God's presence.

The key-word of this Gospel is found in Matthew 28:20, "I am with you always, yes, to the end of time." The newly-Baptized in the school of Matthew have to learn that Jesus, to Whom each of us is given in Baptism, does not live only in memory or in the intimacy of the heart; He is found every day in the community of our brothers. Matthew therefore speaks of pardon for offenses, of obedience to authority, of the role of Peter — all the things which characterize the Christian-communal experience.

If a Christian makes the step of conversion and says: "I follow God," but does not realize that with it he has also assumed the weight of the community, he hasn't yet completely made the step that is asked of him. We Christians serve God and Jesus Christ in a visible, hierarchical and organized community which we call the Catholic Church. And we must find God in this Church. We must find Christ's presence. From this, we understand Matthew when he says: "So far as you did this to one of the least of these brothers of Mine, you did it to Me" (Mt 25:40). And we also recall: "Woe to him who causes one of these little ones to sin." Indeed, the Baptized Christian must learn gradually to recognize Christ's presence in the "little ones," in the poor who apparently do not count for anything.

Matthew then gives us a reasoned catechesis of the kingdom of God. Through the five great discourses and facts about Jesus, he brings us to understand what the Kingdom is, how to accept and enter into it. Matthew presents the principal duties of those who live in the Kingdom; all that characterizes their way of living; their Christian ethic; their missionary tension in the Kingdom; its internal difficulties; the charity and pardon that must reign there; and its eschatological ends. Matthew's is a long catechesis that brings the Baptized to examine deeply the sense of belonging to the Church.

January 8
Luke: The Gospel of Witness

The next stage of the journey is best expressed by the Lukan Gospel, which is united with the Acts of the Apostles. Acts is the Gospel of mission and preaching: "Go, therefore, into the whole world . . . ," to the ends of the earth.

This stage concerns the formation of witnesses. Once the Christian has learned to live in community as one of its responsible members, the question pops into his head: What can I do for and say to others who do not believe? Luke's Gospel gives indications for a gradual, progressive formation of the evangelizer or Christian witness. Luke teaches the Christian to bring the Word to those who do not believe, to those who think differently.

This Lukan guidebook is best summed up in Luke 24:13-34 in which the evangelist relates the story of the disciples on the road to Emmaus. They grow from their first verbal announcement — which is on their lips but not in their hearts (Lk 24:19-24), to a proclamation given from their hearts which are on fire with the Word and presence of the Risen Christ (Lk 24:32-35).

January 9
John: The Contemplative Gospel for the Mature Christian

The "presbyterial" stage (in the etiological sense of the word) concerns Christian maturity. We know that in antiquity, given the short life span, this maturity was attainable by those whom we today call "young." Having journeyed through the previous stages, the Christian at this point asks himself: What is the center of the many different experiences I've had? How can I describe them? How can I reflect on them in their simplest essentials? This is a stage for contemplative simplification in which the many duties, precepts, rites and other things no longer enter into play. Rather, the Christian seeks "the gist of the matter." John offers a contemplative and summary Gospel for those who have already journeyed through the earlier stages of Christian experience. He introduces us to a contemplation of the fundamental mystery of our faith. If you read St. John, you see that throughout all his pages, through the various episodes of Jesus' life which he has

12   JANUARY

put together, as well as through Jesus' words, John develops one theme, always repeated: the Father reveals the Son because He loves the world. "For God so loved the world that He gave His only Son" (Jn 3:16). In the face of this revelation, man feels called to faith, trust, belief and love. John speaks neither of virtue nor of vice. He makes no problem of obedience, nor mutual pardon, nor matrimonial duty or state, nor obligations of justice. All of this is absent from the Johannine vocabulary. He treats important things which look back to the fundamentals of Christian initiation. He looks to those things which make sense out of everything, namely: faith and charity.

Faith and charity, present in the Father, the recognizable God Who lovingly reveals Himself in the Son, draw us to Him and save us. John's is a contemplative Gospel which teaches us to aim at the essentials. Therefore, it is a fitting Gospel for the mature Christian of the "presbytery" who gradually becomes qualified to assume the responsibility for others in the Church.

January 10
The Primacy of the Gospels

By this heading, I wish to emphasize the most profound reality from which everything else derives: the divine initiative that saves us, that comes to us and makes itself known to us. God's saving initiative is the root of all; the point of comparison for everything else; the reality upon which all is spoken and judged.

It is the Good News — as the prophet Isaiah says — that "changes life and fills with joy." It's the crown instead of ashes. It's the song of praise instead of the melancholy heart. It's the Good News, the precious pearl or the treasure hidden in the field, for which one sells everything without a second thought in order to buy it.

The Good News of the Gospel is the center and heart, the fundamentally single preoccupation of the bishop's ministry and of the Church's action. It is the first orthodoxy which concerns the bishop so that it may be authentically proclaimed, contemplated, and made crystal clear in every action, structure and movement in the Church.

Before being certain of the correctness of the words with which the message is being proclaimed, the bishop will take every care to see to it that the message itself, in all its reality, is worthy and resplendent.

All of this is very important. In fact, in every facet of Church life — from those areas which are of a proclamatory nature to those of service, from the teaching of catechetics to the ultimate determination of discipline and of worship, from the formulation of how to live the Christian life to the administrative, economic and juridical structures of the diocese — what is important is to ask oneself if and how that particular area throws light on and proclaims the Gospel.

January 11
The Communitarian Character of the Announcement

The announcement that God's mercy for man is manifest in Jesus Christ is expressed both collegially and organically by the faith community.

In the Letter to the Ephesians, St. Paul tells us that all of us, as a body, seek to grow in everything towards

Jesus, Who is the Good News of salvation. He Himself makes us grow in Him as a well-united and connected organism through a collaboration of every part, and according to each member's energy. This unity is expressed in various ways and forms: apostles, prophets, evangelists, pastors, teachers. Everyone cooperates towards the one and the same end: the unity of the faith and recognition of the Son of God and His presence among us as Savior, Evangelist and Transformer (Ep 4:11 ff.).

I ask God for the grace that in this one body which we are, He may show His presence in our poverty, humility and inabilities. May we make room for the power of the Lord that pervades!

In one part of *De Poenitentia*, Saint Ambrose speaks of his fears and reluctance at being a bishop — how he felt his own unworthiness. I, too, many times am heavily conscious of my poverty. But it is also true that this feeling gets swept away by the certainty that we are the Body of Christ. And that is what counts.

By means of the many different gifts given to each person, the reality of God manifests, in the weakness of human experience, how we are to know, accept, love, forgive and understand each other!

As the Body of Christ, as the Christian community, it is true that we are but a little flock, a mustard seed, a handful of leaven, when compared to the immense disbelief that pervades our world enslaved by excessive power and interests other than those of the Gospels. It is important, however, not to lose one's self in confrontations and trials, but rather, to proclaim: "Lord, You reign in us. We are Your Body. You live through its various parts." Our contemplation of this divine fullness within gives us the strength and serenity to make our journey and be instruments of the Gospel where and as God asks us to be.

January 12
The Christian Community Reveals the Mystery of God

The living reality of the Body of Christ reveals the mystery of God. We are the extension in time of the Son's mission. We are the manifestation of love with which the Father loves the Son and the Son loves the Father. Together They carry out in us and through us the things we can only mutter the significance of, because They infinitely surpass our intelligence. We can only intuit in a limited way the value of that which gives value to every other thing on the earth — the Supreme and Absolute Value Who gives sense to every man's existence. This is the Trinitarian mystery: the Father loves the Son; the Son loves the Father with that perfect and personal love Who is the Holy Spirit.

Poor and limited though we are, in our life we can show "the boundless power of the Holy Spirit" wonderfully operative in the Church (*Lumen Gentium*, No. 44).

Loved by God, graced and pardoned by Him, we go forward together, accepting and pardoning each other. In so doing, we reveal to the world God's love.

How ineffable are the mysteries which are carried out in our midst. How immense are the realities which the Lord accomplishes with the dust of our poverty. What marvelous designs for eternal life does the Lord bring forth in the briefest imaginable segments of our temporal reality, which is marked by weakness, pain and death!

January 13
The Church of Tomorrow

I've asked myself and have often been asked how do

I see the Church of tomorrow, and what do I desire for it. What images of the Church has the Spirit put into my heart?

The Church of tomorrow can't be other than the Church of Jesus Christ and the apostles; the Church of Saint Ambrose; the Church of Pope John Paul II; the Church of the Councils and Synods. But how is this Church? Is it possible to delineate some characteristics?

It is a Church fully subject to God's Word; nourished and freed by this Word.

— A Church which puts the Eucharist at the center of its life; focuses and reflects on its Lord; does everything "in memory of Him" and models itself on His gifts.

— A Church which is not afraid to use human means and structures to serve rather than be served. A Church that wants to speak to its contemporary world, culture, diverse civilizations, with the simple words of the Gospels.

— A Church that speaks more with deeds than with words, and says only those words which spring from and rely on those deeds. People are tired of words! A certain reserve in speaking will give the words more dignity and effect. As was taught by the Messiah: "He does not cry out or shout aloud, or make His voice heard in the streets" (Is 42:2). The truth is strong and does not need to depend on a tone of voice; rather, it relies on the conformity of word to deed.

— A Church attentive to the signs of the presence of the Spirit in our time, however the Spirit may appear.

— A Church aware of the arduous and difficult journey many people face today; of humanity's almost unsupportable suffering; a Church sincerely sharing in the pain of the world with a desire to console.

— A Church which brings the liberating and encouraging Word of the Gospel to those who are heavily burdened, while always remembering the words of Jesus: "Alas for you doctors of the law, because you load on men burdens that are unendurable; burdens that you yourselves do not move a finger to lift" (Lk 11:46).

— A Church able and willing to seek out the "new poor" and not too preoccupied about failing in its efforts to help them in a creative way.

— A Church that does not privilege any one category of persons, welcoming old and young alike. A Church which educates and forms all its sons to faith and love, and desires to make the most of the diverse charisms, services and ministries in the unity of communion.

— A Church humble of heart, closely united in its discipline, in which God alone has primacy.

— A Church which patiently, objectively and realistically discerns its relationship with the world — especially today's society — and which strives for active participation and responsible presence. A Church that has much respect and deference for institutions, but which well remembers Peter's words: "Better to obey God than men." — A Church . . . but we could go on without end! Essentially, we're concerned with building a Church founded in tradition and open to the Spirit of God, to the Magisterium, and attentive to the signs of the times. A Church that lives up to the motto: *"to perfect and add to the old with the new."*

January 14
God's Gift of Community

We must first and foremost remember that community is a gift. It is not founded upon our own collaborative pastoral efforts, nor on our sincere desire for friendship. These things are important and we must always keep them in mind.

But the Acts of the Apostles (Ac 4:43) and the First Letter of John (1 Jn 1:3; 6-7) speak of a "being together" (Ac 1:14; 2:46; 4:54; 5:12; 15:25), and this togetherness, so characteristic of the early Christian community, is a gift from God. It is a new world of being that comes to us from above.

It is the participation God allows us by His mysterious "being together" in the Trinity.

It is the participation by grace — a "being together" — that joined Jesus to His disciples; the ones who were called "to be His companions" (Mk 3:14).

First, this gift is founded on baptismal grace. Baptism brings us together with the Church that is spread throughout the world, with the Pope and his brother bishops, with all the Baptized, and with all those whom God will call (cf. Ac 2:9).

God shares His Trinitarian community with the Church, and in the Church, each person shares the community experience.

January 15
Word of God and Community

By accepting the Word of God we become an authentically Christian community according to the laws of fellowship.

God's Word assures us of a living and immediate contact with Christ Himself, the Living Word of the Father, the source of fellowship. But since the Word gives witness to Christ through the very rich variety of human experiences read and seen in the light of Christ, it offers rich provocations that touch on all the fundamental aspects of life.

The Word tells us how the Father's love touched human situations through Christ and made them true experiences. It enlightened them and purified them from within, and opened them to new and unexpected possibilities.

Life, death, friendship, pain, love, family, work, differing personal relationships, solitude, secret move-ments of the heart, great social phenomena — in sum, all human life comes to us through the Word of God, seen in a new and true light.

When we encounter the Word, we meet ourselves: our past, our future, our brothers. We learn to create a community which, faithful to the laws of fellowship, finds a place, a way, a message of hope for every man and every human situation.

January 16
The Community that Lives Fellowship

Saint Paul offers us a community experience that lives fellowship. This fellowship begins within man's heart. In Saint Mark's Gospel, Jesus said that it is from within, from man's heart, that evil intentions emerge— all of which contaminate man and separate him from his neighbor, often by greed and possessiveness. As it is said in the Letter of James, it causes division and war (Jm 4:2).

But Christ's peace is put into man's heart by the loving God, and with it, man is made able to feel mercy, goodness, humility, meekness and patience — feelings and intentions that build fellowship and peace.

Following a description of a community based on charity, St. Paul's Letter to the Philippians tells us to richly and abundantly breathe the Word as a group of faithful, for the Word of Christ dwells all around and within us (Ph 2:1ff). And it was just this type of community that Ambrose unceasingly nourished with the Bread of the Word; Bread that for him had become daily and indispensable food.

"When I read the Divine Scriptures," Saint Ambrose said, "God returns to walk in the earthly paradise." He continued: "Christ and Divine Scripture are the remedy for every distasteful thing and the only refuge from temptations. Therefore, from this unrenounceable source," St. Ambrose wrote to the newly-elected bishop, Constantius, "the bishop must draw, until filled with the sacred words, he can guide his faithful in a just manner."

January 17
The Center of the Council's Debate

To understand the fundamental message of Vatican II, it is important that we realize one thing: while we can say that at the center of the Council's debate was the relationship between the Church and contemporary man, we must recognize that neither man nor the Church were the center of the Council's message. The Church's difficulties in its dialogue with contemporary man and his institutions were passionately studied, but they did not produce an anthropocentric Council. Similarly, the reflection on the Church progressed enthusiastically and made many discoveries, but it did not produce an ecclesiocentric Council.

Always at the center was God's plan in Christ Jesus.

The serious and heartfelt consideration of man's life neither captured nor exhausted, in itself, the faith of the Church. Rather, it urged it to become a purer and more rigorous faith in truth, in hope and in the salvation of man; that is, in Jesus Christ. The Church of Vatican II discovered its proper fellowship with Christ and the mission that Christ entrusts to it in our times.

With profound awe and with a sense of responsibility, the Church found within itself the mystery of Christ, the mystery which always goes beyond it and lights the way for every man.

January 18
The Church is Mystery

The Church of Vatican II described itself as the mystery, sign and Body of Christ. These expressions speak of the Church's relationship to Christ. The Church does not have complete meaning or consistency in and of itself.

The Church points to Christ, while at the same time, it is a visible and historic manifestation of Him.

The reference to Christ, which animates all of the Council's documents, is particularly explicit in two: *The Dogmatic Constitution on Divine Revelation* (*Dei Verbum*), and *The Constitution on the Sacred Liturgy* (*Sacrosanctum Concilium*), which see the fundamentals of Christ's presence in the Word and in the Sacraments, respectively.

These two constitutions, with their clearly Christo-centric design, have opened access to the living presence of the Lord.

January 19
The Church is Fellowship

The Lord Jesus is the Son of God, the first born of many brothers, the center of human history, and the model of fellowship with God. The Church is the community of those who live in fellowship with Christ and it offers this communion to every man. This view of fellowship or communion luminously affirmed by the Council (*Lumen Gentium*) considers Christ's great gift to the Church: the Holy Spirit, Who then becomes the source of many more gifts through which man enters into communion with Christ. In the light of the Spirit and His gifts, participation in the life of the Church attains new and unexpected depths.

Its structural, functional and societal relationships are vivified by its desire for freedom, spirituality and charity.

The consideration of the common dignity and responsibility of all believers traces the fundamental area in which the necessary diversity of function and vocation stand out.

These same functions and vocations have been redefined with profoundly new treatments. The rethinking of authority, for example — taken in its collegial structure and in its ministerial finality in and for the service of all God's people — especially comes to mind.

One thinks, too, of the impulse given to a reconsideration of the figure of the Christian lay person, an understanding which does not exhaust itself in the idea of the Christian animation of temporal realities, but carries with it the concept of a whole new way of participating in the mystery of Christ with active responsibilities within the Christian community (*Apostolicam Actuositatem*).

Moreover, enlightened by the Spirit, the very real (even if incomplete) participation of the Catholic Church in the life of peoples outside its institutional confines, has been reevaluated. The ecumenical movement, the dialogue with the non-Christian religions, the foresighted and calm consideration of the phenomenon of disbelief are all results of this (*Nostra Aetate, Unitatis Redintegratio*).

January 20
Communion and Mission

Communion with Christ is not an addition to man's life, but is his true goal. Each person, by the very fact of being a person, is called to share in Christ's destiny. For this reason, communion with Christ becomes a real mission towards all people for the Church.

This mission first of all requires going to all people, including non-Christians. More generally and profoundly, the mission asks each of us to go to each person and show theoretically and practically that man is that much more free, autonomous and rational as he responds to Christ's call. In this light, Vatican II drafted a Christian anthropology, that is, a vision of man that begins with his faith in Christ (*Gaudium et Spes, Dignitatis Humanae*).

Two categories have a top priority in this anthropology: fullness and hope.

Christ is the highest and most complete achievement for man. Christ is the ultimate and definitive Good Who gives form and meaning to the divine goods that are the object of our desire, search and hope.

Fullness and hope are categories which require a more rigorous theoretical interpretation and practical translation — by becoming ever more inherent in our cultural situation — which carry with them, at the same time and in compensation, an enormous burden which is both suggestive and challenging.

January 21
Community and Conversion

Vatican II did not offer a ready-made solution for every cultural situation, but rather, uncovered a task: to integrate any given man, both in his concrete historical situation and in his cultural variability, into the proclamation of faith (it is in this sense that the word "aggiornamento" is to be understood).

An undertaking of this type requires patience, hard work and experimentation. Far more than the initial attempts at cultural dialogue proposed by these same conciliar texts the Church underwent a profound crisis due to the rapid change in culture.

The culture of the Council is not the same as that of the post-Conciliar period. It is difficult to put a date on the cultural upheaval, even if the often cited year of 1968 is emblematically marked as such.

It is even more difficult to indicate the contents of the change. We can generally say that from an optimistic frenzy to build a civilization of well being we have passed to a kind of pessimistic disorientation about the sense of man's actions. We have passed from a humanistic culture which centered on the person, to a culture caught up in the anonymous interplay of structures and institutions. We have passed from a compact, industrial society to a restless post-industrial society. We have moved away from trust in international collaboration to a present inflexibility and to the arms race.

How can we understand, critique, purify and save this culture? The Council does not offer the norms for a time it was not able to foresee. Instead, it launches an intense appeal to the person.

Persons apply the norms to themselves and are converted. So, we can see that this post-Conciliar period is not so much a time for tranquil application as it is for strong conversion.

Conversion calls our failures and tardiness to scrutiny, but also puts us in Christ's presence Who is greater than our own hearts. By His Resurrection, He definitively defeated the evil which is in us and in the world. Seen as a call to conversion, the Council conserves its momentum. As the years pass, it remains ever ahead of us. It is not a memory of the past, but a hope for tomorrow.

January 22
Jesus and our Cities (and Countries)

We don't ask ourselves whether or not Jesus had the capacity to understand the mysteries which lie at the heart of every city. Saint John's Gospel notes that during Jesus' first visit to Jerusalem for the Passover, "many believed in His name when they saw the signs He performed." But the evangelist adds, "but Jesus knew them all and did not trust Himself to them; He never needed evidence about any man; He could tell what a man had in him" (Jn 2:23-25).

The problem, then, is something else: the way with which Jesus encounters a city that He knows is filled with hostilities, prejudices, tensions, violence, threats — a city about to reject Him.

Jesus does not enter the city in a fearful, distrustful, reserved or cautious way. Rather, He is open, benevolent and conciliatory. "Do not be afraid, daughter of Zion; see, your king is coming, mounted on the colt of a donkey" (Jn 12:15). The expression "daughter of Zion" tenderly designates the city as a daughter, a woman to love. The king enters simply and seriously, just as a thousand years earlier when Solomon, the king of peace entered full of hope and promise. "Do not be afraid, daughter of Zion, because I don't fear you" — Jesus says — "nor do I accept the judgment of a foreign, unlivable city, to fall on you. I love you and come to you in that love; do not fear." Pope John Paul II reechoed these sentiments when he entered Rome and recalled the words of St. Peter upon his entrance to the city: "Do not be afraid to welcome Christ and accept His power. Do not be afraid. Open wide your doors to Christ." What Jesus did for His own city, entering it as He did with benevolence, openness and without arms or prejudice, I think He would do and, indeed, does do for every great modern city of ours. His entrance into the city of Jerusalem is also the Redeemer's entrance into our own cities.

We Meet Christ Together

The Gospel recounts that the great crowd who came for the feast "heard that Jesus was on His way to Jerusalem. They took palm branches and went out to meet Him, shouting, 'Hosanna! Blessings on the King of Israel Who comes in the name of the Lord!' " (Jn 12:12-13).

We don't know if the crowd that went to greet Jesus was big or small with respect to the immense multitude of people who lived at that time in the city.

Indeed, the Gospel notes that a crowd "had come for a feast." Therefore, many had come from Galilee, from the country, and from those pockets of faith and sanctity which cities have always had. But undoubtedly many citizens of the city were there. And those who cheered Him surely did so in the name of the city they loved, and to which they felt tied by a thousand years of history.

The city was the soul of a people who went out to meet Christ.

They were a people who drank freely from the fountain of the glorious prophetic traditions of Israel. They were people whom Luke, in defense, refers to as those "who looked forward to the deliverance of Jerusalem" (Lk 2:38).

January 24
Jesus' Words for Our Living

Many people welcomed Jesus into their lives. And certainly, there are many men and women in our cities today who have not lost hope and await ''the deliverance of Jerusalem.'' They hail Christ's coming as humble Savior.

To these men and women, and to you, I repeat the words of Saint John the Evangelist as they were expressed by Pope John Paul II: ''Be not afraid, daughter of Zion. Be not afraid, you modern city so proud of your success, your history and your palaces. Sad, too, for the sadness of all your sons in search of true love and meaning in life. Be not afraid. Behold, your king comes.

''Be not afraid! Throw open your gates to Christ and His saving power. Open all your borders; your economic, political, cultural and developmental concerns. Be not afraid! Christ knows all that lies within man's heart! Only He knows! So often today, man does not know what lies within him. He's uncertain about the meaning of his life. We see so many people like this on the streets of our cities. They are filled with doubt and see change only by desperation.

''Therefore I pray — I humbly and trustingly implore you — let Christ speak to you. He alone has the words of everlasting life.''

January 25
The Humanism of the Crucifixion

Jesus' cross negates every image of the divine as an all-powerful despot or a shabby limitation of man, or as holiness irreconcilable with mercy.

The cross is a firm ''no'' to any image of God that does not correspond to a loving Father of the crucified Jesus.

Jesus' cross is a message about humanism. That

humanism is a "no" to any projection of man which is expressed practically in those persons who put Jesus to death. The humanism of the cross condemns the false humanism of excessive power, abuse and envy that these people represent.

At the same time, the crucifixion suggests a new humanism: the humanism of discipleship. Being a disciple means turning around one's mentality and behavior. It means carrying the cross every day, and, if necessary, facing misfortune and persecution.

It is this "new man," born of the cross, that we find in our meditations on Jesus. But at the same time, how far away from Him we feel ourselves to be at times! We can only say, "Lord, we understand something of your love and crucifixion, but how we labor in trying to live it!" And Jesus replies to us: "I am your salvation! I am God's strength, justice, reconciliation and sanctification. I give you the possibility to joyfully accept the humanism of the cross!" Returning for a moment to the humanism that rejects the cross — when it reaches a critical encounter, when it faces sickness or death and shows its impotence — doesn't it really show its inconsistency?

Now compare that with the humanism of the cross and its ability not only to handle the problems of life, but also the problem of death, of salvation, and of everlasting hope. Doesn't this humanism even today point the only way to salvation?

Isn't the cross, in reality, the fundamental question for humanity? Isn't that what man is called to decide upon: whether to accept the humanism God offers or close oneself into a self-styled humanism without hope?

January 26
Violence

The greatest of evils in our times; the greatest plague is violence, in all its forms.

We experience *political* violence, which has produced the cruel aberrations of terrorism. I can still see the blood of those innocent victims who were killed at their work, at the university, and even just a few steps from where they lived. We also experience *criminal* violence. Our streets and our homes are bloodstained over persons' desires to rob or settle some vendetta. Then, there is the violence inflicted upon *nascent life*, which constitutes one of the most grievous and bitter plagues of our time as it cuts down innumerable voiceless and defenseless victims. We face *societal* violence, which expresses itself in every form of injustice. We particularly see the harm from the violence implicit in our economic structures which result in persons not being able to protect their livelihood and savings. And how many millions have died from hunger!

Finally, there is the synthesis of all violence and social aberrations: *war*. War has stained every country of the world with blood. We still feel its menacing presence from the arsenals which are kept and are capable of destroying humanity once and for all.

January 27
Loneliness

Loneliness is another plague that particularly affects our great modern cities. By loneliness, I mean the situation of all those who are deprived of that help and companionship which they should have in some necessary way. They are helpless and they are suffering, often to the point of despair.

There is the loneliness of the *elderly*. How many in our cities are alone in their homes or alone in crowded shelters. These elderly persons are not infrequently ill or suffer from a particular infirmity that does not allow them to easily provide for themselves.

There also is the loneliness of the many *sick* who are not suitably assisted by our public health structures. They often must suffer through long waiting hours for a badly-needed cure. But more important, they don't feel any kindness or attention around them, even when they are receiving physical assistance with their illness.

There also is the loneliness of the *handicapped* (particularly those psychologically handicapped) and their families.

There is the loneliness of those who are imprisoned or awaiting justice. Their wait is long and stressful. There, too, is the loneliness and fatigue of all those who work in prisons.

I also think of the loneliness faced by the tens of thousands of anonymous strangers who live on the fringes of or even outside legality, with no protection or employment.

Finally, I think of those who are alone and isolated within a family and community. Their bitter tears are many, and many never see them.

January 28
Social Corruption

Social corruption brings darkness over the world,

just as in the moment of Christ's death. This corruption, after violence and loneliness, is the third plague that infects our air and screens out the sun in our cities.

Against how many situations must we defend ourselves! How many things gnaw on the social fabric like parasites, and often get rich on our city's degradation!

First, there is the cancer of *drugs*: I think of the desolation that the drug addict causes in the family. I think of the slow drain of feelings and life that the drug draws out of its victim. And with even more indignation and sadness, I think of all those who speculate on drugs and draw immense earnings from them; more than profits from the greatest enterprises. I think of all those who solicit, induce and sell in this vast market. They preach with incredible cynicism this self-deliverance to a non-human existence.

To these people the words of Jesus resound: "It would be better if he were never born." And what shame to hear that this activity may be one of the greatest commercial activities of our regions!

We find more corruption from the "godfathers of pornography" who draw immense profits from a squalid commerce that speculates on vulgarity.

And what about those forms of corruption which join together in society to commit crimes — to rob, kidnap, extort, blackmail? They protect and promote their cause by a code of silence.

We must not be deceived into thinking that we will not be harmed by these evils. Like the plagues of old, they seek to hide themselves and then deny that they ever existed.

Finally, there is *white* corruption. This corruption creeps into the rash management of others' money; into administrative improprieties of every kind; into acts of waste of communal goods and resources; into the various forms of political corruption, favoritism, unjust distribution, privileges, and of serious neglect of civic duty.

January 29
Jesus With Us and Before Us

How does Jesus see our cities? We can only respond by looking to the meaning of Good Friday: Jesus sees our evils with His infinite love and mercy. And to better explain the term "mercy," Jesus tells us from the cross: I am *in* you.

All of those who are plagued and who suffer; all the sorrowful of our cities; all the victims of violence, loneliness and corruption — all these, Jesus says, are in Me and I am in them. Whatever you do to the least, to the poorest, to the abandoned, to the most humiliated and loneliest of My brothers, you do to Me, He says.

Secondly, He reminds us: I am *with* you. I am with all of you, men and women of good will. I am with you, men and women, young and old, who sacrifice your lives in voluntary work or service for others. I am with you. I assist you in your labors. I sustain you with your daily fill of enthusiasm. I am with you the living, in order that you may live and give life to each other.

Thirdly, Jesus says: I am *before* you. I am the goal, the way and the horizon to look toward. It is I Who build the eternal city, the city without walls, the city of fullness and friendship, the city of fraternity in which all are recognized as brothers and sisters under one name and under one heaven. It is I Who build this immense city whose architect is God. It is I Who precede you with this ideal of universal communion, of cosmic fraternity. I am the first, the creator, the artisan, the sustainer and the head of all humanity.

January 30
Fostering Understanding in the Family

I believe that the most sought-after good by the family (beyond its daily bread, the house, work, health, success in study and profession) is that of good relationships, mutual accord, and reciprocal serenity. This concerns the ability for mutual understanding.

This good is not always expressly asked for because to ask for it requires a confession that we lack something. Such a confession is not easy to make.

Reconciliation opens the way to understanding. But it requires patience. It often must be repeated in the home; reconciliation between husband and wife, between father and mother, between parents and children, and between and among the children.

Such repeated reconciliation is needed because good, tranquil, trusting, permanent, attentive and provident understanding is something rare in the family; so rare, in fact, that it can appear impossible to permanently and habitually have such a good. Experience seems to say that it's impossible.

January 31
Four Proposals for Families

Through you, I would like to make four serious proposals to all families who may need them.

First, constantly strive for good understanding. Never give up. To escape or fall into the sin of hatred is actually the resignation to a lack of good understanding.

Instead, we need to reach out with hope every day. I can change for the better, and so can others. Circumstances can always arise which clarify misunderstanding, and thereby remove all shadows.

The perfect good of family unity is reserved to the fullness of the Kingdom. However, we will not be questioned if we reached it or maintained it; we will be questioned if we strained towards it and journeyed towards it incessantly, with the certainty that the Lord is near us.

Secondly, look inside yourselves. Look at the gifts you've received, as well as the gifts others have. Look especially at the gifts of those whom the Lord has put near you.

To look inside the self means to look at the good qualities, such as patience and courage, and also at the profound gifts from the sacramental grace of marriage; graces which remain and grow and support.

Each person has within a treasure given to that person by God. It's important to give a hand in making that treasure shine, in helping the rays of grace to make the treasures of others shine.

The third proposal complements the preceding one: *Look beyond yourselves.*

Looking beyond means going outside the family and opening up to that larger community which is given us by God's loving grace through listening to the Word.

Looking beyond means not closing the self in on one's own problems, believing them to be the unique and decisive problems of living together. Rather, it's necessary to open up to that broad cohabitation that is the

36

Christian community. Looking to other families in need, we can see that there are many problems that can be mended through family action. I think, for example, of problems involving trust, problems involving children and young people in difficulty, problems involving the mutual support of marital partners.

Fourthly, entrust all concerns to Mary.

FEBRUARY

February 1
Accepting Christ

Let us look at the prologue to the Gospel of Saint John (Jn 1:1-18). What is the Word of God telling us? The Word which "was in the beginning with God and was God, and through Whom all things came to be"? What attracts our interest about man's search, man's wait?

John's prologue speaks of the Word and His closeness to the Father. John speaks about the Word's creating action and of the gifts of life and light with which He enriches all things.

We then arrive at a dramatic contraposition between those who accept the Word and those who reject Him: "He came to His own domain and His own people did not accept Him. But to all who did accept Him He gave power to become children of God." At the center, then, of the Johannine prologue, is the drama of human freedom. It therefore speaks to us as well of the choices we, in our humanity, are called to make.

Freedom is to accept Christ and open ourselves to the journey which His love takes us on and which reveals to us the true good that comes from the heart of the Father. The Gospel immediately goes to the heart of human freedom: freedom is the ability to accept or reject.

Rejection of Christ brings about evil. We greatly lament the evil which is in our life and society. We think with pain and indignation of many evils. We think of those imprisoned, those drug victims, and those without a home to name but a few.

But we must also ask ourselves where the evil comes from.

It is born out of our not wanting to accept others, and very often, not even accepting ourselves. Evil comes from our not giving time and attention to persons, from our not questioning ourselves on what is truly the good which we say we want to offer others. If we had the courage and patience to examine all the good that we wish for ourselves and for others, we would discover that these ''goods'' send us beyond — towards a life and light and fidelity which are the divine gifts brought to us by Jesus when He came into the world. Evil, then, is a rejection of Christ.

In a parallel way, the free search for good is a welcome acceptance of Christ.

Make room for Jesus in your life. Make room for others.

Making room for Jesus — which is the key to our salvation — is confronted on the one hand, for example, by the haste and impatience upon which our relationships are based, even in our families. How much impatience exists in the family! How much impatience we find blocking the paths to friendship and love! How many sins are born from an inability to accept others as persons or from a rush to devour relationships!

When we fail to make room, we can become indifferent to the needy, the suffering, the socially uprooted and those who live on the fringes, and become totally engrossed in concerns about our own luxuries and wasteful pursuits.

Ultimately, whether or not we make room for others

depends on our making room in our hearts for reflective attitudes of silent contemplation of the mystery of God.

February 2
Courage

Jesus is the living Word of the Father and a friend and companion for our journey. Jesus, Who speaks to us in human words, is, in the mysterious depth of His being, one with God. He opens our horizons to include the possibilities God has given us, so that we, too, can be one with Him.

So, I exhort you: cultivate the virtue of courage in your life. Not only the courage to question yourself on the profound realities surrounding us, but the courage to freely follow paths founded on truth, justice, serious and competent scholarship, faithful and respectful friendship.

The rejection of every form of possessiveness and greed of the eyes and senses becomes a generous response to God's love, desire, and Word, as well as to the needs of our brothers and sisters and the calls for help which they raise in our presence and in our world.

Courage opens our hearts to understand that to live simply means "to go." It means to accept "being called and sent." It does not mean answering the question "What satisfies me?", but rather, means loving and choosing what is agreeable to God — namely, the good, the just and the true.

Jesus' Obedience: Normative Proposals For Us

Looking to enter more deeply into the mystery of the Last Supper, we are brought to consider the words Jesus spoke at the consecration of the bread and wine. Christ makes a gift of Himself to man, and that enchants us. But we must not forget that Jesus acts to reform the Covenant. He says: "This is My blood, the blood of the new and everlasting Covenant." This biblical word recalls all of God's loving initiatives towards our human race, from Noah to Abraham to Moses.

The Covenant, recalled and renewed by the prophets, now removes Jesus' act from that of a simple relationship of affection, and presents it as the supreme sign of devotion to God on the part of His Son, the sign of the earthly and faithful love with which God nourishes, heals, frees, pardons and builds up His people.

The entire passion account is read in this perspective. In the chain of painful and sorry events which present Jesus betrayed and condemned, and on His part, dedicated to us through His supreme act of testimony, is uncovered the interior event of the filial relationship of Jesus with His heavenly Father.

It is not for nothing that Matthew insists on Jesus' obedience. Jesus says on the Mount of Olives: "Be it done according to Your will." And to His disciples He says: "The hour has come" (the hour of obedience). Then He added: "The scriptures must be fulfilled which say this is the way it must be." Jesus' relationship with the Father is, therefore, the light that enlightens His life, passion and death. We do not mean to say only that Jesus courageously chooses between life and death, joy and pain. Jesus chooses the narrow and difficult path as the way of testimony. As the Son, He chooses between following a life without the Father and accepting death with the Father. He chooses obedience. He chooses the Father's will, being with Him to the end.

Jesus is intensely and passionately aware of His Father, and meditates on His face always. This helps Him to understand that the choice of being a part of the Father, even if it brings pain and death, is above all the choice which brings Him, through love, to the fullness of the Resurrection.

February 4
What Doing the Father's Will Means For Us

When the Christian chooses to give his or her life, to serve others, to take up the cross, to wash the feet of his or her fellow human being, to accept a life transformed by the Gospel, to accept the requirements that life brings at home, at work, at school and in society; when he or she accepts the suffering that is a part of this life, and the solitude akin to Christ's that comes with it — that Christian does not do it out of some strange desire to suffer, but because he or she has discovered the face of the Father and has understood that the spring of life is found in doing the Father's will, even when that indicates a road of sacrifice and dedication unto death.

It is in the Eucharist that we understand all these things and how Christ makes them present in our life. The Eucharist forms us for the great choices we must make in our life and in history, according to the will of the Father.

The Eucharist is not something that suggests to us to do other useful and beautiful things for our brothers and sisters. The Eucharist is the revelation of God's love and His desire for a covenant with us today, now. This revelation comes about through Jesus' total dedication, which creates and consolidates in us the will to dispossess ourselves and fully belong to the Father.

In every Eucharist we are invited to ask ourselves: what is the Father revealing about Himself to me today? What in His unbounded love is revealed? What does He reveal to me about myself and my being created for love and self-gift, just as Christ was? What does the Father reveal to me about all the others who are waiting for this love and this gift?

February 5
Humility

Humility is a word that we use a thousand times. But we never easily grasp all its implications. In a general way we could say that humility is the opposite of what Mary terms in the Magnificat, the "proud of heart" which God has routed. The proud conceive themselves to be so high as to have rights that others must yield to in service. As a result, the proud never thank anyone for their services because these services are looked upon as being another's duty towards them that had to be performed.

This attitude was stigmatized many times by Paul in his letters. For example, in writing to the Romans: "Treat everyone with equal kindness; never be condescending. . . . Do not allow yourself to become self-satisfied" (Rm 12:16). The humble attitude is not self-inflating nor self-deluding.

It is important to reflect on this notion that we do not

know many things. It is indispensable in our relationship with God. In fact, we don't even know the words we are to use when we pray or the things we are to ask for (cf. Rm 8:26).

Often we do not succeed in our prayer because we begin with the presumption that we know how to pray. However, we should always begin by confessing: "Lord, I don't know how to pray. I know that I don't know how to pray." Already this is prayer, because it makes room for the Spirit.

February 6
The Social Aspects of Humility

Humility has three aspects:
— the social aspect: a way of behavior;
— the personal aspect: a certain awareness of self;
— the theological aspect: a certain relationship with God.

The *social aspect* is, on the one hand, an absence of pretense, and, on the other hand, attention to others. Paul would say: "I sought to be with you without pretense, thinking nothing special of myself, but being attentive to each one of you." "It was God Who decided that we were fit to be entrusted with the Good News, and when we are speaking, we are not trying to please men but God, Who can read our inmost thoughts. You know very well, and we can swear it before God, that never at any time have our speeches been simply flattery, or a cover for trying to get money; nor have we ever looked for any special honor from men, either from you or anybody else, when we could have imposed ourselves on you with full weight as apostles of Christ. Instead, we were unassuming. Like a mother feeding and looking after her own children, we felt so devoted and protective towards you, and had come to love you so much, that we were eager to hand over to you not only the Good News but our whole lives as well'' (1 Th 2:4-8).

Humility, in the social context, means being without pretense and filled with affection, attention, and love. It involves distinction, correctness, a certain reserve, a profound education, and a finesse that conquers the heart, because humility is not simply an expression of exterior comportment. Nothing is more moving to those who know how to expect little of society than seeing themselves treated with the extreme respect and value that they are.

February 7
The Personal Aspect of Humility

The personal aspect of humility concerns a simple value judgment of the self. Paul returns many times to this ability to justly value the self according to what our weaknesses and fragility make us understand. In the First Letter to the Corinthians, he speaks about Jesus' appearance before him: "Last of all He appeared to me too; it was as though I was born when no one expected it. I am the least of the apostles; in fact . . . I hardly deserve the name apostle'' (1 Cor 15:8-9). He says it with truth and sincerity, with clarity of self-judgment.

This judgment is a mode of behavior which he attained through the school of life, making him aware of his poverty and weakness. He learned to think of himself

46

in a humble, disinterested and tranquil way — without feeling guilty, but rather, being at peace.

"For we should like you to realize, brothers, that the things we had to undergo in Asia were more of a burden than we could carry, so that we despaired of coming through alive. Yes, we were carrying our own death warrant with us, and it has taught us not to rely on ourselves but only on God, Who raises the dead to life" (2 Cor 1:8-9). It is stupefying that an apostle speaks of himself like this, almost at the risk of scandal.

But personal humility comes from lived experience, and thus it is difficult for a young person to have it. Perhaps he meditated on these things, but was unable to feel it as natural because he had yet to pass through those trials and experiences of true weakness which puts us in our just place and frees us from false assumptions.

It is sad to see that at times we pass through trials without knowing how to live. If, when facing his tribulations, Paul had been moved to curse everyone and everything instead of recognizing his own weakness and fragility, he would not have profited at all from the experience. Instead, he was formed as a true shepherd because he knew to draw from the pain that he experienced in his life a lived humility.

February 8
The Theological Aspect of Humility

Theological aspect: Having profoundly lived his truth before God, Paul asks: "Has anybody given you some special right? What do you have that was not given to you? And if it was given, how can you boast as though it were not?'' (1 Cor 4:7). At the heart of his humility — which is one of the secrets of his ability to win people over — was a profound sense of God, the Creator, the Father, the Lord, the Merciful One, the Giver of all good things.

Before God, Paul is a poor sinner who receives grace, mercy and salvation. Paul's words are not his own; they are God's Word. Paul given to Him as a gift in the measure of Christ. Paul's apostolic zeal is not his own, but was given to him by the Christ Who dwells within him.

This humility is the transparency of the divine within him. It is a Christological transparency. It is the transparency of the Christ Whom he had known and understood, of Christ the Servant of Yahweh, of the humble, humiliated Christ Who did not choose to rank as number one or cause a sensation by throwing Himself from the pinnacle of the temple or by changing rocks to bread. It is the transparency of Christ Who chose not to exercise His reign over the earth, but rather, chose to be the servant of all.

Paul's humility is that of Christ. Thus he can present it to us as a fundamental attitude of one who serves the Lord, just as the Lord served. Christ served with total humility and, in like manner, His servant chooses to exercise authority with the humility and meekness of the Master.

February 9
Vigilance and Sobriety

Chapter Twenty-four of Saint Matthew's Gospel focuses on the theme of *vigilance*. The disciple who waits for the Lord's return does not fall asleep, or allow himself to be dulled by habit. Rather, he continually watches, discerns and penetrates the realities around him.

Vigilance is one of the typical virtues of the disciple in the New Testament. The note in the Jerusalem Bible in this regard is most interesting: "*Stay awake*: abstain from sleeping. Jesus recommends this attitude to those who await His coming. Vigilance, in this state of alarm, presupposes a solid hope and requires a constant presence of spirit that takes the name *sobriety*." We can therefore reflect on the importance of this attitude of the spirit which does not sleep and which does not allow itself to be intoxicated or darkened by the reality in which the spirit lives. This relationship between vigilance and sobriety involves the ability for self-control, as well as a discipline of the eyes, mind, body and imagination.

In particular, we can ask ourselves the question that comes up often: *Is chastity marginal in relation to our faith journey in the Church?*

Without expressly speaking of the serious disorders in the area of sexuality, I believe that it is useful to point out the negativity which is to be found in much of what we breathe in today's society — in the press, the field of entertainment, behavior in public — and which filters into the life of our communities.

The lack of vigilance and sobriety, and the resulting laxity, is one of the causes of a diminished apostolic spirit, diminished creativity, courage, joy, and strong vocations — all of which must be born, nourished and strengthened if they are to eventually achieve their ultimate purpose.

In this sense, the evangelical themes of sobriety and vigilance are related to the community's faith and journey, even if this relationship is understood only as a concrete and well-structured ideal.

Sobriety certainly guarantees the capacity for prayer, a love for spiritual reading and a craving for the Holy Spirit. The New Testament does not use the word "sobriety," which literally means "an abstention from drunkenness." We, however, can translate it to mean "abstention from a drunkenness of images" that we come to use. For example, I can think of the indiscriminate use of television today. I believe that the Holy Spirit will awaken us from this t.v. drunkenness and bring many young people to make drastic decisions regarding these "realities" that magically create a dangerous dependence.

It's true that we are not dealing here with the long-term decisions which touch on the faith or essence of the Church. We are trying to deal with everyday life which has an impact on our ability and readiness to accept the consolations of the Spirit with hearts that are free.

February 10
Being Small and Weak

We begin our journey towards God with the *recognition of our weakness*. The word in Greek for "weakness" can also mean frailty, sickness, inability or inadequacy. Our fragility or nothingness, is recognized, loved and freely accepted without anxiety or fear. Nothingness fears nothing because it has nothing to lose.

The Spirit comes to help: "The Spirit comes to aid us in our weakness," and He does so out of His greatness and goodness. As Saint Paul describes it: "We don't even know what to ask for.'' We don't know what to ask for, what our future will be — we don't know what to fix ourselves and our desires upon in order to journey safely and surely to God! We don't even know in which direction to go.

The Spirit of God takes hold of us, takes care of us, comes to our aid, and assists us. We should never forget this beginning of our journey. God, in fact, will give us tests to make sure that this sense of our nothingness which we find at the beginning will remain clearly in the back of our consciousness, for if it does not, then it will happen as St. Paul says, that believing that we have become something, we end up finding that we are truly nothing.

Our weakness will be put to the test ''in order that we may see that this extraordinary power is not ours, but God's'' (2 Cor 4:7).

February 11
The Poor and Christian Poverty

The Scripture texts do not give us any details about Jesus' birth other than that He was born on the outskirts of Bethlehem and was put in a manger that was used by animals. This detail is repeated three times in Luke's Gospel, and provides us a discreet, but significant key to a reading of the whole episode.

The baby that is born is, in a certain sense, like all other babies. It would be a search in vain to attempt to find any of Jesus' divine origins in the baby. But the extraordinary precariousness of His first bed, unacceptable even to the poor Bedouin shepherds who at least had a proper tent, makes an impression on all who accidentally pass by that manger or are called there by the heavenly voice.

For every person, even the unbeliever, this young family's lack of means and roof overhead is an invitation to open one's heart and home.

For those who come with the eyes of faith, the crib is an unforgettable sign about what is and is not valuable in the eyes of God.

There are many among us — and I think of those who have been evicted from their homes or those who bear the faces of anonymous strangers (some very young) who spend their nights in bus and train stations — who lack a home or work or any kind of security. There also are those whose house is not a home because of an atmosphere of hostility or indifference which seems to reign therein.

And there are many — or better said, that we are many — who profess a belief in Christ, and that the baby in the manger is the Master and Savior. But in the long run, many of us seem to embrace the practical value judgment of preferring "having" to "being." It is not a sin to have — even Jesus had a home, a job and a lifestyle which conformed to the people of His time. But it is a sin to make having the most important value in life.

Everything — personally, socially, politically and ecclesiastically should come under this principle.

February 12
Being "With" and "Like" the Poor

A second aspect of the message of Bethlehem, as exemplified by Mary's and Joseph's loving adoration of the child, calls us to be *with* the poor. It is not enough to be *for* the poor. Understanding Jesus' birth requires us to enter into the soul and suffering of our brothers. It means sharing a sort of communion that broadens to a universal level, because the greatest part of humanity is in a state of poverty, need and underdevelopment. We must be with those who suffer, and, according to one's vocation and the various graces that God gives His Church, we must share their condition to truly understand them, and feel the intolerability of their situation. We must do this so as to be stimulated into effective action and support.

Finally, there is the third aspect of the Christmas message, which is probably the most difficult to accept. We are called to be *like* the poor. This expression, which we sometimes hear in preaching and which we read in the Scriptures, seems to be very far from the values which our society espouses with its cycle of production and consumption. It's very hard to separate ourselves from this mentality of our society, but it is precisely for this reason that we need to stand before the manger and reflect. We need to seize its profound sense of evangelical poverty, which means freeing ourselves from within from those things we possess and which are dear to us: not only economic goods, but cultural goods, and the professional qualities of talent, time and physical energy.

We thank the Lord for what He has given us, and we ask that we be free to share these goods with others, and to know how to share them with love.

We ask to recognize that we must deprive ourselves of our goods, to give to others, to enrich the weak, the least and the voiceless, so that we may all attain a balance in our possession and use of the things of this earth, a living sign of brotherhood.

The Lord helps us in the victory of the Spirit and man over the disintegrating forces in our lives. He helps us to grasp the cosmic sense of today's world that comes from the baby wrapped in swaddling clothes, lying in a manger!

"O Lord Jesus,
that You wanted to be such for us,
that You loved us to this point;
O Invisible and Eternal God, that You made your-
    self visible
in this mysterious and simple sign —
Open our hearts
so that we can understand you!
Open, we pray, the hearts and doors of this society
that it may celebrate Your victory over anonymity
    and indifference
by welcoming You Who are its Lord and
    Redeemer!"

February 13
Newness of Life and Poverty

The Gospels announce a sign of new life, a new way of being which at first glance seems irrelevant. "Here is a sign for you: you will find a baby wrapped in swaddling clothes and lying in a manger" (Lk 2:12).

His coming is nothing short of grandiose as regards the angels and all men, the heavens and the earth — and still the sign is irrelevant.

We note that there is an earlier reference to this sign in the general description of when and where Jesus was born: "She gave birth to her first born son, wrapped Him in swaddling clothes and laid Him in a manger" (Lk 2:7). The shepherds had to find Jesus, therefore, just as He was born.

But why do we insist on this sign?

In this tender expression, its simple words, we can see a profound contrast. The baby is wrapped in swaddling clothes and is lovingly welcomed by Mary. But He lies in a manger — a place where no baby should ever lie — for want of a home. He is poor, alone, abandoned.

We find the sign to be this contrast between Mary's attention and the poverty of the manger. God is historically present in the world in the sign of love and the sign of poverty.

He is present in the sign of Mary's love to show that we are all loved by God and that God asks our love, affection and welcome for Him into our lives in return.

He is present in the sign of poverty to show God's mysterious way of being in history. He provokes and frightens us.

What, then, does the poverty of the manger mean if, on the one hand, it represents the fruit of man's carelessness and sin, and on the other hand, it represents the concrete, historical way that Jesus manifests Himself?

What does the poverty of Bethlehem say to us and to the Church today?

The first aspect of the message is being for the poor; that is, willingly putting ourselves by their side in their need for essential things such as shelter, food, work, affection, health.

To be for them, by their side, doesn't mean neglecting others but it means to be concerned about those who find themselves in the same condition in which Christ Himself chose to be. Giving such a preference embraces all of man's experience in the cultural field and is the way of being Christian: with Christ's mentality, His way of action, His social, political and cultural concerns.

This attention is the fruit of a meditation on the

manger. It goads us incessantly to be for the poor — to seek them out, identify them, help and support them.

Think of the many good works that the Christian community has done and continues to do under the stimulus of the poverty of Bethlehem!

February 14
The Values of the Kingdom and Evangelical Poverty

Christian poverty is a way of being that ultimately is not based upon gestures or acts, but upon the values of the Kingdom which these express. The discerning criterion of our poverty, then, is the life of Christ, His "dignified austerity and simplicity" in public ministry, and His openness to the supreme and final events of His life.

Ours is a contradictory society. On the one hand, it is always producing new poor, emarginated outcasts who are abandoned and who despair. So, our poverty is called to be a sign of solidarity with and help for our brothers and sisters.

On the other hand, we live in an "opulent" society, threatened by the dangers posed by things, exposed to the risks and attractions of consumerism. Our poverty must be a criticism of this world that surrounds us. It must be a sign of the differing value between persons and goods.

Our journey in poverty is a journey of freedom, joy and enthusiasm, because it binds us intimately to Christ. It gives us a taste, in an unforeseen way, of the power of the cross and its ability to renew the most stagnant situations.

A little bit of pleasure, attention and work in the exercise of austerity, poverty, penance and rejection is for everybody the moment of discovery of the Gospel. Without this step, without the effort, they remain muted. With even the simplest of steps, the words of Jesus are actualized and resonate. They stand out. We thus experience something of the joy and enthusiasm of the Twelve who journeyed the streets of Palestine following Jesus after saying to Him: "Behold, Master. We've left everything to follow You."

February 15
The Greatest Commandment

We ask the Holy Spirit to help us to understand Jesus' words on Love.

Jesus summarized His thoughts in response to the lawyer's question on the greatest commandment. The episode is told in Matthew 22:34-39; in Mark 12:28-34; and in Luke 10:25-28.

We all know Jesus' answer: the greatest commandment is to love God and love your neighbor.

With these words, Jesus recalls several themes from the Old Testament. But while He recalls the Old Law, Jesus introduces two new ideas.

The first is the union of the two commandments. For Jesus, love is a powerful and distinct fact. It is rooted in an unreserved dedication to God: the whole person, with his gifts and abilities must entrust himself to the will of God and God's project of love for man. The visible and dynamic manifestation of this duty is the dedication that considers every man as a brother, neighbor or another self. To separate or simplify the different aspects of that unifying event which is Love means to use some of our restricted perspectives against the vast horizon opened up by Jesus' glance.

The second novelty is the surprisingly revolutionary notion of the "neighbor." Only the evangelist, Luke, puts a second question on the lawyer's lips: "But who is my neighbor?" Jesus replies with the parable of the Good Samaritan. The neighbor doesn't already exist. One becomes a neighbor. A neighbor does not already have a relationship of blood, race, business or psychological affinity with us. I become a neighbor when, before another, even a stranger or enemy, I decide to take some step that brings us closer.

It's important to note the relationship between the two new ideas which Jesus introduced. For man, love is born from a dedication to God and trust in His will. But God is the Father of all. So, in loving God, each person approaches others and creates new paths towards togetherness, while knocking down barriers of race, social class, different ideology or different religious beliefs.

February 16
The Radical Newness of Love

A concrete example of this newness may be found in the Sermon on the Mount, which is found in Chapters Five through Seven in Saint Matthew's Gospel. The Sermon describes the life of the disciple who, because he has encountered the Kingdom through the goodness and mercy of the Father, lives a life of love that goes beyond the old law. The disciple's model is the Father's love. "Be perfect as your Father in heaven is perfect" (Mt 5:48).

At the heart of the Sermon on the Mount is the "Our Father," the prayer of God's children (Mt 6:9-13). What follows is a series of concrete acts and attitudes of love which are described with abundant and stimulating examples. These examples demonstrate a love so intense towards everyone, including enemies, that even those who do not believe in Jesus as the Son of God, but consider Him to be a great master of humanity, are deeply touched.

We can find other insights in Saint John's Gospel. He does not employ a question and answer approach. In Chapter Thirteen, verses 34-35, Jesus gives the new commandment to His disciples during the Last Supper: "I give you a new commandment: Love one another. Just as I have loved you, you also must love one another. By this love you have for one another, everyone will know that you are My disciples." We note, above all, Jesus' example: His concrete act of self-sacrifice and death offers the disciples a living image of the Father's love, an insuperable model to imitate, and an inexhaustible source to draw upon.

We must also take note of the disciples: They are all loved and invited to enter into the community of believers in the love of the Father and Jesus. But in order for this universal love to be effectively proclaimed and put into effect, it is necessary that the believers (the disciples) seek good among themselves, offering themselves as examples and prophets of love. Jesus confirms this in His prayer: "Father, I pray not only for these, but for those also who through their words will believe in Me. May they all be one. Father, may they be one in us, as You are in Me and I am in You, so that the world may believe it was You Who sent Me" (Jn 17:20-21).

Charity and the Life of the First Christians

The New Testament illustrates the inexhaustible richness of Jesus' words as they became the source of new life in the concrete history of the first Christian community.

Considering the life of the first Christians from the viewpoint of charity, what immediately comes to mind is the sharing of goods practiced in the community of Jerusalem.

This practice offered immediate and realistic sociological relief, through the community's ability to change things and resolve the problems of poverty and prefigure a new society. However, it also agrees with other aspects as well, which give it a more profound interpretation.

We note first of all that this act of charity is very close to the other of the Lord's gifts and other forms of Jesus' presence within the community. In the two passages of the Acts of the Apostles in which this communion of goods is described (2:42-47; 4:33-37), it is bound together with prayer, with listening to the words of the apostles, with the breaking of the bread, with miracles, with joy. It therefore goes beyond a mere social initiative. It becomes a gift of God, Jesus' presence, an expression of faith in the Resurrection.

Moreover, it is a free gesture. No one is constrained to do it. Peter confirms this to Ananias who had sold a field but then kept back part of the proceeds and gave the rest to the disciples, telling them it was all: "Ananias, how can Satan have so possessed you that you should lie to the Holy Spirit and keep back part of the money from the land? While you still owned the land, wasn't it yours to keep, and after you had sold it wasn't the money yours to do with as you liked? What put this scheme into your mind? It is not to men that you have lied, but to God" (Acts 5:3-4).

All this brings us to see a dynamic relationship between charity and the concrete gesture of sharing goods. Charity is broader than every act. It is obedience to the Lord. It is a celebration of the Resurrection in the words of the Eucharist. It is joy at Jesus' eternal presence amid His own. But charity aims for concrete action. It searches to do all that is possible to manifest the new life of believers in the social arena as well. The communion of goods is a concrete sign, a prophetic and free manifestation of the richness of charity.

February 18
True Worship That Pleases God

Frequently, Saint Paul's letters describe the Christian life as a concrete life of charity. It is interesting to note that Paul uses the words "offering" and "sacrifice" (the language of worship) to designate a life of charity. Here are two examples:

In the Letter to the Romans (12:1-2), Paul begins to describe the life as a response to God's initiative presented in the preceding chapters of the letter. He writes: "Think of God's mercy, my brothers, and worship Him, I beg you, in a way that is worthy of thinking beings, by offering your living bodies as a holy sacrifice, truly pleasing to God. Do not model yourselves on the behavior of the world around you, but let your behavior change, modelled by your new mind. This is the only way to discover the will of God and know what is good, what it is God wants, what is the perfect thing to do." Paul then continues by giving concrete indications on the way to exercise fraternal charity.

In the Letter to the Ephesians, Paul dedicates the first three chapters to announce the central place of Christ in God's loving plan for humanity. With Chapter Four, the apostle presents the Christian life as sticking to Christ and God's plan: "I, the prisoner in the Lord, implore you therefore to lead a life worthy of your vocation. Bear with one another charitably, in complete selflessness, gentleness and patience. Do all you can to preserve the unity of the Spirit by the peace that binds you together" (Ep 4:1-3). Paul then continues to describe the life of believers in Christ and the concrete forms of exercising charity. In the middle of this description he says: "Be friends with one another, and kind, forgiving each other as readily as God forgave you in Christ. Try, then, to imitate God, as children of His that He loves, and follow Christ by loving as He loved you, giving Himself up in our place as a fragrant offering and a sacrifice to God" (4:32-5:2). The life of Christ, spent in love and the life of the Christian, conformed to Christ are true and agreeable worship.

This means first that worship is a whole life's work: the concrete works of charity done in everyday life are important.

But it is equally significant that life is worship: the concrete works of charity are framed in an obedient pathway to God, by listening to His Word, seeking out His will, staying close to Christ Who revealed and fully accomplished the Father's will.

The Famous Hymn to Love

The vision of the charitable life inspired the famous hymn to love which is found in Chapter Thirteen of the First Letter to the Corinthians. It comprises three stanzas.

The first stanza (v. 1-3) distinguishes love from mere acts done at the service of others. The gifts of tongues, prophecy, knowledge and miracles, without love, mean nothing. Giving away one's goods to the poor, or giving up one's body to be burned, without love, is nothing. Love is the greatest virtue that there is. It does not consist in the simple execution of an act, no matter how splendid or costly.

The second stanza (v. 4-7) describes the multi-faceted manifestations of love. It surpasses every act or attitude, and breeds new ones. Paul particularly indulges in a consideration of several fundamental orientations which place the person in a condition of acceptance, pardon, readiness, patience, kindness, understanding, trust, hope and endurance. Love is not unidirectional. It provides an interior orientation which permits a person to choose the right direction.

The third stanza (v. 8-13) tries to say the unsayable: Love is an already-existing thing on earth. It is that complete, everlasting good that puts us in God's dwelling place, where we see Him face-to-face and know Him as He knows us. Love is the supreme, surprising discovery of our humanity, as well as the humanity of our brothers and sisters which is the fruit of our total abandonment into the paternal arms of God.

February 20
God is Love

The First Letter of Saint John seeks to answer the question: "Who is the true Christian?" Many distinctive signs of the Christian are presented and they are bound up in love. But what is love? On the one hand, it is beyond our reach, being greater than we are. It is always ahead of us. It is the initiative of God Who loves us and continues to love us by sending His Son, Jesus, and following with the Holy Spirit. God Himself is Love. I remember a beautiful comment by the Danish philosopher Kierkegaard: "You loved us from the beginning, O God. We speak of You as if You loved us first, only once. However, day by day, for our whole life, You continually love us first. In the morning when I awake and lift up my spirit to You, You are there first, loving first. If I get up at dawn and immediately raise my spirit and prayer to You, You precede me, because You've always loved me first. It's always this way. And we ingrates! We speak as if You only loved us first the first time!" On the other hand, love demands that it become concrete in our lives and operative in our love for one another: "This has taught us love — that He gave up His life for us; and we, too, ought to give up our lives for our brothers. If a man who was rich enough in this world's goods saw that one of his brothers was in need, but closed his heart to him, how could the love of God be living in him? My children, our love is not just words or mere talk, but something real and active;. . . This is the love I mean: not our love for God, but God's love for us when He sent His Son to be the sacrifice that takes our sins away. My dear people, since God has loved us so much, we too should love one another. No one has ever seen God; but as long as we love one another God will live in us and His love will be complete in us. We are to love, then, because He loved us first. Anyone who says, 'I love God,' and hates his brother, is a liar, since a man who does not love the brother that he can see cannot love God, Whom he has never seen . . . Whoever believes that Jesus is the Christ has been begotten by God; and whoever loves the Father that begot him loves the child Whom He begets'' (1 Jn 3:16-18; 4:10-12, 19-20; 5:1-2).

February 21
Love and the Liturgy

Love stretches between the mystery of God and the history of man. It plumbs the depths of the mystery and produces ever-new fruit in history. To better know the mysterious and fruitful ways of love, we must ask the Holy Spirit to help us to understand love as it is manifested in history, how it came about by human events, and how it gave an answer to man's poverty and his needs.

I certainly cannot examine twenty centuries of Christianity. I can only offer several ideas which I believe useful in understanding the ways in which love must be present in our time.

I would like to begin with reference to two places in which the Holy Spirit is particularly clear in teaching us the value and expressions of love.

The first place is in the liturgy, especially the Eucharistic celebration. Through every generation, the liturgy, with its intense language, has revealed to Christians the fruit of God's love — Jesus Himself, Who draws all men together in the mystery of the Father's love. The

Holy Spirit, invoked at the consecration in order that the bread and wine may become the Body and Blood of Jesus, is also invoked after the consecration in order that all believers may become the Body of Christ; that is, the real manifestation of Him and His love for man. The Holy Spirit guides us in this narrow relationship between the Eucharistic Body and the Ecclesial Body of Jesus. He guides us between the love that Jesus lived in His Passion and the love that the Church must live in history.

The liturgical act offers us the instrumentality by which we follow the guidance of the Spirit.

I think of the Word proclaimed during the celebration, commented upon during the homily, illustrated with catechesis, and entrusted to personal reflection and communication of the faith in groups. If the Lectionary is truly used, understood and enjoyed, it becomes a rich source of practical examples, concrete stimuli and challenges, because the celebrated rite can be transformed into lived love.

I think of some of the significant moments at Mass, which, by their nature, form the hinge between liturgy and life.

The penitential rite, for example, helps us to discover and confess our concrete lapses against love.

The prayer of the faithful teaches us to confront the proclaimed Word with the problems of the Church and the world.

The exchange of peace invites us to become neighbors with those who are next to us, not from our own choice, but because it is called for by the assembly of believers.

The offertory collection, whether for ordinary or extraordinary reasons, calls for attention to and solidarity with our needy brothers and sisters.

A second place in which the Spirit speaks to us about love is in the history of Christian sainthood. The Saints, because they allowed themselves to be guided by the Spirit, do not glorify themselves for their work or exceptional tasks for which they sometimes gave their lives. They prayed and humbly entrusted their lives to God. But it is exactly because they dwell in God, very near to His heart, that they have a prophetic kindness and heroic strength to perceive the world's needs and do something about them.

February 22
Charity Builds the Church

We should endear ourselves to the Bible's message on the centrality of charity (with its characteristics of personal sharing, gratuitousness, total and unconditional dedication, and dependence of one's whole being on God) in the life of the Christian and the life of the Church. In so doing, we should see how this biblical message was heard and interpreted in the different ages of Christian tradition, so that we can better apply it to the problems we face today.

We should assume this patient and loving study by limiting ourselves to several summary enunciations which come more from the difficulties and problems that we've experienced in our lived faith in the Church.

It is necessary to clearly confirm that charity occupies a decisive place in the constitution of the Church and the formation of Christian life.

The Word and the Sacraments, in which the Father's love is made present in Jesus and communicated by the

Spirit, objectively and constitutionally aim towards charity by which the whole Church truly, really and actively acts "in memory of Jesus." Every Christian becomes capable of giving himself, body and blood (that is, totally and personally) for the good of his brothers and sisters.

Therefore, the entire prophetic, liturgical, ministerial and charismatic life of the Church aims toward that charism which is above all other charisms (1 Cor 13) and becomes authentic and unchangeable.

The service of love, whether within the community or in its missionary expressions, cannot be considered something to delegate to someone else. Rather, it demands everyone's participation, even though it finds only in some that prophetic and stimulating proposition which would benefit all the others.

February 23
Personal Structure and Love

The fact that love is the indispensable root and seal on every aspect of Christian life, makes it difficult to describe.

Love is not univocal behavior. Rather, it is a context in which many behaviors mature (1 Cor 13). Love is not unidirectional, but an interior sense or orientation which allows us to take the right direction in any circumstance.

Love is a "rediscovery" of ourselves and every other person by the very act of "losing" ourselves in the paternal arms of God. Now, aiming at a closer description of love, we can say that it has a clear, personal structure, in a double sense:

a) First of all, in the sense in which it directly

concerns the person. Love requires initiatives, plans and social interventions, but all beginning with a rediscovery and dedication of the person.

The personal attitudes of readiness, thankfulness, pardon, attentiveness, and anticipation all constitute the indispensable context in which concrete choices and acts of service mature.

From this point of view, volunteer work, which is founded upon the interior disposition of personal freedom, is a particularly significant expression of love.

b) Secondly, love has a personal orientation in the sense that it values and promotes the dignity of every person.

The Bible accounts (e.g., the parable of the Good Samaritan), confirmed by the many preferential choices for charity made throughout the centuries, enable us today to say that love reveals its pure, divine origins in the disarmed, disinterested unconditionality with which one welcomes every person. Charity enables persons to become neighbors, thereby breaking every discrimination of race, culture, social condition and religion, giving preference to those who are rejected, conferring upon them the dignity and value which is rightfully theirs as fellow human beings.

February 24
Love and the Development of Society

What we have previously described as the characteristics of love do not oppose the development of society, technology and science. Rather, we can see that love has an inexhaustible reserve of personal energies and deep motivations which assure a calm development of society.

Love does not limit itself to aid disadvantaged persons, but stimulates justice, and fights those laws, situations and structures which create disparities.

Love pushes science and technology to greater advances in knowledge in order to bring more good for humanity. Love matures the conscience of civil duty, assumes courageous social responsibility, encourages every public intervention in favor of the good of all.

As we can see, the development of society and science do not go against love *per se*, but only against any incomplete or distorted conception of love that society may propound.

It is therefore necessary that our communities' acts of charity clearly aspire to the authentic laws of evangelical love and know how to integrate into themselves those characteristics of scientific rigor, technical organization and social programming which certainly do not exhaust love's potentialities, but reveal love's ability to value man according to those norms and degrees which are truly Christian.

February 25
For Those in Difficulty

Beyond the obviously broad significance of "*For those in difficulty*," I would like to pause at a limited situation which captures the reality of this important concern. I mean, then, by "for those in difficulty" not every generic need of another, to which one responds in some habitual and foreseen manner. Rather, I am concerned with those situations in which a brother or sister and their need puts us into a new, unforeseen and uncomfortable situation for which our ordinary structures are not enough. There are no immediate answers to these situations and they demand that something be done, often at the expense of our bearing some discomfort or pain in the process.

This situation is exemplified in Chapter Ten of Saint Luke's Gospel, which recounts the parable of the Good Samaritan. In the story, the priest and the Levite find themselves in difficulty because the injured man on the street presents a "new situation" for them. Perhaps he is already dead. Perhaps it's not worth all the bother and trouble to get involved. Perhaps it's better to leave him alone because he's part of some vendetta or feud between criminals. On the other hand, the two wouldn't know what to do with him. If I lift him up, I might kill him and end up right in the middle of a real mess. Each man is embarrassed, uneasy, in turmoil. The situation was not foreseen. And while in other situations the priest and the Levite would have known what to do and whom to call, this time they are facing something they don't need. The trouble has turned up at the wrong time and in the wrong place.

It is the person in difficulty that puts us in difficulty because he is something not planned for. We have no script to follow. He disturbs our ordinary way of encountering others. He obligates us to choices for which we are unprepared, and lays bare our lack of desire to be prepared or to act. Our readiness is good up to a certain point, but then we discover its inadequacy.

The world, with its inexorable mechanisms for emargination and suffering, is always creating these "new difficulties" which constrain us to continually reflect on our uneasiness and our unpreparedness.

Moreover, even if they are "old" situations, they often return in a new light and oblige us to a greater awareness of them, so as to better mobilize a larger number of our faculties and powers for them. This, then, is the reference point of the Good Samaritan, which we must bear in mind when we are faced with a brother or sister in need.

We must focus our attention on the Samaritan and ask ourselves how he ever found the proper attitude among the many theoretical, practical, social, civil and political possibilites that were placed before him.

In Chapter Ten, verse 33, the key is: "A Samaritan traveler, who came upon him, *was moved with compassion* when he saw him." He comes upon the man and does not turn away. He "sees" him in the biblical sense of the word, meaning that he notices him, recognizes, understands, values and above all, has compassion for him. He lets his heart speak. He lets his inner being emerge — that being which manifests God's love. He has that compassion which all men can express in a just and authentic manner, even regarding a brother in difficulty.

February 26
The Vigilant Intelligence of Love

There exists a love which not only accepts, but which also seeks out its poor. It's an understanding love with the intelligence to scrutinize society in order to grasp new and negative pockets of degradation and physical and moral suffering.

Referring to Chapter Twenty-five of Matthew's Gospel, we come across a number of welcoming actions: "I was a stranger and you welcomed me . . . I was hungry and you gave me food." There also are those attitudes which search out: "I was sick and imprisoned and you visited me." These charisms underline an attentiveness and active searching which question us continually: Today, who are the socially weak, the "vanquished" of society? What can we do for them?

This charism embraces all charitable and educative activities on behalf of today's poor, and always seeks their highest good.

From Matthew's account, we can draw a further insight: " 'When did we visit You while You were sick or in prison?' 'Whenever you did this to the least of My brothers, you did it to Me' " (Mt 25:31-40).

The word "least" refers not only to the condition of infancy; there are situations in adult life in which there exist the "least" because they do not risk being seen, or are positively avoided. But we must always possess a vigilant and intelligent attentiveness to these situations and be ready to embrace others in love.

This is the charism of the love that searches itself, questions itself, and seeks out the other. It is the love that scrutinizes and continually renews itself in its vigilance. We can see this vigilance in the eyes of Mary who notices before all the servants of the house that there is no wine and foresees immediately that the shortage could create consternation and sadness at the wedding feast. She then acts on her vigilance.

February 27
True Fasting

At the beginning of Lent, the Church exhorts us with the words of the prophet Isaiah, telling us that true fasting and genuine penance consist in sharing your food with the hungry and providing the poor wanderer with shelter; in clothing the naked and never turning away from your own flesh and blood (Is 58:7).

Situations such as those described here did not only exist in Isaiah's time. We see them in our midst today. Others exist in a more serious and generalized way in the third world. In his encyclical *Dives In Misericordia*, Pope John Paul II speaks of the "great remorse constituted by the fact that alongside of those in well-off and affluent societies there are not lacking individuals and social groups in the same human family who suffer from hunger . . . and their numbers reach the tens and hundreds of millions." But along with this situation, colossal and macrocosmic as it is, how many other needy people, both near and far, are knocking on our own doors right now?

It's not a matter of exhausting ourselves in a few concrete acts. It's also a matter of digging deep within ourselves to find that secret place in which our self-gift and loving action are sprinkled by the waters of faith and by the power of God's Word.

To the individual who risks self-division we must offer an image of man and community which live this prayerful expression of the faith and this generous act of love as expressions of a uniquely profound reality: that of man redeemed by Christ and raised to everlasting life by Christ's death through love.

February 28
What Baptism Does For Us

Baptism is: entrusting ourselves to God's loving plan; joining the Church, which is the hope of the world.

For each of us, Baptism marks the Father's embrace. It's an effective sign of vital relationships which the Father, Son and Spirit share with us. It gives us a new heart. It enables us to obey filially — like Jesus — God's plan.

Baptism marks our entrance into the great family that is the Church. It enables us to celebrate the Eucharist, to hear and witness the Word of the Lord, to live fraternal charity, and to put our gifts at the service of all.

Finally, Baptism makes us a sign of hope for all humanity, because it makes us a new humanity, freed from sin, ready to enter into the many ways of human living, but not with aggressive egoism that demands everything selfishly, but with firm openness to be drawn by Christ and disposed to help, collaborate, serve and love.

Meditating on our Baptism is always profoundly consoling. It's a meditation which brightens our world outlook. Then if the problems we face are enormous, Baptism fills us with trust, because through His Baptized, Christ continues to defeat with love the evil that is in the world.

MARCH

March 1
Baptism: At the Heart of Christian Living

There are many important moments of grace in our Christian life where we grasp God's action in us in a remarkable way. These moments are lived throughout the liturgical year in various ways: at Sunday Eucharist, when hearing the Word of God, when reading Scripture. There also are moments when we face great moral decisions and must say "yes" or "no" to God, to honesty, to life.

All of these moments shape our Christian existence. They draw us closer to God and the responsibilities of our faith. These moments which mark God's presence and action in our life have a foundation: Baptism.

Baptism is the founding event which determines all the stages of Christian life. It provides the source and meaning of all that we do, from our prayer at the Eucharist, to works of charity, to the priestly and episcopal ministry, to giving one's life if necessary. All the good that we do and will do is born from this privileged encounter with God at the moment of our Baptism.

I would like to call attention to this fundamental truth: in Baptism, we present ourselves to God as we are. We deliver ourselves to the Father, Son and Spirit, and forego the management of our own life according to principles based on egoism: having, possessing, profiting, and personal success. We accept and desire that our life be guided by God's heart and mind; in short, by His plan. This is the radical change that affects our daily living and broadens our horizons.

We bring our infants to the Baptismal font because we desire that they, like we, no longer live for themselves — as Saint Paul says — but for the One Who died and rose for them. They live an existence founded on love, justice and hope. But it is not an easy life, marvelous though it may be, when we think of how the world exalts personal interest at any cost — even at the loss of the other's goods — and considers justice to include stepping on the rights and the lives of others.

We, however, proclaim before God that man is called to put his whole life, present and future, in the Father's hands, and to be guided by His love, by the Gospels, and by the Spirit Who is given to us in Baptism.

In Baptism, then, each of us delivers himself lovingly and trustingly to the Triune God. And God, the Trinity of Love, welcomes us. From that moment, we are no longer alone and afraid of what will be. We are sons of God, brothers in Jesus, persons who love by the power of the Spirit. If we were truly able to understand the explosive power of this mystery, its ability to renew the world and change the face of the earth, we would be filled with joy in recalling what has been completed in us: "Lord, revive the grace of Baptism in me!"

March 2
Baptism and Our Baptismal Promises

Baptism is the gift of the Risen Christ in us. It opens the way of life to us in the company of Jesus and gives us the certainty that He will remain with us all the days of our life. As Matthew recounts for us at the end of his Gospel, the Risen Jesus invokes the Trinity, and, in so doing, assures all the Baptized: "Know that I am with you always; yes, to the end of time" (Mt 28:20).

Let us prepare to renew our Baptismal promises. They are the promises which affirm the intensity of our gift and its correspondence to God's action. The promises develop along two lines: renunciation and then, profession of faith. Christ comes to us in Baptism. He lives in and with us and journeys with us. But He asks us to clearly and courageously make ourselves known in history and change it, just as Jesus' Resurrection changed the world's course from a journey of death to a journey of life.

We are called upon to reject everything that is allied with death, oppression, egoism and selfish possessiveness, defeatism and despair.

Then, we are called to make a full profession of faith; a faith built and lived around the figure of the crucified and Risen Christ. It is a faith that not only dwells in the heart and is not only professed with words, but that is carried through life in one's open hands, and confronts the world by the courageous choices for freedom that we make.

March 3
Our Conversion Is Baptismal Conversion

We were baptized in Jesus Christ, and therefore, buried with Him in death so that we may live a new life freed from sin and the fears of sin: fear of death, fear of failure, fear of losing others' esteem, etc. (Rm 6:4-14).

We were given a spirit of love, not a spirit of fear or slavery (Rm 8). It is God Himself Who confers the oil and puts the Spirit in our hearts (2 Cor 1). For our part, we give thanks by journeying in faith and calling God our "Father." We ask the Lord that He may give us the grace to walk in trust and love, and never walk like those who groan as they carry a heavy and almost unsupportable burden. Let us walk as free men called to an enthusiastic vocation which, by the grace of God, we willingly carry out before God and before man.

March 4
Lent Is a Journey of Conversion

The Lenten liturgy holds values which, together, solicit and enlighten a journey of conversion. To accompany the Lord as He "goes up to Jerusalem" means renewing the choice of communion in the mystery of His death and Resurrection. This choice finds its particular expression in a faithful abandonment to the Father, and in service to our brothers and sisters. The Word that nourishes — "Man does not live only on bread, but on every word that comes from the mouth of God" (from Matthew's Gospel for the first Sunday of Lent) — shows the spiritual route to believers, and also reveals man's hard-hearted attitudes which separate him from God.

The Lenten liturgy refers many times to Baptism, and invites those who celebrate to renew the Covenant with God and enter onto the road of authentic discipleship. Finally, the liturgy underlines our frailty and the sinful condition in which we live. It calls on us to

80

welcome the signs of penance, and manifest a heart knowledgeable of its faults and poverty, but trustful of God's mercy.

Each of the forty days of Lent brings these messages into our hearts. Let us say "yes" that our prayers as individuals and as communities may transform our hearts and lead to true conversion.

The Values and Attitudes of Conversion

I would like to call upon everyone — we are all penitents in need of redemption — to cultivate several values and to educate ourselves to several fundamental attitudes on our journey to conversion.

First of all, I can think of an openness to judge one's life by the Word of God. We ourselves are not the final judges of our life. But our faith requires us to face the norms that the Word sets out and to judge ourselves and our actions according to these evangelical criteria.

The penitent's spiritual experience further demands a renewed choice to put himself at Jesus' disposal. The *soul* of our journey lies in this fidelity to the Master and in our consistently choosing to follow Him.

Finally, there is the desire to live in full communion with God and with our fellow man. Sin damages or destroys this communion. The convert must always return love in a deeper way.

The invitation towards sacramental Reconciliation reaches many different situations; and here I'm referring to "spiritual" rather than "physical" situations. For example, the person who has broken his Baptismal Covenant must decide to truly return to the Lord by having a penitent heart and a desire to be pardoned so as to start anew.

Another example: perhaps there is someone who has an indifferent or distracted faith. His heart is somewhere else — perhaps on material things. He has no space for nor desire to seek out God. For him, conversion will mean exiting from the gray areas and getting back on track by accepting a different and personal relationship with the Lord.

For the person who journeys in faith, this penitential time leading to Easter allows him to reconfirm his choices, purify himself by understanding his weakness, and better comprehend God's plan for his life.

There is something great in all of us that is worthy of being fully lived. Lent makes an invitation to enter into our life, our choices, our ways of confronting or avoiding problems. Then the spiritual itinerary of conversion can help us to transform ourselves into something relevant, both personally and socially.

March 6
Conversion and the Gospels

I have previously developed the themes of the four Gospels, which are understood as images of the progressive development of the Christian journey.

Mark presents the Gospel of conversion for the catechumen. Matthew presents the Gospel of the Baptized for entrance into the Church and catechetical initiation. Luke presents the Gospel for the evangelist, teaching that the Word must be proclaimed to the world.

82

Finally, John sums everything up, presenting a Gospel for contemplation by the "elders" in the community of believers.

The four Gospels are reread every year. They continually challenge us to ask ourselves: Where am I? What is the next step? Where do we find ourselves as community, group or parish? What path have we taken? How do we stand as a family, living together?

Minimally, we are always called to aim for and to take that step in the right direction. But the Gospels guide us in such a way that, in taking the right step, we can experience great joy, because each step brings us closer to each other and to God.

March 7
The Struggles and Our Spiritual "Arms" for the Lenten Journey

The Bible presents us with many images of struggling: Jesus was tempted and, before Him, the People of God struggled in the wilderness on their way to the Promised Land. Certainly, the first Christian community struggled. In our Lenten journey towards Easter, we must include ourselves, the Church, as the People of God engaged in a struggle.

Lent is not simply a time of major silence and interior quiet. It is a time of spiritual struggle. It is a time in which the inner conflict inherent in human existence — against Satan and sin — shows itself in a stronger and clearer way, particularly in those who seriously make the Lenten journey. The journey will then flow into the joy of Easter in the measure of our ability to fully welcome

Jesus' salvific gift of the cross and Resurrection.

We must therefore begin Lent with great courage, ready to struggle, armed with the arsenal of the Gospels.

The Gospels are not conventional or even the more tremendous nuclear arms. Instead, they are arms of the spirit, man's interior power which wins in the struggle against evil.

The entire Lenten liturgy urges us on to a path of conversion. This means accompanying Jesus in His journey to Jerusalem, abandoning ourselves, like Him, to the will of the Father.

The Gospels give us the spiritual arms and tools for the journey's struggles: the Word of God itself, by which man lives, especially during Lent with its penitential activity, which expresses itself in the Sacrament of Reconciliation and other works of penance. Our confessions during this time must be lived with intense faith. We must be certain that we will receive God's pardon through the mystery of the Church, thanks to the Body and Blood of Jesus.

March 8
The "Lectio Divina": A First Reflection

In English, *Lectio Divina* refers to spiritual reading which is based on Sacred Scripture. The literal translation from the Latin is "Divine Reading." It is very important for us today to understand the value and significance of this precious inheritance that the Benedictine tradition knew how to value, deepen, and hand down through the centuries.

As the Latin word says, by *lectio*, we mean a

"reading." But to fully understand the term, we must go beyond its traditional meaning which conjures up images of a cursory, superficial going through of some written page of material.

Monastic spiritual reading is done by listening, ruminating and repeating our reflection on the Word. The Word is not only superficially read by the eyes, but is listened to with the ears and received with the heart. It is absorbed, repeated and meditated upon. It is a Word that descends into the heart slowly and fills it. You can imagine how much peace this exercise produces. It is completely the opposite of that anxious and hectic reading, hearing and dialogue of our cities' pace which makes our life so tense and tiresome. This monastic reading introduces a slower and simpler pace, just by the rhythmic reading and the slow, relishing meditation which fosters peace, calm and dignity. This sets a pattern for us in our approach to all things: not with the hectic and devouring haste of a consumer, but with the calm of one who is receiving a gift.

Most important, remember that this *lectio* is "divine." Its object is God's Word: the Scriptures.

The Church of Vatican II, as seen, for example, in paragraph six of *Dei Verbum*, repeatedly teaches that this ancient monastic tradition is something for all Christians to rediscover and put back into the heart and practice of the community; that is, a continuous reading of the Scriptures which sets the entire plan of God before us every day, every week, in well determined cycles.

It is the "divine reading" of the Divine Word that opens up the plan of salvation. It's a reading which allows us to touch God in some way, to hear Jesus speak to us, and to put into practice that "true search" for God Who is the soul of Benedictine life and the soul of every man's search. Search out God. Seek to see Him, touch Him and know Him. An attentive, devoted, prolonged reading of Sacred Scripture allows us to see, touch and immerse ourselves in God and His plan of salvation.

March 9
Continuing the "Lectio Divina"

Spiritual reading (*Lectio Divina*) is "divine" not only because it places us in the presence of God's Word, but because it allows us to "read" the book of our life, as God's work. The Bible is the mirror of our life. It tells us who we are, where we come from, where we're going, what each day's events mean, what our sufferings mean, and what excites us in the world today.

The Bible reveals the divine aspect of all these things, the mystery of God's grace. And it is precisely here in the exercise of the *Lectio Divina* that we reach that marvelous moment in existence described by Pope John Paul II in his encyclical, *Redemptor Hominis*: "We find ourselves confronted with an overwhelming sense of awe because we see how great is man for whom God has done so much." Reading the Bible organically, attentively and intelligently we discover the mystery of God in our life. That is why the monastic life (in particular the contemplative life) is the model of the ideal, healthy, human life, able to link one's prayer and one's work. It enables one to understand God's and man's ways, plumb the mysteries of the Spirit and to reach out to all creation. It helps one to look both above to God and out to all people with simplicity and love, and to serve all those who are in need.

86

Educating the First Disciples,
Educating Today's Christian

What kind of instruction is given to Peter, James, John and the other disciples who follow Jesus?

Jesus instructs them on the Christian person; that is, He teaches them all of those attitudes which make up the mature person who is able to account for the needs and sufferings of others. We can think of the instructive value of the miracles that the disciples witness as they confront the many forms of human suffering — from sickness to misfortune, from forms of obsession to other psychic suffering.

As spectators, the disciples see how much evil there is in the world, how much suffering, abandonment and deprivation. They are taught that they need a heart and a sensitivity in order to recognize the suffering. Theirs is an education founded upon goodness, charity and compassion. Peter thus summarized Jesus' actions: "He went about doing good and curing all who had fallen into the power of the devil" (Ac 10:38). Jesus makes His disciples share in His heart-felt and ready compassion by which He is able to see the evil and suffering in others and empathize with them.

The disciples' instruction also focuses on their relationship with Jesus. It is an education in trusting in the Messiah's mission. The apostles witness Jesus' goodness, His success, and His ability to win people over. The apostles enthusiastically put their trust in Him, His honesty, His charity and His sensitivity for the sufferings of others. Through their Master's guidance, their trust grows.

Thirdly, Jesus instructs His disciples to look at

man's basic problems. We think of the episode of the paralytic: "I forgive you your sins," Jesus says. Or, when Jesus says: "I came not for the just, but for sinners." And also to the woman in Simon's house: "You are forgiven much because you loved much." The disciples, like most people who are immersed in their work and its fatigue, probably had limited life and family experiences. They had to learn that there's much suffering, and many people in need of compassion, including those who suffer within.

This, then, was what we can call the education of the Christian person — with emphasis on the word "person"; that is, a being who is able to turn towards others in Christian fraternity.

March 11
Luke's Pedagogical Route (Lk 9-18)

Jesus' words in Luke 9-18 are *the hardest and most uncompromising words of the Gospel*. I wish to summarize these passages into three dominant themes.

1) *Teaching detachment and freedom of heart.* "Sell your possessions and give alms. Get yourselves purses that do not wear out, treasure that will not fail you, in heaven where no thief can reach it and no moth destroy it. For where your treasure is, there will your heart also be" (Lk 12:33-35).

Those who follow Jesus are gradually taught about freedom of the heart; that is, not to become attached to those things which would separate them from their task (e.g., profit seeking, career, personal preoccupations). Jesus uses strong words to emphasize the need for a free heart.

2) *Teaching self-abandonment to the Father*. The disciple must know that his life is in the Father's hands. He must entrust everything, present and future, to the Father: "What father among you would hand his son a stone when he asked for bread? . . . If you, then, who are evil, know how to give your children what is good, how much more will the heavenly Father give the Holy Spirit to those who ask Him" (Lk 11:11, 13).

Or still: "That is why I am telling you not to worry about your life and what you are to eat, nor about your body and how you are to clothe it. For life means more than food, and the body more than clothes. Think of the ravens. They do not sow nor reap; they have no storehouses and no barns; yet God feeds them. And how much more are you worth than birds!" (Lk 12:22-25).

3) *Teaching the meaning of the cross*. This instruction carries an important characteristic for the entire Gospel teaching. Not all of Jesus' teaching is idealistic. Jesus provides principles, draws conclusions, sets a plan, and then provides the way to actualize the plan. *It is an instruction learned by being lived*. The disciples live with Jesus. They see how He acts, reacts, speaks, behaves. His teaching and His life are intertwined. Jesus teaches and He does. This is fundamental to the Gospel instruction from whence it draws its authority.

March 12
Peter: How Jesus Works Through the Disciple

Jesus creates a way for His disciples to follow in order that they may become evangelizers, and we can trace that route through the example of Peter.

His calling is related in Luke 5:1-11.

The background of the scene: There are many people listening to Jesus on the shores of a lake. Jesus sees two boats with fishermen pulling in their nets. One of the fishermen in the boat stands out. He seems so free and secure in his domain of the vessel. This fisherman is Peter. Jesus asks Peter to take Him a little way off from the shore so He can teach the crowd.

We can imagine Peter's feelings at being chosen. He gets a little cocky, probably thinking to himself: "I mustn't be the worst of the village. Jesus must have recognized my modesty and wants to honor me." Peter experiences some moments of euphoria.

But there's a surprise in store for him: When Jesus finishes His talk, and Peter prepares to bring the boat ashore (undoubtedly, he thinks, to the accolades of the others), Jesus, without warning, tells him to go out onto the lake and throw out his nets for a catch. Certainly Peter experiences some change at that moment (Scripture does not say much about people's inner feelings; it leaves them up to our imagination and our own lived experiences). From Peter's reply, we can sense that some doubts rose in his mind as to his Master's wisdom: after all, no one fishes at this hour because there are no fish! In the first part of the answer, Peter says: "Master, we worked hard all night long and caught nothing." In this delicate moment, Peter wrestles with himself. He is giving in to his fatigue, and telling Jesus that he's already tried and that it's useless; it's better to go home.

If, however, Peter decides to risk a little and overcome the oppressive labor and the possible ridicule he is opening himself up to by throwing out the nets at this time, he will pass this test of faith: "If you say so, I will pay out the nets." Here Peter makes his decision. He

takes on the responsibility of a man who must courageously decide big and little things. He leaves his calcula-
tions behind and acts on the Lord's word. This is one of
the typical characteristics that Jesus looks for in an
evangelizer.

Peter's nets fill. Other boats come around and throw
their nets in too. What's happening? Seeing this (and this
is an aspect of *kerygma*: some unforeseen, but notable
act), Peter recognizes God's power and throws himself at
Jesus' feet saying: "Go from me, for I am a sinner."
What happened? Jesus makes Peter realize his sinfulness.

Jesus thus brings Peter to the point where He wants
him — to a purification, a humility, a recognition of his
need for God's mercy. Jesus brings Peter around to this in
a free and human way, without causing him any inner
turmoil.

But the episode ends with yet another reversal of the
situation. Peter expects the Lord to acknowledge his
penitential sentiments. Instead, Jesus says: "Don't be
afraid; from now on it is men you will catch." So, Peter
journeys first from being a conceited person, to being a
person capable of placing his entire trust in Jesus, to being
a person who recognizes his own poverty and weakness,
to being a man who bears the responsibility of his relationship of trust with the Lord.

March 13
Peter's Faith and Insensitivity

By leaving his own values behind, Peter made the
most significant act of his life. He dared to affirm that
Jesus is the One in Whom Peter would place his final

trust. He proclaimed: "You are the Christ, the Son of the Living God." With this proclamation, Peter fundamentally changes the relationship between Jesus and the disciples. And for this, Jesus praises him: "Blessed are you, Simon, son of Jonah." Not the body or blood, not intelligence, observation or reflection suggested the words to you; it was My Father who revealed them to you. Peter thus came to know how to proclaim the truth, namely, that Jesus is the Messiah, God-with-us, the hope for all humanity.

On the other hand, Peter must have thought about the significance of his proclamation: Jesus is the Messiah, the King of Israel. He must have some plan to reign. He knows a way to resolve political, economic, social and civil evils that plague the Israelite community.

So imagine Peter's shock and dismay when he hears Jesus say: "The Son of Man is doomed to suffer, be rejected and put to death." Peter does not accept the contradiction between his image of Jesus as the triumphal King and Jesus' image. Peter reproaches Jesus, and is, in turn, reproached by the Lord. Before, Peter was called "blessed"; now Jesus calls him "Satan," telling him that he does not reason as God reasons.

What Peter did not understand (and will only come to understand in time, after his denial of Christ and Christ's subsequent Resurrection) is that Jesus' mission is Jesus Himself, offered in sacrifice. Peter struggles with this, not just because he can't believe this truth about his King, or because he loves Jesus so much, but because he is unable to understand that man must first fulfill himself by self-giving before he can go out and achieve great things. Jesus says: "He who wants to save his life will lose it, but he who loses his life will find it."

92

March 14
Proclaiming Faith in Jesus, the Word of Life

At the end of His discourse in Capernaum, Jesus receives so many objections and so much criticism that He turns to His disciples and says: "You, then, what do you plan to do?" Peter responds: "Lord, to Whom shall we go? Only You have the words of everlasting life." Surrounding the events which demonstrate man's unwillingness to accept God's Covenant, Peter voices his trust in the Lord.

To better understand the significance of Peter's declaration, we can ask ourselves if in the Bible there are any parallel excerpts with which we can make a comparison. We are looking for a Scripture text which contains a confession amid a climate of hard-heartedness, indifference, or disputation.

One New Testament excerpt, which is used to introduce the Passion, comes to mind. This is the episode of the woman of Bethany, who entered the house of Simon where Jesus was at table, and broke an alabaster jar containing an expensive ointment and poured the ointment on Jesus' hair.

Just as Peter made his confession of faith in the hostile environment of Capernaum, so too did the woman of Bethany, who on the eve of Jesus' Passion, broke and sacrificed her vase and oil—her treasure—to confess that Christ is the center of her life. Her confession is through her *act*.

Peter confesses the truth of Jesus with his *words*. His question, "Where shall we go?" clearly demonstrates that there is no other way to salvation except through Jesus. Peter's affirmation, "Only You have the words of everlasting life," says that Jesus is the bread of life; *He is my life*.

Moreover, Peter adds: "We believe and understand that You are the One Whom God has sent." He means: we put our trust in You with eyes closed. Not everything is clear to us. Although we want to know more, it's enough that we know we must put our trust in you. Through you, our eyes will be opened and we will understand who we are, and thus may live the meaning of our life's journey.

March 15
The Transfiguration

"About eight days after this had been said, He took with Him Peter and John and James and went up to the mountain to pray" (Lk 9:28). In the Transfiguration episode, we can see just how much Peter lived his calling with enthusiasm and with a sense of responsibility. "He said to Jesus: 'Master, it is wonderful for us to be here; so let us make three tents, one for You, one for Moses, and one for Elijah.' He did not know what he was saying" (Lk 9:33).

Here we see Peter in all his generosity. In fact, he does not say: "Let's build a tent for me." He thinks of Jesus, Moses and Elijah. Feeling himself clothed by the Kingdom, he takes up his responsibility. He is ready to do everything for the sake of the Kingdom. At this moment he feels at the height of his power and ability. We can think that when he comes down from the mountain the next day (Lk 9:37) and learns that the disciples were unable to drive out a demon from a young boy, he, too, probably shares the words of Jesus: "How much longer must I be among you and put up with you?" That is, Peter

94

thinks: I truly have faith, I am by His side. These other disciples no longer understand what they're dealing with. They aren't on the same level as I am.

Peter is growing in awareness of his responsibility, the weight he carries on his shoulders.

March 16
Jesus' Prayer for Peter and God's Free Gift

Like a cold shower, the words of Jesus strike Peter: " 'Simon, Simon! Satan, you must know, has got his wish to sift you all like wheat; but I have prayed for you Simon, that your faith may not fail, and once you have recovered, you in your turn must strengthen your brothers.' 'Lord,' he answered, 'I would be ready to go to prison with you, and to death.' Jesus replied, 'I tell you, Peter, by the time the cock crows today you will have denied three times that you know me' " (Lk 22:31-34).

How does Peter take these important words: "You must strengthen your brothers"?

Evidently, he assumes that he is capable of assuming the responsibility that the message contains: "Lord, I am ready to go with You to face prison and death." Because we know what happens next, we think of how presumptuous Peter is in making such claims. But the words are so beautiful; words that every Christian should be able to affirmatively say. So, what is bad about them, which will help us to understand how Peter fell? Peter truly expresses what he feels, but it's clear that he didn't hear what Jesus was telling him: "Satan has got his wish to sift you all like wheat; but I have prayed for you, Simon." If Peter had heard this, he would have said:

"Lord, thank You for praying for me. I am so weak; I can do so little. Stay near to me." Instead, Peter takes the task on as a privilege which he can handle by his own strength. He misses that the task can only be accomplished through the gift of the Lord. He thus sets himself up for his fall. *In fact, the Gospel is precisely the free gift of God. It's the salvation that God freely gives to the sinner.* When we receive it with a grateful spirit, with humility and just recognition of its source, we are in our proper place. We can thus begin to appropriate it, digest it and control any situation. Peter thinks he is not afraid, yet his pride comes from his fear of the cross. He is sincere, but his fault lies in his desire to be first. In a theological sense, we could say that he wants to be the Lord's savior.

March 17
Peter and Jesus on the Mount of Olives

Jesus goes off with His disciples to the Mount of Olives. He is filled with anguish. He sweats drops of blood. Yet, Jesus lacks the support of the disciples, including Peter. Peter cannot bear the image of a weak Jesus. Peter knew Jesus as powerful, successful, as One Who always handled any adversary and any situation.

Here, for the first time, Peter sees Jesus overcome by weakness. Peter's heart becomes restless. How is it possible for God to be with this man? He is weak and afraid.

Peter was taught under the Old Testament to view God as great and powerful: Yahweh the strong, Who wins wars and vanquishes His enemies. Peter transferred this image to Jesus. Now, seeing Jesus so weak, what can he do but shut his eyes to it? It is the act of one who says: "I don't want to know; I don't want to see; I don't want to come to understand." They come to arrest Jesus. Judas approaches Jesus and gives Him the traitor's kiss. What does Peter do? He recalls the images, gathers his strength and says: "Lord, shall we use the sword?" Peter reverts to playing the hero who wants to die for his Master. He is ready to throw himself into the battle, win at any cost, maybe even die to save the Master. He reaches what he believes to be the peak of his generosity: the Gospel calls me to this. I'm called to give my life, so I must give it.

Let us imagine the almost total interior crumbling that happens within when Jesus intervenes: "Leave off! That will do." Peter's idea of God is shattered. God is no longer more powerful, more good, more just. He does not intervene to save Jesus. Who then is this Master that we've followed and believed in? Peter falls into a tremendous internal confusion, which helps us to better understand his later denials.

March 18
The Salvific Quality of Peter's Denials

Peter follows his Master, but keeps himself at a distance. He follows Jesus because he loves Him. He keeps himself at a distance because he can't speak openly of Him anymore. Peter no longer understands: What does He want?

Then Peter is confronted by the first accuser: "This one was with Him." But Peter denies it saying: "Woman, I don't know Him." In reality, Peter's denial, "I don't know Him," has a certain amount of truth to it in Peter's own mind, because Jesus is no longer the One

Peter believed in; that is, a leader and a winner Who could overcome any adverse situation. Peter no longer knows Him. He no longer understands the man who has been abandoned to His enemies. Peter no longer knows what Jesus wants. Peter no longer reaches out to Him.

When Peter is again confronted with, ''You were one of them!'', he denies it, saying: ''No, I'm not the man.'' The text says, ''about an hour passed.'' We can imagine the identity crisis Peter was experiencing. Who am I? What do I want? What has my life been? What was in me that made me follow this man? What or who made me do it? And still, I believed Him and wanted only His good. He shouldn't have betrayed me this way.

These are the twists and turns of a man who generously followed a way, but now no longer understands God's plan for him. What does God want of me now? Before, I was able to say. Until a few hours ago I was ready to die with Him. Now I don't know what God wants. It's a terrible moment for Peter.

Then, ''another insisted: 'Truly he was with Him; he too is a Galilean.' But Peter said: 'Sir, you do not know what you are saying.' '' Peter's trial is one of the most terrible trials a person can experience. Peter came to doubt all that went into his religious formation. Is this God I believed in or have I made a mistake?

If Peter passed through this, he passed through it for the whole Church, for us, to strengthen his brothers, as Jesus foretold. Therefore, it is a trial he experienced as the head of the Church. Peter's dilemma may be expressed as follows: Peter wanted to save Jesus, but in reality, it was Jesus Who had to save Peter. Peter had to realize that he was saved by Jesus. He was pardoned by Jesus. In fact, he was the first confidant of evangelical pardon and mercy.

The trial cost Peter much, because he was very jealous of his fidelity and ability to be honest and trustworthy.

Instead, the Lord made him understand that he too can reach a moment of grave error. Therefore, if he wants to evangelize, he must have limitless understanding of God's salvific mercy and a limitless ability for compassion for his brothers in the Church.

At this point the text continues: "While he was speaking, a cock crowed." At its crowing there is Peter's rejection of his sin: Look at what you have come to, you who wanted to possess the Kingdom and the Gospels, you who wanted to be the defender of the Master.

March 19
Saint Joseph: Mature in Faith

Even before Jesus was born, Joseph was a believer mature in faith. The events surrounding the conception and birth of Jesus reveal how differently he behaved and struggled as he moved towards a greater knowledge of God.

There are two key words in the Gospel account that help us to understand the positions he took: "Her husband Joseph, being a man of honor and wanting to spare her publicly, decided to divorce her informally." The exegetes have devoted much time to the meaning of this excerpt, as the text and its translations are not so clear. For our purposes, it is enough to say that even persons of honor (or to use New Testament language, believers mature in faith who act charitably) find themselves caught in anxious and difficult situations.

It may be helpful to consider what the Jerusalem Bible notes: First, Joseph's "integrity . . . consisted in wanting to withhold his own name from a baby whose father he did not know." This involves a legal honor. Joseph cannot give his name to a child who is not his.

The note continues: Joseph's integrity also consists in the fact that "he was convinced of Mary's virtue," and therefore, "he refused to expose to the rigor of the Law a mystery he did not understand." Here, Joseph's integrity approaches what Paul describes in Galatians 5:22 as "*agathosune*": comprehensive goodness.

Naturally, his conflict of conscience causes him to suffer. Joseph was well aware of the Law, and knew that it was rigorous. But at that moment, his mature faith and charity shows through. He chooses the person, Mary, rather than the Law.

We can think of how often Jesus rebukes the Pharisees for their way of interpreting the Law, and their hardness of heart. He does not chastise their material attachment to the Law, but their approach to justice which has no depth because it lacks charity.

Joseph, then, through his struggles, reaches a balance. His holiness and mature faith do not exempt him from the anxiety that comes with difficult situations. However, having taken upon himself the decision to do the honorable thing, which was the fruit of an attitude of charity, his maturity of faith is summarized as an openness to the power of divinely illuminated grace. In fact, the angel of the Lord arrives to resolve the situation. "Be not afraid" (implying that Joseph was afraid!). The angel reveals to him the deeper meaning of the event, thus overcoming all his anxiety. He is filled with pure joy!

The figure of Joseph allows us to grasp a fundamental teaching: we need to have a hope that is patient, that can wait as Joseph did, a hope that knows how to suffer with a humble spirit through difficult situations, sure that God will answer.

March 20
Jesus Looks Upon Peter

"The Lord turned and looked straight at Peter, and Peter remembered what the Lord had said to him, 'Before the cock crows today, you will have denied three times that you know Me.' And he went outside and wept bitterly." The Lord brought Peter, almost inexorably, to the point where he truly recognizes who he is in Jesus' plan. Peter probably prays, "Lord, I too am a poor man like everyone. Lord, I didn't believe it would come to this. Lord, have mercy on me. Lord, You are going to die for me and I betrayed You. You are giving Your life for me, Your unfaithful one." Peter finally grasps the meaning of the Good News of salvation for sinful man. He realizes the truth of God's being: He is not some moral reformer of humanity, but limitless, boundless and pure Love, the Giver of Mercy Who does not condemn, confuse or rebuke. Jesus does not look upon Peter with the eyes of an accuser. He looks upon him with mercy and with love. "Peter, I love You just as you are. I knew how you were and loved you knowing you were such." We could sum this up by saying that Peter probably makes the easiest and hardest act of his life at this moment: *He lets himself be loved.* Up to now, he has always been very proud, wanting to be the first at everything. Now he understands that before God he can do nothing other than let himself be loved, forgiven, saved.

The Good News is precisely saying thanks to God for everything, nothing excluded; it is knowing how to draw strength from God's saving mercy. Peter's great step allows him to be the first evangelist; the first to proclaim the Word and thus strengthen his brothers. Peter wanted to die for Jesus. Now he sees that it is Jesus who wants to die for him. The cross that Peter would have wanted to take far away from the Lord is the sign of God's love and salvation for him.

This, then, is the key to religious conversion. Conversion is the result of our understanding that our God is a God Who serves, Who puts His life on the line for us. He says: "I am among you as One Who serves," and "This is My body, given for you." Before I ask something of you, I ask simply that you allow yourselves to be loved.

March 21
We Believe

We believe that Jesus, God and man, is the Risen Christ Who remains with us always in the sign of bread and wine.

We believe that Jesus willingly offered Himself up to death in order to give us new life, redeemed and sanctified. The Passion continues every day in the Eucharist.

We believe in His living presence and His sacrifice that is repeated at the Mass.

We know that through the Mass He is the source of our redemption.

We believe that repeating His act of self-sacrifice for our neighbor is not only a Christian duty, but the only way of living a truly human life.

We believe that it is only in Jesus, present through His total and final gift which is the Eucharist, that we find the truest response to our expectations of peace, justice and love, thereby offering an ability to change and reform a new humanity.

We are certain that all the pain, injustice and cruelty which causes our brothers' blood to soak the earth merges in Your blood, O Lord, and becomes redemptive for all.

We are certain that the sacrifices hidden in men's hearts, the courage in those who struggle for love, the pains of daily labor, are all precious and fruitful moments offered in Christ's death and renewed in the Eucharist.

March 22
Let Us Break Our "Alabaster Vase"

In seeking a symbol to show how Christ is the center of our life, we want more than words. Just like the woman of Bethany who broke her precious alabaster vase, we seek acts which proclaim that we give all that we are to Christ.

We can all think of different ways we can break our "alabaster vases," whether by breaking with our "going-through-the-motions" prayers, making them patient, loving and trusting; or by breaking from a lazy intelligence that contents itself with received slogans and ideas, making it something which lovingly seeks the deeper meaning of things. To break from all that keeps us from dedicating ourselves completely to the Church.

Breaking something of ours means allowing labor, sacrifice, or whatever is costly to us to enter into our lives. It means doing courageous acts, however simple, to make it possible for others to make this journey.

Breaking the alabaster vase means, for many of us, saying "yes" to our life's calling. Repeating that "yes," saying, "Lord, I'm not turning back. All that I have I now give to You. Ask me whatever; I don't want to betray You."

March 23
The Adult Christian and Faith

The faithful adult Christian can be described as the person who allows himself or herself to be stretched to the fullest in the exercise of charity. It is only this perfect expansion of charity which provides the complete image of the Christian adult in his ethical physiognomy. By this, I do not mean his interior maturity, or even his prayer ability; but rather, the final fruit of his growth: charity.

The New Testament presents a moral teaching in terms of "enlightened positivism." It is not a "don't do this, don't do that" morality. It says instead: "Be imitators of God, as His children, full of love, goodness, meekness, esteem for one another, and centered and supported by charity." If we assimilate these characteristics and tie them together under the banner of charity, we will be on the right road towards constructing a spiritual ethic of the Christian adult.

Among the New Testament texts which may be helpful in this regard, there are certainly two:

The first is Chapter Thirteen of the First Letter to the Corinthians. Paul speaks of the attributes of love. We could say, "Love is patient." The mature Christian, aware of his ethical responsibility which comes from the social teaching of the Gospel, is a patient person. He is kind, not envious, not one to blow up in anger. He doesn't take a count of the evil he's received, nor does he delight in injustice; rather, he rejoices in the truth.

The second text is the Letter to the Galatians (5:22), where Paul describes the *ways,* rather than the acts, of being a mature Christian. "What the Spirit brings is very different: love, joy, peace, patience, kindness, goodness, trustfulness, gentleness and self-control." These nine characteristics can be viewed as the departing point for a description of the faithful, mature adult.

Another way of describing these nine fruits of the Spirit is according to the triad of human expressivity which Scripture continuously refers to as the hand, tongue and heart — work, word and affection. We can compare these three elements with the characteristics we find in Galatians: love, kindness and goodness. Love, expressed better for our purposes now as "sincerity" (coming from the Greek "agape"), signifies an openness of heart. Kindness concerns communication. Goodness involves the work of the hands.

Let us begin with the hands. The Greek word which we translate into "goodness" is *agathosune.* But it can also mean "generosity" or "wide-open-hands." It is, for example, the money paid to the vineyard workers at the eleventh hour in the parable of the vineyard. The owner, having a great heart, knows that his workers must eat that day, and so he gives them all that they need. "Goodness" is also the money given by the Samaritan to the innkeeper: after having done all that he could for the injured man, he opens his hands in goodness and generously fills them, so that the man may lack nothing. In a great measure, it is the immense debt which the king forgave of the first servant in that parable. In each instance, we find an attitude about work which leads a person to go beyond his duty.

The lips. When we translate the Greek word *chrestotes* by "kindness" or "benevolence," these words describe our ability to offer welcome. They thus involve communication, a way of speaking. We find this, for example, in Jesus' approach to Zacchaeus: He calls him, invites him to share a meal, takes the initiative of dialogue. It is an ability to overcome polemics and open the way to communication.

The heart. This aspect, which I've called "sincerity," involves a readiness to offer sympathy. In reality, from the point of view of this characteristic, the mature Christian is said to be in a position of "openness of heart."

March 24
Three Fundamental Characteristics of the Mature Christian

Whenever we try to conjure up some image of the mature Christian, that image must include at least three characteristics.

The first is *a positive attitude*. This quality is expressed by the person who continuously builds bridges, patches up difficult situations and forever looks ahead. If we consider St. Paul's characterization in his hymn to love, which "always trusts, always protects, always hopes," we must conclude that there cannot be depression, mistrust, bad humor, melancholy or indifference in the Christian adult. There is no place for the kinds of animosity or resentment which often color the Christian's way of being today: I could do so much if only . . . If only

106   MARCH

there weren't so many roadblocks in the way or monkey wrenches thrown into the works . . . If I could just . . . If only the Church were different. . . ." These are expressions that we all can and do say, but if they become a *way of looking at all of reality*, they are no longer exemplary of the Christian adult.

The first characteristic, then, is of a figure who is positive and constructive; a person who begins by looking at what there is to see, and then discovering its virtue, helping it grow, bettering it. The mature Christian tries to create the best out of each situation, using all the powers he possesses and can give.

The second characteristic that we mustn't forget may be called *a sense of being conflicted*. Where does this concept come from? Saint Paul explains it clearly in his Letter to the Galatians: "What the Spirit brings is *very different*" (Gal 5:22). Paul describes certain "very different" postures which contrast the preceding verses (v. 19ff) in which he describes the works of the flesh: "fornication, gross indecency and sexual irresponsibility; idolatry and sorcery; feuds and wrangling, jealousy, bad temper and quarrels; disagreements, factions, envy; drunkenness, orgies and similar things." The Christian character develops through conflict; through the frank separation from, opposition to and condemnation of all that in man and in society try to explain the Christian person differently. It is therefore a character which, being totally positive, is explicitly in conflict and continually aware of the need to separate the self from the world of darkness.

The third characteristic is *a profound sense of oneness*.

Although each person is fragmented by many attitudes, there is a profound unity or oneness which is apparent on the philological level. Saint Paul speaks of the "fruit of the Spirit." It is the one ethical and social fruit of Christian growth. Saint Paul further explains this one fruit as the one love which impels us to do this and avoid that (1 Cor 13).

If we ask ourselves what is this one fruit, one love, we can find the answer in many other Pauline texts and in the whole of New Testament spirituality: the one fruit or love is God acting in man; it's being like Christ; it's living in constructive and conflicting love.

The Christian who is mature in faith tries to be like Christ in the multiple ethic of his behavior, defined by the Gospel and summarized by the New Testament exhortations. At the same time, he tries to imitate Christ in His obedience to the Father, and through grace, to participate in Christ's divine Sonship.

March 25

Contemplating the Cross and the Experience of the Burning Bush

Contemplating the cross is experiencing the *burning bush*: God's appearance to Moses through the burning bush — a bush that burns but is not consumed. Moreover, it is experiencing the fire that burns, heats and entices: it is both affable and involving. It is *a mysterious, unadorned fact*.

The second moment of the burning bush is the *experience of the call or message*. God speaks from the fire. He explains, admonishes; *He gives meaning to the mysterious vision*.

We live the burning-bush experience when we face

the cross of Jesus. The Passion account presents the naked facts and cruel events; that is, the fire. It's an account that burns, heats and entices. The facts are solemn, painful, dramatic, tragic, terrifying and involving — we don't understand the sense of it.

The two Songs of the Servant of Yahweh help us to better understand the significance of the fire of the cross, and thus, the interior dimension of the Passion. Jesus is prefigured by a mysterious servant of the Lord who offers himself with full and free obedience to a destiny of suffering and death. The prophet Isaiah, the author, divulges the soul of the servant who experiences the reality of the Passion. We thus understand three things:

The suffering Christ, Whom Matthew speaks of, is the One Who prays and entrusts Himself to the Father. As we can see from the Gospel accounts, Jesus' deep trust mirrors the trust of the servant in the prophetic writings.

The suffering, trusting servant is not only a luminous sign of God's love for all men, but represents all men before God. He is the true man, obedient and reconciled to God. He suffers the tragedy of sin and opens the way for other men to come back to God.

The servant of Yahweh is in union and in sympathy with all the people. He takes all their sins upon Himself, bringing His human family onto His loving, powerful and atoning journey.

March 26
Towards an Understanding of the Message of the Cross

Jesus' cross is a message. But it is a message that we do not understand if we do not make Moses' journey; if we do not grasp the meaning of the fire of the cross.

It is impossible to understand the cross of Christ — and, indeed the cross of every Christian — *without having a spiritual direction.*

The cross makes no sense for those who trust only in material efficiency, technical developments or social programs. It makes no sense for those who do not want to make space for an interior life, or think that all human problems can be resolved by stepping over man's freedom and his heart.

The cross offers nothing — even more, it's an obstacle — to those who do not open themselves to its mystery; to those who reject the Wisdom that comes from above; to those who do not respect God's actions which patiently unfold over time; to those who pretend that God's love corresponds to man's superficial desires. The cross is an obstacle to those who do not have the courage to be detached from self so as to put themselves completely in God's hands. The cross is a pure, silent symbol of pain for those who are not open to living in solidarity with Christ and His brethren; to those who call only for quick, automatic solutions to every problem, without lending their own contributions to the cause; to those who see others' pain as an annoyance and not a call towards closeness and fraternal communion.

If we lack deep spiritual values, our attempt to understand the message of the cross is in vain. We see the cross in our churches. We put crosses up in our homes. We wear them on our bodies, but often without the courage to carry our cross together with Christ's.

The Cross Opens the Way to Life

The cross is ever before us. It wants to speak to us, if only we contemplate it with love, drawn by the power of the Spirit Who is the gift of Christ crucified. If we look upon it with awe and affection, the cross becomes an enticing, warm and all-consuming fire: *it gives us a challenge*.

It asks us many things. The cross asks us, our communities, our societies and our cultures to confirm *that there do exist paths from the cross to resolve human problems*.

Our experience reveals that pain, suffering and death fill our history.

Jesus did not invent the cross. He, like every man, found it on His journey. The newness in His message was to plant a seed of love into our bearing of the cross. The element of love turned the Way of the Cross into a way that leads to life. The cross itself became a message of love; a means of our transformation. Our cross is also the cross of Jesus!

This cross first embraces each of us, and entrusts us with a duty in our personal life, in our families, among our friends and acquaintances -- in sum, with whoever else's cross we encounter. I think of the many broken families, the many illnesses which have not been accepted, of hardened hearts which have become embittered, resentful and brooding. How many crosses have been borne up and down in the elevators of our buildings. How many cross-bearers walk up and down our streets, populate our cities!

There are crosses without a name, and often, without a hope. There are crosses of doom which, at best, are merely tolerated. Those who bear them lead lives of quiet desperation and silent resignation.

From His cross, Jesus invites each of us today to put *all* these crosses, and not just our own, into relationship with our own. Jesus invites us to do as He did — plant the seed of love and hope in the soil of each of the crosses we encounter.

March 28
How Can We Celebrate Pain and Suffering?

It is very important that we open wide our hearts to the message of Sacred Scripture which invites us not to celebrate pain and suffering, but to celebrate love.

Why did Jesus die?

A first response is this: Jesus died because He wasn't understood or accepted; because He was met with hostile hearts. But there's also a second, more profound and decisive response: Jesus died because He did not stop loving men, even when they prepared Him for the cross and death. The biblical texts powerfully underline the freedom and awareness with which Jesus went to meet His demise.

He knows and accepts His death, making Himself Isaiah's suffering servant of Yahweh: "And yet ours were the offenses that He bore . . . through His wounds we were healed. He surrendered Himself to death and let Himself be taken for a sinner, while He was bearing the faults of many and praying all the time for sinners" (Is 53:4-5, 12).

We must pause attentively and feelingly on Jesus' voluntary acceptance of suffering. Jesus does not desire pain; He does not invent the cross. Like every man, He wants life and happiness. But He encounters evil, suffering and death on His journey — the same journey that each of us takes. He wants to eliminate evil, but His way of doing so amazes us.

God eliminates evil not by ignoring or sidestepping it. Rather, He embraces it and transforms it from within by the power of love. Jesus lives with men, and loves and pardons them, even while they prepare to murder Him. In so doing, Jesus reveals the point to which we must go in filial love and obedience to the Father: not even the cross and death induce God to tire of loving man or to abandon him to his destiny. The pain of the cross becomes an ardent cry to love; a free, unexpected and prodigious human potentiality. It becomes a sign and occasion of freedom, courage, obedience to the Father, and unconditional dedication to man. The Resurrection reveals the mysterious and overflowing vitality that is born of the cross.

But all this is possible because we speak of the cross of *Christ*, and not just any cross. The Christian disciple receives the same task from his Lord and Master: to transform man's cross into the cross of Christ. Man's cross is ambiguous and without hope. Christ's cross is bright and luminous. It bears the name of love. In hope, it prepares for the victory of life and the Resurrection.

March 29
The Language of the Cross

Death on the cross had a precise language and meaning for the Jews and pagans of Jesus' time; and therefore, for the first Christian community as well. For the Jews, death on the wood of the cross clearly demonstrated that God had abandoned an individual.

The dramatic way with which Saint Matthew's Gospel presents the crucifixion emphasizes this solitude and abandonment. The last words of Jesus come from Psalm 22: "My God, My God, why have You abandoned Me?" (Mt 27:47).

The Psalm presents the cry and prayer of the virtuous man. The opening line, which Matthew quotes Jesus as saying is a word of lament without rebellion. But it nevertheless gives the sense of a tremendous distance from the Father. This echoes the similar feeling that the Jews had about such a death on the cross.

For the pagans and the Jews, the cross pointed out just how foolish and absurd was Christ's pretense at being the Messiah, the man of God. In the eyes of the Greeks and pagans, the qualitative value of the crucifix could not in any way be of value to God. The crucifixion has nothing of the power and omnipotence which ought to characterize divinity. Rather, it is a demonstration of inferiority and weakness. They cannot envision God or hero in the crucifixion. Christ's death on the cross cannot even be compared to that of a wise man, such as Socrates, who calmly and with dignity freely chose his own death.

Thus, we can only see gross insult, blood, darkness and cruelty.

The death of Jesus on the cross seems all the less divine the more one has a sublime idea of what is divine: of a God Who is incapable of participating in the affairs of this world and unable to suffer or have compassion on those inferior to Him. The cross puts our values and conceptions — whether human or divine — into crisis. And the crisis is only overcome when, in light of the

114

Resurrection, we have the courage to look with faith upon the crucifixion and see that in it is where God's power and wisdom lie, along with His justice, sanctification and redemption. The cross reveals the Father.

In contemplation and adoration of the cross, we can see the perfect way towards deliverance: through obedience, sacrifice and love. Jesus' obedience to death reveals His constant filial relationship to God. Jesus, the Word Who was in the beginning, cannot live if not in the way of the Word obediently accepted.

March 30
A Love That Dies

Let us reflect on the two groups of actors in the drama on Calvary: First, there is Jesus by Himself, Who follows His painful way of the cross alone, yet fully aware of where He must go — towards the gift which He was to make of Himself through His humiliation and death.

The other group is made up of all those around Him: the disciples and friends, Judas, the high priests, the soldiers, Pilate, the crowds of people. Each person is disturbed by this drama according to the measure of interest that is touched by Jesus' actions. If His act was authentic and true, we should change our way of living and put ourselves at the service of others. We should want to be the "least" and care for the least.

But because of this, each person ends up defending himself, seeking a way of escape or attack, while keeping a certain distance from it all. Those who are most angry with Jesus put Him to death. Everyone speaks, discusses or schemes over Jesus, but no one asks the essential question: Why is He doing this? No one, therefore, finds the fundamental answer: He is dying for me, because He loves me; because God loves us in Him.

"Grant, O Lord, that in our contemplation of the mystery of Your Passion we do not run away from the essential things. Help us to contemplate you, Your Eucharistic love, Your crucified love as the sum reality necessary to understand all the rest, as the one reality from which all the others receive light and clarity.

"We ask You this through the intercession of the One Who had the eye to see all essential things: Mary, Your Mother."

March 31
The Cross: School of Humanism

Jesus' painful death expects not only our compassion, but our participation. It becomes a school of life. We, too, must follow a "way of the cross" with Him if we want to be fully human and desire life and salvation.

Nevertheless, in confronting this great mystery of the cross, we ask ourselves: Is it true that the way of the cross makes us more human?

At first glance, it seems impossible that the cross can be any kind of school of humanism. Man seems to be flattened and humiliated by it. Nevertheless, true humanism — true love for man — is exercised on the cross.

Let us pray: "Lord, teach us by and in Your cross to know God. Teach us to know man. Teach us to know who we are." Meditating in silence, reflecting on the mystery of the cross, we see that, by His Passion and

116   MARCH

death, Jesus loves man such as man is. He loves man in his sinfulness, separation from God and his tragedy. This is a hard realism, but Jesus does not withdraw or turn His back on man. Rather, by His limitless love, Jesus seeks to reawaken in man the beautiful attributes of penitence, conversion and rediscovered faith.

The humanism of the cross, understood with this realism and fidelity, unmasks and challenges certain of our idealisms which unfortunately remain more on the ideological than the practical plane. How often we lack the courage to look at the real man! We always seek to invent from our fantasies, desires and even repugnance, an ever-compromising image of man that does not or cannot exist.

When our human situation calls for a total rejection of ourselves, we all instinctively seek a compromise, or look for a way of escape. We unite with the apostles who ran away in the face of Jesus' Passion.

From the cross, Jesus proclaims God's love for us. He assures us that we all have been granted an ability to love. He invites us to once again see, with courage and faith, the criteria which inspire our relationships with others, our dedication to man, and our service to our brothers and sisters.

And we must unmask these forms of escape which characterize our humanism and which are manifest on many levels.

On the level of the family, how many times do we seek self-gratification or self-affirmation, and thereby not accept those who are close to us, such as they are. We always want them to be different, and so they drive us crazy!

In our friendships, how many times we don't go beyond a certain comradeship and superficiality in order to avoid communicating the most profound values which we hold because we're afraid of the differences in viewpoints and opinions they might present. We prefer to remain comfortable in our convictions!

In our professional environments, how many times do we just drag along and not serve the heart — a service that demands our letting go of the self in order to share in others' crosses.

When facing either the sufferings of others or our own, how many times do we just close our eyes, rather than firmly take hold of Christ's cross and squarely face reality!

When encountering those who are on the fringes of society, how many times do we play the role of Pilate and wash our hands of the whole affair, because they aren't worth our competence!

How many times do we plainly express our uneasiness, anger or refusal at our brothers' needs!

The many simple encounters of our daily life call for the work of profound conversion. They call for us to get on our knees before the cross and grasp the realism and fidelity that has the power to change our life!

APRIL

April 1
The Church and the Paschal Mystery

The Church relives Christ's Passion in a very real way through its own flesh and blood suffering, not just through the mystery and symbol of the Eucharist. We, too, must continue to express ourselves, as part of Christ's Passion, through the Church.

During Holy Week, the Church enters into Christ's infinite pain. It achieves solidarity: with the high price Jesus paid for man's sinfulness; with His unique ability to offer words of conversion and reconciliation; with His ability to raise Himself in the most aberrant situations of existence, and not by uttering words, but by an act, albeit painful, of obedience to God and in solidarity with the most terrible of human suffering. The worst suffering is that which comes from sin, because it creates the loneliness that a person feels when, through sin, he effectively abandons God.

A very important moment in the Good Friday service is the solemn Prayer of the Faithful. In this solemn prayer before the raised and uncovered cross, ideally there will be assembled all groups of people, with all the problems and needs of humanity. The Church need not fear or be overwhelmed by this ideal assembly, because it knows that the cross of Christ which stands at the center of the liturgical celebration is able to take upon itself all man's drama, pains and sin. God assures us that death cannot defeat His love, marked by the cross. He also assures us that there is no human condition that can remain outside of the cross' embrace. Hasn't Jesus said: "When I am lifted up from the earth, I shall draw all men to Myself"?

April 2
Christ's Passion Continues

Christ's Passion continues today in the many people who are suffering: the unemployed, those who fear the events which are happening around them, the anxious and afflicted in prisons, the victims of absurd and ruthless violence. The Passion continues for the elderly who have been drained of their energies through the years by society, and who now have been cast aside and are all alone — and how many suffer this loneliness! The Passion continues in those who are awaiting justice that is not forthcoming — how many people, for whatever reason, have had to leave their homeland, but do not find welcome in their new lands, many of whom probably are in our communities right now and have no real sense of "home." The mystery of the cross renews itself in all those who feel themselves on the fringes of society, such as the handicapped; or those who are shown ways of escape which are, in reality, solutions leading to death, such as addiction to drugs or a life of crime. Those engaged in such activities over which they no longer seem to have any control and who should be in places of rehabilitation or reconciliation are oftentimes forced to remain in a climate of violence and death because of their

120   APRIL

past. Finally, the Passion and its suffering continue on in those who are despairing because they see their daily sacrifices and fidelity to their responsibilities as being unappreciated and generally futile.

Reading the newspapers, it sometimes seems impossible to us that man, so small, can create so much evil in the world! And when we read the Passion, we see that the sentiment behind the accounts are not much different.

The Lord's Passion teaches us not only to recognize those who suffer in order that we might help them, but also to break out of the matrix of violence which seems to perpetuate itself in man's heart and human history.

An act of forgiveness and prayer, similar to the dying Christ's, which others in our day and age seek to render alive and effective, is the good news that helps us believe that the mystery of Good Friday still looks forward, and always will, to the dawning of an Easter morning. Christ does not want to have any other hands than our own today in order to care for our brothers and sisters who are in need.

April 3
By His Wounds We Were Healed

Isaiah, the anonymous prophet, is a man called to speak new words: "God has given me a new tongue," a tongue that listens to things unknown in order to tell them to others. These words encounter opposition and cause suffering, but the prophet cannot resist speaking them: "I gave my back to those who beat me, my cheeks to those who plucked my beard." This suffering saves the people, and saves us: "By His wounds we were healed." These mysterious words which speak of the rejected messengers who nevertheless save, are key to an interpretation of the history of Jesus and His Church. The words find their maximum intensity in Jesus' prophetic proclamation of love for the world, and in the repudiation which we, with all our sins, have made and continue to make of Jesus.

Today, we must remember our sins with humble hearts. Our strictly personal sins, which we alone know, affect others through the lack of solidarity which our sins create. They contribute to the growth of injustice in the world.

Even with all these sins, with our resistance to the love and the Word of God, we are called *now* to repent and in humility, challenge ourselves before the cross.

We are called to meditate on Jesus, the victim of our sins, the real figure and tangible sign of how sin can badly treat and disfigure a man. By assuming the condition of the defenseless prophet, Christ wants to force us to open our eyes to the blinding reality of poverty and its misery.

If our conversion is authentic, if it is the fruit of the love and pardon of the cross, it will provoke a social transformation in the world around us.

April 4
Death Is Conquered

The Preface to the Eucharistic Prayer for Easter affirms: ''By dying He destroyed our death; by rising He restored our life.'' This is the central message of Easter: By Jesus' death, our death — even if it preserves its biological reality — is no longer a dark end, a desperate termination, or an exit into nothingness. Death is a conquered reality, a tamed ferocity no longer able to dominate all our thoughts and expectations.

On the contrary, our thoughts and projects can assume a greater dimension and security which are given them by the possibility of entering into communion with the perpetuity of life proper to God alone which comes to us in the Risen Christ.

Our liberation from death is a liberation that conditions everything else, and opens the way to every constructive project which is lasting and full of hope for history and humanity.

We ask ourselves if this is so for us. For the believer — even the one with but a morsel of faith — the true vision of life includes space for eternal life by the grace of Christ's redemption. Being open to eternal life changes one's way of living and thinking; a thinking and living illuminated by the light of Easter.

What would happen to us if we were to let this light enter our lives, and not just by a glimmer, but by throwing open ''the doors and windows'' so to speak?

How different we would view our work, our family relationships (which in these days are all too often strained and cold), our maladies, the sufferings of others, especially those dear to us! In the light of Easter, everything makes sense; everything takes on a divine tone. Everything is susceptible to being redeemed by hope!

April 5
Who Are You Looking For?

Saint John's account of Easter morning finds Jesus speaking to the woman at the tomb. He asks her: ''Who are you looking for?'' (Jn 20:15). This is a significant question in John's theological presentation. Jesus began His public ministry with that question, which He presented to His would-be followers.

And now, at the end of the Gospel, He returns to those same words: ''Who are you looking for?'', meaning, ''you are looking for *someone*.'' This is the *fundamental question* that the Resurrection event presents to us: You are looking for someone who will dry your tears; who will faithfully love you; who will save you. You may not know who you are looking for, but *you are looking for your God*.

When Jesus, His Word and His Spirit, presents this question to us, we feel all the power of the Resurrection. *It is our Easter*, lived by each one us. It is our opening of the tomb of our heart to the power of the living Lord.

If we hear the question — if we challenge ourselves to respond to it — then we, too, will hear Him call us by name, just as Jesus called the woman, ''Mary.'' Mary recognizes Jesus only after He calls her name; when He reawakened her inner being and regenerated her freedom, renewing in her the creative potential by which God calls each person into existence and entrusts them with a special mission in life.

''O Risen Lord Jesus, we ask ourselves why we weep today; which are our deepest sufferings? It is only through you that we can reach into the depths of our hearts to see what we're looking for; to find out what is the object of our endless search.'' If we pray in this way, Jesus will help us to understand that we seek a person — He, Himself, Who died and rose for us. He will help us to roll away the tombstone which seals our lives, opening the way to life with Him Who is alive now and forever.

April 6
Christ's Victory Is In Us

The power of the Resurrection reaches into every place and every time. We are called to prepare ourselves with a new mind and heart to be able to grasp that power.

Our pain and sadness, which so often bring us to reject this word of comfort, probably comes from the fact that we do not have an exact idea of the liberation which Jesus' Resurrection brings us.

We cultivate the fantastic and illusory idea that everything can and must change in the blink of an eye; that from today to tomorrow, there can be no more sickness, pain, social agitation, injustice and war. When we see that people continue to suffer, we feel defeated and we despair.

We wait for fraternity, peace and disarmament, but they aren't happening. Tomorrow, or the day after, there will be more arms, more violence, more death and destruction. *What, then, does Christ's Paschal victory mean? What joy does it bring*?

We must understand that Jesus' Paschal victory, which certainly concerns all the evil in the world — sin, violence, arms, war and death — must *first* begin in us!

Christ's victory, already present in the Resurrection, has a time and way for complete fruition; but we cannot know them. What is certain, however, is that the victory happens first in us.

It happens in me. It happens in you. Through us, it happens in the community, in the city, in society. *We* are the first work of the Resurrection; we are the revelation of His victory.

If our free will pulls together all our forces to trust in Christ, and to make room for His love, we become the principals of the new world that is founded on each of us as loved, pardoned and renewed persons who witness the living presence of the Risen Christ.

April 7
Jesus, Present Throughout History

We may ask ourselves what happens in the Risen Christ between the journey of the past (memory) and the journey of the future (hope)? What happens to the relationship between tradition and freedom? What happens to all that is behind us, in our history, and that of the Church and the world? And what about all that is before us, our life in the future and that of the Church and mankind?

The liturgy provides us with an answer to the questions: The Risen Jesus *does not obliterate the past* of Israel, but resurrects its memory in His own body, uniting in Himself both yesterday and tomorrow, memory and hope, tradition and freedom.

The Easter celebration both proposes and actualizes a wonderful joining of the traditions of the past and the creative freedom of the future.

It may at first seem strange to think that the future of man can, in some way be tied to the past. We tried to believe, as do many of our contemporaries, that tomorrow is an absolute beginning, with its origin in ourselves. We tried to think of our freedom as autonomous in setting our own course, creating the future in our own image.

We generally view the past as some far away, outgrown time which is better off forgotten, a period full of sad regrets. At most, we view it as an accumulation of experiences which provide the backdrop for our present and future conquests.

If, however, we look deep within ourselves, we will agree that within us there are many varying, sometimes opposing feelings, thoughts and emotions. Besides our passion for self-sufficiency, we find deep affection for parents and family, recognition for friends and acquaintances, and awe and wonder at the many mysteries of life.

If we open ourselves, even if only as persons, to understand these things, we will realize that our freedom is not an absolute beginning. It loves to set its course, but it is, at the same time, faithful to the life we've been given, to the history that preceded us, and to the task that has been assigned to us by the One Who is greater than we are.

Our freedom is also faithfulness to a name that someone else gave us: our Baptismal name. Faithfulness and trustfulness to a Father Who came to us, revealed Himself in history, declared His love for us in Jesus, accepted to die for us, and thereby, destroyed our death. Our freedom is also a faithfulness to our brothers and sisters whom God has put in our care.

By joyfully and confidently adhering to our faith, our freedom finds its roots and the strength to go forward into the future, in a journey of hope.

We rediscover that the Risen One, the Living One forms the unity of our life. He fills our present with a dimension of the eternal. He is able to embrace things, persons, situations affections, past sufferings, and fill them with love and fidelity, projecting them towards the future — a certain future — with Him always at our side.

April 8
The Signs of the Risen Lord

John's Gospel recounts to us Mary Magdalen's weeping near Jesus' tomb. He presents four images in just a few lines: Mary is crying outside the tomb; she bends over to look inside; two angels in white ask her, "Why are you weeping?"; then, Jesus appears and asks her the same question.

The evangelist immediately gives us her answer. She is weeping for two reasons: her Lord is dead; and she also fears that someone may have profaned His tomb: "They have taken away my Lord and I don't know where they have put Him." Beyond the immediate answer which refers to a succession of facts and events, there is a more profound significance to Mary's *continuing* to cry, notwithstanding the fact that she has seen the signs of the Resurrection in the empty tomb and the two angels.

The true answer to, "Why are you weeping?" should be this: "I am weeping *because I have not succeeded in understanding the signs of the Resurrection. My eyes are so filled with tears that I cannot see the signs of life; I don't comprehend sufficiently to accept words of consolation.*" Mary Magdalen has affixed Jesus' death in her head to the point that she can no longer admit that there may be some other possible way of being; that there may be a way to overcome the irreparable cycle of death.

The inconsolable weeping of the woman helps us to foresee something else. First of all, we Christians who seek the Lord, who believe with our lips, who profess His Resurrection — must also struggle to recognize the signs of the Risen One in us and around us. We block ourselves to this reality by underlining the suffering, the loss, the signs of death and desolation. Just like this woman who didn't want to be consoled and persisted in her desire for her Lord's dead body, so too, we have difficulty in accepting the transforming joy of the Resurrection. It is certainly true that to weep is a painful thing; and still it may be much easier than to accept a great joy or to open our heart to a disturbing hope. *Mary Magdalen is the image of us as Christians, and, even more so, she is the image of our fallen race.*

April 9
The Banquet and Words of Promise

Let us reflect together on the Book of the Prophet Isaiah, Chapter Fifty-five. We may subtitle the meditation: *An Invitation to Messianic Well Being.*

The first part of the chapter presents an invitation to a banquet, but the words are imperative: "Come to the water all you who are thirsty; though you have no money, come! Buy corn without money, and eat, and at no cost, wine and milk . . . Listen to Me, and you will have good things to eat" (Is 55:1-3). The images are of food and wine, prepared by the mysterious master of the house.

The second part expresses a promise for the future, but no longer as an exhortation: "With you I will make an everlasting covenant out of the favors promised to David . . . You will summon a nation you never knew, those unknown will come hurrying to you" (Is 55:3-5). The image of the banquet is followed by words of hope; the promise of a covenant, of universal importance, in the light of King David.

The key words of the first section evoke man's nourishment and the satisfaction of his desires. Man is one who thirsts. Besides his physical hunger and thirst, we know he has a desire for community, for deep and authentic relationships with others, and for peace. The images of food and drink remind us of man's great primordial needs; those for which he thirsts — truth, peace, justice, community and love. The satisfaction man yearns for; his striving for the bread of truth and peace, and the water and wine of friendship, is the answer that God gives. God will satisfy man's hunger.

I am not speaking here about abstract desire. I am talking about the desires which are innate to us, stirring our hearts. I'm talking about desires that shake our humanity. God answers these concrete desires with His covenant. He is telling us that He will make a stable, everlasting friendship with us; a friendship that will be expressed in a united and peaceful messianic community which enjoys God's favor, will not be touched by death, and will have universal influence on all people.

These are the favors about which Isaiah speaks. These are the promises made to David. These are promises of a great and everlasting Kingdom.

The Church reads this promise as the promise of Christ's glorious Resurrection. He is the head of a new messianic people; a people who are certain of everlasting life. We are the community of the new people of God. We are a community in which each of us can see that fullness of peace with God and with our fellow man.

April 10
Easter Reveals the Face of God

In the Resurrection of Jesus Crucified, God makes Himself known in a different way than man first imagined Him. God is not totally different, but there is a certain contradiction. With our limited, imperfect human language we can try to explain these opposite and complementary images:

The first deals with the new way in which God reveals Himself to man, of the way He "*communicates*" the affectionate warmth, intimacy and fecundity of His fullness.

The second deals with His spirit of *sacrifice*: His selflessness, His giving of Himself to the point of losing Himself, reminiscent of His own affirmation, "It is better to give than to receive." In other words, the Resurrection is a revelation of God as Trinity: of the Father Who raised His Son to life. The Resurrection permits us to recognize in all the affairs of Jesus as a man the story of the Son of God as well; that the Resurrection is the Father's great "yes" to His Son as God as well as man. It reveals to us the divine value of sacrifice, of going out of oneself, of losing one's self as Jesus did on the cross. Jesus, betrayed, killed, obedient unto death, Who from the cross gives the Spirit of life, shows us that the power of self-giving unto death is divine. It is the prerogative of the highest principle of being. It is the norm for authentic human life in the image of God.

The Holy Spirit, the gift of the Risen Jesus to believers, makes all who are prisoners of their fear of death into free, courageous and loving witnesses to life.

The Easter event, therefore, reveals a new face of God which appears as the Trinity, as paternity, as intimacy, as gift, as sonship, as company, as enthusiasm, as love, as fullness of life, as communication.

And we, the Church celebrate this new image and knowledge of God in history. We speak of and give witness to God by the way we make Him a lived experience, and communicate our knowledge to others.

We can ask ourselves what kind of Church communicates this image of the Trinity? A Church that is enthusiastic, prayerful, courageous, sacrificing, trusting, self-giving, and loving; one that puts itself in the Father's hands.

April 11
Easter Attitudes

When we find in our lives and the lives of those around us pain, illness and moral suffering, what is our attitude? Do we walk away from these moments, avoid them, try to obliterate them from our senses and thoughts, close our eyes? Do we satisfy ourselves by stepping over them and relegating them to just an afterthought? Or does the Risen Lord, the Spirit of Christ that is in us, give us the grace to enter into that pain to help them find the possibility for a full life, trust in God, fraternal solidarity, spiritual growth and patience? How often do we experience in such situations mature love, life, friendship and a new meaning in life?

When in our social life, among the many promising values, we find delusions, injustices, mortifying or insufficient structures, what is our attitude? Do we look for remedies only outside of ourselves, such as more just laws? This is important and necessary, but Easter involves much more. It teaches us that we must ask ourselves: What can *I* begin to do, with my love, openness and personal presence, with my own sense of optimism that was born from having drunk from the Spring of life that is Christ? Does a change in our personal and community attitudes make us want to dedicate ourselves to these situations — even the most painful — and commit ourselves, with God's strength, to change them from within?

Our life is risen now with Christ. Christ living in us enables us to give life and to give witness to life.

April 12
Two Essential Moments of Easter

We are invited to explore the depth of the relationship between the two essential moments of Easter: Death and Resurrection. The second event surpasses the first, but does not cancel it. The Resurrection brings to full development the life already present in dying for love. The light of the Resurrection does not make the cross disappear, but helps the believer understand the mystery of life and love that bursts forth from it! If we disregard this connection, which is the intimate structure of the Paschal mystery, we can become deluded, sometimes in a dramatic way. The Paschal joy must be felt in connection with our historic reality that nothing materially has changed: we still experience sickness, death, hatred, social upheaval.

Easter does not immediately take these realities away, but rather, tells us that, if Christ is living in the glory of God; if Christ is living in the Church and in history (and therefore, in each of us), all this does not keep us from loving, but rather makes it possible to love and hope more. Christ, Who understood life and love, assures us that he who lives in love, but also in suffering and death, is not abandoned by God. He is welcomed, loved, and brought to the fullness of life and joy. He who loves receives the life of Christ. Easter joy, then, is not superficial or forgetful; it is not a joy of the moment. Easter joy is able to make the memory of the cross a serious thing, and as such, fit for showing us new ways to announce true hope to all people.

April 13
Easter Joy

What is our Easter joy? What does it mean? What does it say? What does it contain? Doesn't it run the risk of being something superficial which we utter with our lips only; that we would like to interiorize, but do not know how?

Or, if we look with faith at the true source of this Easter joy — the Risen Christ — don't we run the risk of expressing a joy based on forgetfulness of the cross which preceded it?

We must, of course, speak of the joy of the Resurrection that we've received and we must proclaim it in faith. But it's possible for us to forget the Passion and death of the cross; forget the nails and the scourging; almost as if they didn't really happen, or were part of some bad dream.

But, in reality, there are many people among us today who are suffering. And, what's more amazing, the proclamation of the joyful Easter message does not take away the world's suffering. After a brief euphoria, we find ourselves tomorrow, the day after tomorrow, or perhaps even today, facing the same problems: sickness, injustice, hunger, violence.

How then are we to understand Easter joy, in order that it doesn't become just a formality; in order that it may not be founded on a false hope for the physical removal of sufferings?

The Word of God tells us that the Risen Jesus is the same Jesus Who suffered and died; indeed, as Luke tells us, He had to die. We, therefore, understand that the Lord's new life is not simply a cancellation of His death on the cross, almost as if it never occurred or should be forgotten. Rather, it is an awakening of the prodigious vitality that it already presents in the life and death of Jesus, from His abandonment in love and dedication to the Father. This life already present was what Jesus carefully laid down for His disciples in the Sacrament of the Eucharist. He declared that He freely gave up His life for them out of love.

April 14
Like the Disciples of Emmaus

We must live meditating on the reality of the Church and of its powerful mission, which the Spirit actualizes in us through our poor and simple works. We must be filled with that same joy as the two disciples of Emmaus while they were listening to Jesus trace the figure of the Messiah through the history of salvation. We are all, at times, like those disciples at Emmaus: We get caught up in the events of the day and our surroundings. At times they weigh on us, sadden us, worry us.

In the same way, if we get caught up in the reality of the Church, look upon it too analytically, we can find ourselves burdened with that same sense of heaviness, and thereby miss the complete picture of the plan God set out for the disciples while they journeyed on the road together.

The disciples, even though they had everything

about salvation right there before them in the person and message of Jesus, persisted in not seeing it, even deploring everything around them, as if they were wandering in the wilderness without a map, without even feeling that they were part of God's plan. But Jesus walked with them. By His words and amiable presence, He was able to lead them towards a wonder-filled acceptance and enthusiastic participation in the richness of the plan of salvation that connected their life to Jesus' death and Resurrection.

Each person, from the fragments of his own life, can grasp the fullness of the Resurrection that enlightens him and makes him a part of the Church, the Kingdom of God. All human history is brought into the Church and brought along in it to a transformation of the self and of society by the power of the Spirit. By this same gift of the Spirit, we are led to want to give our modest contribution, with all the sacrifices that will be asked of us, and with the great hope that is in our hearts.

April 15
Christ Is Our Life

We have heard and we have expressed with our words, deeds and symbols that fundamental proclamation: Christ lives! He is our Life!

This proclamation comes from a time both long ago and far away. It comes from the angel of the Resurrection; from the women who discover the empty tomb; from the apostles who witness the Lord alive. The message goes from them quickly, from person to person, from group to group, stirring up the community of believers. By studying the New Testament texts, we can follow along the journey that this message takes, and rediscover the original formula and its original flavor: The Lord is truly risen! The Lord is risen and has appeared to Peter! God has raised the Jesus Whom men crucified!

All of primitive Christendom stands or falls with this proclamation. Our faith is not born of an abstract word from on high. It's born from a *fact*, witnessed and proclaimed by those who experienced it, shared it: Christ is truly risen! So, although this proclamation comes to us from a faraway time and place, it comes through an uninterrupted chain of witnesses.

But it is also very much right here, right now, among us. How? Peter, whose voice we hear in the Acts of the Apostles, expresses it this way: "We are witnesses to all this, we and the Holy Spirit Whom God has given to those who obey Him" (Ac 5:32).

To this testimony of the apostles we add the testimony that is the gift of the Holy Spirit. The Spirit of the Resurrection works in our hearts. The Spirit worked in the Church of the Council and the period after the Council, and guides it towards the completion of the second millennium.

The Risen Christ, then, is not only our life, but our living as well. His love, His prayer, His vital energy take possession of the Church, through the Spirit, and the Church witnesses His Resurrection and continued life for all centuries.

April 16
Opening Doors to Christ

What does it mean to open doors to the loving Christ in the world?

This reflection touches on the cosmic aspect of our opening doors to Christ.

The heart of Christ Crucified is like an observatory, from which to look out at all history. It challenges us to enter into love relationships which alone are able to overcome the bloody course of human events.

Christ's death for mankind is the objective measure of the truth of love. It is an ever-present measure because He is risen and alive. He is always present so that man can trustingly turn to Him in order to transcend himself and seek the Authentic One: God, the Word upon Whom all existence and truth are based; the *Logos* in Whom my life makes sense.

We say that only love is believable, but it must be a love that can be touched with the hands and verified through its fruits. ''It is to the glory of My Father that you should bear much fruit . . . You did not choose Me, no, I chose you; and I commissioned you to go out and bear fruit; fruit that will last'' (Jn 15:8, 16).

But how do we recognize in history this supreme, necessary and ever present instance of love? How do we encounter it and listen to it?

The *Spirit of Christ*, Who spoke through the prophets; Who in the risen Jesus gave back to the world its hope to love, is present and active in the Church that does not cease to re-present to man today the supreme instance of truth and love.

The Church, in fact, has a humble and ardent, while at the same time, poor and confident mission to lovingly reconcile society and restore *unity to the world*.

As a community of love, as a place of perfect friendship, we are called, starting from our poverty and sin, to be the origin of authentic life. We are called as Church to be the ''we'' of a reconciled world that has as its supreme law (and, in a sense, its only law) that free, authentic love we call "charity."

April 17
Christ-Love in My Life

What does it mean to open the doors to Christ in my life?

First, it means not running to meet Christ, but letting Him enter, letting Him love me, letting Him forgive me — believing that He died *for me*.

What, then, does it mean not to open the doors to Him? It can simply mean being far from Him; not praying or reading the Gospels; not thinking about Him. It does not mean *only* this, however, because a person can be near Him but still close the door to Him. For example, Judas kissed Jesus, but did not love Him. He kissed, but at the same time, because he neither understood nor accepted Jesus, he closed the door of his heart.

Not opening doors means not entering into a posture of love; not trying to understand Jesus; not understanding that He first loves us. Not opening doors to Christ means having a self image other than the one Christ offers.

The one who opens his door to Christ is the one who puts himself in a position to be loved; who learns to love Christ; who, together with Christ, loves all others, every group, race or people; who puts himself in a position to pardon and make peace.

The closed doors to Christ are the doors of racism, diffidence, closed-mindedness, and even, spiritual elitism. In closing doors to Christ, one closes doors to the universe, dividing it in two: myself and others; friends and enemies. Closed doors lead to a vicious cycle of opposition to others: I can only define myself when I'm against another.

The fundamental question for us is this: *Who is Jesus for me*? What presence does He have in my life, and I in His? It is only this way in which we can determine our ability to love, not by questioning our feelings and what things we can do. We must ask ourselves if we have truly opened up to Christ the doors of our very existence so that He can enter in and be with us and us with Him.

There's also an ecclesial sense of this opening of doors: it concerns not creating divisions within the Church. It means not dividing the Church into "us" and "them," "us this" "they that." The ecclesial aspect of opening the doors to Christ requires that we look at everything from the vantage point of the heart of the Crucified Jesus. From that place, even though inside, we are higher than the world and all things. The heart of Christ is the place of contemplation that loves and embraces the Church as Jesus loved and embraced it Himself.

April 18
Christ: Freedom and Truth

"Christ" means "Messiah" or "Anointed One"; the One consecrated by God and responsible for history and its proper journey towards peace.

The Messiah exemplifies the authoritative fulfillment of man's desires regarding every personal and social good. *The Messiah* is He Who brings man to the full achievement of the ideal of *Shalom*; that is, fullness of peace, goodness, justice and truth in each of his social relationships.

Nevertheless, the truth of every relationship demands the ability to love; to establish relationships in which persons make an authentic gift of themselves to one another. Christ is the truth of love. He teaches me to be myself in love. There is, then, a close relationship between the Messiah and love.

Who is Christ-Love?

Christ-Love is God's ecstasy for man. It is God Who truly loves and goes out to meet man in history.

Christ-Love is Your shining self for me, O my God! It is You, my God, Who loves me and wants to come to meet me!

Christ-Love is divinity enamored of man Who empties Himself in some way of His divine power and life; Who does not count Himself as important, because to Him my life is more important than His own.

Christ-Love is the culmination of Christ-Truth, and Christ-Freedom. Christ-Love is Christ crucified, Who loved me and gave Himself in death for me. Christ-Love is Christ-Eucharist Who offers His body and pours out His blood for me.

When we encounter Christ-Crucified, we get an authentic taste of what it means to be loved with no strings attached; of being important to someone. It teaches us how to love others as we have been loved.

Love, then, is not, in the first instance, a feeling or emotion of the soul. It is not the result of effort on our part — or better, it is this too, but only after we've accepted Christ and His grace.

When we open our hearts to the real events — the Incarnation, the Passion, Death and Resurrection of the Son of God for us — we learn the truth about love.

In fact, Saint John, in his Letter, says: "This has taught us love — that He gave up His life for us; and we, too, ought to give up our lives for our brothers . . . God's love for us was revealed when God sent into the world His only Son so that we could have life through Him; this is the love I mean: not our love for God, but God's love for us . . ." (1 Jn 3:16; 4:9-10).

But who can speak the name Christ-Love, but he who makes the encounter an affecting experience? Who can give him the name, but he who encounters Christ-Love as friend, and as the everything in his life?

Christ-Love, then, is Christ-Crucified Whom *I meet*. It makes no sense to speak of Christ-Love if not in relation to my encounter with Him. I can say that I truly begin to understand Christ-Love when I allow myself to meet Him.

April 19
The Sign of Jesus: Serving Others

When John the Baptist's messengers ask Jesus if He is the One to come or must they wait for another, Jesus does not respond directly and say: "Yes, I am the One." He is satisfied to specify the facts about Himself which the Baptist already knew. The Gospel excerpt, in fact, begins by telling us how much John had come to know: "Now John in his prison had heard what Christ was doing and he sent his disciples to ask Him, 'Are You the One Who is to come, or have we got to wait for someone else?' " (Mt 11:2-3).

Jesus replies by singularly and straightforwardly listing certain works. In His answer, *He puts man at the center*. Jesus' six answers are six proclamations of the centrality of the human subject: the blind recover their sight, the crippled walk, the lepers are cleansed, the deaf hear, the dead are raised, and the poor are evangelized.

This is the messianic sign of Jesus: MAN, man who suffers; man who needs attention; man who is the object of mercy and love; man whose dignity must be restored. Jesus does not speak of the Kingdom of God, which was the nucleus of His activity and mission. And this amazes us.

Jesus says "yes" to the Good News, but puts man and the poor as the subject of the Good News. He presents this as the specific sign of the mission. He describes His messianic action not as the exercise of His power, or as His taking possession of His empire, being the ruler that He is (as Lord of the world); but rather, He describes His messianic action as a work of service ("*diakonia*" in Greek) towards man and his needs.

April 20
Jesus: The Good Shepherd

"I am the good shepherd. The good shepherd is one who lays down his life for his sheep; I am the good shepherd, I know My own and My own know Me" (Jn 10:11, 14).

These two affirmations are preceded by another: "I tell you most solemnly, I am the gate of the sheepfold." With these three affirmations, Jesus represents in the first person, the parable which is found in the beginning of that chapter and which explains how the Good News has not been understood (Jn 10:1-6). In John's Gospel, we find many metaphors of Jesus: water (chapters 4 & 7), bread (chapter 6), light (chapter 9), life (chapter 11), vine (chapter 15). These are images of things. Jesus is man's refreshment, just as water that quenches our thirst. He is nourishment, like bread. He is clarity, like light. He is communion, like the vine. But in the personal image of the shepherd, Jesus is for each of us the loving leader Who is always with us with supreme and untiring affection, patience, devotion and self-giving. In this image, there is the profound closeness of Jesus, more profound than any of the other images. The figure of the shepherd is able to keep the flock together by the weight of his own personal attention. We can recognize a progressive personalization in these affirmations: "I am the gate of the sheepfold. I am the good shepherd." But these expressions which John has recorded for us are, at the same time, very difficult: "I am the good shepherd: the good shepherd is one who lays down his life for his sheep . . . I am the good shepherd; I know My own and My own know Me." Jesus speaks first about giving His life for the sheep, and then about knowing His sheep. He seems to be saying that He loves by making the supreme offering.

The Scripture text gives us more insight. Jesus says: "I know My own and My own know Me, *just as the Father knows Me and I know the Father*, and I lay down My life for My sheep." To give one's life is a great thing, but it is always a human work. As Paul says: "Even if I let them take my body and burn it, but I am without love, it will do me no good whatsoever" (1 Cor 13:3). It has its root in Jesus' mysterious transparency, in Whom we see the Father, and in and through Whom the Father works. The good shepherd who knows his sheep is the one who draws them into the relationship Jesus has with the Father. This is the ultimate reality which explains all others.

Jesus is tied to us not simply as a hero Who gives His life, but as the expression of the Father's tender concern for each one of us. He knows us as the Father knows Him — and there isn't a relationship that's greater or a transparency more perfect.

April 21
Our Fears and Jesus' Consolation

Saint John's Gospel says: "In the evening of the same day, the first day of the week, the doors were closed of the room where the disciples were, for fear of the Jews. Jesus came and stood among them" (Jn 20:19). This excerpt describes for us the circumstances of time and place in which Jesus presented Himself after the Resurrection: "The first day of the week, the doors were closed in the room where the disciples were. . . ." John has his reasons for putting together these details: the night, the night of the same day, the first after the Sabbath, with the doors all shut. What image is the evangelist creating?

Certainly, the night evokes images of solitude and sadness. But more, it was the night of the same day, the first day after the Sabbath. With these words, John refers to all that took place in Chapter Twenty up to this point. He's referring to the day in which Mary Magdalen went to the tomb. The account begins with the words: "It was the first day of the week [first day after the Sabbath]." So this was the night of the empty tomb; the night of the announcement; the night of the Resurrection.

The Gospel writer continues: "The doors were closed in the room where the disciples were, for fear of the Jews." An atmosphere of fear pervaded. The announcement and the signs of the Resurrection were not enough — they wanted something more.

Their fear is expressed by the image of the closed doors: fear and locked doors go together. While joy is the mother of communication and opening up, fear is behind our closing in on the self.

It is to this situation that Jesus comes. Furthermore, the text says: "Jesus came and stood among them." This Gospel expression "stood among them" is new. Jesus put Himself in the midst of His Church to console it in its fear and to announce to it His peace.

Today, we might express this fear that gripped the apostles in the closed room in this way: fear of the environment that surrounds us; fear of the dominant culture; fear of appearing different, strange or innovative; fear of being persecuted or derided; fear of freely and courageously proclaiming the Gospel message from our heart.

The Gospel says that Jesus "stood among them." He did not stand above them, as He could have done, to show His superiority. He did not stand off on the side, as if to judge them. No, He stood among them, on their level, in a fraternity that is itself most significant.

Continuing with the excerpt, Jesus says: "Peace be with you" (Jn 20:21). This greeting should not be over-looked or discounted. Jesus could have begun by reproving them with harsh words, such as, "Why did you abandon Me, O men of little faith? Where are all your promises? Where were you, Peter, who bragged about your fidelity unto death?" Jesus could have embarrassed them, humiliated them, or scolded them — but He doesn't. Instead, He greets them with sweet words of encouragement, mercy and trust.

The text tells us that Jesus "showed them His hands

and His side''; that is, He showed them His wounds. ''And the disciples were filled with joy when they saw the Lord'' (Jn 20:20). They didn't get frightened, or sick at the horrible signs of the Passion. They rejoiced in the Risen Lord!

April 22
Jesus' Power and Authority

When we hear the last words that Jesus spoke on earth (as recounted by Matthew's Gospel), we are struck by the totality of His pronouncement: ''*All* authority in heaven and on earth has been given to Me. Go, therefore; make disciples of all nations; baptize them in the name of the Father and of the Son and of the Holy Spirit; and teach them to observe the commandments I gave you. And know that I am with you *always*; yes, to the end of time'' (Mt 28:19-20).

Jesus has been given all power in the heavens and on earth, and from this emerges His mission to all nations so that they may observe the commandments.

Jesus speaks with the messianic fullness of His power. He, the Lord Who is in glory at the right hand of the Father, contemplates all human history. And it is exactly this mystery of Christ's glorification which we celebrate in the solemn feast of the Ascension.

The words of the Gospel, framed in this mystery, invite us to reflect on Jesus' power over all the nations. What kind of power is this? I would like to explain with the words of Pope John Paul II: ''We think of power in terms of categories which refer to dominion over the social order, or to justice in the world. Jesus Christ is beyond these categories. The power that was given Him in heaven and on earth — the power which properly belongs to Him — is the power to offer Himself for the life of the world. It is the power of Redemption through love. This power reached its zenith in the Paschal mystery: the sacrifice of the cross and Resurrection are the culmination of this power. Through the Eucharist, the Church shares in that universal power of Christ (to offer Himself for the life of the world). It becomes the very heart of her mission and service.'' All this is part of an organic design: from the cross, Christ radiates His power over the universe. That power is then realized day by day in the Church, through the Eucharist, which is the center of the community and its mission.

Jesus' power is born from His incredible ability to serve and dedicate Himself to every person. In Jesus and His dedication, man finds the intimate definition of his being, which is that he is a gift, made in the image of God, the supreme Love and Gift.

Beyond this global interpretation of Christ's universal power, we could ask ourselves if there also may be an historical or empirical reading of this power. Can we see any concrete sign of it in the events of our daily life?

I think that beyond the Church and its constitution centered on the Eucharist; beyond its attractive presence in the midst of humanity; there may be what I call a political sign.

We can grasp this ''political'' aspect of Jesus' power in the extraordinary nostalgia that pervades humanity. It is a nostalgia for the unity of the human race; a nostalgia for universal fraternity. This nostalgia — and I believe it is more evident these days — for unity among men, for breaking down barriers and reconciling adverse factions and forces, is interpreted by the Church in its recognition

148   APRIL

that Jesus is the sign for the times. And thus, the Church puts itself at the service of this thrust for unity.

April 23
The Lord Is Always With Us

Whenever we "look up" to the Kingdom that Jesus has attained as the final condition for humanity, and then we look around us we can be filled with bitterness and consternation. We see that we are not yet in our final state of being; we are on a journey. We lack many things; some never come; others about us we deplore. So, we suffer and, in such a moment look beyond all the negativity around us towards that day when we will experience perfection. But that perfect reality which we seek is not very far from us. It isn't only the object of our desire. The same words that announced to us that Jesus is in the Kingdom also tell us that Jesus will return one day. This is to say that the Kingdom is destined to permeate everything; it is destined to enter into our life and transform it according to the power which it has already fully manifested in the life of Jesus.

Back to our question: When will He return? When will this final state of existence come? The Acts of the Apostles tells us that this return begins with Pentecost.

Pentecost is the first act of Jesus' return to take possession of the world. We are reminded by the last words in Matthew's Gospel: "Know that I am with you always; yes, to the end of time" (Mt 28:20).

Jesus is with God in the Kingdom. At the same time, He is with us, every day. He is with His Church. Jesus — in all His glory and power — is in and with us. He is in our hands in order that we may build a more just society. He is in our minds so that we may reflect on all that is good and true. He is in our hearts so that we may make choices which bring life and love. As a man, He lived in us with the fullness of a life close to God. From the moment of His Ascension, He lives in us, through the gift of the Spirit, "the extraordinary richness of His power," as St. Paul says.

If, looking above to the heavenly Jerusalem we find many things about ourselves to lament, we must learn to look to Christ within us. We must see how He has been given to us through the presence of the Spirit in our hearts. Then we can perceive how His power works within the Church. We will see Him in all aspects of the Church's life where the power and love of the Spirit is manifested.

April 24
The Salvific Event of the Ascension

With His Ascension into heaven, Jesus, in His human nature (and in Him, each of us) is definitively seated next to God. Jesus, the mediator between God and man, the judge of the world, and Lord of the universe, has not abandoned us to the poverty and misery of our human condition. He has preceded us to our eternal home in order to secure the hope that where He — the head and firstborn — is, we, His members shall also be.

The Ascension makes us think to the future and our hope. It makes us look above, just as the Gospel tells us that the apostles do.

And from this image a question arises: This looking to the heavens, couldn't it distract us from our daily tasks?

150

Perhaps that is the point of the reproach in the angels' words to the disciples: "Why are you men from Galilee standing here looking into the sky?" (Ac 1:11).

The answer to this question may be found in the same Scripture passage: "Jesus Who has been taken up from you into heaven, this same Jesus will come back in the same way as you have seen Him go there." Let us reflect for a moment on the significance of these words. They speak of the Jesus Who lived among us; Who traveled the streets of Palestine where we, too, can travel in pilgrimage. They speak of Jesus, a man like us Who suffered and was filled with joy — suffered because He was misunderstood; filled with joy whenever He was understood. They speak of that man Jesus, Who was killed by His enemies, but raised to life by God. Jesus, being the Son of God, lived a life experience similar to ours, from birth to death. That is why the Gospel passage speaks of Jesus as being one Who lived among us and has now ascended into heaven.

He is one of us, made like us. He knows our experiences. With His presence in heaven, our experiences, our life and our desires have been brought up to God. Now, in His full humanity, He lives that full reality with God. In the ineffable and definitive mystery of God which has ruled since the beginning of history, He is the aspiration of every human heart because it is only in Him that the heart finds solutions to the most profound questions and problems that keep us in turmoil.

As man, Jesus is present in the perfect light of the Kingdom, the heavenly Jerusalem, the city of God, the place of perfect peace and justice, the place where everything is free and clear.

April 25
We Are Jesus' People

We must not envy Jesus' contemporaries. Instead, we must consider with great joy our fortune to be able to encounter Him and remember and relive His Passion.

Jesus is in our midst. He gives us His Word. He is present among us to help us understand the mystery of His life.

Above all, it is in the mystery of the Eucharist that He reveals Himself to us, gives us His love, enkindles a new fire in our hearts, changes our lives, entrusts to us the mission to speak His name to everyone.

The major events of Easter did not just take place in the past: through the Eucharist, Jesus is glorified and present among us here and now. He helps us to remember those events in an intense and realistic way.

He establishes a profound relationship between His history and ours; between His life and our life. In Him, we become new creatures reliving our Baptism. We become His people, announcing His love to the whole world.

Through the Eucharistic body, which is given to us in real food, we become His body, His reality in history; one being with Him.

These great and mysterious gifts, present in the Eucharist, ask to be contemplated and assimilated each time we participate in the Eucharistic sacrifice.

April 26
Cross and Glorification

John the Evangelist uses a word that invites reflection: the disciples understood what happened when Jesus

152

entered Jerusalem and was "*glorified*" (Jn 12:16). The term "*glorified*" does not necessarily refer to Jesus' Resurrection. In fact, when John does want to refer specifically to the Resurrection, he knows how to use that vocabulary. Narrating the episode of the Jews who were seeking a sign, he quotes Jesus, "Destroy this sanctuary, and in three days I will raise it up," adding the notation that when Jesus rose from the dead, the disciples remembered what He had said and believed (Jn 2:19, 22).

Here, however, John is speaking of "glorification." John uses the term many times throughout his Gospel, but here I will use but one citation to include them all. In Chapter Twelve, Jesus speaks of His imminent death, saying: "Now the hour has come for the Son of Man to be glorified" (Jn 12:23). In other words, Jesus proclaims that His glorification comes through His death.

"Glorification" helps us to see that the sense of Jesus' life lies not only in the Resurrection, but also in the cross: *in His way of dying for love and with love*.

From the cross, we can focus on the true meaning of His Kingship: His is a Kingship not of dominion, but rather, of attraction. Jesus draws every person to Himself by the power of love.

It is from this glorification and contemplation of the cross that we are called to know and understand a little better the mystery of Jesus.

April 27
Jesus: Interpreter of Scripture

John makes an observation which calls us to reflection: "At the time His disciples did not understand this;

but later, after Jesus had been glorified, they remembered that this had been written about Him and this was in fact how they had received Him'' (Jn 12:16).

Their direct participation in the events which surrounded Jesus was not enough to enlighten the faith of the disciples. Another intervention was needed. We immediately think of the appearances of the Risen Lord to the disciples; how He enlightened their faith, gave them the gift of the Holy Spirit, and helped them to understand all that He did and taught them while He was with them.

Such, for example, He did with the two disciples of Emmaus. He encountered them in depression on their return journey to their home after the crucifixion events. He walked by their side, and explained the meaning of the Scriptures. He lit the fires of their hearts. He accepted their prayer that He stay and eat with them, and then revealed Himself in the breaking of the bread. Jesus helped them to ''do this in memory of Him''; to recall and even become themselves a living memory of Him; a living witness to the Resurrection. In that moment, the two disciples understood everything: they remembered the events contained in the Scriptures, and understood the words that explained those events:

''Then, starting with Moses and going through all the prophets, He explained to them the passages throughout the Scriptures that were about Himself. When they drew near to the village to which they were going, He made as if to go on; but they pressed Him to stay with them. 'It is nearly evening,' they said, 'and the day is almost over.' So He went in to stay with them. Now while He was with them at table, He took the bread and said the blessing; then He broke it and handed it to them. And their eyes were opened and they recognized Him; but He had vanished from their sight. Then they said to each other, 'Did not our hearts burn within us as He talked to us on the road and explained the Scriptures to us?' " (Lk 24:27-32).

Clarity and Darkness in Christ's Passover

Jesus enters His city for the last time, in order to fulfill His mission. He enters as a king, and the people recognize Him as such: "Blessed is He Who comes in the name of the Lord, the King of Israel." He enters under the clear and precise signs of kingship — He rides an ass (a reference to the history of Solomon, and more particularly, to the messianic prophet Zechariah, who said: "He rides the foal of an ass").

On the other hand, Jesus' entrance has something of darkness about it which makes little sense: Jesus the King enters the city meekly and humbly, without exercising His sovereign powers, without the acts of imperialism and dominion which usually characterized the solemn entrance of a king into his conquered city. Jesus enters in such a humble, simple way — John tells us — that not even His disciples understood these things.

Thus, there is the *clarity* of Jesus' action which shines for all those who know the Scriptures and understand the reference to prophecies. But there is also the *darkness* created by His humble entrance that does not make sense to those who apply worldly criteria of dominion and kingship to Jesus' actions.

By His actions, Jesus makes no one happy. Those who stand for absolute clarity would have wanted Jesus to exercise His authority. But Jesus is entering the city where He will be imprisoned, judged, tortured and killed, meek and humble and seated on an ass. Those who would have insisted on His humility are amazed at His acceptance of other honors usually reserved to an earthly King: the shouts of hosanna, the praise of the crowd. These things disturb them and raise doubts in their minds about Him.

Jesus begins His Passion with that clarity and darkness which previously had characterized His ministry, and had particularly been manifested in His enigmatic parables. Those who wanted to, were able to understand. Those who didn't want to, remained in darkness.

The mystery of Jesus is gradually manifested through this darkness and light which must be attentively evaluated and made part of us in such a way that we come to know Him as He is. He is not the Messiah according to the world's conception of Him. Jesus represents the newness of God, of God Who enters our lives in ways different from those in which we expect Him, of God Who calls us to a new mode of existence, and who rightly turns our expectations of Him upside down.

April 29
"Chiaroscuro" in the Mystery of the Church

Christ's clarity and darkness are reflected in the mystery of the Church. The Church, too, in a way, has the clarity and power of God's Word; the ability to promote human, civil, social and political works which favor an insertion into society — this is the glorious aspect of Jesus' entrance into Jerusalem.

But the Church is also itself when it retires in prayer,

156

in adoration, in humility, almost hiding itself in its adoration of the Eucharistic host. It is also itself when it accepts humiliation and trials. The Church is itself in both of these situations; one is not separate from the other and neither is one privileged in relation to the other. It is only in this unity of power and humility that the Church goes forward as Jesus did, and reveals God's strength and mercy, His justice and goodness, His becoming one like us.

We must jealously conserve this mystery of the Church's unity: a mystery of the Church as sweet, humble and loving — like Mary — and strong and courageous, like Peter; a mystery of a Church that withdraws in the silence of prayer, and which openly proclaims the Word of God.

This double reality of the Church's life must appear in our own lives. Each of us lives in himself the mystery of Christ and the Church. We experience moments of strength and clarity, as well as moments of humility and hiddenness. We have moments of generous and responsible action, as well as moments of contemplation and prayer. And we grasp the key to this mystery of Christ and the Church in the Paschal mystery.

We, as Christians and as Church, go through this world just as Jesus did. We desire to hold firm to this resolve: to follow the Lord, such as He was and as He revealed Himself to be. We desire to be a Church not different from that which Jesus founded.

April 30
**Mary Introduces Us to Jesus'
Humanity and Goodness**

Mary's devotion introduces us to the "humanity and

goodness'' of the Lord Jesus Christ. I have transcribed these two terms from the Latin Vulgate of Titus 3:4, where the Jerusalem Bible today reads "kindness" and "love." My use of the terms "humanity" and "goodness" are meant to designate the fraternal and friendly posture which must always show through our Christian actions.

It is true that our faith must express itself in strong decisions, and in works that are taken seriously and continued consistently to a conclusion — always maintaining an inflexible opposition to every injustice that may show itself. We also need to truly live the novelty of the Gospel life; to clearly and openly reject the many easy forms of living, choosing for ourselves rigorous discipline and self control.

But all of this can bring about a certain rigidity or hardness which is inevitable when we are striving to achieve a certain result. The Church assures its own unity, and explains and protects the faith of individuals, through a strong organization which demands the respect of precise rules. Without this, the "Body of Christ" would loses members and fall into the mediocrity of its surroundings. At the same time, as Urs von Balthasar noted, this "Petrine" aspect (organization and hierarchical aspect of the Church) must always be accompanied by what he calls the "Marian principle." The figure of Mary calls us to the simple and ready faith of her "who believed that the promise made her by the Lord would be fulfilled" (Lk 1:45); to the humility of the "handmaid of the Lord" (Lk 1:38); to the human warmth of Mary who "set out . . . as quickly as she could to a town in the hill country" to be with her kinswoman, Elizabeth (Lk 1:39).

Mary's way of being present highlights the value of kindness and discreet attention which led her to notice the

158   APRIL

problem at the wedding feast of Cana (Jn 2:1-11); to look tenderly upon the baby cradled in her arms in the stable (Lk 2:7); to remain in silent anguish at the foot of her Son's cross (Jn 18:25). Her example leads us to give our considered attention to the value of human life and to be compassionate in the face of suffering and death, approaches which we find sadly on the decline in much of the world today.

MAY

May 1
Ours Is a God Who Labors

Sacred Scripture, in Genesis, speaks to us about *God's work*: "On the seventh day God completed the work He had been doing" (Gn 2:2). In speaking of this "work of God's," even if metaphorically, the Bible is not afraid to make God out as "One Who works." And if we read the first pages of the Book of Genesis — this book that speaks of the world's beginnings — we can see *the object of God's labors*: the earth, creation, vegetation, life. We, ourselves, are the object of this marvelous work. We are the fruit of His labors.

We can further ask: How does God work? What are some of the characteristics of this work? The Scriptures can also provide the answers to these questions.

God's labors are freely done. They are the means for Him to spontaneously express Himself. His are creative works, inventively rich and full of satisfaction.

After each work, God pauses and says to Himself: This is good! "God saw all that He had made, and indeed it was very good" (Gn 1:31).

The Scriptures, then, in their limited human words which try to capture the great mystery of God, call God's work free, spontaneous, creative; something which bears fruit and gives much satisfaction.

For our part, we, who are made in the image and

likeness of God, must do our work in the image and likeness of God's work. This work is destined (by God's design and will) to be free, spontaneous and creative. It must satisfy the laborer and be a means for his or her self-expression.

Here is the reality of God's plan: He labored for us, and continues to do so. We, in turn, have been placed in a responsible position to likewise work. Our tasks must be similar to His; done in love and joy.

May 2
Human Labor as Part of the Reality of Sin

Confronting the work of God's plan, however, is the *dramatic reality of human work in the history of sin*. It is a reality that we all know and which we can define with almost the exact opposite characteristics to what we first used in describing what work is about.

We are now speaking of a work which often is not free (and this goes well beyond the mere talk of any work imposed by conditions of slavery which happen from time to time in the world). This non-free work is often imposed by circumstances and situations that we can neither calculate nor control. It is a work that goes against our will and attitudes, and therefore causes uneasiness.

The labor we often have in our hands — however free, creative or self-expressive it may be — obligates us to the monotony and fatigue of repetition. This fatigue, with the physical and psychological discomfort it brings, often detracts from the satisfaction we might otherwise feel by our completion of the task.

Moreover, in today's society, it often happens that

we never get to see the fruits of our labors, as the fruits may be far from us. Therefore, we cannot say: I have produced this thing and it is good.

So, it appears that God's plan for free, spontaneous, personally expressive, creative and fruitful work is denied by the harsh reality that in our hands, work often becomes tiresome, painful and heavy. Sometimes, we go so far as to say that we are ''condemned'' to our labors!

May 3
The Plan of Redemption in Human Labor

Here is where the redemptive plan of salvation comes into consideration; the *plan of redemption as it relates to human labor*. This not only concerns God's work, but the work of Jesus, the labors of Joseph and Mary, along with the work of all those who have experienced firsthand the world's redemption.

This is the marvelous task before *us*, the task that from the earliest of times has been very important to millions of people in the world who have embraced it by means of an immense workers' movement which takes in all persons of good will: to bring their work ever closer to God's plan, ever closer to His Person, in subordination to their own person, expressive of their humanity, in such a way that it becomes something which they can enjoy and in which they can take real satisfaction.

This may seem like a dream, but it is rather *a long and difficult road to travel*. It is especially difficult because from time to time we think we've reached one of the objectives (e.g., we've been able to diminish the fatigue of our physical labor), but then we run up against other barriers (such as our falling into monotony, repetition or anonymity).

It is then, when we renew our efforts *to work better* — that is, to make our labor an expression of the freedom and dignity of every person — that we create something true and good. As I have been saying, this is a long journey, with some stages already behind and others still ahead. What makes it difficult is that along the way we have to rethink our way of living, our way of wanting, enjoying and consuming.

We are speaking about *putting human values first* — putting them ahead of immediate satisfaction, profit, consumption for its own sake. We must put these human values before everything that threatens us, and at a certain point, mysteriously but rapidly break down these enslaving mechanisms in our society.

We cannot make our journey in sadness, as if things would or should never change. Neither can we fool ourselves into thinking that some miracle will come from who knows where and bring us to the desired objectives. This journey is entrusted to us — to our courage, to our hope, to our faith.

May 4
Mary: Most Excellent Fruit of the Redemption

I would like to reflect upon the words which the Second Vatican Council, in the Constitution on the Sacred Liturgy (*Sacrosanctum Concilium*), dedicates to Marian feasts. The Council says: "In celebrating this annual cycle of Christ's mysteries, holy Church honors with special love the Blessed Virgin Mary, Mother of God, who is joined by an inseparable bond to the saving work of her Son. In her the Church holds up and admires the most excellent fruit of the redemption, and joyfully contemplates, as in a faultless model, that which she herself wholly desires and hopes to be'' (SC 103).

There are three important affirmations made here: The first affirmation teaches us that all the Marian feasts are a part of the cycle of Christ's mysteries — the *only* cycle that the Church celebrates in its liturgy. There aren't three cycles (one for Christ's feasts, one for Mary's and one for the saints'). Mary's feasts share in this one cycle of Christ's mysteries by the indissoluble bond which joins Mary to the salvific work of Jesus. The Virgin Mother, along with the Church for which she is the model, is in total relationship with Christ. She is significant in our salvation history because of her nexus to the Redeemer.

''In her,'' the document says, ''the Church holds up and admires the most excellent fruit of the redemption.'' Mary is strictly tied to Jesus' redemptive action because she is first of all the most excellent fruit of His salvific work. We habitually pray in the ''Hail Mary'' that Jesus is the fruit of Mary's womb. But here the Council is going further, and tells us that Mary herself is the fruit of the redemption; that she is joined to Jesus because she received everything from Him.

Our Lady fully opened her arms and heart to receive the fullness of God's gift. In this way, she is the model for every man and woman to recognize their duty to God; to let themselves be loved by God.

''The Almighty has done great things for me'' (Lk 1:49). With these words Mary recognizes that everything is a gift from God, and thus, she feels fully loved by God in Christ.

We must carefully note the expression that the Conciliar document employs: in Mary, "the Church holds up and admires the most excellent fruit of the redemption." The Church praises God for the gifts He has given to Mary by using the same words with which the Virgin praised the work of the Lord: "My soul proclaims the greatness of the Lord and my spirit exults in God my savior" (Lk 1:47). In the liturgy we celebrate, there is a lived identification between Mary and the Church. We, as Church, feel understood and represented by Our Lady.

The document's third affirmation is more explicit: in Mary, the Church "joyfully contemplates, as in a faultless model, that which she herself wholly desires and hopes to be." The Church looks beyond itself, beyond the events of its daily life to Mary who is in God's glory. Mary is the concrete image of all that the Church desires and hopes to be. She is the icon of the goal of all that is to be done, of all that is to be prayed for, of all that is to be worked toward, of all the sacrifices of the Church.

Mary represents all that each of us ought to be: totally dedicated to the Lord; totally attentive to the work of Christ; totally caught up in God's great mysteries.

Mary, glorified in body and soul with the Father, is the transfiguration of the body, of our daily historicity. She is the goal for all humanity called to share the fullness of her glory.

May 5
In Mary, the Work of Christ is Perfected

There is a person who has already accomplished all that humanity desires and hopes for, a person in whom the work of Christ is perfected. It is the Virgin Mother of our Lord.

Each person can look to her and say: Here is God's work made perfect. Here is the place of true joy and true peace. And, since Mary is the Mother of the Church, all those who conform themselves to her in the Church, live, by the measure of their correspondence, the splendor of God's gifts.

But what do we mean when we say that we should imitate Mary's adherence to God, and express that in our lives?

It simply means three things: To listen to the Word, to say "yes" to God, and to serve.

Listen to the Word. Mary is a person who made space in her life so that the Word of God could enter in. Mary let the Word resonate within, from the first words of the angel until the last words of Jesus on the cross.

Mary created a zone of silence within and about her so that she could hear: "She treasured all these things and pondered them in her heart" (Lk 2:20).

Say "yes" to God. From Mary's contemplative silence is born the second characteristic I've mentioned: the ability to say "yes" to God — to put oneself at the disposition of the divine call. "He called those he intended for this; those He called He justified, and with those He justified He shared His glory" (Rm 8:30). These somewhat obscure words of St. Paul mean to tell us that we have nothing to fear when we say "yes" to God in our life. He guides us, but always in His fidelity.

To serve. Jesus' mother then demonstrated her adherence to God. She allowed Him to manifest His reign in her, through her humble service as the handmaid, from the Incarnation to the cross, and then in the early Christian community.

The Church was born out of this openness and readiness to serve. And the Church is continually sustained and advanced by the generous service of all the Baptized, and the service of the priests and bishops — each one in his or her right place. And it is also out of this spirit of service that civil society is served and supported.

May 6
O Mary, Forever Immensely Loved

Mary Most Holy, in her Immaculate Conception, presents us with the perfect case and example of the dignity of life received from the beginning as grace, and expressed throughout its existence as obedience. This dignity is the fruit of grace; that is, the fruit of God's love.

As the Gospel says, Mary is full of grace. The expression in Greek is actually in the passive tense, which expresses something received. Even more, it is in the *remote* past. Therefore, we could interpret it this way: "O Mary, you have been loved for a long time." This is the dignity of Mary — forever immensely loved.

With the help of St. Paul's Letter to the Ephesians, which speaks of God's eternal plan, we realize in our contemplation of Mary that we contemplate the dignity of every person — each person born, each person conceived, each of us. Just as the words applied to Mary, they apply to us: creature forever loved, forever present in love and in God's plan. "Blessed be God the Father of our Lord Jesus Christ, Who has blessed us with all the spiritual blessings of heaven in Christ. Before the world was made, He chose us, chose us in Christ, to be holy and spotless, and to live through love in His presence, determining that we should become His adopted sons" (Ep 1:3-4).

Man's dignity, seen in this mystery, is grace, gift, and being loved.

But to be loved also means letting oneself be loved. It therefore concerns obedience: listening to God's Word. The sincere and loving acceptance of that Word — which has always spoken our name and which always loves us — is perfectly expressed by Mary's response to the angel: "Let what you have said be done to me" (Lk 1:38). Our dignity, then, is a dignity that we receive and express in obedience.

May 7
A Woman at the Center of God's Plan

At the center of God's plan we find a woman, and this is key to our understanding of woman's dignity in the world and in history.

Mary is the first in the human chain of believers. She is the beginning of the Church, the Mother of the Church. God Himself was interested in her from her conception.

This means to say that not only is life sacred from the first instance — a human sacredness to respect, love, protect and defend in the name of human dignity, but it also means that from the beginning each person is truly alive and already the object of God's transcendent loving plan. From the beginning each person is a being who is forever loved by God, and not just a purely indifferent biological existence.

God puts His love into our hearts. We are all invited to listen to the voice of love which He put into us at the beginning of our life, venerating the beginning of the Virgin Mother of God's life without sin.

Repeating the words of the "Hail Mary" is not simply a devotional exercise, but an evocation of the mysteries which conquer our fears and illuminate the dignity of every man and woman, beginning with Mary. The "Hail Mary" is the proclamation of a hope-filled event for us. It proclaims the certainty of life, not the fatality of a death that we fearfully await each day.

May 8
Mary: The First Believer

The Scripture texts describe the dark and negative existence into which God intervenes, bringing the light of salvation.

In Genesis the text says that Adam was afraid (Gn 3:10): it is the first time in the history of humanity that the Scriptures tell us of our fears. This fear, which is the root of all that follows, does not come from an outside threat or enemy, nor from the insidiousness of nature. Rather, it comes from within. We are a spectacle to ourselves and our uneasy awareness of ourselves tends to want God to disappear. We fear God. Thus, we find ourselves facing one of the unconscious roots of atheism: the desire to hide ourselves and our dissatisfaction with life from God.

Saint Paul's Letter to the Ephesians responds to this fear. It allows us to contemplate the positive, luminous aspect of human existence: "Before the world was made, He chose us, chose us in Christ, to be holy and spotless, and to live through love in His presence" (Ep 1:4). God chose us. St. Paul uses "us" to refer first to himself and his brother Jews, the heirs of the Covenant who were chosen by God ages before. The Church refers in particular to the daughter *par excellence* of the Covenant: the daughter of Zion, Mary. She is the first of believers; the first who fully hoped in God's promise of Christ. For Mary, the Mother of Jesus, these words of Scripture are more important than any other: Mary was predestined "to be the adopted daughter, to be holy and spotless in His loving presence" (SC).

Our Lady, the Mother of God — our holy and immaculate Mother — is our light. She shines on this world and makes us feel proud to be a person. We share in her life and mission.

Mary, who was a creature of such interior cleanliness so as to challenge any of our moral dissatisfactions, helps us to contemplate her sincerity and humility before God. Even though we at times may be constrained to say along with the psalmist, "no one is honest, no one is sincere, no one is pure in this world"; even though we may feel bitterness and desolation, we can always rejoice because we have Mary before us!

May 9
The Handmaid of the Lord

Because it is difficult to reflect on the entire Annunciation story, I've decided to offer some thoughts only on the last, simple words of the account: "I am the handmaid of the Lord," Mary said. "Let what you have said be done to me" (Lk 1:38).

These words express, without a doubt, a clear recognition that there is a relationship present. Mary calls herself a handmaid, indicating that she is in a relationship with another.

At first, this servant relationship presents a problem. The word in Greek (*doule*) refers to bondage or slavery. However, if we consider the spiritual and biblical context from which the term "handmaid" emerges, we understand that it contains a deeper and more tender meaning.

Mary's words parallel the words of Isaiah: "Here is My servant whom I uphold, My chosen one in whom My soul delights" (Is 42:1).

Our Lady was certainly nourished by reading the prophet Isaiah, and that verse resounds in every fiber of her being and her words. We see the similarity of the first part in Mary's words: "I am the handmaid [servant] of the Lord." We see the similarity to the second half of the Isaian verse in the words of the angel: "Mary, you have won God's favor" (Lk 1:31).

Mary identifies herself in relation to God because He decided to put Himself in a close relationship with her, a relationship of favor and support.

We find another beautiful similarity: "I have endowed him with My Spirit" (Is 42:1b) with the words of the angel to Mary: "the Holy Spirit will come upon you" (Lk 1:35).

Mary accepts and responds, "I am the handmaid of the Lord" within the same framework of the predictions of grace and mission with which we place the figure of Yahweh's servant, as told by Isaiah.

She has the same awareness as the mysterious servant who is loved by God and pre-chosen by Him to be filled with the Spirit. But this awareness is not just an individual awareness; it is an awareness of the people. Mary speaks in the name of the people whom she represents. This we also find in Isaiah: "You, Israel, My servant [here referring to the people of Israel as a servant], Jacob whom I have chosen, descendant of Abraham My friend. You whom I . . . called from the ends of the world; you to whom I said, 'You are My servant' . . . do not be afraid, for I am with you'' (Is 41:8-10). "The Lord is with you," the angel tells Mary, "do not be afraid" (Lk 1:29, 31).

Mary lives in unity with the people who feel loved, who know they are chosen and experience God's sustaining power.

There is another parallel in Isaiah: "I am Yahweh, your God, the Holy One of Israel, your Savior. . . . Do not be afraid, for I have redeemed you; I have called you by name . . . you are precious in My eyes" (Is 43:3, 1, 4). In Mary's soul there is a dedication to her God, the God of all Israel: Mary is the soul, the voice, the expression of the vocation of her people. Because of this, she responds to the Lord as an individual and as the Virgin of Israel, the Daughter of Zion.

But beyond this sense of her people, Mary has an awareness of all humanity: "I, Yahweh, have called you to serve the cause of right; I have taken you by the hand and formed you; I have appointed you as a covenant for the people and a light to the nations, to open the eyes of the blind, to free captives from prison, and those who live in darkness from the dungeon" (Is 42:6-7). "My servant shall justify many . . . hence I will give whole hordes for his tribute" (Is 53:11-12).

Mary lives on the wave of the biblical revelation which becomes actualized in her through the angel's words. Mary lives the triple awareness of her personal relationship of dedication to God, her choral expression of her people, and her responsibility towards all humanity.

The Prophecy of the Magnificat (I)

The Magnificat is the joyous hymn Mary proclaims at her encounter with Elizabeth. Mary, feeling herself welcomed by her kinswoman, feeling herself understood in her intimate secret (her maternity by the work of the Spirit), breaks into a song of joy, an exultation to God's work in history.

If we closely examine the structure of the Magnificat, we can see that its central part is composed of a series of verbs in the past tense: ''The Almighty *has done* great things . . . He *has shown* the power of His arm, He *has routed* the proud of heart. He *has pulled down* princes . . . He *has come to the help* of Israel'' (Lk 1:49-54). These verbs indicate actions which are considered to have already happened. But Mary says these words when she has just begun to experience God's greatness within her. Furthermore, while Mary was proclaiming these words, the proud were not being routed, nor were princes being pulled down from their thrones, nor were the hungry filled with good things. Jesus Himself had not yet proclaimed how blessed are the poor!

This canticle, then, which in linguistic terms expresses past actions, can also be considered a prophecy. It could be said that a prophecy in the remote past is a proclamation of events which, in part, must be verified; events which the prophet, putting himself or herself on God's side in the light of faith, already sees completed.

The canticle expresses the joy in Mary's heart which began with the end or goal of the salvific action. This action, for Mary, ended in her glorious Assumption to God. When Mary speaks this prayer, she has not yet experienced the fullness of God's great work in her, but she is sure of it, and can describe this reality as an already completed plan: "The Almighty has done great things for me . . . He has shown the power of His arm" (Lk 1:49, 51).

We too can contemplate Mary as the fulfillment of God's plan. She revives our hope in the power of God's plan that works throughout history.

May 11
The Prophecy of the Magnificat (II)

A second important observation we can make is that the Magnificat begins with a reference to the individuality of Mary: "*My* soul proclaims the greatness of the Lord and *my* spirit exults in God *my* savior" (Lk 1:47). It is Mary, the individual, historical person, speaking of herself and her destiny. Nevertheless, the canticle, so rigorously individual in the beginning, ends with a collective reference to all the people. Mary makes an expression of the historic consciousness of the people: "God has come to the help of Israel His servant, mindful of His mercy — according to the promise He made to our ancestors — of His mercy to Abraham and to His descendants forever" (Lk 1:54-55).

Mary, the handmaid of the Lord, whose glorious destiny is sung in this hymn, becomes the "servant of Israel," that is, all of us who, in union with her faith, are children of Abraham, God's people, inheritors of the Covenant. Therefore, we read in the Magnificat the prophecy of the coming of the Church — exactly what the Holy Fathers read in the many pages of Scripture. As one scholar put it: "From the beginning of Scripture, on the frontispiece of history the mystery of the Church was already present." This mystery of the *Corpus Ecclesiae* takes shape in history, and has light thrown on it in a privileged way by Mary. And this, our human condition, taking into consideration its experience within the history of salvation, must aim towards its perfect completeness in the Kingdom of God.

The Magnificat is not just a lyric expression of a personal event; it is the epic of a people. The Assumption is not only Mary's personal destiny; it is exemplary of what we are all called to as individuals, as Church, as humanity. The Assumption lets us look at ourselves as the new creation, the new community reconciled in peace with God, in shalom, in messianic peace. Mary attained the fullness of this peace.

We pray in order that all humanity — and in particular, "Mary's people," the historic people of Israel — may understand the ways of God's peace.

We pray in order that each of us may collaborate in this work of understanding and peace, putting aside any resentment, until we realize the promise of God's mercy, as He promised to our fathers, to Abraham and his descendants forever.

May 12
The Small Seed for the Big Earth

An important mystery which we find in the salvation history of the world is "the mystery of the one for all," "the singular for the plural," "the one for the many," "the small seed for the big earth." We celebrate this same

176   MAY

mystery in the Eucharist when the priest prays over the chalice that the blood poured out for all of us is for the remission of sins.

Our salvation begins from a "little." And this means that we are joined by a solidarity that spreads like a stain of oil. Our salvation manifests itself through an infection from one to another, from the few to the many. Throughout history, humanity has always taken account of these two polarities (the individual and the group) and at the same time, has recognized that it all begins and spreads out from one — from Mary, Mother of Jesus. It becomes a mass elevated with love.

To those who ask us where the great crowds of Christians of days past have gone, we answer by presenting individuals and small committed groups, such as the "300 of Gideon" which the Bible mentions; a yeast which may truly be such and cause the mass to grow.

Our responsibility is great. We are "the salt of the earth." We are called to continually listen to and heed the voice that is within us, wherever we hear it and in whatever life we lead. Only in this way can our solidarity grow.

May 13
The Disproportion of the Sign

The pages of the Gospels help us understand that the ultimate realities of which Mary is a sign or symbol enter into our daily life. And they enter in through familiarity, friendliness and proximity — all of which are exemplified by the great meeting between Mary and Elizabeth (Lk 1:39-58).

Elizabeth is an elderly woman. She is forced to carry her special secret inside herself because it is something that's hard to communicate. Mary is a young woman who carries an even more incommunicable secret.

The two meet and they understand one another. They look into each other's eyes, feel the vibrations of the Spirit, and embrace in joy. Each understands the truth of the other. They share and respect each other's secret.

The Magnificat (the hymn which anticipates the fullness of time) is born from this mutual understanding, friendly closeness, and trust. We must note the prophetic force with which Mary recalls the events of the past that will happen in the future: "He has shown the strength of His arm, He has routed the proud of heart. He has pulled down princes from their thrones and exalted the lowly" (Lk 1:51-52).

These are man's hopes and Mary gives them a voice. She puts things in place. She is the fullness of God's Kingdom, the Kingdom towards which humanity irresistibly journeys.

In this moment of friendship, when the two housewives exchange greetings, Mary is the prophet of humanity, and she presents every person on this earth the possibility to go from their daily life, their profession and place of work, from the kitchen, and accept the dimensions of salvation which regard all of history: "He has come to the help of Israel His servant, mindful of His mercy . . . forever."

May 14
The Mystery of Joy and Closeness

The Assumption of Our Lady is a feast of great, great joy. It is the clap of joy at Mary's being freed from the burden of earthly existence. It is a jubilation, a hymn of the Madonna because she is with God and delivered from every suffering and every tear.

Her Calvary is ended and she lives in the fullness of joy. For her part, she wants to share even just a bit of the joy she tasted in the moment of her liberation.

But there is another aspect of the feast which we glean from the pages of Scripture. It is the aspect which I call nearness or closeness.

The Gospel presents us with two women — Mary and Elizabeth. One is young and the other, old. Each one has her own secret that she shows to no one. Their life, because of the secret, is characterized by a certain amount of solitude, until that special moment when the two women meet and immediately understand each other.

Elizabeth understands the mystery within Mary — her baby. Mary understands the mystery which Elizabeth silently lives — her baby. Each woman feels understood by the other and so they break into a hymn of joy: the Magnificat.

It is a cry of joy that bursts forth each time that we feel understood at the core of our being. We are all worth something, but we often do not know how to express it or we express it badly. But the values are there, and when someone else comes close to us and seeks to understand us, we break into joy!

We need this mystery of closeness. We need dialogue. We need to listen to and to understand each other. This is an important lesson for our society, where people often are not heard or hide themselves from others. To live in closeness or nearness frees the heart and recognizes the first signs of each person's dignity.

May 15
She Knows How To Rejoice

The mystery of Mary, in the visitation and Magnificat, is a mystery of exultation. Mary knows how to be joyous; she knows how to exult. She recognizes and embraces the consolation of the Holy Spirit.

Thus, we as Church must know how to rejoice and receive this consolation of the Spirit. The joy we recognize in God's gift is the definitive way of being in the Church.

We try to reflect in our assemblies and meetings and encounters a Church that knows the content of God's treasures and lives by rejoicing, all the while carrying the weight of its sufferings and preoccupations. In reality, I have the impression that we often have the image of the Church which is disturbed, afraid and exhausted by its burdens and by the darkness; a Church that never heeds the call to be what Mary was and is.

If we read the Acts of the Apostles, we notice right away that true joy founded the Christian experience: the early Christian community witnessed the joy of the Resurrection!

The Church, therefore, is called to rejoice, to exult in the fullness of God's gift — not only for the future, but now — in the humility that was Mary's. This is true even when we join this joy with our sufferings, fears, tribulations and persecutions.

Contemplating Mary, *we contemplate and admire the Church's fundamental dimension in all time*: the Church which finds repose in the power of God and His Word.

May 16
Mother and Child

In the background of our life, its past and its future, as in a mysterious point of time and space, there is the figure of the *Mother*, Mary and her *Child*, Jesus. It seems to be too simplistic a scene in the middle of the world's complexities and the particular problems facing humanity. Furthermore, this simple mother-with-baby scene turns our eyes towards the mystery of Christmas. We would love to ask the mother how she feels and lives the profound reality of Jesus, her Son, in her life. What words can she offer us to express the central core message which, in its smallness and simplicity, enlightens the world?

Imagine her in the stable with Jesus in the manger: she doesn't say a word; she looks upon her Son, embraces Him, caresses Him, covers Him with kisses, adores Him in silence. She teaches us the attitude which we are called to live: silent adoration of God in our midst.

I can't explain it to you in words. It is not a mystery that we can rationally declare, because it goes beyond us; it leaves us in awe. Just like Mary before her child, in spite of the appearances and everything else, we are amazed.

God loves us. Each of us is the object and subject of the unspeakable mysterious love that comes from on high and shows itself in time, in this baby that Mary puts before our eyes. From this baby is born a great light for the world, a great hope for our weakness and our frightened hearts. God's infinite love is come to us. He chooses to make Himself man to share in our life, our suffering, our death, and to teach us to live in trust, in hope and in love.

Mary's Gift of Synthesis

"The mother of Jesus was there. . . ." At the center
of the Gospel account of the wedding feast at Cana (Jn
2:1-11), is Mary. Even Jesus and His disciples appear in a
somewhat hazier light: "Jesus and His disciples had also
been invited." It is without a doubt that the figure of the
mother is central for the evangelist. It is from her that our
attention to Jesus is shifted. The miracle, the manifestation of Christ's glory, emerges through Mary.

I would like to offer three points of reflection on this:
Mary sees the whole picture; she identifies herself with it;
she is brave in her action.

I begin with a beautiful anecdote of St. Therese of
the Child Jesus who, in her autobiography, recounts her
infancy: "I was a cheerful character, but I did not enjoy
entering into the games for children of my age. Often
during recreation, I would sit under a tree and from there I
would contemplate whatever my eye would fall on,
abandoning myself to serious reflection!" This excerpt
offers a splendid image of the quality Mary showed at the
banquet at Cana.

The Gospel account tells us that everyone had something to do — who was in the kitchen, who served, who
supplied the music. But only Mary sees the whole
picture. She has that knowing glance and understands the
essential things that are happening. This is Mary's contemplative spirit, her gift of synthesis: it is her ability to
focus her attention on details. Certainly, she too had some
helpful task while there. Nevertheless she observed the
little things and, like the Saint of Lisieux sitting under the
tree, she contemplated the scene with her knowing
glance.

The gift of synthesis is typically feminine: to know how to see the focal point with intelligence of heart, and not by mere reasoning or immediate and practical analysis of all the elements.

Mary perceived the unexpressed sigh of the world and expressed it simply: "*They have no wine.*" She is the only one to say this. It is probable that others were aware but as in a dream: they saw that the wine was becoming less and, not knowing what to do, preferred to keep on going, pretending that nothing was amiss.

Every woman ought to desire this marvelous gift of contemplation: it is not a skill or dexterity in doing this or that, a specialization within a human being's capacity, but an all-embracing perception by which one knows how to conserve a sense of the whole. It may be difficult to express, but it is important, even necessary to the life of the Church. In the Church there is in fact the gift of governing, of administering, of careful programming: this is the gift of Peter, a fundamental gift for the ongoing functioning of the ecclesial body. The gift of contemplation is something more subtle, almost undefinable, which gives unity, gusto, taste, and consistency to the Church overall. It is Mary's gift, and were it to be lacking, the Church would risk becoming a society of experts, of *periti*, of specialists, where everyone tried to promote his or her own particular vision, even arguing with others over it and precisely in the name of one's own expertise.

The charism of Mary is her comforting watchfulness over the whole ecclesial body which renders her attentive to every part that is suffering and ready to express herself, to provide by advising those responsible, causing others to intervene. At Cana, in fact, Mary did not directly provide for their need for wine, but she threw the spotlight on it, put it into relief and entrusted the need to her Son.

May 18
Mary Helps Us Discover What Is Lacking

When the Madonna had acted in this contemplative manner, she might have stopped there. That is not the way things happened, though. Quite the contrary! Mary became so much a part of the situation that she came close to being rebuked by Jesus. Exegetes have written volumes about His mysterious words and yet have failed to reach full agreement regarding their exact meaning: "*Woman*, what is that to you and Me? Why have you turned to Me?" Certainly it is not an encouraging expression no matter what meaning we try to give it. Mary accepts it because she has got involved with the situation as if it were her own: "*They* have no wine" means "*we* have no wine." It expresses her identification with those poor people whose names we do not even know and about whom the Gospel account tells us nothing else.

Actually, the fact that the banquet runs short of wine is not all that important. The people could have gone home satisfied, regardless. This means that the shortage Mary notices is not something essential. It is not a life and death issue. It is the lack of *well-being*, of *that indefinable something* which makes things go as they should. And this is the very thing which is often missing in *our* lives. We are frequently lacking "that indefinable something" in terms of joy, or enthusiasm or fervor required to make things go right.

Mary has to help us discover what is missing, not as an accusation or rebuke, but because she suffers with us and loves us. And above all she must help *me* discover what *I* personally lack, "that indefinable something" which would make *my* life more worthwhile. Maybe I am only short of little things: little steps I should take in disciplining my body, my spirit or my mind; little acts of forgiveness, little daily renunciations, little tensions I can conceal or little words I can avoid saying. Maybe I only need a little to become "good wine." The good wine Jesus is looking for in all the baptized and, perhaps especially in the women in the Church, is that they radiate His charisms, His vivacity, His promptness in serving.

May 19
Mary Is Intrepid

Jesus never says that He is going to provide the wine, but Mary nonetheless tells the servants, "Do whatever He tells you." Her words have, so to speak, a time-tested biblical sense. They are in fact the very same words spoken by Pharaoh in Old Testament times during the famine in Egypt when the people were short of everything. " 'Go to Joseph and do what he tells you.' Now there was famine all over the world. Then Joseph opened all the granaries and sold grain to the Egyptians" (Gn 41:55-56). The figure of Mary is put into relief by the man who satisfies the hunger of a whole country. Mary is the woman through whom the power of Jesus is shown on earth for all humanity. She is *sure* of her Son, because He is the Son of God.

Perhaps this is the certainty we are most likely to lack. Maybe we notice the shortage of wine and perhaps we can rather gloomily identify with the aridity of our life, of our communities, of our local churches. But we are unable to pass over the "chasm of faith" and get bogged down in the bitter consideration of our situation or seek out inadequate solutions for it.

We need remedies but we do not have that confidence in Jesus which alone gives strength to our total activity. We do not believe enough, and hence we fail to make that qualitative leap which does not consist in seeking the key of the hidden treasure but rather in feeling certain of Jesus even in the simplest things and even in life's most self-evident manifestations.

Mary at the Foot of the Cross

There is a person who, under the cross, fully lives the reality of our redemption, and that person is Mary. She represents an immense treasure for Jesus Who makes her the custodian of His gifts of salvation and sees in her, in the name of the Church, the first fully human response to His action of unlimited love.

As we contemplate Mary at the foot of the cross, we should try to grasp what happened in her at that moment.

Mary lives here the dramatic climax of her life, the real deprivation of her Son Whom she offers to the Father for humanity. And, in that instant, she receives all humanity as a gift from her Son. This is the center of the scene in the Gospel of John who, through the figure of the disciple, shows us the Church placed in intimate communion with the mother of the Lord as the fruit and the result of the Passion endured by Mary together with Jesus (Jn 19:25-27).

So what does the Madonna represent at this high point of her faith journey and of her close following of the will of God? She represents all humanity. She represents the Church. Because she has completely followed the plan of God, has made it totally her own and now has reached the point of that total giving in faith to which Abraham was called, she receives the fullness of the Church as a gift. Because she has put her whole self in the hands of God and has abandoned herself to Him together with all that she held most dear, her Son, she receives from God what is most dear to Him, the Body of His Son which will live in the Church born from the Passion, death and Resurrection of Jesus. Mary is the woman who, more than any other person, understood the meaning of Jesus' sacrificial offering, of His love for humanity and of the fullness of dedication to the plan of God which this offering implied. More than anyone else, she can thus receive the gift of a new humanity.

May 21
The Woman Clothed with the Sun

Chapter Twelve of the Apocalypse presents a great symbolic vision of the way the author understands human history. *It is a history moving towards cosmic harmony.*

Its sign is a woman *clothed with the sun* with the moon under her feet and on her head a crown of twelve stars.

So we are talking of a human being and the symbols of created reality are arranged in order all around her. These represent universal harmony: a harmony of nature and of history, of nations and of the cosmos; a harmony towards which human history tends as it marches irresistibly under the gaze of God towards total reconciliation, towards a definitively ratified alliance, towards the handing over of Christ's glorious Kingdom to His Father.

Thus we have the evangelical vision of history, or, in other words, the good news that, by the grace of God, history is moving towards a fullness of cosmic, human, inter-human and divine harmony.

But this having been said, we are immediately made aware of the fact that the Apocalypse in this passage introduces another image, viz. that of cosmic realism. *The human journey is marked by conflict and drama* and this is shown by the presence of the red dragon and the two beasts representing the excesses of political power and all the exasperating confusions and forms of erroneous spirituality.

We might explain the meaning of this Scripture passage in these words: although human history is moving towards an ideal of harmony, it is shot through with conflict and drama. And it is a very crucial history because in it the existence and the happiness of individuals and of all humanity is at stake. And so human history is a history in which progress is made only by a clear determination of the goal, by a constant effort for good against all adversities, by overcoming all misunderstandings, all the disguises of evil and all confusion. It is a history calling for courage and for the strength to witness to the point of shedding one's own blood.

This vision of conflict does not clash with the absolute certainty of God's final victory and the manifestation of Christ's Kingdom to those who have accepted to fight with faith and hope and who have not run away from the assaults of the beast and of the Evil One.

What part has the woman in this vision of history? She represents all of humanity, God's holy people.

And this *woman*, representing all humanity because she is the one who receives the Word of God and from whom the Son of God Himself is born, is, on closer examination, *Mary the Mother of Jesus*. We see in her our point of departure (viz. hearing the Word) and our point of arrival which is total reconciliation and that eternal life which we are called to share with Mary even now.

Mary is the living symbol, the sign of humanity on the move, of a reconciled humanity, of woman reconciled with herself and with her mission. She is the sign of a renewed humanity in which woman regains her place and role and so gives rein to universal reconciliation and brotherliness among people.

May 22
The Holy Spirit, Soul of the Church

The Church receives the Spirit and is shaped and formed by the Spirit so as to be the living Body of Christ in the world and in history. The Church is enlivened by this vital breath, just as the first human being was enlivened by the breath of God, so that it may be the expression of the glory of the living God, the presence of the Risen Christ, the meeting-place of unity and peace, the sign of convergence for all peoples and the sign of hope and light for all nations.

By the Spirit, the Church is shaped as Catholic and universal. The Word of the Church, aroused by the Spirit, is heard by everyone. It becomes a universal word, a word of salvation for every generation, every tradition and every culture. The Church becomes a universal organism of hope whose voice every human being may listen to. This is a wonderful mystery of the Spirit Who, through some people placed in a clearly-determined social, cultural and historical context — indeed, almost enclosed in it — creates an open, universal body which is at the same moment free and also capable of finding a place for everyone, of giving everyone his due, of respecting individual characteristics, personalities, customs and habits and of transforming everything into the Risen Body of Christ.

The worldwide Church is also a ministerial one. Scripture speaks of one Spirit and of many gifts (1 Cor 12:4-11). The multiplicity of aptitudes, services and ministries making up the richness of the ecclesial community is brought to unity through its unique Source which is the Holy Spirit of God.

The Spirit is also the Spirit of peace and of universal pacification. The first word the Risen Jesus says to His disciples before giving them the Spirit is: "Peace be with you" (Jn 20:19). The Church is truly itself, as the Spirit raises it up in history, through its continual, tireless, offering of reconciliation to all.

May 23
The Holy Spirit, Extraordinary
Daily Breath of the Church

Let us ask for light, grace and spiritual insight to understand the meaning of the words of Scripture.

1. *Chapter Two* of the Acts of the Apostles transports us into an extraordinary atmosphere. There is the roar of the wind from the sky. There are tongues of fire and a reaction of collective amazement. "They were bewildered . . . amazed and astonished . . ." (6, 7). So we are talking about an event which goes beyond the ordi-

nary contingencies of everyday life and confronts us with an unheard-of and inexplicable mystery.

2. On the contrary, *Chapter Twelve* of the First Letter to the Corinthians takes place in an atmosphere of ordinariness. The invocation, "Jesus is Lord," which no one can utter unless by the power of the Holy Spirit is the most commonplace invocation of Christian life and is necessary to all for salvation. It does not require either ecstasies or new tongues. It takes place as one of the everyday experiences of each baptized person. All forms of service, ministries and activities which St. Paul mentions in this letter are equally part of daily life in the Church. They are forms through which the body of the Church expresses itself every day in a down-to-earth way.

3. *Chapter Twenty* of John's Gospel brings together the relationship between the extraordinary and the everyday. Thanks to the words of the Risen Jesus the apostles receive the power to carry out a specific service: "Whose sins you shall forgive, they are forgiven them." And this service actually belongs in practice to the daily unfolding of Church life because every baptized person learns to say each day: "Forgive us our sins." Yet this daily service, belonging to the ordinary frailty of human and ecclesiastical existence, is extraordinary and superhuman and derives its efficacy from the Spirit of the Risen One. It is an action, a service and a grace which presupposes the death of Jesus out of love; the most extraordinary event of the Redemption.

In the light of this intertwining of the extraordinary and the commonplace, we might thus define the Spirit's action: it is the extraordinary daily breath of the Church.

And so it is a necessary grace but also an imperceptible one, like breathing which is present in all the most hidden and most basic human operations and which yet is an extraordinary and wonderful gift, enlivening and raising up people's tired daily existence and daily giving fresh impetus to an otherwise decadent common burden.

The person who senses this capillary, and at the same time widespread, presence of the Spirit in the world is also able to read in today's many concrete happenings the signs of this divine and active force.

May 24
The Holy Spirit Leads Us to the Truth

It is in John's Gospel that we find the words, "guidance of the Spirit," and, "but when the Spirit of truth comes, He will lead you to the complete truth" (16:13). Taking my cue from this Johannine text, and with special attention to the verb "will lead," let me offer some reflections.

A more accurate translation of this Johannine verse — a translation I found in a recently published Commentary on John's Gospel — reads: "The Spirit of truth will lead you *progressively* to the complete truth." So we are talking about being led, but step by step.

And so the translation of John 16:13 which best gives the import of the original text might be: "The Spirit of truth will introduce you to the complete truth," meaning a world, a complexity of situations which have to be taken in with a single glance. The reference is to the multiplicity of historical realities in which the truth of Christ for people is expressed.

We are not dealing with a number of small indications, or fragmentary behavior. We are talking of an overall vision, a guide to the fullness of Christ in history.

What John the Evangelist promises is that the Church will be conducted, and progressively made present, by the Spirit as it becomes aware of the historical dimensions of its existence which makes the Body of Christ come alive in the diversity and complexity of human situations.

May 25
Many Names for the Same Reality: The Holy Spirit

At the experiential level of the individual Christian the fullness of truth to which the Holy Spirit guides people has many names. These names are not completely synonymous and yet they are linked together and shed light one on the other. Different historical epochs and the history of spirituality and culture may decide in practice why one name rather than another prevails.

The fullness of truth to which the Spirit progressively leads is the *new heart* which the prophet Ezekiel speaks about in the Old Testament. In New Testament interpretation the new heart expresses that vision which embraces in one overall glance the fullness of the mystery of God lived through Christ in history.

St. Augustine uses an expression which had a great deal of meaning for the culture of his day: *the blessed life*. This refers to the fullness of joy and of inner serenity which includes the totality of things and situations and sees them in God. It is a prelude to the perfect life and an anticipation of the glorious vision of God.

In the Middle Ages and at the beginning of our modern era, the fullness of truth to which the Holy Spirit leads is indicated by the word *devotion*, a word about which St. Thomas comments in depth and which will reach its maximum meaning in St. Francis de Sales. For the bishop of Geneva ''the devout life'' is the totality of this fullness of truth to which the Holy Spirit leads people.

Later, another word is more common, a word which has more of a psychological meaning: *fervor*. Particularly in Christian asceticism, ''fervor'' was often understood to mean the fullness of life in which one is able to grasp and express with zeal the whole mystery of Christ.

Sometimes the word *contemplation* is also used, generally to indicate the way by which the Spirit leads to the fullness of living truth. Today, the term *communion* which we use frequently might perhaps be understood in this same sense.

There may be other synonyms, but what is basic is to realize that the fullness of truth to which the Spirit leads is not simply the sum of minor actions but is a decisive orientation, a radical revision of life. This profound change, however, suggests a deeply meaningful name if it is linked to the words already mentioned: *conversion*. Christian conversion in its totality is a new way of seeing things, events, situations and oneself. It is the ability to grasp the fullness of Christ reflected in history.

May 26
The Holy Spirit Converts Us To Christ

The Spirit of truth guides us to the fullness of truth: to Christ, the Incarnate Son of God. The word, ''conversion,'' has to be understood here in all its rich meaning. We are not talking about conversion from this or that weakness or wretchedness or about being converted from this or that sin. Conversion means to turn oneself completely to Christ and to seek every perfection in Him, rejecting every self-justification which would shut us up in ourselves.

Conversion means to leave the dried-up wells of a pharisaic religion, dominated by a too personal and rather ambitious religious way of acting, and to enter fully into Christ's way of acting and being.

Conversion of all human life to Christ is the goal of the entire action of the Holy Spirit and this goal is absolute and total.

The process of *discernment* which the Christian is called to make can never be directed toward the goal but will rather have to do with the choice of means through which one is progressively introduced to the living of this totality.

This total conversion to Christ, the goal of the Holy Spirit's guidance towards which individual acts of discernment are directed, is impossible to human beings.

In the depths of his historical reality, man is actually a closed, diffident creature continually striving to defend his limited personal patrimony and lacking self-confidence. He feels destined for death, and is caught up in the toils of egoism and ambition, unable to get free. When he becomes aware of his true position, he can recognize himself perfectly in the Apostle's description:

"The fact is, I know of nothing good living in me — living, that is, in my spiritual self — for though the will to do what is good is in me, the performance is not, with the result that instead of doing the good things I want to do, I carry out the sinful things I do not want. When I act against my will, then, it is not my true self doing it, but sin which lives in me.

"In fact, this seems to be the rule: that every single time I want to do good it is something evil that comes to hand. In my inmost self I dearly love God's Law, but I can see that my body follows a different law that battles against the law which my reason dictates. This is what makes me a prisoner of that law of sin which lives inside my body.

"What a wretched man I am! Who will rescue me from this body doomed to death?" (Rm 7:18-24).

This awareness of one's personal inability to reach the fullness of conversion to Christ is the starting-point in allowing oneself to be guided by the Holy Spirit.

May 27
The Life of Christ in Us Through the Holy Spirit's Action

The grace which is Christ's life, His human way of living and being, is offered to our innate human impotence. Christ, Who did not come to be served but to serve, instills in the Christian His own power of self-offering, the possibility of being gift, of being "for." To be gift, which is characteristic of Christ's human life and is even more the secret of the Word — to be the gift *of* and *to* the Father — is poured into us by the action of the Holy Spirit.

And so the Spirit of truth guides towards total truth, revealing to the Christian and bringing into being in him the ability to assimilate the life of the One Who "did not cling to His equality with God" (Ph 2:6b), the ability to avoid evil and to enter into the "supreme advantage of knowing Jesus Christ my Lord" (3:8).

This action of the Holy Spirit begins with the sacrament of Baptism which renews man in the depth of his being. It continues with Confirmation and has its climax in the Eucharist.

Only with the gift of the Spirit can we arrive at total conversion and total living of the Gospel. The Spirit carries the mystery of the Trinity within Himself and draws from it. The Spirit is an outpouring of the Father in the name of the "Son and an outpouring by the Son as a gift of the Father to Him" and the Spirit lets the Trinity overflow into the Church, making of the Church something wonderful, "never before heard." No need to recall the past, no need to think about what was done before. "See, I am doing something new, even now it comes to light . . ." (Is 43:18-19).

Clearly, the Christian cannot avoid the daily struggle to fill the whole of his earthly existence with the Spirit. Trinitarian conversion enriches man with the Spirit of truth through a slow and patient journey and through a painful struggle in which the sacrament of Reconciliation has an important place. And yet the power of the Spirit — ready for every confrontation with the world, for every clash, for every provocation, for every risk — takes over the guidance of the Christian so as to make of Christian existence a creative translation of God's love for people.

May 28
Signs Revealing Life in the Spirit

It is not enough to have understood the meaning of our journey. The Christian is always likely to experience aridity, to hinder and impede the Spirit's action. And so it is important to know the *signs* revealing life in the Spirit.

If the Spirit's action shows itself in us as a radical

conversion to the person of Jesus, the first sign is given us by the way Christ lived: in charity, that charity which is opposed to carnality and is the opposite of worldliness.

"When self-indulgence is at work the results are obvious: fornication, gross indecency and sexual irresponsibility; idolatry and sorcery; feuds and wrangling, jealousy, bad temper and quarrels; disagreements, factions, envy, drunkenness, orgies and similar things" (Gal 5:19-21).

And so life in the Spirit emerges as a dramatic and continuous confrontation between the fundamental carnal and worldly tendency and the basic evangelical one. The Christian lives in the thick of history either sharing in Christ's existence or cut off from Him.

If we read attentively the list Paul gives in his Letter to the Galatians, we note that the unmistakable result caused by the egoistic and possessive man is division of hearts and of communities. The Apostle speaks about feuds, wrangling, jealousy, bad temper, disagreements, factions and envy. These are seven carefully-chosen attributes of the flesh and indicate an attitude opposed to the character of Christ, to the essence of the Eucharist and to being "for" others.

To this degrading spirit is opposed the Spirit of truth with His fruit of "love, joy, peace, patience, kindness, goodness, trustfulness, gentleness and self-control" (Gal 5:22). These are the privileged signs of a journey guided by the Spirit toward the totality of truth.

Clearly, we are not talking of just any love, joy or peace, but of the result of a daily struggle with the works of the flesh. This is not love which coincides with pleasure, joy going hand in hand with a certain type of enjoyment, peace as the absence of contradictions or the result of a superficial balance of power.

The fruit of the Spirit is the powerful presence of Christ urging us on and turning us against the fleshly desires which are also in us. It is the crucified love of Christ, it is joy born of self-sacrifice, it is peace with God on which peace with others is founded and maintained and from which it spreads.

May 29
Guided by the Spirit in the Reality of the Resurrection

To be guided by the Spirit means to live the reality of the Resurrection. It enables us to overcome discouragement, desperation and everything which cuts us off from hope, and this is because Christ, our hope of glory, dwells within us.

The very desolation which may strike us on our spiritual journey when it becomes particularly dramatic or obstructed, can be conquered if we turn our thoughts to this hope which is ours. That does not mean that as Christians we will never experience desolation, dejection and defeat. But we experience these things in the certain hope that the dynamic power of the Spirit is with us, guiding us towards the resurrection, life and peace, and that this power will ultimately triumph.

If as Christians we allow ourselves to be led by sadness and depression, even distress for our own sins, and cease to continue believing in the power of Christ's Resurrection, we are not under the action of the Spirit of truth.

We can understand why St. Ignatius of Loyola, in his rules for the discernment of spirits, advises us not to make any decisions in times of desolation and sadness.

We may make mistaken choices because we are unable to clearly perceive in those moments the action of the Spirit of truth. Decisions should be made in a time of "spiritual consolation," in a moment bathed in the peace and joy of Christ which are characteristic of the Spirit's action in us.

St. Ignatius takes the word "consolation" to be synonymous with the names we have already mentioned: a new heart, blessed life, devotion. Consolation, for Ignatius, means the total presence of the Spirit of truth in human existence and that is why he invites us to make all our big decisions in the "time of the Spirit." And so, practical daily life is the consequence of a continually new presence in us of the Eucharistic mystery and of the Paschal mystery of Jesus. Anything outside of life in Christ, the work of the Spirit, can conceal the illusion of self-justification, pride, lack of purity and poverty of spirit as desired by Jesus. Anything can become an idol.

On the contrary, the contemplation of Christ to which the Spirit of truth leads us, brings back the vigor of evangelical unworldliness, of humility, and of peace.

May 30
Prayer in the Spirit

We may ask ourselves what is the attitude which best enables us to be guided by the Spirit of truth in prayer, one which is characteristic of a Spirit-filled existence?

It seems to me that it is the attitude running through all the Psalms of the Old Testament: *Praise*. "Praise" is the word which in modern Hebrew means "thanks." Actually, to say "thanks," the Hebrews say "praise,"

praise to God, that praise which is thanksgiving. All other aspects proper to prayer — petition, supplication, compunction — draw their most profound truth from being immersed in an atmosphere where the glory of God takes precedence over everything else.

It is prayer in the Spirit when joys, sorrows, problems and personal needs — though they exist and are very real at this particular moment because they are part of the woof and warp of human life — still become in the end a hymn of praise to divine mercy. Every time God takes the place of our ego in a living human act, there we find the presence of the Holy Spirit of love, in Christ, with Christ and for Christ. And there is another word in this connection: *Eucharist*, the mystery which totally includes the life of the Church and the genuine reality of being Christian.

May 31
Mary, Queen of Welcome

The mystery of the Visitation is the mystery of mutual communication between two women, different in age, background and characteristics, and of their respectful welcome one for the other; of two women, each carrying a difficult secret to share, the most intimate and profound secret a woman can experience at the level of her physical life: to be expecting a child.

Elizabeth finds it hard to speak of this because of her advanced old age and because of the unusual and strange circumstances surrounding the conception of her son. Mary has a problem because she finds it difficult to tell anyone of the angel's words. If, according to the Gospel story, Elizabeth lived for some months in a kind of solitude, the solitude of Mary was infinitely greater. And maybe this is the reason why Mary leaves "as quickly as she can." She needs to be with someone who understands her and, from what the angel has told her, she has sensed that Elizabeth is the most suitable person. She leaves as quickly as she can so as to be helped and not simply because she wants to help her cousin. Is it not nice to think of Mary's readiness to allow herself to be helped in this way?

When the two women meet, Mary is queen because she gives the first greeting. And she is queen because she knows how to honor others. Her queenly qualities show themselves in the care and foresight and attention which she pays to her cousin. And all of this produces an extraordinary result: "As soon as Elizabeth heard Mary's greeting, the child leapt in her womb." Elizabeth feels that she has been thoroughly understood and what previously caused her fear is now a source of her joy. She understands herself in the thrill that she experiences and she exults in the child that she is carrying. But at the same time, she also intuits something of the mystery which Mary had not yet revealed to her: "Of all women, you [Mary] are the most blessed. And blessed is the fruit of your womb." Logically, she might have said, "*I* am full of joy!" But rather than speak of herself — indeed, with the power with which she herself is speaking — she instead tells Mary who she is: the blessed among all women.

We can easily imagine Mary's exultation and astonishment. Without having spoken a word, she feels herself understood, accepted, acknowledged, loved and exalted.

"Why should I be honored with a visit from the mother of my Lord?" Elizabeth knows everything now.

She has grasped it all. But, what revelation has she had? No special revelation. She has simply allowed herself to be swept up in Mary's greeting and, thanks to this greeting, she has understood Mary's secret and accepted her in the fullness of joy. ''Blessed is she who believed that the promise made her by the Lord would be fulfilled.'' Mary recognizes that she is being praised for what was specifically hers: namely, her faith in the Word. She could not explain that faith to others, but here it was acknowledged.

And so the mystery of the Visitation speaks to us of a mutual co-penetration of souls, of a mutual and most discreet welcome, not spoiled by a multiplicity of words, not requiring a torrent of eloquence but a welcome which, with simple flashes of light, that light which penetrates the darkness, allows perfect communication and full recognition. These are the regal graces Mary contributes to history and to humanity.

JUNE

June 1
The Eucharist: Sign and Reality of Divine Attraction

I would like to dwell briefly on this biblical phrase: *"I shall draw all men to myself."* Even though this does not refer directly to the Eucharist, it can help us grasp the profound meaning of the Eucharist if it is read in context (Jn 12:20-36) because it throws light on the interior power of Easter of which the Eucharist is the manifestation and the realization.

Some Greeks who had gone up to Jerusalem for the Paschal festivities desire to see Jesus (Jn 12:20-21). Even the non-Hebrew world is beginning to take an interest in Him. The great moment of His meeting with all peoples is on its way. Jesus could draw them to Himself with some striking deed but in fact His reaction is, apparently, disappointing. They do not see anything remarkable. All they observe is a "grain of wheat" falling to earth, disappearing and dying (Jn 12:23-24). But it is this very death which will glorify the Son of Man, will give a definitive revelation of His Father's love and will be the beginning of new life. When He is raised on the cross, Jesus will appear publicly as the Savior of the world. And He will draw all people to Himself to involve them in His own personal action of dedication to the love of His Father (Jn 12:32-36, 44-50).

The Greeks who have gone up to Jerusalem for the

feast of the Hebrew Passover will see the new and definitive Pasch, the exodus, the passover and the return of Jesus to His Father, the beginning of the great return of all reconciled and saved humanity.

In this light we sense that Easter, by the very fact that it must bring about universal reconciliation and communion, will have to leave a gesture, a sign, an instrument of some kind to reach each and every person, attracting them to Jesus and, together with Jesus, lead them to the Father.

This gesture or sign, because it is the convocation of many people in Jesus following an attraction toward the mystery of God, will have among its fundamental characteristics at least the following: It will express and bring about the communion of human beings with Christ. It will call them together, gathering them in a saving assembly, in a kind of fellowship. It will draw them toward the transcendent in its reality as a celebration of the mystery, a sacred rite making human beings part of Christ's sacrifice in the adoration and filial obedience with which Jesus accepted and fulfilled the loving will of His Father.

That is what the Eucharist is. It is attraction, convocation, communion and sacrifice, all lived in a ritual celebration.

June 2
God With Us

People today seem unable to believe anybody, to trust anybody. Many things we thought fundamentally just and honest, delude and surprise us. Many relationships we believed true turn out to be false. And people are tempted to see themselves abandoned and alone. They are tempted to be afraid to share or to make others part of their lives. They are afraid to give life or promote life.

There is a message for people who think they are abandoned and are unable to believe anybody anymore. The message comes to us from the Word of God itself: God nourishes us with His Word and He nourishes us with His life. Christ makes us live in Him and with one another as members of the same household. Christ leads us to share a common existence.

The Eucharist, center of the community, is the source, the origin and the motivating power of this sharing of life and possessions. It is the final and incontestable reason for that trust we are called to give creatively one to another overcoming all inclination to suspicion and diffidence. It is to be a creative trust, not closing its eyes on evil and injustice but rather creating through goodness and the power of love not just a personal renewal but also a renewal in those we meet.

Just as Jesus nourishes us with His Body and His Blood and gives each of us — who are so unworthy of trust because of our sins — the ability to entrust ourselves to Him and to receive from Him the trust of our brothers, so also, because of the Eucharist, our mutual encounters must make each of us grow in our ability to trust others and to build trust around us.

June 3
Sunday Mass: A Living Action and Experience

We want the Spirit of Christ to produce in us the same prodigies He initially produced in the Apostles and to build up our unity and the unity of the entire human race. We want to be freed by the Spirit from the divisions, the opposing viewpoints, the factions and the egotisms which are a tragic burden on our society. Unity, for us Christians, is visibly manifested and mysteriously generated in the Eucharist which, for this reason, becomes "the center of the Christian community and of its mission." We want to rediscover the value of the Eucharist and not limit ourselves to repeating the rite of Mass every Sunday as an action cut off from life and from our daily choices. Rather, we would like to make it the center, the point of comparison, the criterion of our vocational search and of the revision of our Christian life.

The action of Jesus who gives Himself completely to His Father for the salvation of mankind and which He Himself repeats in every celebration, must call for our continuous attention. By this I mean that it must fuel in us commitment, courage, the capacity for self-donation to others, for serving our neighbor and for seeing all life as a sign of love.

As we attend Mass each Sunday we have the opportunity of renewing this commitment in the certainty that we are not alone and that we can always count on the help of our brothers who share the same faith and are nourished by the same Body and Blood of the Lord. And so the Eucharist, too, becomes a luminous and fascinating testimony to a new way of understanding human society. It becomes an impelling source of justice, of fraternity and of charity overflowing all our society.

This mystery of love which we celebrate in the Mass and which we adore in its presence in our churches, must produce its daily fruits and must heal today's most widespread ills. It must bring each of us to take an interest in and to help his or her neighbor and to change structures and situations which are gravely offensive to human dignity.

Celebration and Life

The interior efficacy of the celebration consists in the fact that it puts us in the presence of God's mystery. Because this mystery is not just one element among others but is the common stuff of all reality, it throws light on every aspect of life, dissolves resistance, and instills in every human event the thrill of liberty and the joy of hope.

Celebration takes time if we are to enter into the mystery in this way. It requires exterior time to ensure that those gestures giving shape and direction to our thoughts, desires and affections are made according to some specific plan. It requires especially interior time so that, by a series of spiritual actions a twofold path may be followed: the path leading away from areas of dissipation, of disordered and manifold interests, of distraction and of wasteful relationships with people and things toward the mysterious center of life. And the path leading from that mystery giving meaning and vigor to all the other facets of our existence.

All this, for the Christian, is enlightened with the certainty that the mystery of God has not remained a vague shadow towards which human beings direct their uncertain steps but that God Himself has come to meet mankind. God has revealed Himself, has spoken, has taken a face and a heart in Jesus and in the community of those who have received the Spirit of Jesus. The Christian's encounter with the mystery takes place in Jesus' presence with the interior guidance of the Spirit in the light of the Word and within the fraternal assembly.

The Christian celebration of the mystery blends the rites of human religious feeling with the actions instituted and performed by Jesus, in line with that plan for celebration established by the Christian community. In addition, it takes place accompanied by the Word announced and assimilated. It leaves room for interior silence so that our docility to the Spirit may be continually renewed. Finally, it envisages that both the journey toward the mystery and the journey from the mystery to daily life be undertaken with our brethren by means of song and common actions favoring life concentrated in the mystery and the irradiation of that mystery into life.

June 5
The Eucharist at the Center

The Eucharistic food makes of many people one single body, the Body of Christ in the Holy Spirit. And so it shapes in time a people which expresses at the social level — and not just at the individual level — the power of the Spirit of Christ transforming history. It makes of humanity a new people, according to God's design.

In this way the Eucharist makes the Kingdom real in the world, not by human power but by the action of the Spirit of the Risen Lord. Putting the Eucharist at the center means recognizing this formative power of the Eucharist and being ready to allow it to act in us not only as individuals but as a Christian community, accepting the conditions and implications of this unique and revolutionary event: Easter cast into our own human time.

Why is it important to put the Eucharist at the center? I will explain with a comparison which, at least, has many affinities with the Eucharist. I am thinking of the role which a meal fulfills or should fulfill in the life of a community. It is just one more event and yet it is full of meanings and values which go well beyond the exterior action.

We speak during our meals, discussing events of the community and getting our bearings on the current situation as we think of the future. These goods (words), exchanged and shared at a common meal, are seen as a concrete symbol of the goods toward which family and community tend. Something similar happens at the Eucharist. From certain points of view, it is a precise and limited episode in Church life and yet, without losing any of its concrete nature and precision, it increases to a point of synthesizing, as well as shaping, all of life.

Actually in its real though mysterious identity with the Lord's Easter sacrifice, it guarantees our living contact with Christ, the objective center of Church life and of all human history. And because the Eucharist draws all human existence in Christ towards the fullness of the Kingdom and the Father (1 Cor 15:28), it has the function of placing every facet of life, fragmentary and singular, within the unifying breath of a plan and of a destiny which is simultaneously the synthesis, the summary and the creative matrix of every moment of Church life and human history.

June 6
Is the Eucharist at the Center?

It is not easy to place the Eucharist at the center! It is not easy to accept the message of the sacrament of the Eucharist in its power. The New Testament texts often refer to the incomprehension the Eucharist meets among those for whom it is destined. For example, the first New

Testament document on the Eucharist condemns the incorrect manner in which it was celebrated by the Christians of Corinth (1 Cor 11:17-22). And Luke tells us how during the Last Supper the disciples argued about which among them was the greater (Lk 22:24-28). In John, Chapter Six, the themes outlined by Jesus in the Eucharistic discourse are matched by His listeners' lack of understanding: "This is intolerable language. How can anyone accept it?" (Jn 6:60).

In the Eucharist the love of God manifests itself in its purest and most disconcerting form and meets human beings disoriented by things immensely greater than they themselves. The Eucharist at the center is the goal of a long journey. To humbly confess our faults or even simply our uncertainties and difficulties is the first step required to rediscover the inexhaustible riches of this mystery.

The fundamental, "serious" question remains: do we really know how to celebrate God's mystery? Is it really a value for all of us, a supreme value? Does the Mass transform our life? Do we feel drawn to the Mass? Is the Eucharist truly the center of everything for us, or as Christians do we at least live our commitment to try and make it the center, to try and open ourselves to the inspiration that comes to us from the Word, from the breath of the Spirit which invites us to put it at the center?

June 7
The Eucharist and Hardness of Heart

Let us seek enlightenment from a page of the Old Testament (2 S 7). After King David had built himself a royal palace in Jerusalem, he felt the desire to build a house for the Lord as well, a temple in which to put the Ark of the Covenant which was still under a tent. There was a sincere religious meaning in his desire, and great thankfulness for the role which God had given him. But there was also the pride of appearing grand and munificent towards the Lord. There was a subtle complacency in being able to count the Lord Himself among his city's inhabitants. There was the secret hope of having God at his beck and call, of being able to count on Him and of being sure of His powerful protection.

Consulted on this point, the prophet Nathan at first gave his approval but later, having received a sudden nighttime revelation, he came back to the king to dissuade him from carrying out that project. David would not be the one to build a house for the Lord but rather the Lord would build a house for David and would guarantee his progeny.

Time and again we, too, approach the Eucharist with the identical mentality of David. We already have our plans. We already think we know what the Eucharist is and how we can calmly list it among our possessions. In a word, we have already built our life according to a program with ourselves at the center. And this is the dark mystery of that human "hardness of heart" or that slowness to believe of which the Scriptures so often speak.

Sometimes this concentration on ourselves is so radical that it makes us reluctant or indifferent about our relationship with God. This explains why many neglect the Eucharist or consider it a sentimental phenomenon, all very well for youngsters or to produce a vaguely religious emotion in us as we take a nostalgic glance back over our mature years.

In other instances, a general kind of relationship

with God is acceptable to us but we want a God conformed to our own ideas. We human beings want to decide how, when and where we will meet our God. The Eucharist, a gratuitous mode by which God gives Himself to us in the Christian community, is neglected in favor of other incomplete or ambiguous expressions of religious feeling.

We know that in the Eucharist Easter is operative and "the flesh of Jesus for the life of the world" (Jn 6:51) is present. And so we try to grasp what message Easter conveys to our life through the Eucharist. But this search is not entirely honest and above board. We have formed an idea of our life through our personal experience and contacts with others but we do not do this analysis in depth. We stop at the point where our life seems to us to be a good which is actually in our power, something needing simply to be shaped by us alone.

June 8
What Use is Easter to Me?

Instead of asking ourselves what radical changes Easter requires of our life, we try to find out what advantage it can bring us. In general we are not clearly conscious of this attitude of ours. It surfaces in hidden ways and takes various directions. For example: some of us consider the Paschal mystery to be a great reservoir of grace, but we tend to look at it from a subtly utilitarian point of view as if it were a quantity of goods to somehow be obtained. And so we see the Eucharist as a kind of sacred vessel from which the grace of Easter is transmitted to us.

214   JUNE

Others, however, see Easter as a collection of ethical values putting a seal on human moral ideals. They admire Jesus' courage, His freedom, His fraternal forgiveness, His fidelity until death to His love commitment. They believe that the memory of Jesus' death, rich as it is in such highly symbolic examples, must reach and benefit today's people also, as they tackle their increased moral responsibilities. And so the Eucharist is seen as the living memory of Jesus' Passover able to produce moral benefits.

All these are values but they do not yet make the Eucharist the ''center'' of everything. If people — and each of us is constantly tempted to do this — limit themselves to a utilitarian concept of the Eucharist and are not prepared to go beyond it, they fall into the error of those who, after the multiplication of the loaves, sought Jesus out to make Him king (Jn 6:15) thus ensuring themselves of a life without problems. Jesus cries out to them, as He cries out to us: ''I tell you most solemnly, you are not looking for Me because you have seen the signs'' — He meant that they have not drawn from His miracles the stimulus for an unconditioned faith in Him — ''but because you had all the bread you wanted to eat'' (Jn 6:26).

And so we have to complete a process of conversion to enable us to discern in the Eucharist not just a good at our disposal but the living presence of Christ, the power of His Holy Spirit drawing us into the power of the Son's obedience and availability to the merciful love of His Father.

The Eucharist and Church Conflicts

In Chapter Eleven of the First Letter to the Corinthians (17-34), Paul is very clear: the way the Corinthians celebrate the Lord's Supper is blameworthy. It does not lead to salvation but, rather, condemnation because they do not allow the charity of Christ present in the Eucharist to attract and transform their hearts. They continue to be divided among themselves. Indeed, at those very meetings in which the Lord's Supper is celebrated, they underscore divisions and cause offence to the poorer members among them.

The Eucharist is incompatible with divisions in the Church! And so Christianity runs the risk that, when it is not complemented by the dynamism of a charity flowing from it, the Eucharist may not be able to overcome egoisms and misunderstandings which spring up continually in the life of a community. In turn, this weakness and meanness of ours, not reached and purified by the Eucharist, makes us still more unprepared and deaf before the Eucharistic mystery. I am thinking of the tensions afflicting the life of the community which most frequently disturb us.

A look at these tensions in the light of the Eucharist would help us know how to recognize them. Because in fact, the Eucharist draws all aspects of life into the mystery of Christ and the Father, it calls for total fidelity to the reality of Jesus and to the ritual and institutional forms which unite us to Him. At the same time it calls us to be present in a many-sided, detailed and intimate way to all those facets of our human life which we must orient towards Christ.

On the other hand, a less than full understanding of

216   JUNE

the Eucharist hinders us from interpreting community tensions in a broad and unified sort of way. Instead of a vision deriving from the Eucharist we are inclined to substitute visions based on our own prejudices or on our own way of understanding the life of the community. The different perspectives, far from complementing one another, become rooted in opposing viewpoints leading us to bitter judgments, harsh behavior, fiery discussions and inveterate stubbornness. In this way we run the risk of increasing tensions, explosions, nervousness, resentment, and slowness in grasping the needs of others, etc.

If we accept, though, a concept of a community life project based on the Eucharist, we would at the same time come to a true evaluation of our judgments, and would especially experience the power of the love of Christ drawing us into the Father's heart and winning a victory over our sins.

June 10
"You Have Done Well . . . in Maintaining Our Traditions"

This is how Chapter Eleven of the First Letter to the Corinthians begins (v. 2): "You have done well in remembering me so constantly and in maintaining our traditions just as I passed them on to you." This letter is the most ancient of the pastoral letters, having been written most probably a little before Easter in the year 57. St. Paul is the author and he is penning this letter some 25 years after the death of Jesus, giving the exhortation we have just mentioned. The reason why at the beginning of the chapter he praises the Corinthians is their fidelity to tradition, indeed to the very special tradition going back to Jesus Himself and to the Lord's Supper. The community desires to make this a living tradition for the very reason that it is a gift Jesus offers His disciples to make Easter perennially present.

And so Jesus' Paschal gesture, unique and unrepeatable in its historical setting, becomes — at Corinth and later at Rome, then all over the world — sacramentally repeatable in the Eucharistic celebration which reaches every person to share God's friendship with him or her. This fact gives us, too, as we celebrate the Lord's Supper in our own day and age the same joyous certainty that the early Christians had: we come together to celebrate the Eucharist, to recall the Passion and death of Jesus out of love for us.

We do this with the certainty that it is not merely a souvenir of the past but a present reality: Christ's gift to each of us and His irrevocable devotion to His Church.

This is why the community of Corinth — and, indeed, every community — should be praised: because it wants to celebrate the Supper as a memory, yes, but more importantly as a living and present reality; as a look back at the past, yes, but also as an awareness of the present and a hope and prophecy for the future.

June 11
"I Cannot Praise You For This"

However, in Paul's First Letter to the Corinthians, the Apostle states that there is also a reason which absolutely prevents him from praising the community. It is, in reality, unable to have total trust in the Supper of the Lord

Jesus. It is — as we would say — unable to courageously place the Eucharist at the center of all. It is incapable of postponing the regular supper, postponing its own plans, its own way of approaching the mystery. The community gets its human projects mixed up with the divine and by so doing it becomes divided, weakened, sick and even reaches the point of death . . . "eating and drinking its own condemnation" (11:29).

The Lord's Supper — and everything concerning the Eucharist — does not tolerate being put at the service of other interests. It wants an undivided heart and gift because it is destined to form the one Body of Christ, the Undivided One, all through time and up to the parousia.

And so we may ask ourselves what all this means for us, what it says about our lives and about our Eucharists. It says this to us in rebuke: "I cannot praise you for this." It points out that our Eucharistic sharing is sometimes, regretfully, somewhat like the Corinthian situation: listless and not very fruitful because we do not cultivate the spiritual dispositions which are at the same time the basic requirement for the celebration and also its fruit.

We approach the Lord's Supper lacking the serious will to ask ourselves honestly what is the meaning of our life. We go to the Eucharist to do something religious and not to allow the totality of our life to be challenged by the total gift of Christ to us.

At the Last Supper, and later in the Agony in the Garden and in His entire Passion up to the crucifixion, Jesus did the exact opposite. He is the One who renounced Himself, His tastes, His will so as to taste the will of His Father and put Himself at our disposal, the One who serves, the One who washes the feet of His disciples.

He asks for our commitment at every Eucharist and

simultaneously He gives us the grace to renounce ourselves so as to become children of God and brothers and sisters to all people.

June 12
Conversion Approaches in the Eucharistic Journey

Paul, in his exhortation in 1 Cor 11, shows by some practical spiritual approaches the deep conversion which the Eucharist requires of us and produces in us. We may usefully reflect on each of them:

First of all, there is the invitation to "examine oneself." [N.B. The Jerusalem Bible uses the term "recollect" instead of "examine" which is a more precise translation of the Italian text]. To learn to examine ourselves (to reflect on ourselves), we have to know more about contemplation and seriously ask questions concerning the final end of existence and the meaning of our life. We may also seek to reflect and to think in the company of our brethren, including those who do not share our views, and we can share with them whatever is closest to our heart.

The second approach which Paul requires is "to be able to recognize the Body of the Lord." We must try to discern the Body of the Lord in the poor and simple signs under which it presents itself: in the poverty of the sacramental signs of bread and wine as well as in the poverty of the bodies and spirits of the poorest of the poor; in the poverty and limitations of our communities; in the confusion caused by many difficult living situations; in the distress of so many of our marginalized brothers and sisters. Let us open our eyes and hearts to the Apostle's invitation: "Recognize the Body of the Lord." Finally, Paul asks us to "wait for one another" when we come together for the Supper. Training ourselves in this respect means training ourselves in that fullness of good manners which is called "hospitality."

June 13
Lord, I Am Not Worthy!

The sin which frequently corrodes the Eucharistic tone of our communities is our taking the Eucharist for granted, as something to be given to us anyway.

We have a similar attitude with regard to the Word. We think we know it already, that we are acquainted with it because we have heard it so many times. We believe that it doesn't have anything more to say to us. Sometimes we have the same attitude towards the crucifix: we've seen it so often, we've grown accustomed to seeing it, we feel that what happened had to happen!

But the real attitude we ought to have is one of attention, reverence and wonder before the awesome mystery of God, His Word, His cross, His Body and Blood given under the appearances of bread and wine.

It is the attitude of wonder and awe which immediately stirs up in us the feeling of our own unworthiness of such a great gift. Real unworthiness on our part, on the other hand, would be to believe that we deserve to receive it, that the gift is something due to us, that the grace is really payment of a debt and that love is something that can be calculated.

An example of awe, wonder, attention, adoration and gratitude for the gifts of God is to be found in the example of Elizabeth the mother of John the Baptist: "Why should I be honored with a visit from the mother of my Lord?" Another example is to be found in the attitude of Mary who is "disturbed" by the angel's words because she does not feel herself to be worthy of such a solemn message. So, too, is the attitude of the centurion which the Church places before our minds every time we are offered the Eucharistic bread: "Lord, I am not worthy to have You enter under my roof." Such also is the attitude of Isaiah: "I am a man of unclean lips . . . and my eyes have looked at the King." The attitude of John the Baptist is exactly the same: "I am not fit to undo the strap of His sandals." Such, finally, is likewise the attitude of the publican: "God, be merciful to me, a sinner!" Eucharistic unworthiness, on the other hand, is expressed by the Pharisee: "I thank you, God, that I am not like the rest of mankind." I'm fine. I have no problems. I have a right to your gifts. I have nothing to forgive anyone.

The one who approaches the table of the Lord without being hungry and thirsty for Christ's pardon, eats and drinks unworthily. The person who thinks he or she is in order before God and with people and has no need to be reconciled with anyone, eats and drinks unworthily. The one who thinks he owes nobody anything and almost believes that it is God who owes him something for coming to church and for making the effort to approach the Eucharistic table, eats and drinks unworthily.

Presuming to think that one is *worthy* of the Eucharist opens the door to a self-sufficiency and self-satisfaction which makes the Eucharist almost useless because it no longer is seen as a uniquely, infinitely great gift before which we must always fall down in grateful adoration.

June 14
Letting Oneself Be "Pierced" by the Eucharist

I would like to note some approaches which might prove very helpful to the community in allowing itself to be shaped by the Eucharist.

The first of these is that one allow himself or herself to be "pierced," as it were, by the Eucharist. Recalling and applying the word of Simeon to Mary — "A sword will pierce your own soul" (Lk 2:35) — we may even go so far as to say that we must allow the Eucharist to "pierce" our hearts. We must allow it to act in us, give it some freedom of movement as far as we are concerned. This is fundamental.

Allowing oneself to be shaped by the Eucharist means making oneself receptive and open. The opposite of this is the attitude of one who refuses to listen or receive. We ought not presume that we know all that the Eucharist has to offer. In fact, its power is the very power of Christ of which St. Paul speaks in his Letter to the Philippians. Paul is ready to jettison everything if he can but have the "supreme advantage of knowing Christ Jesus . . ." (Ph 3:8). "All I want is to know Christ and the power of His resurrection," he says. It is this knowledge of Christ which causes the Apostle — and us — to forget what is behind and to reach out for what is to come. It is a transcendent knowledge, an inexplicable knowledge of the Lord based on analogies.

The Eucharist is a gift which God gives us continually and it is God who continually instills in us the attitude of silence and of listening to the Eucharistic mystery.

Walking With the Church

The second approach which applies to the entire community is *walking with the Church*. There comes a time when we do not understand the Eucharist any better either by racking our brains over books or contemplating it in the tabernacle. It is really a dynamic force and anyone not linked to the living body of the Church, walking in step with the local church and allowing himself or herself to be called by it, cannot understand the Eucharist's full power.

There are varying groups who may have a knowledge of the Eucharist from the biblical or ascetical-contemplative points of view, but as long as they do not attempt to journey totally with the local church they will not be able to grasp that it is the Eucharist which produces the whole community. And so they will understand community in a very individualistic way.

We have to go forward humbly with the Church, be linked to its total living body and to the total dimension of the Church's progress, locally and universally because every Mass does not reveal the Eucharist, every Communion does not reveal the fullness of the Eucharist nor does every Eucharistic Visit. It is the totality of human life in the ecclesial context which reveals that the Eucharist is the shaper of Church, of Christian culture and civilization. It is not a private good to be understood in depth through elaborate studies. It is a journey which one undertakes.

June 16
Listen, Adore, Serve

The third approach in understanding the Eucharist involves making room for hearing and meditating on the Word. In other words, the Liturgy of the Word must expand in the context of personal and community life because otherwise the Eucharist does not exercise its power.

Basically, we are asking the question: why does a Mass, which has infinite value, not change the world? Because its power has to extend over all life and this occurs principally through the dissemination of the Word. The Eucharist is Easter made present. And Easter cannot be understood except in the context of the whole of salvation history. Thus the person who does not know the totality of salvation history does not understand Easter, does not understand the Eucharist and finds little meaning in the Mass.

Certainly it takes a long time to understand that the Eucharist unites us with the journey which the Church has been making down through the centuries. It means to understand the Eucharist in the context of Christ's life, of His choices, of the Beatitudes, of His miracles of mercy, of His strong language, of His self-giving. There is no other way.

To understand the Eucharist we must understand Jesus totally. We must understand the Gospel in its entirety. We must understand Mary, John the Baptist, Paul, Jeremiah, David, Moses and the People of God because all of their experiences have been written for us.

The fourth practical approach is to prolong our Eucharistic adoration. *Eucharistic adoration* was born in the West from an instinctive need to prolong the celebration of the mystery. And so it is not a distinct devotion. It is strictly linked to the celebration of the Mass. And for this reason it must also be Eucharistic in its internal structure and not just one more silent prayer before the tabernacle.

It has to begin with the Eucharistic state of Jesus, from His being immolated for us and being the witness to the Father's truth until death, the perfect adorer of His Father, the destroyer of idols, the source of perfect communion between people and with the Father. It must nourish in us the continuous search for dialogue and the ability to offer our life.

Finally, the last approach: to enable the Eucharist to reveal its power, we must acquire an altruistic Eucharistic mentality, one that is born of the conviction that we do not exist for ourselves but for others.

As Church, as assembly, we must identify with the Paschal attitude of Christ, and be assimilated into His method of being, of doing and of giving. This brings us to considerations such as attention to the poor and the disenfranchised, to having a missionary awareness and a preferential option for society's rejects.

June 17
A Eucharistic Existence

What does a Eucharistic existence mean? Isaiah tells us (61:1-3) that it is a life "to" and it is a life "for." It is a life that is not closed in on itself in a yearning for self-realization or in the preoccupation "to be somebody," to have personal triumphs, to be happy.

It is a life open to a task beyond myself, a life of

which I am not the center. Isaiah describes this life in these words:

> "to bring good news to the poor;
> to bind up hearts that are broken;
> to proclaim liberty to captives,
> and freedom to those in prison;
> to proclaim a year of favor from Yahweh."

These are four "to's" describing a life dedicated to a message.

In the second part of the prophet's text, there is a reference to life:

> to console;
> to make joyful;
> to give them a garland for ashes; the oil of gladness
> for a mourning robe; praise for despondency.

Here we have three "for's" which characterize a life lived for the joy and comfort of others. What new self-understanding, we must now ask ourselves, generates this life "to" and "for"? The reply is to be found in the Second Letter to the Corinthians (4:1-2). This new life generates a fearless conscience and an uncompromising attitude because the "ego" is no longer involved.

St. Paul writes: "There is no weakening on our part. On the contrary, we will have none of the reticence of those who are ashamed, no deceitfulness or watering down of the Word of God." We are not really talking of ourselves and we do not preach ourselves. "For it is not ourselves that we are preaching but Christ Jesus as Lord and ourselves as your servants for Jesus' sake." It is not our cause, it is His. We are free from all worrying about personal success or the lack of it because it is His problem and we are His servants "for you." Where does this quality of life come from? Who is its author, the one responsible for it? It is Jesus Himself who has given His life for love of us. The Eucharist is the guarantee, the permanent power of the Eucharistic person.

June 18
The Eucharist Forms the Church
Through its Celebration

The Eucharist forms the Church in at least five ways: through celebration, consecration, communion, imitation, mission and witness.

The Eucharist forms the Church through celebration. In the Eucharist the assembly is led to express its adoration and praise along with its gratitude for the mystery which is a constitutive experience for the people. The Eucharist is the celebration of the mystery and the mystery is "God-with-us," the "Other-with-the-world," the "Unreachable," the "Most Intimate," the "Closest-to-us," the "Neighbor" who is at the same time the "Completely Other." Every Eucharist educates people in this fundamental sentiment on which depends the meaning of being creatures and of the moral law as a relationship with the Other, and, therefore, not just with the immediate neighbor but with the Absolute One.

It involves a sense of searching for God above all else, the acceptance of the primacy of His Kingdom in our lives. This stance is fundamentally unwelcome in our modern civilization, but the Eucharist creates it in the souls of those who participate in the celebration. Moreover, it continually restores and renews it.

The celebration builds up the person who is open to mystery, to unselfishness, to adoration, to the meaning of providence, to giving and to all those traditional virtues of our people, of the simple, unlettered men and women who had, all the same, a highly developed understanding of God as an absolute mystery to be adored and grateful for. God knows what He wants. He leads us. Our life and our death depend on Him. All the rest comes from this feeling of mystery. When it is missing, human beings act according to secondary absolutes: truth, justice, equality and fraternity. Eventually, these prove to be inadequate and give rise, for example, to the problems of life such as abortion and euthanasia. All these point to the fact that people have lost their moorings with respect to the sense of the mystery which we call the Absolute.

June 19
The Eucharist Forms the Church Through the Consecration

It is Jesus' Paschal sacrifice which unites us to His "yes" to the Father. It is also the sacrifice of human beings to the extent that they die to the world and live for God, of human beings who recognize the mystery and say "yes" too. When the Eucharist represents to us the death of Jesus freely accepted at the Last Supper and repeated in His Passion, it prepares the human person and urges that person internally to say "yes" to the mystery.

To better understand this power of the Eucharist, we might say that it unites us to Jesus in Gethsemane and at the same time that it moves the Church and the assembly to say: "Yes, Father. Let Your will, not Mine, be done."

It is the second stage of the person who has grasped the mystery and concurs with it, dedicating his or her life to God.

The Church says "yes" to its mission, to its destiny, to its trials and persecutions. The Christian says "yes" to family, to love, to life, to sickness, to death and to all the commitments which daily experience requires whether one likes them or not. Each of us says "yes" to the brother or sister nearby even when they are not congenial and even if we are unable to bear them because, in the power of the death of Christ, we accept all.

June 20
The Eucharist Makes the Church
Through Holy Communion

By this we mean that it leads the assembly to live its "yes" to the Father in an experience of full and unspeakable communication with God Himself, in Christ and with their neighbor. Thus the Eucharist makes of the assembly a single body united in a full and naturally perfect communion with God Whose full glory is still hidden but Who makes the profound desire of every person to be in communion with God come true.

All human anxiety, all the ancient sacrifices, all the yearning of religions for communion with God are made real in the Eucharist. And, just as Christ is in perfect communion with His Father, so His Body is in perfect communion with His Father and for this reason lives a fraternal experience.

The Church's awareness of being a body is a fundamental and most important awareness. By this we mean that a person is no longer himself or herself but is the Church, is one body with the Church. The person's voice is the voice of the Church and it is no longer a matter of what he or she says or does. It is the Church which acts, speaks and operates.

This is the fundamental experience of the priest and bishop: to be a man of the Church, to lose oneself in the body of the Church, to lose one's idiosyncrasies and one's individuality; to desire what the Church desires; to want not only what God wants, but what the Church wants, because it is the body of Christ, an instrument which has lost its individuality like a grain of wheat which has become this dough, this bread.

Only by the power of the Eucharist can one renounce something so "essential" as one's subjective reality. The loss of one's life in the body of the Church is a fruit of the Eucharist.

June 21
The Eucharist Makes the Church Through Imitation and Mission

The Eucharist makes the Church through imitation. In this case, words fall short and we look to symbols. The picture of the washing of the feet comes to mind. We know that John places this episode in the setting where the other Evangelists have located the celebration of the Eucharist at the Last Supper. And he does this because the act of washing one another's feet gives us the greatest clue as to what the Eucharist is all about: "As I have washed your feet, so you must wash each other's." The Eucharist constitutes the Church as a network of services and reciprocal ministries. Even Peter's ministry is understood in the light of this great love: "I am among you as one who serves." The Church is an organic unity structured according to humble services. To wash people's feet is a life-giving symbol. It is modeled on the example of the total service of Him who gave His all, "His body and His blood." The Eucharist constitutes the Church in imitation of Jesus as the assembly of those who are ready to give their body and blood for others. "Body" means one's daily life with all its burdens, problems and needs. It means not seeking oneself — as St. Paul says, not seeking one's own profit or interests "but each one seeking what is useful for another and for the utility of others." "Blood" means total self-giving: in sickness, in inaction and in passivity, putting everything at the community's service and offering everything for the community.

The Eucharist makes the Church through mission. This means that the Church, animated by the Eucharist, understands that Jesus desires to attract all people to Himself and it identifies itself with Christ who draws all people and all things to Himself. It continually goes out of itself, feels itself sent by Christ to all peoples, and cannot be at peace until the Easter Gospel has been preached everywhere.

June 22
The Eucharist As Witness

As it studies the charity of Christ present in the Eucharist the Church discovers that her charity must continually go beyond community limits to open itself to all people whom Christ loves and wishes to draw into His love for His Father.

When the community does not become self-centered about its projects, its institutions or its needs but is centered on Jesus present in the Eucharist, it sees itself objectively placed in a state of mission toward each person, each situation and each human circumstance needing to be reached by the good news of Christ's Easter and needing to be involved in the celebration of God's love.

In addition, the comparison with the Eucharist not only continually renews the missionary need in the Church's awareness but also points out its fundamental law. That law is elucidated in Chapter Twenty-one of John (17-25) which speaks of the mission of Peter and of the beloved disciple. It is the law of witness. We are talking about showing other people a life that is really drawn into the love of Christ toward His Father and which finds a special human fulfillment in this attraction.

The needs of one's brethren are not the ultimate criterion of mission. The criterion is our sharing of the love of the Father and the love of Christ. This love goes in search of human needs and allows itself to be caught up in their urgency. It evaluates the reactions they have aroused. It utilizes the instruments of social analysis clearly highlighting the needs. But it also uncovers their new and unsuspected aspects, revealing human beings according to the real dimensions of their humanity. It unmasks incorrect and sinful desires. It gets to the bottom of purely superficial tensions and stirs up more noble desires.

It opens human hearts and activities to the presence of God in history. It announces a pardon capable of destroying egoism and of regenerating the finest human powers.

"It Is The Lord!"

The analysis of our difficulties with regard to the Eucharist suggests that we approach its mystery without preconceived ideas, schemes or projects which might hinder us from grasping its fullness. And so we should go back over what Catholic doctrine teaches us about it.

Any reflection on the Eucharist is fundamentally a reflection on the very special life of Jesus Christ and, as a result, is a reflection on Christian community. But, far, far more it calls, in the beginning, for a reflection on human beings open to mystery and, in the end, for a reflection on the witness to the love of God given by people today.

Such a reflection keeps Chapter Twenty-one in mind as a point of reference. The story of the appearance of Jesus to some of His disciples after their fruitless fishing expedition on the lake, sums up the principal themes of salvation history.

The account begins with a fascinating description of the human condition. The background is the darkness of the night which gradually gives way to the light of morning. But it is an uncertain light, not allowing us to see things clearly. In parallel with this environmental situation is the spiritual situation of the disciples. They go out to fish, full of the daring and certainty expressed in Peter's decision: "I'm going out to fish." But they catch nothing. They become painfully aware that there is not a full and certain identity between goods people want and those they really attain. As it seeks happiness and joy, human freedom must also take into account extraneous factors. It has to make allowance for waiting, for patience and for failure. It has to learn to hope, to ask and to accept.

What the disciples sought in vain with their fruitless labor in the night is given them miraculously by Jesus. He bridges the gap dividing human desires from their object. The miraculous happening moves the disciples to ask themselves who is the mysterious person standing on the lake shore. But the miracle also gives rise to a faith journey: the journey the beloved disciple makes with the rapid steps of the heart and which Peter covers as he swims through the waves of the lake.

The key point of this journey lies in recognizing that the Risen Jesus Who grants human desires is still the Crucified Jesus who has entrusted to the Father the carrying out of His own desires. He has aligned His will with the will of His Father. He has accepted the loss of His life on the cross as He accomplishes His mission of proclaiming to a sinful people, separated from God, that the Father does not abandon them in their failure and does not refuse them even though He is refused. On the contrary, He gifts them with His own Son to show that not even sin stops God from loving them and drawing them to Himself in a gesture of pardon, conquering both sin and death.

All this is implied in the cry of the beloved disciple (v. 7) breaking the morning silence: "It is the Lord!" Actually, this expression re-echoes the early Church's profession of faith. Jesus, humiliated in death, in obedience to the Father and for love of humanity, has been glorified by the Father and proclaimed Lord: One who bears fully in Himself the power of love and salvation proper to God Himself.

"Jesus Took Bread and Gave it to Them"

"Jesus then stepped forward, took the bread and gave it to them" (Jn 21:13). This common meal between Jesus and His own, even if it is not a Eucharist in the full sense, takes up again the Eucharistic language of the New Testament and invites us to reflect on the Supper and the Eucharist.

As it is accepted in the faith of the Church, the Eucharist presents a surprising aspect which disconcerts our minds and moves our hearts. We are confronted here with one of those sublime gestures of God's love before which our only possible attitude is one of adoring surrender full of boundless gratitude.

As we have already said, the Eucharist is not only the way Jesus desires to make forever present the saving efficacy of Easter. It does not only include the will of Jesus instituting a saving action. In the Eucharist, quite simply, Jesus Himself is present. But what mysteries there are in this simplicity!

Jesus gives Himself to us in the Eucharist. Only He can leave Himself as a gift to us because only He is totally one with the limitless love of God Who can do all things.

Of course, we must also pay attention to the human instruments Jesus uses but all this is covered and surpassed by something absolutely new: so great is the power of communion manifested and made to come alive in the sacrifice of the cross that it makes Christ Himself present in the Eucharist, Christ giving Himself to the Father and to us so as to remain with us always.

Jesus, Who already draws the Church to Himself in many ways with the power of His Spirit and His Word, raises up in the Church the will to obey His command:

"Do this in memory of Me." And when the Church, in the humility and simplicity of its faith, obeys this command, Jesus through the power of His Spirit and His Word, brings this attraction of the Church to Himself to the level of such an intense communion that it becomes His true and real presence. Through a mysterious transformation called "transubstantiation" the bread and wine really become the Body given and the Blood shed on the cross. In the joyous signs of eating and drinking and feasting a real communion of believers with the Lord takes place.

The Eucharist is thus presented as the sacramental manner with which the Paschal sacrifice of Jesus is rendered perennially present in history, revealing to everyone how to reach the living and real presence of the Lord.

We are dealing with prodigies multiplying on that prodigy of inexhaustible love which the Easter mystery is. On the other hand, we might say that we are dealing with the simplest thing in the world: God, in Jesus' Eucharist, takes seriously His desire for a covenant and His decision totally to remain with us, to receive us as His children and to draw us into His intimate life.

June 25
"Simon, Son of John, Do You Love Me?"

"After the meal, Jesus said to Simon Peter, 'Simon, son of John, do you love me more than these others do? . . . Feed my lambs . . . Feed my sheep' " (Jn 21:15). These words invite us to study thoroughly the relationship between Eucharist and Church.

On the one hand, the Eucharist is celebrated in the Church and by the Church. It takes place only within the faith of the Church which is faithful to the command of Jesus.

On the other hand, it is the Eucharist which makes the Church insofar as it is the perennial presence of Easter.

To understand these points, we must think of the "drawing power" by which Jesus constitutes the Church and gathers it around Himself through the Holy Spirit and the Father.

To form a simple and practical idea of this drawing power we are led to consider the threefold profession of love on Peter's part (Jn 21:15-17). It is charged with psychological reactions, with painful human awareness and with a passionate and intense feeling. But, in the long run, it is not the product of human ingenuity.

We can definitely apply to this profession of love in this chapter (21) of John's Gospel what is said of the profession of faith which we find in Matthew 16:17, viz., it is a gift coming from on high, the result of the Father's initiative.

The mystery of the Church is hidden in this love of Peter for Jesus. The Church is the loving spouse of the Lord whose love for Christ is a totally practical love, involving the very finest powers of human freedom and giving life to generous and broad-minded initiatives. But the Church knows that it is able to love only because it is itself loved.

In any case, an impulse to trust shines forth in every authentic love. And so the Christian accepts the love of the Lord and responds to it in fidelity. The Eucharist embodies what is signified by this fidelity.

Peter's Slowness To Understand

Let's begin with Luke 9:20, complementing it with
the parallel passage in Mark 8:29. Luke gives us Peter's
confession but not Peter's denial as he tries to stop Jesus
from choosing to go up to Jerusalem and the crucifixion.
In Mark, Jesus asks: "But you, who do you say I am?"
And Peter replies: "You are the Christ." Peter reaches
the apex of his mission in this statement and truly becomes the one who, as an evangelizer, prophet and
apostle, can sum up the thought of others and express it
clearly. Peter is overjoyed at this moment because the
trust which Jesus had placed in him was justified.

So we can imagine his dismay when he hears Jesus
saying, " '. . . the Son of Man is destined to suffer
grievously, to be rejected by the elders and the chief
priests and the scribes and to be put to death and after
three days to rise again.' And He said all this quite
openly. Then, taking Him aside, Peter started to remon-
strate with Him. But turning and seeing His disciples He
rebuked Peter and said to him, 'Get behind me, Satan!
The way you think is not God's way but man's.' " Let's
pause for a moment to reflect on the impression these
words must have made on Peter's heart and on the change
of mood which they occasioned in him. Peter could well
have thought: "But what harm did I do to be treated in this
way? Deep down I wish Jesus well. I only wanted to
prevent His having such a sad end. I wanted Him to be
honored as He deserves. Really now! I just cannot fathom
this Master of mine Who is never satisfied! His ideas are
too avant garde for me and now maybe He will be out of
humor with me and will never speak to me again." As we
can see, Peter is going through a very difficult phase in his

life. He thinks that he understands the Lord, but by no means does he do so totally.

June 27
Jesus Questions Peter

"Simon, son of John, do you love me more than these? Do you love me? Are you my friend?" (Jn 21:15). These thrice-repeated words of Jesus, preceded as they were by the repetition of the name, "Simon, son of John," form the introduction to the pastoral mandate: "Feed my lambs. Feed my sheep." As He went to His Passion and death, Jesus Himself indicated the reason: "That the world may know that I love the Father." Jesus loves the Father and so prepared Himself to offer His life for His sheep. Peter loves Jesus and must likewise prepare himself for any eventuality in the care of the Lord's sheep.

Why does Jesus ask Peter, on whom He is going to confer the pastoral office as chief shepherd, this question and not others? There are many other questions which we can imagine His having asked him concerning his suitability. For example: "Simon, son of John, are you aware of the responsibilities you are taking on? Do you realize your weakness? Have you thought that it is difficult to bear others' burdens? Do you appreciate that one can reach the point of crying out as did Moses, 'If this is how You are to deal with me, I would rather that You killed me!' (Nb 11:15), so much did he feel the burden and the responsibility that had been entrusted to him? Simon, son of John, do you understand? You must not preach yourself but Christ the Lord. Are you aware of how many people about you are in need of help: the poor, the sick, the needy, the lonely? Where will you find bread enough to give them something to eat?" All these questions are very important. And there are many others.

But Jesus sums them all up in a single, basic question, repeated with two different verbs in Greek to indicate the different nuances of love and friendship which are being referred to: "Simon, son of John, do you love me? Are you really my friend?" This question appears to be the central, indeed the only one, because it goes directly to a person's heart.

June 28
Saul's Background

In the autobiographical text of the Letter to the Philippians, Paul states that the Word of God struck him while he was in full possession of all that he held most dear, values which he had made his own in part at a high price: "If it came to relying on physical evidence I should be fully qualified myself" (Ph 3:4). He is talking about realities that come to a human being from his nature and background and from his personal talents: "I am even better qualified." Some of the salient points of Paul's life which he lists and takes pride in are:

— *I was circumcised when I was eight days old*: he was not like the pagans, derisively called "the uncircumcised" in the sense of being accursed or abandoned, those whom God does not seem to bother about;

— *of the race of Israel*: of God's Chosen People, the light of the nations;

— of the tribe of Benjamin: I know my past and my ancestors and I can trace my lineage back to the son of Jacob;

— a Hebrew, born of Hebrew parents: those who hold fast to what they have received, i.e., father, mother, grandparents and all of this glorious generation;

— as for the law, I was a Pharisee: in other words, I was a Hebrew of the strict observance, of the most absolute moral propriety, one who knows the law better and lives more thoroughly the deep spiritual tensions of Judaism. Pharisee was a glorious name which emphasized the commitment of a life lived within the law with great interior moral force;

— regarding religion, I was a persecutor of the Church.

— as far as the law can make you perfect, I was faultless: this is the same word of praise applied to Joseph: a "just man." The parents of John the Baptist, Zechariah and Elizabeth, are similarly described: "they were both just," the maximum praise, from the biblical point of view, that can be given to anyone. Paul applied it to himself.

— faultless: he might have said, "Which of you can convict me of sin?"

— there was nothing in my conduct for which I could be accused from the viewpoint of the law: we know how detailed the commandments, the ceremonial prescriptions and the complicated rituals of the law were. Even nowadays a Hebrew meal is very complicated, marked by many regulations concerning food, mixtures to be avoided, etc. To be observant calls for much spiritual tension.

And so Paul is caught up in a situation where his traditions, his personal commitments, his zeal and his love for justice are in apparent conflict with his new found faith. He lists with deep emotion some of the things which had once been of supreme importance to him. Indeed he had taken great care in defending them, expended considerable zeal in spreading his beliefs, and engaged in much violence against the early Christians who threatened his treasured way of life. Now he counts them all as a "disadvantage," "loss," and "rubbish." Knowing all of this, we can better understand the self-accusation which we find in his First Letter to Timothy: "I used to be a blasphemer and did all I could to injure and discredit the faith" (1 Tm 1:13). He was not a blasphemer in the sense that he had turned against God, but in the sense that, without knowing it — and herein lies the real meaning of his conversion and of the drama he lives — he turned against Christ the Son of God in the course of defending his treasured way of life.

He did not see God as God, the Author and Origin of every good, but rather he placed *his* possessions, *his* truth, *his* treasured way of life at the center of all else. His was a blameless life externally, but internally there was a possessiveness so exaggerated that it radically disturbed his relationship with God the Father and Creator.

He was not living the Gospel of grace but the law of self-justification which led him to forget that he was a poor man graced by God, not so that he could become personally important but simply because God loved him.

Paul's drama is a subtle and difficult one, the sort of drama a profoundly religious person might live and which threatened to become a radical distortion of the image of God in him. That was Paul's background and the reason for his ideological struggle.

The Last Exodus of Peter

After having said for the last time, "Feed my sheep," Jesus adds:

" 'I tell you most solemnly,

[Jesus normally used this special form of speech to indicate that He was speaking about the absolute and definitive reality of the Kingdom of God or the absolute nature of the signs of God in history]

> when you were young
> you put on your own belt
> and walked where you liked;
> but when you grow old
> you will stretch out your hands
> and somebody else will put a belt around you
> and take you where you would rather not go.'

In these words He indicated the kind of death by which Peter would give glory to God. After this He said, 'Follow me' " (Jn 21:18-19).

This was Peter's final exodus.

He had experienced one exodus when he threw himself at Jesus' feet in the boat after the first multiplication of the loaves saying, "I am a sinful man." He then heard the words, "Come, follow me, and I will make you a fisher of men." And he left everything to follow Jesus. Many other times he heard the invitation and left familiar surroundings to follow Jesus: for example, when he jumped out of his boat to go to meet Jesus on the lake. And again, separating himself from the rest, he proclaims that Jesus is the Christ, the Son of the living God. He did the same when he replied to Jesus' question, "Will you, also, go away?" "Lord, to whom shall we go? You alone have the words of everlasting life." Each incident was another break with the past, and the entire life of Peter is composed of these successive breaks. Some were less successful (as when he jumped into the water and risked drowning), others were more felicitous. But in each of them he is invited to go beyond himself, to risk the leap of faith, to embark on a kind of exodus.

Jesus speaks to him here about the final break, the final leap of faith.

How does He define it? By contrasting "activity" with "passivity." "When you were young you put on your own belt and walked where you liked." Certainly, Peter had already lived through a period of very difficult and fatiguing ministry, but basically he was active and free to do as he wished. Now the moment was coming when he would have to make the fundamental transition which every human being has to make: "When you grow old, you will stretch out your hands and somebody else will put a belt around you and take you where you would rather not go." The final leap, the definitive exodus, that Peter will be called upon to make will not be from one activity to another, with constantly increasing responsibility and difficulty, but from activity to passivity. This is the most dramatic leap: now Peter will truly come to learn what it means to know the crucified Christ who Himself had to pass from activity to passivity in the course of his "passover." "(Others) will put a belt around you . . ." You will be surrounded by events, conditioning and situations which will force themselves on you and you will be unable to control them (imprisonment, martyrdom, death).

". . . and lead you where you would rather not go." You will note in yourself a repugnance and a resistance. Your spiritual efforts will not be enough to enable you to look with a serene eye as you encounter physical and moral suffering and death. In this "where you would rather not go" we can read the parallel to Jesus' prayer in the Garden: "Still, let Your will, not Mine, be done." Peter is called to enter into this bitter prayer, the prayer of total human self-giving to the mystery of God. Not what I want, not what would appear to be useful to me at this moment, not what I believe I could insist on, but what You will.

June 30
Paul the Apostle

First of all, the Lord led Saul to a total *detachment* from what originally seemed to him supremely important: "But because of Christ, I have come to consider all these advantages that I had as disadvantages. Not only that, but I believe nothing can happen that will outweigh the supreme advantage of knowing Jesus Christ my Lord. For Him I have accepted the loss of everything, and I look on everything as so much rubbish if only I can have Christ" (Ph 3:7-8).

The Lord had brought him to the awareness that all this is worthless compared to having Christ; not without value in itself, but having no value apart from Christ. He brought Paul to a completely new vision of things. It was not an immediate moral change but an enlightenment. Paul speaks of "revelation" because when he viewed things from this new standpoint, the standpoint of Christ, everything appeared in a different light to him.

When Jesus asks him, "Why are you persecuting Me?" (Ac 9:4), he suddenly understands that he has got the truth of things badly mixed up.

In Chapter Thirteen of his Gospel, Matthew similarly describes a merchant who, when he has found a really valuable pearl, realizes that all the rest have no value in comparison. In the same way, the man finding a treasure hidden in a field suddenly grasps that all the rest have no meaning for him any longer.

What happened to Paul was a revelation of the reality of Who Jesus was, a revelation such that it led him to change his judgment and attitude about what *he* was and what *he* was doing. It was a revelation which turned his thinking upside down.

We find the second aspect especially in a chapter of his Letter to the Galatians: "God . . . chose to reveal His Son *in me*" (Gal 1:15), "so that I might preach the Good News about Him to the pagans." This is the *mission* entrusted to Paul. The two things happen simultaneously, a very disconcerting thing for him. In the same moment in which Jesus lets him understand: "You've got everything wrong," he also came to understand the Lord's saying to him, "I am entrusting everything to you. I am sending you." This instant sums up for Paul all he mistakenly thought about God. What was obscure becomes clear and the violent man becomes merciful.

All you have been gifted with. On Paul's part there had been no effort, no meditation, no spiritual exercises and no long prayers or fasts. Everything was a gift to him so that for all peoples he could become a *sign* of the mercy of God whose search for us always anticipates our search for Him.

JULY

July 1
Praying with the Emmaus Disciples

Lord Jesus, I thank You because You let Yourself be recognized in the breaking of bread. Though we are running toward Jerusalem and are almost breathless from anxiety to get there quickly, our hearts are pounding but for a much deeper reason.

We should be sorrowful because You are no longer with us. And yet we feel happy. Our joy and our hasty return to Jerusalem, leaving a half-finished meal on the table, show our certainty that You are still with us. Our path crossed Yours a few hours ago on this very road when we were tired and disappointed. You did not abandon us to ourselves or to our desperation. You disturbed us with Your rebukes, but even more You entered into our inner selves. To us You revealed God's secret about Yourself, hidden in the pages of Scripture. You walked along with us like a patient friend. You sealed our friendship when You broke bread with us. You inflamed our hearts to see in You the Messiah, the Savior of all. And You did this when You entered into our lives.

As evening fell and You hinted that You wanted to continue Your journey past Emmaus, we begged You to remain with us.

We shall address this spontaneous and impassioned prayer to You time and time again in the evening of our discouragement, of our sorrow and of our immense desire for You. But now we understand that it does not touch the final truth about Your relationship with us. In reality, *You are always with us*. On the other hand, we do not always remain with You, do not always stay with You. And so we are unable to make You present to our brethren.

For this reason, Lord Jesus, we ask You now to help us to *remain with You always*, to be close to You with all the ardor of our hearts, to take up joyfully the mission You entrust to us and that is to continue Your presence and spread the good news of Your Resurrection.

Lord, Jerusalem is now near. We have grasped that it is no longer the city of broken hopes, of desolate tombs. It is the city of the Last Supper, of Easter, of the supreme fidelity of God's love for humanity, of a new fraternity. We shall set out from it onto all the roads of the world to be witnesses of Your Resurrection.

July 2
Mission: 1 (Jn 13-17)

Mission is born of a profound love for Jesus Christ, from the contemplation of the Crucified One. As we contemplate Him, we see in the cross the supreme act of God's love for all mankind. As we share in the mortal agony of Jesus we, too, feel almost "torn" between absolute fidelity to the Father and the unrepentant fidelity to a humanity which refuses Jesus and His Father. We share in His "compassion" (Mt 9:35) for people who do not know how much God has loved them or, even if they do know all this, do not correspond to His great love.

Such compassion becomes "missionary." It urges

believers to review their lives and to become converted so that every action and every relationship with other people may become a herald of this love of God.

The seal of all this is to be found in a reality surpassing every institutional reform and giving a definitive measure of one's obedience to the mission of Jesus: works of *charity* embodying the unconditional love of Christ for mankind and especially for the least fortunate and the least loved.

An important insight into the Church's mission is to be found in the Last Supper discourses in Chapters Thirteen through Seventeen of John's Gospel.

a) The central theme is the disciples' preparation for imminent death. Death for Jesus does not mean ending in nothingness but rather going to His Father, carrying out fully His Father's will and showing definitively the unity existing in the Holy Spirit between Father and Son.

When Jesus returns to His Father He makes more real through His Spirit His indwelling among His own. The Last Supper discourses elucidate the close relationship between the absence of Jesus and His presence. But His absence is required for a new form of presence through the disciples themselves, guided interiorly by the Spirit. And so these discourses are missionary ones.

b) The background of mission is made up of the world seen as a reality under the dominion of evil but equally capable of being called to faith. The life of the disciples, conformed to Jesus through the Spirit's action, becomes a judgment of condemnation of the world if it closes in on itself, but is the road to faith if it has the courage to open itself up.

c) And so the emphasis falls on *the disciples' life* which must produce *in* the world a life different from that *of* the world, a life which conforms to the Spirit of Jesus.

Mission: 2 (Mt 28:18)

The most obvious facet of these discourses is the universal dimension of mission. The disciples have to preach the Gospel all over the world, to all peoples, to all mankind. But we must understand the basis for this universality. The New Testament founds missionary universality on the special relationship which the Risen Jesus has with each and every person.

The Gospel has to be preached to everyone because Jesus is mankind's truth and has received from His Father all power in heaven and on earth because He did the Father's will to the point of death and so opened for everyone the way to fullness of life. John presents the Risen Jesus in a very meaningful way in the act of breathing the Spirit on the disciples. This is an allusion to Genesis, Chapter Two, which presents God in the act of forming human beings and pouring into that human being a living spirit. Jesus is the new and true man, associated with His Father's creative work, the source of new life for everyone. Jesus shared our human existence. He lived it from the inside and He opened it fully to the design of God, Creator and Father. All people should know this so as to unite their personal life to the life of Jesus and find there truth and salvation.

This gives us the characteristics of mission:

— The power of the soul is the Holy Spirit Who is promised to the disciples by the Risen Jesus and is given to them as the beginning of a new life, a life to be announced to mankind and even shared with mankind.

— The content of the mission involves the following of Christ, obedience to the Gospel, the observance of Jesus' commands, baptismal fidelity to the life of the

Father, Son and Holy Spirit, detachment from a life of unbelief, imploring the remission of our sins and accepting their remission.

— The hope which sustains the missionaries in weariness and difficulties is the certainty that Jesus is always with them until the end of the world.

July 4
Mission: 3 (1 and 2 Cor, Ac)

From the Acts of the Apostles and from the Letters of St. Paul we can assemble a very bulky documentation about how the early apostolic communities understood and put into actual practice the mission they had received from the Lord. Here are just a few pointers:

The missionary effort shown by the first generation of Christians is impressive. In the course of a few decades the Gospel had been preached in all the then known world. At the back of all this lies an *exact missionary conscience*. The Christian communities felt they were founded totally on the power of the Gospel which, because of its intrinsic importance, is destined for all mankind.

Some of St. Paul's expressions have become famous: "I am not ashamed of the Good News: it is the power of God saving *all* who have faith" (Rm 1:16). "Not that I boast of preaching the Gospel since it is a *duty* which has been laid on me: I should be punished if I did not preach it!" (1 Cor 9:16). "I have never shrunk from announcing to you God's design in its entirety" (Ac 20:27). ". . . the love of Christ overwhelms us when we reflect that if one man has died for all, then all men should be dead; and the reason He died for all was so that living men should live no longer for themselves but for Him Who died and was raised to life for them'' (2 Cor 5:14-15).

The Gospel's internal power derives from the One Who is announced in it: from Jesus Christ Who is the salvation of every person. In the initial speeches of St. Peter recorded in the Acts of the Apostles the statement keeps continually cropping up: it is that very Jesus Who has been crucified Who has been appointed Lord and Savior by God. Only Jesus Christ can bring us salvation: ''For of all the names in the world given to men this is the only one by which we can be saved'' (Ac 4:12).

From the missionary conscience, *missionary life* is born: a new style of personal and communitarian life, the fruit of full belonging to Christ. It is the first and fundamental form of missionary witness.

Apostolic communities are also aware of an explicit *missionary work*. This in the first instance involves going out to other peoples. Just think of the journeys of Paul and the other apostles. But detailed evangelization through daily contact with people is also important. Even when he is tied down in prison, Paul stirs up interest in Jesus and takes the opportunity to announce the Good News even there (Ph 1:12-19). And it is supremely important that our going forth should truly involve dedication to others, entering into their mentality, becoming all things to all people as St. Paul himself says (1 Cor 9:19-23).

We may also briefly refer to the content of *missionary preaching*. This is rigorously Christocentric. The apostolic Church is not tempted to talk of itself and of its problems but rather resolves its very serious problems by preaching Jesus Christ, His life among the people, His death and His Resurrection.

The Life of the Disciples (Jn 13-17)

The Gospel endeavors to describe how believers were conformed to Jesus. In the first place, conformity implies obedience to Jesus' commands. Just as the Old Covenant involved a law, so the New Covenant, ratified by the blood of Christ, also entails a new law. John does not mention the institution of the Eucharist and the mystery of the New Covenant which was already well-known through the account in the synoptic Gospels. He is concerned to recall the new commandment of fraternal love founded on the example of Jesus and with the power of Him Who washed His disciples' feet and laid down His life for His friends.

Obedience has to become interior conformity. The disciple must be united to Jesus as the branch is to the vine. He must live in Jesus, meaning he must inhabit Jesus' spiritual world, and must make his own the motivations and the profound origins of Jesus' love. For this reason he has to live with Jesus in the Father and in the love uniting Father and Son. Living in the Father and the Son by the power of the Spirit, the disciple himself becomes a dwelling, a temple, the habitation of the Father and the Son.

This dwelling in love becomes communitary and missionary. The dwelling of all believers in the unique mystery of the love of God revealed by Jesus becomes the basis of a very profound communion of believers among themselves. The communion is later expressed in communitary life marked by a search for unity. And unity among believers becomes such a vivid testimony of the love between the Father and the Son that it attracts the world to faith in the mission Jesus has received from His Father.

July 6
The Disciple's Missionary Stance (Mt 10:1-42)

Matthew is one who most feels the need to give an order to the words Jesus said to His first disciples, putting them in a kind of "manual" for every disciple sent out on mission. Let us take from him some essential elements of this which are particularly relevant to our situation today.

Jesus reveals His clear will to associate others with Him in the mission He has received from His Father. This means that Jesus esteems and trusts human freedom called to collaborate in the preaching of the Gospel. We are talking here of a *call*, an *association*, and a *collaboration*. The disciple takes part as a disciple, by which I mean with a freedom that is interiorly animated and guided by the will of the Divine Master. Disciples must do the same things Jesus did. It is He Who freely chooses them and sends them out. The Church's mission comes from Jesus and is carried out under the guidance of the twelve designated by Him.

The Gospels are very measured when they speak about the things the disciples must say. They refer to the Kingdom which has come nearer. With the advent of Jesus, the loving and merciful will of God is here present in the midst of the people to heal, pardon and bring them peace. However, the major emphasis is placed on how the disciples should behave. The profound essentials of the Kingdom are reflected in the new lifestyle of its messengers. This new lifestyle requires some distinct and absolutely necessary attitudes. A preferential attention and a practical tenderness is recommended towards the sick, the poor, the lepers and the possessed. Jesus' miraculous powers are shared with the disciples but most of all they share in His compassion for the poor and suffering. The disciples' behavior must be founded on temperance and on minimum demands in terms of poverty, food, dress, daily needs and interpersonal relations.

The Kingdom is such an important and high-ranking fact that everything else is secondary to it. Mission must take place in a climate of freedom and availability. The disciples must be ready to give everything, without thinking about what they receive in return. So they must be ready for everything. This is so because the Kingdom consists in the gratuitous love of God putting Himself freely at our disposal without reservations or conditions.

The maximum measure of poverty and availability is found in our ability to bear contradictions and refusals. Matthew foretells the possible rebuffs the disciples will encounter. They must be prepared for sorrows and persecutions following the fate of their Master (10:16-25). But they must not fear: the Spirit will speak in them (10:19-20) and the Father will take care of them (10:24-31). All they have to worry about is to be publicly and courageously faithful to the radical demands of the Gospel and to the cross of Jesus (10:32-39).

July 7
"Testing" Disciples in Mission

The New Testament texts dealing with mission bring to our attention the urgency of the missionary task.

If we merely let ourselves be caught up in this atmosphere of urgency and compare it with the factual resources of our communities, we run the risk of getting bogged down in those paralyzing mentalities the Gospels attribute to the apostles when Jesus gave them the task of feeding the crowd in the desert (Mk 6; Mt 14; Lk 9; Jn 6). How are we to get beyond this mentality? The Gospel of John adds a stimulating note to the account of the multiplication of the loaves. After having told us what Jesus said to Philip when he asked, "Where can we buy enough bread for all these people to eat?" John adds, "He only said this to test Philip. He Himself knew exactly what He was going to do" (Jn 6:6). The emergency situation in which Jesus puts the disciples is a "test." It brings them up sharply before their poverty and prepares them to accept the revelation of Jesus as the Messiah Who has pity on His people, Who celebrates the banquet of messianic joy with His people and miraculously provides food for them in the desert.

For us, too, the emergency of many missionary needs are a "test" for us leading us to become more aware of our own poverty and opening us up to the possibilities of the Gospel solution. In practice the New Testament texts on mission not only present its urgency but also its deep relationship to obedience to the power which the Gospel itself unleashes. The very crisis which urgent missionary need causes can lead us to rediscover what it means to be sent by God. Our neediness can bring us to a decision to be obedient, to trust blindly in Divine Providence, and to be totally dedicated to doing what we can.

July 8
The Way to Pass the "Test"

I would like to outline for you a way to approach and to successfully pass the "test" which missionary difficulties offer us as we move from the work of man to that of Almighty God. This way embraces three stages:

a) The first stage brings us to the discovery of God's wisdom, making us aware of the poverty of our own efforts. This is the stage of *humility*.

Our very suffering, lived in the light of His cross and with simplicity, teaches us to understand that the missionary role entrusted to us by the Lord is greater than we are in every way. Nobody has any ready-made solutions. All of us need the help of others. We can learn from every one of our brothers and sisters in the faith as well as from all persons of good will.

b) Unfortunately, when we are confronted with complicated situations our will, not finding the road of free and joyful action, may take the route of resentment, of discouragement and of pride: in brief, the way of sin.

In comparison with those who have a strong faith, we recognize how often we are guilty of rash judgments, unworthy acts and gestures of mistrust. Before those who do not share our faith, we shrug our shoulders and say: "But what can I do?" Faced with so many people with great material and spiritual needs, we find it difficult to study their cases carefully and lovingly, and to give them all the help we can. These are the most painful "tests" because they uncover the tremendous reality of our hardness of heart. But these trials can also give us the opportunity of getting close to the power of the Gospel if they inspire us *to ask for pardon* and *to give it*. In the joy of being forgiven and of forgiving, the originality of the

Gospel starts to become real for us, that originality which is the good news of the Father's mercy on us who are, indeed, sinners.

c) When pardon has melted our hardness of heart and has opened us up to evangelical joy, we will begin to see things in a new light.

In the same way, community tensions, our tiring missionary efforts and those of our companions, our defective initiatives (perhaps in need of review), now begin to appear before our eyes purified by humility and pardon as the first sign and beginning of an unceasingly active presence of God. This way — which brings us closer to God — becomes *prayer*. We celebrate, we adore and we thank God for His multiform presence in our midst and we call on Him so that our uncertainties, our poverty, our personal limits and the limits of our communities may not be an obstacle to His presence, but be penetrated and transformed by it.

July 9
Characteristics of Mission

There is the *existential mission*: all persons are called to offer their very existence to Christ and to allow that existence to be moulded by the Spirit by becoming disciples of the Lord. The *life of believers* which, through their daily search for sanctity, grows in conformity into the life of Christ, becomes a missionary witness. From this point of view the essential element is the enthusiasm of the believer who has discovered Christ and feels the need of sharing with everyone the joy of encountering Him Who is the source of all truth and hope.

The believer, however, takes on this mission in obedience to Christ knowing that he has been *sent* by Him, and he clings to those forms and means which allow him to maintain some kind of concrete link to Christ's historic will. This is the *institutional mission* which challenges the life of the visible Church. The decisive element in this case is the vigilance with which Christians open themselves to the spirit of Christ through rites, initiatives and traditions which are part of the life of the Church so that they become a living sign of the will of Jesus, a city built on a hill, visible and accessible to all, persons whose lives point to Jesus.

The Church truly manifests the Lord when it shows that in Him every person is understood, loved, pardoned and saved. And so the Church must approach every individual as he or she is and show them what they can become. The Church must embrace all humanity with all its talents, hopes, sins and problems so as to point out the path — or better, so as to journey along with humanity on the path which leads to Jesus. This is the *cultural mission* which involves a decisive element of spiritual discernment, as well as a profound acquaintance with the spirit of the Gospel and of Christian tradition. It also involves such a living, real, interior and immediate experience of differing human situations that one can say: in this case we're dealing with a human factor open to the Spirit; or this goes against the Spirit and is incompatible with the Gospel.

July 10
Jesus Encounters Zacchaeus

The mission of the Church is finalized with the encounter between Jesus and all of humankind. Therefore, it can be useful to contemplate some of these meetings with Jesus which are narrated in the New Testament.

The Lord's meeting with Zacchaeus is a good example. The episode, which is recounted in Chapter Nineteen of Luke, begins and ends with the verb "to seek." In verse three, Zacchaeus "seeks" to see Jesus; in verse ten, Jesus reveals Himself to be the Son of Man come to "seek" and to save that which is lost. The encounter takes place therefore, in the strength of Jesus' love which seeks Zacchaeus, overcoming all the obstacles which are placed in the way. But even Zacchaeus' search undergoes a transformation, becoming purified and changed from a vague initial curiosity to a joyful welcome of the Lord, to a generous conversion of heart.

Overcoming the obstacles takes place through the interplay between the two persons: Jesus looks up and sees Zacchaeus, He speaks to him, asks him for his hospitality, dines with him, shares the atmosphere of his home. And Zacchaeus climbs down from the tree with all haste, accompanies Jesus joyfully, makes himself right before the Lord and prepares to begin a new life.

Even the believer who tries to be a witness and an evangelizer has to have faith in the power of the Word of God to overcome all obstacles, which may include the personal inadequacies of the listener, psychological problems, and laziness in searching for the truth. Or they may include disturbances which come from the crowd, that is from the prejudices, the current mentality of the times, the customs of a certain locale. Victory over these obstacles comes through personal contacts, friendship, visits to the home, the sharing of problems, listening to spiritual difficulties, help in overcoming prejudices and unfortunate mindsets, the habit of reasoning and dialoguing about things, avoiding the taking of preconceived positions.

July 11
Saint Benedict

I remember the frequent trips I used to make to Subiaco when I was living in Rome. I would stop to pray for some time under that great rock which seems to hang over that holy place of prayer, almost ready to fall. But it remains suspended there as if through the power of St. Benedict who commands it not to harm his sons.

How many times have I gone to this formerly abandoned land of hills and cliffs high in the Aniene valley. Near *Lo Speco* I would pray and then descend the stone steps to the place where St. Benedict is said to have met the shepherds; next to the briar patch, I would try to sense in these rocks and in these places the various stages of Benedict's youthful life and prayer.

I still recall my stays at St. Scholastica. There I would take part in the monastic prayer of the community, always with a haunting question in my mind: What drove Benedict to come here and isolate himself so in prayer? What did he say to God during those colloquys? How did he spend his nights? What kept him here, so far from everything? And even more, what urged this young man (who had become such an accomplished man of prayer) to gather others around him to pray together? What did they do here? What meaning did their experience have for the Church at that time?

I would proceed through the high Aniene valley looking for traces of the oratories scattered around the base of St. Benedict's mountain. These were those numerous places for prayer where small groups of young people from Rome would come to escape the suffocating air of the city with all its vanity and dissipation, retreating with Benedict in order to rediscover the roots of their Christianity and to experience life authentically once again.

Reflecting on the values which Benedict had sought and lived, one understands the meaning of the monastic experience for the society of that time, an experience which would later become increasingly clear and precise with the publication of his Rule and its application.

July 12
Jesus Encounters the Samaritan Woman

Jesus took the initiative in His encounter with the Samaritan woman and the development of the meeting is entirely measured by His interventions. However, in this instance Jesus' saving mercy cuts across a human search, a vague, and in part, distorted desire which is gradually purified and expanded.

First, the woman is looking for water and Jesus invites her to think beyond the sort of water she initially desired. Then she senses that He bears the mysterious gift of prophecy because He knows her past life and so she tries to fit Him into the scheme of well-known biblical personalities — Jacob, for example, or "our fathers." Jesus invites her to leave these schemes aside, directing her desire for salvation and for truth towards the mysterious messianic prophecies. At that point the woman tries to bring Jesus back to the conventional expectancy of the Messiah to come. Once again Jesus widens her expectation beyond the conventional one and opens her mind to the unforeseeable event of the salvific "hour" and to the messianic presence already contained and active in His person.

This encounter highlights the approach of Christian truth which begins with the concrete human situation, not ignoring it but neither allowing oneself to be stopped or conditioned by it, rather opening that concrete situation continually towards the radical newness of the Father's design. The truth of the Gospel, for the very reason that it is the full and total truth, is able to utilize that tension towards the truth to be found even in ambiguous situations. It purifies and orients them toward a more authentic outcome. Applying this principle to the spiritual approaches of the believer who is open to commitment to the Church, I list some powers which the Holy Spirit communicates to such a believer:

— the ability to interpret the different circumstances of life as a challenge to reflect, to ask oneself questions, to seek a profound meaning, to open oneself to the Gospel;

— the ability to highlight the unifying power of the Gospel founded on Jesus' centrality in human history;

— the ability to assimilate at that stage the power of biblical, liturgical and dogmatic theological language, being able to express it without devaluing it or making it sound banal while still using the language commonly employed in personal relations.

July 13
Jesus Encounters Paul

I want to take a look at another encounter. It is the meeting of the Risen Savior with Paul on the road to

Damascus (Ac 9). In this case Paul was obviously not only unattracted in some way to the Gospel but he was actually driven by open and positively violent hostility to it. Yet this meeting, too, involves fulfilling a desire and going beyond it. Basically, Paul's aversion to Christians came from his desire to observe the Law which, for a Pharisee such as he, not only included justice but also revealed the way to resurrection in the new world. When Jesus presents Himself as the Risen Lord and as the beginning of the new world, He interprets, purifies and orients Paul's desires. He helps him understand that life does not come from observance of the law but from faith in the Christ, repudiated by people but glorified by God.

This *encounter of Jesus with Paul* on the road to Damascus shows the vocational power of the Word of God, its ability to take the situation of a person bursting with desires and projects and make that person enter into the designs of God by assigning him the missionary task of helping other people know God's plan and accept it.

The believer committed to pastoral work must find in meditation on the Word of God the criterion for planning his or her life and for giving a meaning to family, profession and social commitment with a clarity persuasive enough to help other brothers and sisters in the faith. This help is aimed at enabling them in their personal and communitary reflection on the word of God to find a point of reference for the discovery of their own commitments and responsibilities in the diverse fields of life and checking on them.

July 14
Being Witnesses

What does it mean to be a "*witness*"? It means that you do not want to express your own ideal, that you do not want to communicate your own teaching, something you have found and which seems important to you, but that you are witnesses to Another and that your life is totally dedicated to Another. To witness means to give testimony about Someone you have seen and heard. And so the witness is one who has seen Jesus, has listened to Him and testifies to that fact.

The basic qualification of a catechist is to be a witness to the faith, to have first of all encountered Jesus personally, to have enkindled in one's own heart and mind the light of awareness of Jesus, to have listened to the words of Scripture and to have become aware of the power of the cross of the Lord to Whom one is witnessing.

If we have met Jesus rather superficially, by tradition or by habit, if we have no exact idea of Him, if we do not know Him as power, as salvation, as the Lord of our life, as the life of human beings, as the solution to human problems, as the reply to our questions, as the bread of our life, as the medicine for our sufferings and wounds, as the One Who fulfills our desires, then we cannot be His witnesses.

And so witness is a specific, lived and intense relationship with Jesus, Lord of humanity, Son of God, revealer of the Father and Truth enlightening history. All of this should encourage us. We are not preaching ourselves, we are not agents of the Church but witnesses to Jesus and to what He is for humanity and for history.

And still it is not enough to be witnesses, to have

seen and listened to Jesus, to have contemplated His mystery and His action through the Spirit in the Church of all times.

We must be catechists and witnesses. This description adds to the first one the ability to explain, to make understandable, and even to transmit with words, gestures and signs the profound, organic, systematic meaning, the total understanding, of what Jesus is for us.

Being a catechist does not mean simply proclaiming, as one does in giving witness before others, that Jesus is the Lord, that Jesus is our very life. Being catechists means explaining the mystery of Christ in relation to life, to experience, to people's desires. It means explaining His relevance to human experience, and making it understood with adequate words and gestures that Jesus is truly a person's life.

And so being a catechist requires that ability to transmit by words, by gestures and by personal witness the meaning of the relationship between Christ and life. It requires that we make the listener understand what he can of the Christian message so that this understanding will widen his heart, add itself to other understandings of the mystery and produce a global, satisfying, positive and enthusiastic grasp of the mystery of Christ.

July 15
Why Not Believe In Jesus?

Public opinion likes the figure of Jesus. All people know, at least vaguely, the purity of His message, His preference for the poor and humble, the coherence of His life and words from the simplicity of the stable of Bethlehem to the dramatic power of the cross.

If, in addition, one does not limit oneself to the vague recollection of one's catechism but begins to read or re-read the Gospel, one meets an unforgettable personage Who has uttered strong and profound words on some of life's most important problems and Who reaches out to every man and woman in the world from the greatest to the least with an impressive authority, tenderness and lucidity.

A careful reading of the Gospel, however, obliges us to go even further. Through many words and incidents Jesus openly allows us to grasp that the special intensity with which He sees and lives His existence as a man among others flows from a profound relationship with God, His Father.

Jesus said stupendous things about the love of His merciful but exacting Father. He proclaimed that He desired always to do the will of His Father. In the terrible moments of His agony in Gethsemane, He asked His Father for courage to give all His life for the salvation of mankind. Dying on the cross He entrusted His life into the hands of His Father and from Him awaited the Resurrection, the fullness of life and joy.

In all His human life, Jesus revealed the mysterious unity existing between Him and His Father. Why should we not believe in this honest, wise and generous man, able to heal the sick and raise the dead? Why should we not believe that the totally human life He lived among us reveals the designs, the desires and the projects of God for all of humanity? Why not believe that God in His immense love came among us in Jesus and truly lived among us on earth? Why not believe that God calls us to live forever with Him together with the Risen Jesus?

The Servant of God: Cardinal Ildefonso Schuster

On August 30, 1954, the servant of God, Cardinal Ildefonso Schuster, Archbishop of Milan, died in the Venegono Seminary. A moving reminder of his last hours and his final words was given some years later by Cardinal John Colombo who witnessed his passing. Among other things he recalls a typical moment in Cardinal Schuster's prayer.

One morning the door of his study was partially ajar. From outside, the Cardinal could be seen seated at the middle table in the full light of the window. His hands were joined, his fingers clasped and resting on the edge of the table. Before him was his open Breviary. His countenance was inflamed; his eyes were closed and raised to heaven; his lips trembled while he murmured in prayer. It was a saint talking to the invisible presence of God. One could not contemplate him there without being shaken by a thrill of religious fervor.

The witness continues, recalling that some time previously Cardinal Schuster had confided to him about his personal recitation of the Breviary on days when he was so weary that he did not have the energy to follow the meaning of individual prayers.

"In this case I close my eyes and, while my lips are murmuring the words of the Breviary which I know almost entirely by heart, I leave aside their literal meaning so as to feel myself in the wasteland where the pilgrim and militant Church is passing on its way to the Promised Land. I breathe with the Church in the light of its every day, in the darkness of its nights. On every side I see the evil hordes trying to trap and assault it. I find myself in the midst of its battles and its victories, of its anguished prayers and of its triumphal hymns, of oppressed prisoners, of the groans of the dying and of the exultation of victorious armies and captains. I find myself in their midst, not as a passive observer but rather as an actor whose vigilance, skill, energy and courage may play a decisive role in the outcome of the struggle between good and evil and in the eternal destinies of individuals and of multitudes." I feel that he is living again amongst us with words such as these, present by the power of the Lord's Resurrection: "I breathe with the Church in the light of its day, in the darkness of its nights . . . I find myself in their midst, not as a passive observer." After the lapse of many years, we still contemplate him in this way: in the midst of his church, of his diocese, of his children who to this day remember him with much veneration and affection.

But his leadership role did not flow from any human pretension. On the contrary, he was by temperament a shy and humble man, a lover of simplicity. Cardinal Roncalli, who had known him very well, described him like this in the eulogy he pronounced in the Cathedral: "And so he has left us for heavenly realms. But only his spirit has gone. He has left us his body, the little frame of Cardinal Schuster which for twenty-five years the people of Milan were used to seeing here and there in different places in this huge archdiocese. Sometimes they saw him far away, curved over like a faint light almost more concerned to hide itself than to shine out, and yet always there. The way he would come, speaking in his thin yet resounding voice with those personal inflections entirely characteristic of him, that likable and interesting voice, those blessed hands always raised in benediction, those eyes, those smiling eyes, devout as a prayer but sometimes widened as a warning and a rebuke." And so we can apply to him the words of the Scripture we have heard today:

> "My son, be gentle in carrying out your business
> and you will be better loved than a lavish giver.
> The greater you are, the more you should behave humbly,
> and then you will find favor with the Lord;
> for great though the power of the Lord is,
> He accepts the homage of the humble"
> (Si 3:17-20).

"The words of Cardinal Schuster," writes someone who knew him, "his voice, his conduct, showed his serene, suave, humility so pleasing to God and to men. It was born in him from his habitual thought of God, from his sense of the presence of God, so that he could write: 'The whole world with all its praises would not be able to make proud a person who knows in God that he is nothing.' With humility he asked for the prayers of his faithful: 'Pray for your bishop, pray for your poor bishop.' Before God he was truly a poor man. Always and everywhere he loved to be hidden and withdrawn. He never wanted to take the first place or to be seen. 'Let us be with God — that is enough' was his motto."

July 17
Cardinal Ildefonso Schuster

The liturgical texts and in particular the excerpt from Luke's Gospel invite us to think again about some characteristics of Cardinal Schuster, reading between the lines of what the Evangelist says about Jesus.

The Gospel starts out by saying that "Jesus went

272

down to Capernaum'' (Lk 4:31). He had been refused at Nazareth but, as if nothing had happened, he continues tirelessly to go around through the cities, synagogues and villages of Galilee, urged on by his missionary zeal that nothing can stop.

This first incident brings to mind a characteristic of Cardinal Schuster which I extract from one of his letters from the year 1936 where he set forth his impressions of his apostolate in the diocese of Milan: "Our life,'' he wrote, "is a missionary one. We live on the mountains or in the plains. We travel by car or on foot with a stick in our hands to avoid tripping over the rocks. We sleep where we can and go on preaching the Gospel in all of the 900 parishes.'' He saw his life as that of an itinerant missionary like Jesus, destined to bring the word of the Gospel to all the corners of his diocese and wanting to do so.

There is another particular aspect of the Gospel and his missionary preaching which is brought out in the next point in the Good News where it says that the people taught by Jesus were struck by His teaching because "He spoke with authority.'' This is the key to Jesus' behavior: He acts with authority and speaks with authority. It is a word indicating Jesus' evangelical-missionary line of transmission to the apostles. He transmits His authority to them.

And it is equally the Word which leads us to reflect on the mysterious and extraordinary fascination of the figure of Cardinal Schuster in his life and after his death. The people said, and say, that his teaching was given with authority. He conveyed a feeling of authority which attracted and impressed their minds and hearts. How many people even to the present day come to me as I make my way around the diocese to say that he confirmed them and that they met him and listened to him! It was an encounter, a sacramental sign, a word which impressed them for the rest of their lives.

If, however, we ask ourselves where he got this authority, this ability to speak the Gospel with power, we find it hard to indicate in precise human terms the source of that which came forth from him. It was certainly not his imposing stature, because he was actually slender and small as Cardinal Roncalli mentioned in his homily at the funeral Mass in which he described the archbishop's appearance. He certainly was not showy. Yet he was found in every part of his diocese. It was not his exterior bulk or his eloquence: he spoke and preached a great deal in a kind of plaintive voice. And, especially in his last years, many had difficulty catching exactly what he was saying, particularly if there were no microphones. It was not the authority of his intelligence. Though he was cultured, studious and capable of profound research, he never used his authority as a scholar or scientist in his public appearances.

No. The ultimate, profound basis for his authority and for the radiant power of his presence, was to be found in his sanctity. People felt his holiness, the fascination of an authentically evangelical life of such power as to surpass the limits of the time-restricted confines of those who came to him moved by a spirit of faith. Many people still feel the power of his personality even though they did not know him personally.

If we wanted to be even more specific in expressing his special way of living a Christian and episcopal holiness, I think we could point to at least two typical characteristics which are easily understood.

Cardinal Schuster was a man who looked to God alone and was able to lose himself completely in Him in prayer, with closed or half-closed eyes, even during the longest church functions, because he felt that he was the representative before God of all his people and he wanted to offer to the Lord the adoration and petition for pardon and grace for all the people entrusted to him.

Each one approaching him noted that his point of reference was God alone and that he had no regard or consideration for worldly realities unless they were appraised in this light and this light alone.

And on this foundation in his daily life was based his exceptional, heroic, detachment from every personal task, comfort, interest, rest, or self-pity and his attachment to a penitential spirit which accompanied his prayers both night and day.

July 18
I Have Called You Friends: Pope Paul VI

Today we celebrate the anniversary of the death of Pope Paul VI. Too few years have passed to allow us enough distance for an overall historical judgment of his personality and his extraordinary activity which would go beyond the passions and impressions of our time. And yet many years have passed if one thinks of the swirling changes that have taken place in the climate of world culture.

As I go back over those days and recall the day news of his passing reached me — I happened to be in Ain-Karim at the time, the place where the mystery of the courtesy and delicacy of Mary to Elizabeth is celebrated — I still feel his death as the departure of a good, generous and faithful friend.

I believe that many today think about him as I do,

many who had the opportunity of just a few moments of immediate relationship, person to person, with him apart from his many contacts with groups.

Paul VI had a marked capacity for friendship, a surprising respect for whomever spoke to him, a rare ability to show that two were needed in a dialogue, not just one. He made one feel, truly and unpretentiously, that whomever he was speaking to was important to him and that from that person he mysteriously expected something decisive. He was ready to give very generously but without ever making his giving a burden. Indeed he seemed to be excusing himself for it, asking that it be seen as something obvious, so that the real, personal aspect of the relationship might not change.

For this reason he did not see dialogue merely as an instrument but as a method reflecting the dialogical make-up of his personality. And so, without being compelled to say so, he felt close to modern people, close also to those who were distant or who opposed him in theory or in practice. That is why his pontificate, moving rapidly forward in the way prophetically indicated by Pope John XXIII was to provide for the Church an audience and a worldwide respect in which the charism of mass encounters with people, characteristic of Pope John Paul II, could be freely prepared.

I remember Pope Paul VI especially as the one who had the "Gift of the Cenacle," those moments of intense communication in faith in which Jesus had said: "I call you friends." I remember him during the meditations given in the last course of Spiritual Exercises in his life: his recollection and his attention encouraged me to speak freely and easily as one does before an audience of humble, expectant people.

All through the rapid succession of historical events

276

the Church must always remain a Cenacle Church, faithful to its origins and to its fundamental approach, making it a fraternity in which the friendship of God with people creates the capacity for friendship among people themselves.

As I read again about the hour and the circumstance of his very brief illness and death, I think once more of the power of this message reminding us of our origins. The fact that I experienced them personally at Jerusalem reminds me of his great love for that land of our Christian and religious origins, a love which one day he personally spoke about to me, underlining the great fruit he had derived from his visit to the holy places and his desire that the greatest possible number of people should have this experience.

Now he is alive in the Resurrection of Jesus, in Whose glorious Transfiguration sign he closed his eyes on earthly cares. He is interceding for all his friends, for the whole Church he tenderly loved and also for the peoples of those lands visited by Jesus for whom he did so much and suffered so much. We, too, on this day, remember him as one of the ''great friends'' who let us feel on earth the joy born of the Risen Lord.

July 19
He Spoke To Today's People as One of Them: Paul VI

As the passing of time moves us further and further away from the earthly existence of Paul VI, his spiritual figure comes closer to us. More and more we understand that he was truly one of us, a man of our age who freed us from the danger of shutting ourselves up in our age, who helped us dialogue with the past, who gave us the courage and the joy to become contemporaries of Christ.

I would like to begin with an impression occasioned by listening to his discourse and reading his writings.

Let me clarify my thought with a biblical episode: the miracle of tongues which took place on the Feast of Pentecost. Those who heard the apostles perceived a mysterious, exceptional reality, different from daily events. This was the intervention of God in the Risen Jesus and in the Spirit. But this reality reached them with and through a common, daily, familiar means: their mother tongue, the way one speaks to oneself, names things, communicates with other people.

It can be said that Paul VI repeated the process of presenting the "different" within the "commonplace." Like few persons of our time he succeeded in awakening in today's people the thrill of mystery. He stirred up amazement for the exceptional, unique, absolute figure of Christ and the sense of the superhuman realities contained in the totally human life of the Church. But he did all this using the potentiality, the nuances and the resources — together with the limits, the opaqueness and the subtlety of the language, the sensitivity, the mentality and the culture of today. He was a believer and a master of the faith who spoke not just "to" today's people but "as" one of them. His faith was so limpid and mature that he was able to express himself even in the era and the culture of disbelief, of secularization, of a grown-up humanity proud of its progress but desperate because of its loneliness. And his assimilation of contemporary culture was so interior, so personalized, so critically sensitive that he was able to discern in it the backward glances, the contradictions and the secret chinks through which it could prepare to accept the message of faith.

A Message for Our Time: Cardinal Stefan Wyszynski

Today let us recall the figure of Cardinal Stefan Wyszynski, archbishop of Warsaw whom the Lord called to Himself at the end of a long and fatiguing life of hard work. He was a great figure in the Church of our times, a person who was able to make a profound contribution to the history of his people. Anybody reading and studying with love and attention the history of the modern Church would find it poorer if it had not been made luminous by the figure of this dedicated pastor.

The Lord called him to a difficult task, one of guidance and of service, in periods of exceptional upheaval and transformation. He accepted this challenge with all the energies at his disposal in spite of his human weakness. In a time of persecution such as the Nazi one, and in a period of profound social revolution such as those he subsequently lived through, of conflict with atheistic propaganda enforced by institutional and cultural power, he gave an extraordinary example and rendered dedicated service.

It is impossible to think of the figure of Cardinal Wyszynski apart from his people and his nation. I recall that I saw him in this way myself when I visited him in Warsaw many years ago and perhaps you, too, have seen him in this light during the visits he made to Italy, including one to our city of Milan, to our Cathedral, and especially in his encounters with Archbishop Montini.

Today many glorious things are known to us about his people whom the election of John Paul II to the See of Peter brought so close to us. But we know above all the story of the dramas, the injustices and the oppressions to which they were subjected. He drew on this tradition, rich in grace and suffering to garner the best fruits of it. And at the same time he gave it new life.

Seeing him intimately united to his people should not diminish his significance for us, as if he were limited to only one part of the world. Each of us is called to live our mission to the utmost where life and the will of God calls us and within the time the Lord assigns to us. If we know how to carry out this duty with coherence and courage, then our witness becomes valid for the whole Church and for all time.

That is why in everything he lived through culturally, historically and religiously, this pastor of the Polish Church was a gift to the whole Church and for us too.

He carried out a *service of responsibility* for his people, similar to the one Moses once rendered to his people during their days in the desert. He agreed to remain as a point of reference in the midst of the struggle, as a tireless mediator between parties in violent conflict among themselves and as a fearless witness notwithstanding the solitude of his high office. In spite of his weakness he was ready, patiently, to teach everyone that we must be eager to carry one another's burdens. Alone in his obligation to give responsible leadership, unafraid to make choices and take action — though some of his actions were not immediately understood in spite of the fact that they had been taken in the light of his mission — he became a person who not only had authority because it had been conferred on him but because he earned it as a beloved and acknowledged guide.

He was able to use his authority in the *service of unity*. People looked to him as a national symbol in difficult times. Even in the recent history through which he lived, his nation experienced massacres, deportations, divisions and persecutions, but he was able to keep the country united thanks to his learning, his religious sense and his faith. The one who works for unity must be ready to become a sign of contradiction, often accused by all sides and frequently left alone in his choices. He can expect to be judged a moderate by those who want revolution and a liberal by those who want the Church to stay out of politics. He will find himself caught between those who would have him opt for subjection and those who would prefer sedition. Criticized by all and as fragile as the weakest among them, Cardinal Wyszynski remained a sign of unity and never once betrayed the message which he bore.

His homilies and his pastoral letters are full of love for his nation and for his native land. In them he incarnated and translated his faith.

July 21
A Man Totally United to Jesus: Marcellos Candia

When a great and luminous figure such as that of Marcellos Candia dies, it is easy to fall into the error of wanting to judge his life. It was a very intense life, lived with ingenuity and dedication to various forms of service to society and to the Church. At the end he was working as a lay missionary among the poorest of the poor.

Much has already been said about him. Our reflection will strive to cast some light on his character. First of all, though, let us meditate chiefly on his death, the death of a Christian, of a baptized believer, of a man who lived his life with an intense consistency. He loved those realities which nourished his life in his infancy and his youth. At the same time he was open, through the grace of God, to the cries, the pleas, the calls of the suffering.

We are invited to reflect on the life of a Christian who, in the words of the Apostle Paul was "completely united to Jesus" in his own suffering and death, from the time of his baptismal union with the Lord which he always professed with great pride, up to his union with Him in the physical sufferings of his final illness. I still recall his glance, his countenance as it was barely three days ago. He was in intense physical pain at the time. His eyes were bright and his lips, murmuring in prayer, gave a hint of his intimate union with the sufferings of Christ for the Church. In that moment, that brief conversation with him, I grasped the burning authenticity of his whole mission in life: commitment, effort, enthusiasm, organization, attention to every need, ability to engage the energies of others. And all of this lived with detachment, humility and utter correspondence to the will of God.

Let me quote you a few of his last words: "Today Jesus allowed me to experience the most beautiful moment of my life and helped me understand that it is not enough to pray to the Lord. It is more important to accept pain with humility and readiness whenever and however God permits it. This is a most beautiful experience. I was, of course, aware that pain exists, but in my vanity and ignorance, I had never embraced it completely. It is a most precious thing to accept suffering as God sends it and to accept it with joy because the Lord gives it to us for our good." This is the final message of a man who, on account of his highly intense and many-faceted life, could have given many messages to people committed as laity in every type of service to society and to the Church. All his teachings may be summed up in the ability to place the whole of his life in the hands of God, closely united to the suffering and pain of Jesus.

The Gospel we have proclaimed reminds us of so many things he did: "You gave me to eat, you gave me to drink, you visited me when I was sick. . . ." This Gospel is the living Rosary of his experience and it is his witness for each of us. The multiplicity of these services is summed up in the fundamental *diaconia* which Jesus Himself lived for His Church and which is the gift of life.

Marcellos Candia seems to be telling us — all those who knew and admired him: "I may have done many things, but I did them with the grace of God and with your help. I may have accomplished many things for my friends among the poorest of the poor. But the most important thing is this" — and these are his last words: "I offer my life, and I invite all my friends to unite themselves with me in prayer and in the offering of my suffering, for the poorest of the poor, for the universal Church, for priests and sisters in the missions, for my city of Milan and for the parish community of the Guardian Angels." Such is the life of a Christian, of a believer, of one who is baptized. It is a life which has become an offering in union with that of Christ for all those actual, daily realities for which He spent Himself in a thousand ways in everyday service.

July 22
Charity in the Form of Alms

Personal dedication to our brothers and sisters as human beings is an indispensable aspect of charity. It is the fundamental point of the Good Samaritan parable. Certainly, we find reflected in this fact a characteristic of the society of past times when help to the needy was assigned prevalently to personal initiative. But a perennial value is also highlighted here, a value which must not be eliminated but rather integrated in the wider possibilities of social assistance characteristic of our civilization.

The typically personal dimension of charity suggests some pointers to me. We have to rediscover the value of giving alms, of providing that immediate assistance which does not presume to settle everything but does all in its power at the time. It may be an ambiguous action. It may encourage laziness and falsehood in the recipient while making the one who gives feel that all has been done that must be done and so put off a radical solution to the problem. This means that in giving alms we need to be realistic and above all to avoid letting it become a surrogate for more comprehensive and efficacious assistance. Nevertheless, even with those risks, almsgiving embraces many values.

First of all, it is a gesture which causes us to face up to reality. Even in our civilization there are situations of poverty which are hard to find and to heal at the government level. Indeed, some of our culture's mechanisms aimed at progress and well-being tend to produce rejects, marginalized people and social outcasts. Certainly, we should work to correct these mechanisms to avoid their directly or indirectly producing negative effects and to ensure that there are remedies at the government level for these. Meanwhile we can do something, and what that is charity will suggest to us.

It is precisely in doing something while we know that much more ought to be done that we begin to detect a second value of almsgiving. It is an educative and prophetic gesture. It proclaims that no earthly civilization, no matter how perfect, can solve all problems. Only

God with the final advent of His Kingdom will wipe away every tear and will cause every sorrow, fear and pain to cease. In this light, almsgiving trains us to approach our brothers and sisters with great humility, without any feeling of superiority but asking pardon because we are able to do so little for them. This in addition helps us understand the true value of charity: it has a value in itself and not only or even especially for the fruits it produces.

July 23
Charity in Caring for the Poorest of the Poor

In the light of charity, understood as a sharing in the Paschal love of Jesus as it confronts the most difficult and dramatic situations, we can grasp a theme especially emphasized in Church programs in recent years and that is a preferential option for the poor.

Attention to the poorest of the poor is founded on obvious and immediate motivations. They are the most needy, the most neglected. They have reached the limits of their resistance. We must urgently intervene on their behalf as an absolute priority.

In reality, people's attention is generally directed towards the average needy case. The poorest of the poor are such not only because of the situation in which they find themselves but also because they are unable to make themselves heard, to attract attention.

For this reason, it is important that our instinctive reasons for intervening on their behalf should be made effective and audible by the peremptory demands of charity. The poorest of the poor are to be preferred because they are the ones Jesus especially loved. They are the ones who have the greater need of the hope which comes from His Paschal sacrifice. Easter reveals more clearly in them its power to win a definitive victory over the most incurable of ills.

To them, in a special way, we must say that Christ is near; that even in their situation it is possible to find love; that if they succeed in believing in this love and living it, they have found salvation.

I suggest that we interrogate ourselves, check our positions and renew our thinking regarding the following points:

a) How can we give voice to the voiceless by seeking out the growing number of new kinds of poor and helping them to make their plight known?

b) How can we equip our communities, from the diocesan to the parish levels, with more easily handled, personalized and efficacious instruments to assist immediately those difficult cases which cannot be tackled by normal means of social assistance?

c) How can we set up procedures which will speed up the passage from short-term to long-term and more organized assistance?

We have to drive home the importance of living this nearness to the poor in a faith perspective. The charity which approaches them must be rooted, through faith, in the Paschal love of Jesus. Otherwise we risk an ephemeral, passing enthusiasm or a sentimental or ideological slant towards the poor and thus fall into a strange contradiction: on the one hand wanting in the name of the Gospel to lift them out of their poverty-stricken condition, and on the other hand declaring that their condition allows them a more Gospel-oriented life. This contradiction can be resolved if we understand that the condition of poverty is not a true value. Nor is the struggle to come out of it.

What is of value is the love which can be developed either by living in poverty or in the struggle to emerge from it. And it is the wisdom of faith within this love which points the way, case to case, and indicates when and how we are to live in poverty (becoming poor ourselves following the example of Jesus) and how and when we are to escape from it.

July 24
Sexuality and Responsibility

Whoever knows the position and the thought of the Church on sexuality knows well that, in the final analysis, its intent is educative. Reflecting on human experience and especially drawing light from the word of God's revelation, the Church proposes the integral truth about male and female sexuality, a truth which simultaneously casts light on values and meanings and on needs or responsibilities built into the very structure and into the profound dynamics of human sexuality. In this sense the Church has both a doctrinal and a moral message, but its teaching is above all for the benefit and growth of human beings. And so the Church's intervention is in the nature of a service.

From this point of view, Christian morality on various sexual problems and in particular on the transmission of human life, is totally centered and articulated in the basic concept of "responsibility." Understood in its totality, responsibility embraces the refusal to entrust the consequences of one's conduct to technical, as opposed to human or self control. It is a justifiable refusal, in the first place, because human sexuality involves the whole human person and extends beyond that which technology alone can reach. It is justifiable, in a second instance, because not all means are to be considered good simply because of the goodness of the end one proposes to attain in their use.

Responsibility says something positive about the human being. It is the consequence of values which are known and loved. And it is respect for the truth about human sexuality, the structures which make it up and the dynamics which give it its finality for the total good of the person and of society.

July 25
The Church in Defense of Unborn Human Life

I would now like to point out two fundamental motives urging the Church to be particularly careful and concerned about all problems touching life in its origins.

The first motive is the religious view which the Church holds with regard to human life. The Church always sees every reality in its essential relationship with the Absolute, with God. This is especially true of human life. As the Italian bishops have written: "The Church believes that God is the provident creator of every human life. 'He made us, His we are' (Ps 100:3). And so we are a gift of the living God. Our life has not been given us as our absolute property but as a treasure to be administered and of which we shall have to render an account to the Lord (Mt 25:14-30; Lk 19:12-27). God in His love watches over human life (Gn 9:5-6). He defends it with His commandment: 'You shall not kill' (Ex 20:13). For this reason human life is sacred and untouchable in the total span of its development from the beginning to the end." When the Church intervenes in the various problems concerning human life, it is aware of the mission it has received to guard and defend the highest value of human life, the religious value, the value of an essential and inalienable relationship which every human life has with God, even a life barely conceived. God is a God "not of the dead but of the living" (Mt 22:32) and the Lord is a "lover of life" (Ws 11:26).

But there is a second motive which stimulates the Church to take to heart problems concerning human life: the motive of love. The Church is well aware that the defense of God's rights is none other than the defense of human rights. This was once expressed in terms of exceptional theological depth by St. Irenaeus of Lyons who said: "The glory of God is man fully alive" (*Adv. Haer.* IV, 20,7). More to the point: the motive is that of love towards human beings seen as "responsible." The "lordship" of human beings as individuals made in the image and likeness of God reaches its apex in responsible liberty. Human dominion is not over things only. Nor is it over the reality of another's human life. Rather it is dominion over the self.

A similar responsible liberty is a gift offered by God to all of us collectively. At the same time, it is a task given to us by Him: a fundamental duty to become increasingly human through free and conscious decisions.

July 26
Respect for the "Specifically Human"

A correct ethical attitude must pronounce in favor of a movement towards conquest of the universe in terms of knowledge and direction, toward the discovery of its influxes and energies and towards the part played by human beings in all it can give for increasingly improved living and working conditions. Actually, research forms a part of that intellectual instinct which constantly drives human beings to know. It is an impulse born in the depths of our human nature and from a vital craving to investigate in ever greater detail all that exists around us so that we can take advantage of new possibilities for our survival and well-being against every form of threat, suffering, sickness or death.

All past history confirms the uncontainable yearning that we have to investigate the realities around us which we must direct and administer. Every period has handed on to the next one new medical knowledge, technology, and programs at the developmental stage which gave promise of a growing stock of remedies and of means for our physical and psychical perfection.

Today the pace of research is beginning to touch the most delicate and basic human structures, especially in the field of the biological sciences. All science is passing into a new phase of its history: from being able to manipulate the world to the possibility of manipulating human life itself through molecular biology, thus opening unexpected further developments in knowledge and practical action.

Naturally, while the stimulus towards increasing conquests can on the one hand contribute to enormous gains in the field of medicine and disease prevention, on the other hand it exposes us to the risk of involving, directly or indirectly, what is "specifically human," that is, characteristically human values which place human beings at the apex of every reality.

The "specifically human" may be said to be especially those things which touch upon the dignity of life and action which is proper to human beings: human intelligence, affectivity, the ability to conceive ideas and to create programs. It is found in the harmony of human functions and in the practical exercise of freedom of choice and of speech. It appears in the right to one's own moral, religious and political convictions, in the exercise of one's own profession and in other ways.

However, any technological or scientific manifestation touching this "specifically human" area negatively would clearly not be "human" any more. Indeed, it would put us in an absurd position.

What is involved here is the premise that every expression of science has as its "reason for being" human perfection in its differing expressions of being and acting. And so if it should eventually be revealed as harmful to a characteristic which is fundamentally human, science would cease to true science or technology and must be called inhumane and unabashed experimentation.

July 27
The Conspiracy of Silence Surrounding Death

It has been correctly noted that desperate decisions, such as the one to seek the death of someone apparently cut off from the possibility of a healthy and "normal" life, often arise in the context of the loneliness into which the family circle of such people are forced by their task of providing for them.

The most immediate conclusion commonly drawn from such a comment is that there should be hospitalization and general social structures for the handicapped, the old and those who are gravely ill. And certainly much still remains to be done from this point of view. But one cannot forget that many of these structures are already available and yet they appear incapable of remedying solitude and the sense of abandonment.

For example, take the case of someone suffering from a terminal illness who is being looked after in a hospital ward. He is surrounded by many people, doctors, nurses, friends and relatives who visit frequently, offer a thousand services and chat away about a thousand trivialities. But all too often he can find nobody ready to talk to him about the most important thing in his life, the fact that he is dying.

Not only does he not find anybody ready to talk to him about this — after all, it truly is a difficult thing to talk about! — but neither can he find anyone who wants to listen to him talk about it. Everybody's behavior all too clearly shows the sick person that one is not supposed to bring such matters up. It's simply unacceptable, embarrassing and taboo.

So we are faced with a question that demands an answer: doesn't this rigorous silence surrounding imminent death, this continuing to behave as if people never died, cause one to feel abandoned and alone?

We not only evade the thought of death, we also evade the idea of suffering. And the thought is no more evaded than is the reality. The only question people bother to ask today in this regard is: what can be done; how can my suffering be relieved; how can I get well; how can I get back on my feet again, away from the monotony of this meaningless and unproductive waste of time, this time of illness?

July 28
Euthanasia

There is no point in solving problems by eliminating them, as happens when difficult pregnancies are resolved by abortion, when population increase is resolved by the unnatural and simplistic method of sterilization, when family crises are settled by breaking up the family, when acute sexual tension is calmed through precocious and indiscriminate promiscuity, when sexual permissiveness is resolved through pornography, and so forth.

Human problems must be faced and tackled in a human way, employing typical human gifts of courage, generosity, self-discipline and self-sacrifice, patient scientific study, responsible liberty, unconditional dedication and, eventually, the acceptance of mystery.

A society which gets rid of its problems in a business-like and artificial way and does not cultivate the gifts mentioned above, is a society inexorably condemned to decadence.

I would like to give my attention now to an especially difficult case, both because it is a dramatic problem in itself and because it is symptomatic of the crisis in our society today. I am speaking about euthanasia or the choice of self-inflicted death out of exhaustion or as a protest, or of killing another for motives of compassion to relieve a person close and dear to us from unbearable and terminal suffering.

Faced with these individual problems, if a word can be said — and how hard it is to say it! — it cannot be pronounced from a distance, ignoring the facts, but must be addressed person to person, directed at whoever is the protagonist in the matter or perhaps its unwitting victim. I believe that the effort to give justification, meaning and plausibility to these painful individual histories by generalizing about the "right to die" seems, first of all, a false and inhuman statement to the conscience of every right-minded person, but, secondly, is even wider of the mark and irrelevant to the one who has given in to such a temptation — with no thought, certainly, of any "right" but confused by a multiplicity of distorted factors.

Still, even if we can say nothing about individual cases, they do make us think as they must. They must inspire us to meditate not only on those cases highlighted by the media but on ourselves, our own life, our own sense of love, of suffering and of hope. The idea of a love which kills must appear "monstrous." And "monstrous" is the compassion which wipes out the one whose pain we cannot bear, the philanthropy which does not know whether it intends to free another from a burdensome life, or to free oneself from a presence which has become an intolerable nuisance. Such a situation appears "monstrous" and so in a certain sense something remote and incredible about which we speak as a far-out possibility.

A very sad modern fable tells us that one morning a man woke after a bad night and saw that he had been changed into a horrible insect (Franz Kafka, *The Metamorphosis*).

What in normal times appears to us as monstrous and alien can, in reality, suddenly show itself as being very near, as a reality we have hidden in our bosom, as an eventuality we ought to have long since recognized and vigorously dismissed before it seduced us to give in to it.

The Church, Guardian of Man's Future Destiny

The Church is guardian of a memory which in no way can be stored on floppy disks. It is the memory of the human journey towards cultural and moral religious transcendence, a journey which has the Gospel of Jesus as its focal point of reference. In the light of the Gospel every human experience having a dynamic transcendence can be understood. It is a journey looking to the absolute future of our human race, to the new Jerusalem coming down from heaven and from God, looking ahead to the city of the eighth day when God, not we, will make all things new.

But we, too, are able to do worthy things for the Lord. I would like to tell here an ancient rabbinic story.

One day some people achieved something wonderful which up to that point had been considered impossible. One of their number became afraid, thinking that people would come to the point of not having any further need of God. Several religious people were very worried.

That very day, Rabbi Nathan met the prophet Elijah and asked him: "What did God do the moment He saw that those people were going to do better than He ever did?" The prophet replied: "God smiled and said, 'My sons are doing better than I did! My sons are doing better than I ever did!' " God is not afraid of our human ability. He encourages it so as to prepare us for the wonder of the eighth day.

And so the believer journeys towards the perfect city where there is no more sorrow, tears or cries. But he does this, passing through the words and paths of human culture and sustained and accompanied on his journey by the memory and the journey of the whole human tradition.

Which means that the preoccupation of the Church to ensure that the memory of the human family is integrally safeguarded, will have to manifest itself on the one hand in keeping an eye on proper preaching of the Last Things and on the other hand in the form of an interest in and an active collaboration with all those realities and initiatives of civil society which work together to keep that memory alive and thus facilitate communication between peoples which is more than simple, coded information. Without memory, there is no communication.

July 30
Gospel-Oriented Vacations

"You must come away to some lonely place all by yourselves and rest awhile" Jesus said one day to His worn-out disciples (Mk 6:30). And to this day we hear again the power of these words.

Vacations are needed in which we can be free to be ourselves, to have our time and our choices. They are needed both to help us rethink and reorder our life in more human terms and to check what our real and truest interests are.

Actually, work, our profession, family and home life, our essential relationships with a certain number of people, tend to wear us out through the anxiety involved in living and the crises which pile up. In fatigue and in worry the criterion of the true and the just tends to fade.

The criteria of profit, of material well-being and of our career — the most common criteria today — come to the fore and they suffocate other values and ideals which we deceive ourselves into thinking we possess. We Christians are becoming too bound to things. We are slaves of a mentality which does not respect our dignity as free people and which dims and cancels in us every sign of resemblance to God.

Vacation is a useful time for a change and it may be the only time we have available in this sense. But let us be sure that at least during these days we find the courage to make choices according to Gospel criteria. If vacation time is taken up only with those entertainments and idle pastimes which do not allow us to reflect, if we pass purposeless hours and days following the latest fads, we risk becoming idol-worshippers and less and less available for the great things God offers His creatures.

We should free ourselves from the fear that if we give our vacation another tone we will not amuse or replenish ourselves. Let us not think that we should let our head or our heart, our spirit or our conscience take time off so as to live our human adventure more fully. Let us not think that human enjoyment always is the fruit of satisfying our whims or letting ourselves be swept along by the most powerful fad. Rather, let us take charge of ourselves. Let us make a schedule and a program of practical things to do which truly will refresh us in body and in spirit.

July 31
The Value of Vacation Time

Among the many values which vacation time offers us, I would like to underline silence, reflection, prayer and contemplation. These are values we feel necessary for our "humanity." Only in silence do we succeed in perceiving the most meaningful and decisive voices of human history, our own personal history and that of our brothers and sisters. Only by reflecting can we conquer our superficiality, descend into our innermost being and find our truest self. Only in prayer do we meet the Lord as the source and goal of our life and from Him receive power and encouragement for our daily journey, winding, as it does, among some joys and many pains. Only in contemplation can we sense the infinite beauty of God and taste the unspeakable joy of His presence in us.

As Christians we have an even graver responsibility: we ourselves have to live these values and present ourselves in a humble and simple but convincing way, witnessing to the value of silence, reflection, prayer and contemplation to the people whom we meet and with whom we pass our vacation.

Our life has to be enlightened and guided by the example of Jesus. The invitation He gave one day to His disciples has a meaning for us today and in particular for our vacation. He said to them, as He says to us:

"Look at the birds in the sky. They do not sow or reap or gather into barns; yet your heavenly Father feeds them. Are you not worth much more than they are? Can any of you, for all his worrying, add one single cubit to his span of life? And why worry about clothing? Think of the flowers growing in the fields; they never have to work or spin; yet I assure you that not even Solomon in all his regalia was robed like one of these. Now if that is how God clothes the grass in the field which is there today and thrown into the furnace tomorrow, will He not much more look after you, you men of little faith?" (Mt 6:26-30).

Do not think it is arbitrary to apply the word of our Lord Jesus to the way the vacation must and ought to be passed by His disciples, this time of repose and joyous serenity. The invitation is to look at and observe all created things. They fall all the time under our eyes but we have lost the habit and the ability of letting ourselves come under their spell and be swept away in awe and admiration and contemplation. The eyes of the disciple of Jesus must be alert to find in creation the presence and the hope of the love of God the Father. Through these things, too, the love of God passes and, as always, His love is a gifting love.

Beyond the creatures, the Christian can always find the Creator.

AUGUST

August 1
In the Land of Jesus: Bethlehem, the Divine Initiative

Beginning our pilgrimage back to the origins, we shall try with the Lord's help to arrange an itinerary for our daily life and for our Christian commitment. Actually, a pilgrimage would be pointless if it were just a stage or a parenthesis instead of being a reference point for our life in the Church's service. On the other hand, the pilgrim coming to the Holy Land for the first time is impressed in a multitude of ways owing to the excess of sights and sounds. This was the very thing that happened to me when, twenty-five years ago, I came here for the first time. I had the sensation of being almost lost as I suddenly came up against three thousand years of history in a small patch of land where some of the most formidable events of all times have taken place.

Clearly, there is a very easy way to get over this confusion and sense of loss: to return often to Palestine! But there is another important thing to be done: viz., to arrange an order, a line of approach, an essential reference-point to guide us in our many-sided journey.

The *unique* and *fundamental reference point* is that here a *divine initiative* is being manifested. We are not going to look for traces of human history but to discover manifold manifestations of the gratuitous initiative of the God Who loves mankind. This is the only thing we look for beyond the rocks, the events, the souvenirs, the people. We look for a God Who has revealed Himself for mankind's benefit and Who wanted to express in these places, persons and situations the fullness of His interest in mankind. Only this do we want to heed: God's manifest initiative, still going on — and destined to go on — in the life of every individual in the world.

And God's initiative has a *center*, a *focal point*: *Calvary and the Basilica of the Resurrection*. Everything we do as pilgrims revolves around the cross and the Resurrection. Everything is a preparation for this and a consequence of it.

August 2
In the Land of Jesus: Bethlehem, Waiting

The itinerary I have thus outlined begins here, in the shepherds' field. At this stage we want to live in expectancy, the shepherds' expectancy, the expectancy of humanity for the birth of Jesus which we shall celebrate later at the grotto of the Nativity.

What does this waiting tell us? It links us up with the world still living in expectation for the full manifestation of Christ. It puts us in touch with our own waiting. I invite each one to reflect on this waiting in our own lives. What are we waiting for? What am I waiting for in my life from the power of the coming Lord? What consolation, what interior fullness, what escape from bitterness, what pacification and what respite do I ask for?

Each one should allow the power of personal longings to be expressed. Lord, what do I want for myself, what do I expect from the power of Your coming? What

302   AUGUST

do I expect from the glory of Your name before which everyone is called to bow? Let the power of Your personal desires for the community be expressed. What do we want, what are we expecting for our communities, for our families, for the people with whom we live, for our Christian and diocesan family, for the world community in search of peace? Are there — deep inside us, either as individuals or as communities — burning desires and a sense of great expectancy which we often try not to think about because they frighten us so, because they are so great? Actually, no desire is too great in comparison with the infinite power of God Who fills the human heart and Who is coming. And if we wish seriously to celebrate the coming Lord we have to celebrate Him with total openness.

A thousand aspirations, running the whole gamut of human desires, seek to find a voice in us. Right now, though, at this time, we yearn to be humanity's voice, the voice of the waiting shepherds, knowing that God surpasses our hopes and fills them in a wholly unique way. We know that the Lord asks us to open our hearts as wide as possible so that He can fill them. Nothing is impossible to the one who believes. And if we have faith like a mustard seed, one of these mountains will move and cast itself into the sea. How many of the snow-capped mountains of hostility and war must be made to melt into gentle, warm streams of peace!

So we live this moment of waiting in expectation, entrusting to Mary, the Queen of all of our desires, who knows what it is to wait in longing for her Son at Bethlehem, and who understands this limitation of our interior aspirations. Let us allow the power of the Holy Spirit to blow on the fire of our yearning, fanning it into a blaze as great as all the universe.

In the Land of Jesus: Bethlehem, Receiving the Gift

What meaning can the celebration of the Nativity of Jesus by the Church here present have for us today? What meaning does it have for our situation as Church and as a society? It seems to me that there is an attitude recommended and presented to us as one which would be proper for our Church today in this place. It is the *attitude of Mary receiving the gift, Jesus*. It is the ability to accept the gift which God Himself gives us and which is not the fruit of our work but the initiative of the God of love which puts it into our hands.

In coming to the Holy Land, we enter into a civilization and culture different in many ways from those we are used to. Even if we note the presence of Western culture here, we can also perceive vestiges of an oriental culture which is very different from our own.

Our Western civilization is totally bent on seeing what comes from human effort and what human beings are capable of planning and accomplishing for the present and for the future. As followers of Christ we have been trained to remember that our doing and accomplishing must make sense, must have a meaning for our life. We have been taught to remember that what we produce is not basically our own but is the product of talents and gifts which we have received.

At the root of everything there is a Gift: the perfect and supreme Gift. Jesus, the Infant, is God's Gift to mankind. As I received the image of the Infant in my arms at the entrance of the church, so mankind receives Him in its arms, as a Gift which God Himself has placed into our hands.

At this moment we are called to renew and restate

our acceptance of the Gift and our pledge of obedience to the One making it. The important thing is to preserve within us — and not merely in our mind or intellect — the conviction which is a fundamental reality: God first loved us. It is God Who always takes the initiative. God's initiative is a gift. Jesus is the origin, the beginning, the exemplar, of everything we are as individuals and as Church.

August 4
In the Land of Jesus: Bethlehem, "Lord, it is You Who Speak to Us"

"O Lord, we want to see in Jesus, become an infant, Your preeminence! It is not we who work, who act, who speak. It is You Who speak to us, You Who come to us. You form us as a gift and whatever we may say, think, do or program has a basic, necessary and fixed point of reference: Your person, Your presence, Your word and Your life.

"Lord, allow us to experience this truth! We do not want to give our assent to it as a simple idea. We supplicate You to impress it on our hearts as Life, just as You became life and flesh in Mary's womb, just as You showed Yourself visibly as life and flesh in the manger to be acknowledged and adored by the shepherds.

"Fill our existence, Lord Jesus! Grant that nothing in us may resist You or oppose You. Grant that our activity as individuals or as people responsible for a family, for a job, for a community, for society, may be transformed by our experience of You.

"Sometimes one has the impression that enormous,

almost unbearable burdens have piled up on those responsible in society, so numerous are the necessities, the worries, the sorrows and the tears of our society. That is why, Lord, we want to go back again to Your Gift which makes all things new, which makes our hearts new by making them sensitive, throbbing, able to accept the burdens of reality and bearing them with serenity and joy!''

August 5
In the Land of Jesus: The Judean Desert, Christian Orthopraxis

Christian orthopraxis. Christian life is a journey and our travel across the desert of life is the symbol of it. But it is not just any journey. It is one with the right destination, like the one that Jesus made.

When the prophet Isaiah (58:4-10) speaks to us about true fasting, he helps us understand that the proper way to travel is by way of authentic and true Christian orthopraxis. We have to take an interest in suffering and put ourselves at the service of our neighbor in difficulties.

If we walk in this way, the justice of the Lord goes before us and His glory follows in our wake. And so, on this first stage of our journey, we can reflect on our Christian life and ask ourselves if we are on the right road, on a journey committing ourselves to others. And we can also ask if the direction of our communities is just, right and lived in truth.

If it is true that light shines out in darkness, if it is true that darkness is illuminated by the midday sun which splits the desert rocks, then this reflection may encourage us to ask the Lord to illumine our way and for the Madonna of the Way to guide our steps as they accompany us on our journey.

August 6
In the Land of Jesus: The Judean Desert, Christian Orthodoxy

Christian orthodoxy. We have covered some ground and can begin to understand the desert as a place where one finds oneself face to face with the bare essentials and, on the other hand, loses the trivialities with which one's life was filled. We find ourselves confronted with temptations, with the truth of the evil within us and with the mystery of God.

As we go along this road, let us try to imagine how Jesus travelled it when He went to the Mount of the Temptations, the fear and anxiety He felt, how much He must have suffered as He approached the full revelation of the mystery of His life. Above all, we must try to imagine how Jesus went along this road when He was going up to Jerusalem, to the final and most tumultuous temptation: the cross and the grave where the mystery of His life would be fully revealed.

As we meditated on Isaiah at our first stop we were able to grasp the first point about Christian orthopraxis or the way that we, as followers of Jesus, ought to behave, viz., like people attentive to others. The Gospel reading at this point (Mt 4:1-11) shows us the roots of this orthopraxis: *orthodoxy*. This is the basis behind every way of helping others, of being for them, of taking care of them, of serving the poor. This orthodoxy is nothing more than having a correct notion of God, a clear sense that God is God and that He alone is worth serving.

Jesus in the desert succeeds in expressing the fullness of this orthodoxy, of this truth which mankind learns about God and about the journey of life. On this desert road, Jesus situated His story about the wounded traveller and described the unfortunate behavior of those who failed to assist him, contrasting that behavior with the proper mode of acting as exemplified by the Good Samaritan.

August 7
In the Land of Jesus: The Judean Desert, "Lord, Show Yourself on Our Way"

Here Jesus tells us something more. He tells us that we must have a proper concept of God if we are to act in a proper manner. Orthopraxis and orthodoxy *go together*. They cannot be separated. Both reveal the truth about the one true God, both reveal what God lets us know about Himself.

The desert is the place where, through trial and temptation, we are called to learn the true meaning of God. And we, as a pilgrim Church, as a Church journeying through history, through our culture and in our civilization, are often confronted there with these difficulties. Sometimes there is really something of the desert in our day to day living, surrounded as we often are by anonymous individuals who do not even salute us or exchange glances. How do we live through these trials?

Let us ask the Lord to help us live in full awareness of His presence. Let us ask Him to be able to recognize

Him as the root of all true awareness along our human journey. "Lord, You showed Yourself through Your Christ in His trials in this place. Show Yourself also in our life so that we may know that You alone are great! In order that we may know that we live by the words which come forth from Your mouth, may we adore and serve You alone to Whom we desire to entrust our entire existence!"

August 8
In the Land of Jesus: The Judean Desert, Contemplating the Face of God

Contemplating the face of God. When we shall have come to the end of our desert journey, I think that many of us will have a glowing complexion because of the intense radiance of the "Son." This is the image of all contemplation, of the individual who looks upon the face of God, and like the Son instinctively reflects and irradiates Him.

First of all, we began with Isaiah. Then we recalled the parable of the Good Samaritan, remarking that the root of all Christian orthopraxis is to be found in orthodoxy, an appreciation of the true meaning of God. But how can we make this root grow within us? Through contemplation! And for contemplation, the desert is the proper place.

I believe it is almost impossible to live a Christian experience, in the society in which we are immersed, without rooting oneself, each of us in a personal way, in deep contemplation. And so the desert is the expression of what we want to do in our daily life. We want to search out moments, desert pauses, so as to live, not in pure solitude, but in listening to and dialoguing with God alone, being illuminated by Him. When our countenance is radiant from contemplating the countenance of God, people notice it. When we live a certain contemplative experience, we radiate God around us even without wanting to.

This is one of the few signs of the presence of God in the world today, a world in which there is certainly a marked absence of the sacred. The presence of God is revealed in those men and women who have established it on the Mount of Contemplation in the desert.

So let us ask that we, too, might be granted to live in this way, because it is the only way the temptation of atheism and of idolatry in our society can be conquered. Let us ask it for ourselves, for the whole diocese, for those who are overburdened with a thousand things and thus run the risk of not giving a place to the radiant contemplation of the face of God.

August 9
In the Land of Jesus: The Judean Desert, Towards the Fullness of Life

The end of our journey. We have come at last to the very edge of the desert. A short distance away begins the oasis which is the end of our journey and marks the passage from non-life to life, from aridity to fecundity.

Everything Israel did, and which we do today as we journey through the desert, conquering temptation, acknowledging the One God as Lord, helping our neighbor whom we find on the side of the road, seeking the depth of contemplation, all this must lead to the fullness of the oasis, or of life which, in biblical language, is also the fullness of consolation or of messianic peace, the fullness of goods and of fraternity rediscovered in the abundance of human and divine gifts. All must flow into the heavenly Jerusalem which is the goal of our journey, the reference point of the Church's life and of human life journeying towards the fullness of messianic peace, the goal lying in the desert of life just as the oasis lies in the dryness of our desert journey.

And so, what is the important thing? It is certainly right to enjoy messianic peace as far as possible, to enjoy the consolation and the fullness of God's gifts coming to us from a fraternal community, or from an anticipated possession of God in our enjoyment of prayer or from a well-organized community which fills us with satisfaction. And yet the important thing is to have the proper orientation, to know where we are going, to know that there is an oasis and that we are going toward it, to know the right and the wrong road, to know that we are taking the right steps on this journey even if it is a tiring one.

We should ask for each one here and for the whole Church that we not allow ourselves to be ensnared by, tired by, or stopped by overly immediate problems, but rather have our eyes fixed on our goal, on those espousals between humanity and God which give a meaning to every human journey and are its goal.

Let us ask the Madonna who is the image of this journey's goal and the icon of the Church's purpose. She already contains the fullness of Israel at its beginning, in its offspring, in the reality of Jesus who must be shown fully in history and give us a great clarity about this goal. We ought to ask the Madonna that all our individual initiatives or choices be those in which there has clearly been some discernment with regard to this goal.

In the Land of Jesus: Jericho, the Presence of Jesus

Let us reflect a bit on the meaning which Jericho has for the spiritual life of Jesus. As we know, Jesus lived a great part of His life and ministry around the Sea of Galilee and later at Jerusalem.

But Jericho is what we could call — translating it into our language — the place of His spiritual maturation, the place where Jesus lived the decisive moment of His interior life, where He determined in a definitive, permanent way the orientation of His life.

Jesus lived what we call our vocational choice right at Jericho and near Jericho in two fundamental episodes of His earthly existence.

These two episodes are, on the one hand, the prayer, fasting and temptations during His forty days in the desert and, on the other His Baptism and experience of the Spirit in the Jordan. These two moments finally define Jesus and His life.

He will not have to act — as His temptations seem to suggest — but will instead respond in a way coherent with the experience He had at His Baptism where God the Father revealed Himself in a singular way to His Son.

In these two episodes, the disciples of Jesus saw the whole life of Jesus summed up. And that is why Jericho, and the episodes in His life which took place there, constitute a link between His past and His future.

In the Land of Jesus: Jericho, Jesus' Visit

The story of Zacchaeus (Lk 19:1-10) is the application of this decisive moment to the life of an inhabitant of

Jericho. A man living here had suffered a number of negative experiences, but in spite of these he heard Jesus say to him: "That's enough!" He had desires and expectations and he heard Jesus say about them: "Be of good heart. I am with you!" It is the decisive experience for Zacchaeus. He learns what part of his life has to be put behind him and what, on the contrary, constitutes his salvation as a son of Abraham and constitutes his call.

Let us ask that we, and also our Church, may be able to live something of this experience, that we, in other words, may be able to live the meaning of the visit of Christ in our personal and communitarian life and live it so profoundly that from it we may receive a new vocational light. Let us ask that we may understand in a practical way what things are to be avoided and what the Lord wishes from us. Your bishop, in the first place, must ask for this grace of clarity, of confirmation and of discernment because he is called to reflect in the name of the whole Church just as Jesus reflected in the desert on the ways of Satan and the ways of God. He is called to understand, as Jesus understood at the Jordan, the way of being an authentic servant of his people.

You must ask for this grace for me because I need it. And then we must ask it for everyone: for the diocesan community, for the life of each person. All of us desire to know the ways of God. Jesus calls us while we are in this place and tells us: "Look, I am coming into your life. I confirm what you have decided to leave aside and not to do any more. I am guiding you along this new road and I am with you."

In the Land of Jesus: Jerusalem,
With Jesus in His Agony

To remain in the company of Jesus in His agony in the garden of Gethsemane is a difficult mystery to explain verbally. It is a mystery whose hidden attraction all feel.

I recall that from my childhood this page of the Gospel made a great impression when it was explained to me. The fact that Jesus had felt fear, that he had experienced anxiety, anguish of heart and what we call a sense of rebellion, seemed extraordinary to me, almost incredible. And at the same time it seemed very beautiful and very true.

At that time I did not know the words of Pascal: "Jesus is in agony until the end of the world." And I would not have understood what those words might mean. I do understand their meaning today, though. In fact, the basilica which rises above the place where all these events took place is called the "Basilica of All the Nations" because it truly represents and symbolizes all the world's nations with their individual cups of grief. Thus the agony and suffering of each of them is united with the anguish and pain of Jesus.

The mystery of Jesus' agony in the garden is incredible and yet we feel it to be profoundly near us, near us in our most difficult trials, trials which we are not able to share fully with others so deeply personal are they. We feel that Jesus, though, does share in these experiences — or better — that we share in His.

And so we understand the reason for the night vigils that take place in this basilica and which are the prelude to all the vigils taking place in churches and oratories

314   AUGUST

throughout the world particularly from Thursday to Friday evenings.

August 13
In The Land of Jesus: Jerusalem, "Ours are the Sorrows He Bore"

This mystery surrounds us. It represents us. No part of it is foreign to us. It is not foreign to our personal life which, without our being able to foresee it, is exposed to moments of anguish, of refusal, of disgust and of rebellion. It is not foreign to people's ordinary living, even to unbelievers who, because of their unbelief, live even more agonizing days and nights. It is not foreign to communities and nations which many times live their own agonies. Think, just now, of the sufferings of Lebanon and of many other places throughout the world where war is raging.

We are talking of historical realities to which, by His admirable providence, God associated Himself in Christ, not rejecting them or considering them unworthy of His greatness but on the contrary seeing them as part of His mission.

True, in the passion of Jesus there will come moments of greater suffering than these in Gethsemane. And yet it is the daily Gethsemane that is commonly present in so many of our personal, familiar, communitarian, social and cosmic realities.

Adoring and contemplating the mystery of Jesus in agony, is perhaps the truest expression of our faith.

In the Land of Jesus: Jerusalem, "Watch and Pray"

But we have an inner question: What does this mystery teach us? It teaches us and it invites us to three ways of thinking which we can deduce from the Gospel (Lk 22:39-53).

The first is that we should not be surprised by these events as Jesus experienced them. So we are not to be ashamed. Jesus was not ashamed and, indeed, He desired that we should be told about them by His disciples. He wanted to say, "I am afraid." Often we fear to tell others that we are in anguish. Jesus, though aware of His responsibility and of the big and little traumas He would create in His disciples' minds, said how He truly felt: "I am afraid." He did not want His own to be amazed at Him, or as a result at themselves when they, too, found themselves afraid.

The second approach that we are invited to take is to stay awake. Stay awake! And this is the very thing we find hardest to do because we generally want, at these times, to sleep or amuse ourselves or to do something else provided we do not have to think, to face up to our situation. One person takes refuge in one thing, another in something else. A person may go to the limits with drugs and alcohol because of fear or anguish.

We do not want anxiety and we refuse to see that this, too, is a travelling companion which should not be evoked in a uselessly masochistic way but should be accepted, knowing that every now and then it shows up and can reappear. Anguish ought to be looked in the face as Jesus in this place looked it in the face.

The third approach is that of prayer. Actually, when we are in anguish we think that even God cannot help us.

If we had the basic awareness of the help of God we would not be entirely in anguish. We feel trapped, believing that not even God knows what to do for us and for this reason we feel no obligation to pray. But Jesus said: Stay awake and pray. Pray with the simplicity and the fatigue with which He Himself prayed. Pray that you enter not into temptation.

August 15
In the Land of Jesus: The Kidron Valley and Mary, Mother of the Church

Not far from the Garden of Gethsemane, near the Church of St. Anne, the mystery of the Madonna's birth is venerated. A few yards away, on the Temple Mount, we find the spot where the mystery of her Presentation is commemorated. And, beyond Jerusalem, in the hill country to the west, at Ain-Karim, the mystery of her Visitation to her cousin Elizabeth is recalled.

Across the road from the Garden of Gethsemane we venerate the mystery of Mary's death and Assumption into heaven. Thus we contemplate all the mysteries of her life as a sharing in the mysteries, the suffering, the glory and the Resurrection of Jesus.

The Book of Revelation (11:19; 12:1-6, 10), provides us with a curious synthesis, not always easy to explain, of the mystery of the Church as a participation in the mysteries of Jesus. And so when we remember Mary we remember, too, the mystery of the Church dying and rising with Christ. We celebrate the mystery of our life and our communities which are equally called to share in the mystery of Christ and Mary.

I invite everyone to ask for the grace that our Church be like Mary. May it be a Church which reflects Jesus, which is entirely related to Him, which has no meaning in itself except for its relationship to Him and which, therefore, manifests Him and lives Him. And let us ask, too, for each of us the experience of this same mystery in our own lives. It is a mystery of combat and of struggle. In fact the Apocalypse speaks of a mysterious struggle. To be with Christ, to be in the Church, means combat. An easy existence is not promised or foretold.

To be with the Lord in His victory over death also means to be together with Mary in all the humble and joyous service which she renders to humanity. Think of Lourdes, of Fatima, of all the places in which the Madonna has appeared to assure us that she continues to be near the daily life of the Church. The place where we are now is, so to speak, the source of all the other Marian presences. Because Mary is alive in Christ she can show and manifest herself to human history.

August 16
In the Land of Jesus: Emmaus, The Parable of a Journey

At this hour of the day many of you are probably tired. So were the disciples of Emmaus when they arrived at eventide in this village. And yet this was an important moment for them.

Therefore, let us ask the two disciples to intercede for us so that our eyes may be opened and we can recognize the importance and meaning of the moment we are now living. May we be able to recognize Jesus

318

revealing Himself in the breaking of the bread. May we recognize the meaning of the path He shows us. It is a journey that is at the same time the *parable of a journey*. It is the sign of the permanent stages of a constantly recurring trip.

We shall always have to become contemplatives over and over again. We shall always have to make our own the word of God which so far we know so inadequately. How many of us over the years have meditated seriously on the Gospels? How many have a profound knowledge of the Letters of St. Paul or can say that the Letter to the Romans or the one to the Galatians is a part of their own lived, Christian experience? For how many of us is the Eucharist truly the foundation and dynamic center of his or her life?

The journey still to be made remains open and we have to go back to it constantly. It is also true, however, that the journey continues and does not ask us to stop only to refresh ourselves and take a backward glance at the stages completed. It asks us to *interiorize* what we have covered by looking ahead.

And it is Emmaus which invites us to look ahead — to look at the road still before us. We may ask the disciples of Emmaus a question as they rise in great haste from the table and run to Jerusalem. We may ask them: "Where are you going?" And they will tell us: "To Jerusalem." And we may answer: "But Jerusalem is a big city, and there are all sorts of things there — good and bad, faith and disbelief. Where are you people going?" Then they will tell us the exact spot. "We are going to the Cenacle!"

In the Land of Jesus: Emmaus, The Love Which Sets the World on Fire

The Emmaus disciples are not going randomly toward an anonymous city. They are going to seek out an environment, a situation, a place where in due course a great conflagration will break out. They are going to the Cenacle where the fire of the Holy Spirit will flare up, that divine charity capable of setting the universe ablaze.

This is the program which faces us. Our witness must overflow into the great and fundamental Christian approach to the world: *charity*. This is not a charity which is simply interest in others, attention to them, help and care for them. It is the charity which is the fire of the Holy Spirit flaring up in us and which becomes love, attention and vigilance in all human situations, e.g., in situations of poverty: material, spiritual, cultural, social, political, cosmic or universal.

This is a charity which comes forth from the Holy Spirit and which is as broad as the dimensions and the confines of the world itself.

From the table in Emmaus, from the simple conversation that the disciples had with Jesus in which He explained the Scriptures to them, come the universal horizons of missionary charity which is capable of setting the world on fire and for which we feel a special vocation and mission.

What we are saying at this moment is not presumptuous. It is simply our sense of reliving the experience of these first Christians. It is feeling again within us the apostolic and missionary consciousness of St. Paul to whom the Risen Jesus appeared, giving him a deep sense of his own mission together with a sense of gratitude for the gift he had received. For this reason Paul could say and mean it, "I am worth nothing; I am able to do nothing on my own. But I can do all things in Him who strengthens me."

August 18
In the Land of Jesus: Emmaus, "Lord, Speak to Our Heart"

"Lord Jesus, Whom the disciples met in this place, You Who showed Yourself to them in the breaking of the bread, speak to our hearts so that we may feel deep within the warmth which the disciples knew. May they make their experience new and unforgettable to us as we seek to discern Your presence in our midst.

"Lord, You Who moved the two disciples so that they passed from a state of confused and resigned bitterness to the decisive certainty of a missionary and charitable journey, do not abandon any of us in our uncertainty and confusion.

"Become our guest, Lord Jesus, so as to reveal Yourself to us, Your love, the meaning of Your death and the meaning of our life. We want to walk and to run with the two disciples towards the great city of many names: Jerusalem, New York, Milan, the universal cosmopolis of the world where all people seek brotherhood and peace.

"We approach this city with the certainty that our journey is marked by a direction, a security, a clarity of ideals that nobody will be able to take from us. We are certain that our journey is good and just, that every step of it — even a simple and modest one — is a step towards the goal: the fullness of life and joy in the Holy City, Jerusalem, come down from God in heaven.

"O Mary, you who already live the grace of this heavenly Jerusalem, you who are the icon of the journey and of the Church's perfect goal, live in each of us and bring alive in each of us the presence of your Risen Son so that we may journey towards that ideal destiny and make travelling companions of those near us, proceeding serenely and trustingly towards the same destination."

August 19
Human Activity Must Show Forth the Works of God

The activities with which we want to fill our days are like the reflection and radiation of a task which surpasses us, does not depend on us, is a gift and — for this reason — builds and shapes us. It is the work of God culminating in the Jesus event. In their profound truth human works are the reflection of the work of God in Jesus. Jesus — whose name, in the sense of a person's ultimate reality and of his or her mission — was not chosen by human beings but, as the Gospel of Luke tells us, was brought to earth by the action of God.

And so time opens before our eyes, and does not present itself as an empty reality waiting to be filled with our works. It is already filled, already specified by the work of God. Each day is the day of salvation, of sacred history. Each day is the day of the Lord.

A new light beams forth from this truth illuminating all our human activities. Our deeds are not a vain attempt to fill a void yawning before us, but express the joyous and trusting commitment to perceive in actuality the active mystery of God, to accept it, to manifest it, to walk responsibly in its light towards the Lord Who is the ultimate and definitive Good, and to pass over those secondary and transitory goods in which He allows us to see some ray of His love.

And so our life is lived in the *hope* of a good which is in the hands of God and with a sense of *responsibility* towards the goods entrusted into our hands. Hope stirs up and sustains responsibility. Responsibility gives witness to and actualizes hope.

August 20
The Wonderful Work of the Father

Because we are believers, we consult the Bible to learn the work God proposes to each of us. The word of God certainly does not refuse this enquiry of ours but it asks us first of all to shift our attention from the work we want to do to the wonderful work God has done for us: revealing Himself and the mystery of His love to us in Jesus His Beloved Son. It is a change of perspective and is a request to entrust ourselves totally to God's action, an invitation to become part of God's design which He lets us know through His Son Who thus shares in the joy of building up our life day after day together with our brothers.

In Jesus, beloved Son of the Father, the most profound human values, the high dignity of each of us, are blended. This dignity is not always respected in a full and unconditional way because we fail to discern its ultimate and universal foundation: the individual relationship of each person with the mystery of Christ. This vision of humanity which sees that each of us is closely linked to Christ Jesus and that we need to be understood keeping Him in mind, is a vision which also explains the drama of existence. Human dignity is a marvelous gift flowing from the loving gaze with which God looks upon Jesus and each of us. But the effective historical actuation of these gifts depends on our free human acceptance.

August 21
Walking in the Newness of Life

We are invited to walk in newness of life, to undertake new things. These new things will not come to life if we are unable to look in depth at our society's suffering, if we do not make this effort and accompany it with incessant prayer, invoking light from above to enable us to discern the signs of hope so as to bring them to reality.

Actually, it is not enough to lay aside a wasted life (a positive note in the lives of many young people) if one does not rediscover the true meaning of existence and avoid introspective evasions of responsibility, a purely selfish life or even self-destructive choices such as drugs which continue to reap victims in our cities. It is not enough to abandon a violent life if we do not rediscover the meaning of service to people and the primacy of ethics over organization.

We have to discern the just aspirations of the poorest, in an effort to satisfy them. We must discern positive projects of renewal so as to sustain them. We must foster scientific discoveries and technical innovations so as to use them for the good of all.

The Lord's light must give us the courage to denounce everything that offends mankind, the absurdity of the arms race. It must give us the courage to make prophetic and meaningful gestures, with humility, without exploitation and without useless presumption, as a gift to the world and as a sign of hope which will be all the more credible and efficacious the more the world finds believers in agreement between themselves and capable of true conversation with God and with others.

August 22
Rise Up! You Have a Mission!

A human reality (Jerusalem, the Church) may also be — and is — the luminous destination of a voyage, light for people's journey. This is a surprising fact and makes us aware of the grave responsibility of those of us who are the Church, a bright beacon for the world, bearers of the destiny of modern history, enlightened by the Spirit of God.

The prophet addresses Jerusalem, a city-symbol of a state, a nation, a people. Today he addresses the People of God, the Church, and says to all: "Arise!" (Is 60:1).

This word is said to someone lying prostrate on the ground in a position signifying sickness and death. Jesus said it to the little, twelve-year-old girl lying dead on her mat and in the presence of her weeping father: "*Talitha, koum*. Little girl, I tell you to get up" (Mk 5:41).

But the word of the prophet is a word of resurrection. Indeed it is the announcement of a mission: "Arise! You have work to do!" To the prophet Elijah, walking dejectedly in the desert to run away from his responsibilities, the angel also said: "Get up and eat or the journey will be too long for you" (1 K 19:7). And when Jonah was wondering if he would be able to resist — and, indeed, was filled with repugnance for the work he had been assigned to do — he was told: "Up! Go to Nineveh the great city and inform them that their wickedness has become known to me" (Jon 1:2).

The word of the prophet signified that these men who seemed defeated, who felt lost and without a future, on the contrary, had a great mission to carry out.

On the Feast of the Epiphany in 1980, the day of my "birth" as a bishop, while I was lying on the ground in the act of prostration preceding ordination, someone said to me: "Rise up! You have a mission to accomplish." This word which was said to me, I now repeat to each of you: "Rise up! A great mission awaits you!"

August 23
"Shine Forth"

The text of Isaiah continues in a way that amazes us. "Shine forth!" In Hebrew this very strong expression literally reads: "Be light! Illuminate!" (Is 60:1).

To better understand this we can go back to the words of Jesus pronounced after the Beatitudes: "You are the light of the world." How was this little group of disciples, simple people without pretensions and without much hope for the future, the light for the world? By the way they lived: expecting the Kingdom, poor, single-hearted, workers for peace, persecuted. In this way they became the source of a new morality and taught what it means to be a moral person.

The exhortation "Shine forth!" means that the

people of God, that each of us must be aware of his or her function as a moral leaven in the world. We must realize that we have to light up the journey of other people just as the star of Bethlehem did, that star of which Matthew says that it brought tidings of great joy.

Do we spread joy around us or are we more inclined to pour out our irritability, our sadness and to unburden on others our bad humor and our fears? Do we really grasp that we, as baptized and confirmed individuals, are asked to be the Lord's stars, communicators of true joy?

Will we also know how to be a sign of light for people who come from afar, for cultured people, people of breeding and of a different mentality? Do we know how to be an absolutely clear light with the transparency of our works which proclaim the truths of the Gospel?

This is the responsibility entrusted to each one of us. That is the mission of the Church in the world today. In its humility, poverty and meekness, in its special love for the poor and humble, in its love for peace, the Church has become a luminous sign for the world.

Pope Paul VI said: "We must come to appreciate this stupendous phenomenon, this luminosity of the Church in today's world. We must become aware of its messianic aspect."

August 24
Jesus, Light of Joy

It appears presumptuous in a world such as ours to be agents of a healthy and solid morality, of an austere search for joy-producing good. But Isaiah tells us again: "Your light has come. The glory of Yahweh is rising on you . . . Above you His glory shines." These three phrases tell us that the light with which the people of God must shine and which we are called on to spread is not the fruit of our personal search but is the light of God in us, the person of Jesus Who shines out in His people, the glory of God which shines out in Jerusalem. The star of the Magi is also totally relative to Christ. It depends on Him and leads to Him reflecting the light of the Word become flesh, "the true light that enlightens all men." And so it is Jesus, loved and acknowledged as the light of our journey, Who fills us with joy and enables us to show it. Jesus is the epiphany of a God Who loves mankind with a serious and unrepentant love. Jesus is the light of the Church and enables it to be the light of the world. Jesus — living in our midst with His pure, free, modest and disinterested lifestyle — is the source of the Church's luminescence.

Think of the Saints and those whom we call Blessed. They were luminous persons who irradiated joy and a strong, healthy morality. With them and with so many among us who take their Baptism seriously and show forth the power of the Spirit of their Confirmation, the Church revives the scene of the Magi who came from afar seeking the brightness foretold by Isaiah. In the midst of the fog and darkness about which the prophet speaks, in the midst of a society blinded by hatred and darkened by indifference, the light coming from the pure and simple life of true Christians makes the Epiphany prodigy come alive again. Men come from afar, men of different cultures, of different civilizations, men who knew nothing about the God of Israel. Immediately they recognize the presence of God in the luminous humanity of Jesus the Lord, in the simple goodness of Mary, in the simple lifestyle of the faithful. And they are fascinated by this irrefutable light.

Christian Service in a Christological Context

We should recall the fundamental ''Christian'' (meaning, ''related to Christ'') value which underlies all forms of disinterested commitment and of service to basic human needs. And for this reason we must go back directly to Jesus, refer to Him and to how He lived in the world of His day, how He worked, how He served society, how He cultivated human relations and how He gave His life for the good of all. It is impossible to define the relationship between a service commitment and its profound spiritual motivation without setting it in its Christological context.

1. Jesus Who lived in His world in a particular time and in a specific human society is the center of the world, the Lord of all times and all things, the lightning rod which attracts all people to Himself, the center of all human and cosmic reality.

2. The New Testament proclaims the love with which the Father and Jesus have loved the world to the point of giving it life and salvation: ''God loved the world so much that He gave His only Son'' (Jn 3:16). ''. . . the bread that I shall give is My flesh for the life of the world'' (Jn 6:51). ''I have come so that they may have life and have it to the full . . . The Good Shepherd is one who lays down his life for his sheep'' (Jn 10:10-11). These texts tells us of a world, of a human reality which in fact is not

open to the creative action of God, has not acknowledged the centrality of Jesus and has not corresponded to the designs of God. They characterize a world which is separated from Christ. And yet God continues to love this world, to desire its good and salvation. And so the love of God is a suffering love. The Son of God sent by the Father into the world with the very mission of loving the world, separated Himself from its pretended autonomy and takes on Himself sin, hate, sorrow and death so as to destroy them in an act of supreme obedience and love of the Father.

3. Jesus shares His service to the world with His disciples. He sends them into the world, desires that they be in the world, immersed in history and in time and thus in temporality and in society. However He asks them not to be of the spirit of the world, both because their presence in the world derives from a principle which transcends it — that is, God's loving plan — and because their service to the world must also oppose its egotistic and rebellious orientations which separate it from God's design.

August 26
The Christian Journey of Service: The Baptismal Option

The Church has the duty of educating us in our journey of charity and faith and must aim at solutions. We ought to know how to link service to someone in difficulty with the community's heart, with daily life and growth. I shall confine myself to indicating briefly some stages of the Christian journey which the New Testament sensed from the beginning and formulated in different ways.

The first stage is the *baptismal option* for God in

Jesus Christ. This option is fully expressed in the centurion's words in Mark 15:39 when he comes face to face with the death of Jesus on the cross: "The centurion who was standing in front of Him had seen how He died and he said, 'In truth this man was a son of God.'" Mark presents us the centurion in this crucial moment of Jesus' total journey as the image of the one who, faced with the cross and seeing Jesus die on it, made the leap from a pragmatic, utilitarian pagan faith which tried to use God as the means to one's success and prestige, to a faith of dedication, self-abnegation and the discovery of the God of Jesus. This God apparently abandons His Son on the cross. He does not give Him success in this life. And, yet, Jesus is full of love for Him, of trust in Him, of exemplary dedication to Him.

The option for the God of Jesus is also a personality shift, passing from a concept of a God Who is useful to me, to my path in life, to a baptismal attitude in which I put my life and my death with total trust at the disposal of the God of Jesus. And when I do this, I begin to share in His attitudes of availability, of abandonment, of life-giving outreach to others which are proper to Jesus, the Christ, the only begotten Son of God.

That is the baptismal option in which everything else must be rooted if we are to formulate a correct, charitable vision of our Christian community. Certainly there can be, and there are, very many charitable actions of service which do not refer explicitly to the baptismal attitude indicated above. But when we consider the overall difficulties which the Christian community must undergo today if it is to offer the right kind of authentic brotherly service, we ask ourselves how it can give an original and congenial reply to the problems it encounters if it does not allow itself to be brought back to its baptismal roots.

August 27
The Christian Journey of Service:
The Community Option

The second stage, particularly highlighted in Matthew's Gospel is the *community option*. We are dealing here with a fundamental text in Matthew: "And know that I am with you always. Yes, to the end of time" (28:20). What do these words mean? They say that the Risen One is alive and is present in the community. The person who has made an option for the God of Jesus Christ has not made merely a generous option which will change his or her life in an isolated way. Such a person is self-given and is a part of a visible group of brothers and sisters. To such an individual the rules of the community must apply: mutual forgiveness, understanding, help, the laws of living together which are recalled in Chapter Eighteen of Matthew's Gospel and which are based on authority, the word of God, prayer and hierarchy. In this community the presence of the Risen One is revealed above all in the person of the member in need.

"For I was hungry and you gave Me food, I was thirsty and you gave Me drink, I was a stranger and you made Me welcome" (Mt 25:35). And so through baptismal education and through one's cordial participation in the everyday life of the body of the Church with its problems and sufferings, one discovers the Risen Lord, the King of the Ages, the God of Glory in the very one who is in need. This type of service is in the context of a light which illumines a progressive journey towards the discovery of the glory of God and the manifestation of His Kingdom here on earth.

August 28
The Christian Journey of Service:
The Option for Those Far Away

The third stage is pointed out especially in the Gospel of Luke and in the Acts of the Apostles and it is the option for those far away which might also be called the option for those in greatest need. The listing in Chapter Twenty-five of Matthew refers to situations of visible, obvious and immediate need which at once challenge us. But there are deeper existential problems, often linked to insuperable difficulties. For example, rarely is the drama of drugs separated from something much more deeply personal. Rarely are prison cases of neglect, particularly among juveniles, not linked to some deeper existential need, at times hard to discover but touching the intimacy of the psyche and emerging from the very depths of the personality. It may be the need of welcome within the family circle, the need to give meaning to one's life, the need for affection. All this cannot easily be provided by short-term institutional help or assistance. And so we have the evangelical stage of Christian community described most vividly in the Acts of the Apostles in which the community becomes aware that there are also these kinds of personal need. They are to be found in dramatic circumstances which only an evangelical type of outreach and dedication can assist and which places at risk one's very own life right to the end as a gift to the other in charity. Think of the many people who have reached the outer limits of suffering and sometimes of hatred for self and life all because of existential needs for which, in practice, no organization or group was able to provide satisfactorily.

**The Christian Journey of Service:
Contemplative Love**

This journey terminates in the Gospel of John where a certain degree of contemplation in charity is reached — that is, the mature community conscience which, through exercises and efforts and sometimes also through mistakes, becomes increasingly sensitive to all human necessities, even the deepest, and is able to take them on in an orderly and exciting way. John shows us the love of God manifested in Christ, urging us to love everyone and to becoming the visible, concrete and nourishing foundation of Christian community. The community becomes the support of each initiative because it embraces a global, contemplative vision of life in which all matters are reviewed in the light of their profound origin: God-Father, God-Love Incarnate, God-Gift of Blessing. The contemplation of divine love gives us a transparent attitude towards all situations so as to live them with that same charity which is summed up and has its permanent expression in the Eucharist. The Eucharist is actually the center, the symbol and the apex of the evangelization of God-Love Incarnate, loving us, urging us on to give ourselves especially to those in need. Gathered together around the Eucharist the Christian community feels a continuous need to understand what it is and to what it is called.

August 30
The Work Exceeding All Others: The Offering of Self

''Think of God's mercy, my brothers, and worship Him, I beg you, in a way that is worthy of thinking beings, by offering your living bodies as a holy sacrifice, truly pleasing to God'' (Rm 12:1).

I believe it will be useful to reflect on the spirit of sacrifice. St. Augustine, disciple and profound student of Paul, defines Christian sacrifice as *''any operation whatsoever done to enter into filial, loving communication with God.''* So sacrifice is an Easter, an entry into divine territory. What is important in the Augustinian concept — shared by all the Fathers — is not the action but the scope of the action. And so the grace of the Holy Spirit, stirring up the spirit of sacrifice in the redeemed person is founded on the spirit of faith. In other words, we may say that sacrifice understood in an objective sense is the action of a human being, moved by love, who passes from attention to many things to the single-minded dedication of their existence to God, giving to their life the meaning of an act of love. This is sacrifice *par excellence*.

We can say more. If we are to call it *Christian* we must reach the final point of our reflection, the fundamental, principal sacrifice, the sacrifice of Calvary in which Christ offers Himself with the whole Church, His spouse, to the glory of the Father in the Resurrection.

In the Eucharist, the sacrifice of the altar is related to that of Calvary and it places whoever lovingly participates in it in the Easter of Jesus. As a Christian sacrifice, all our life is thus related to the Eucharist which in its turn is related to the cross, the perfect sacrifice, the total dedication of the Christ-Man to the love and will of His Father and capable of attracting to Himself the whole of humanity.

How does sacrifice enter into our daily life? Through the ''correct orientation of the heart'' which at one time used to be called ''right intention.'' Christian asceticism is summed up in it. The person who has concentrated a whole existence in the determination to please God alone, enters into the sacrifice of Christ and so into the Father's Kingdom, sharing in the fullness of God and making reality, sanctified with the proper orientation of the heart, share in it too.

The correct orientation of one's heart, in its essence, has another name: *fundamental option*. But an option must be understood in a dynamic sense: it is not enough to direct it once only. Rather, it is a living out of the tension of love, striving to fulfill the desires of God the Father, doing what He likes. It is a disposition which informs the whole of one's life.

This option, renewed in prayer and principally in the Holy Sacrifice of the Mass, is like a living flame giving vigor and form to all our moral choices and making them truly Christian.

August 31
The Prophecy of Peace

The glimpses of peace possible on earth are nourished by the biblical proclamation of peace which is a gift of God. From them is born the prophecy of peace. This involves first of all a farseeing gaze, helping us track down in the human heart the roots of that evil which tends to explode in social violence and war. The enormity of the arms race, of terrible nuclear weapons, of war, of terrorism are prepared by those monsters which we cultivate with irresponsible indifference in our hearts: for example, subtle forms of arrogance, exploitation of others, daily offenses against the life and dignity of other human beings, the search for economic well-being as an end in itself.

We have to be on guard. We have to shout aloud the monstrous nature of a civilization built on prosperity and pleasure, of a life without a soul, without traditions, without a common language or common objectives, of a social communications media which does not serve the truth.

While we create this beneficial and necessary sense of alarm we must also decipher the positive signs present in our civilization: a deep and serene faith in God Who gives peace should help us speak out in prophecy, by which we mean "to give their true name to those anonymous, vague, indistinct but sincere cries to God which vibrate with the search for justice, in the need for a new and authentic morality, in the nostalgia most feel for brotherhood, in the rediscovery of family warmth, in protests against violence and in the questioning of pain and death." The prophetic cry for peace which comes from God finds its expression still more clearly in those courageous forms of witness which stem from conscience, pass over the ambiguities of the present situation and, with exemplary insight, point out a future direction. We must thank God for the gift of these prophetic testimonies. We must pray that they may become increasingly more numerous, varied and complementary.

We have, most of all, to pray that they may always have the characteristics of true prophecy: the humility of the one who does not show off but proclaims an ideal; the respectful courage of the one who is personally committed and does not pretend to impose behavior on others, recognizing indeed that other behavior is plausible; the sweetness of the one who is not concerned to accuse but rather endeavors to proclaim a good that has been revealed and given.

Finally, our prophetic commitment asks us for a profession of hope.

SEPTEMBER

September 1
The Path To Peace

One point stands out with special clarity: the road leading to peace is complicated. It is made up of successive steps and needs different and complementary efforts. Every simplification of the issue, even if it proceeds from good will and a sincere desire for peace, is dangerous and counterproductive.

I don't believe we have to insist on a simplification which fails to link peace with moral good, even in its mysterious and transcendent aspects, and limits itself to suggesting strategy, political methods or the balance of power.

At this point in time it may be more important to be on one's guard against the risk of the opposite type of simplification which does not take into account the difference between peace as a definitive value — a goal never reached in a final form on this earth — and forms of peace which from time to time are possible in terms of human coexistence.

Certain pacifist expressions which are beginning to spread in our time occasionally take on this simplistic aspect. They are characterized by generic accusations rather than by guidelines to attainable goals. Their approach invites simple discrimination between good and evil people. Their method is the abstract affirmation of ideal principles but without a patient analysis of the actual situation. Even if we can appreciate the considerable idealism at the bottom of these things we have to avoid the risks to which the lack of realism exposes us: the risk of instability, of pushing ideological positions which favor themselves, even the risk of exploitation by people needing to cover up their violence with pacifist motives. Sometimes even Christians confine themselves to affirming the value of peace as a deep need of the human heart and as a luminous evangelical concept but fail to face up to the work of giving concrete political credibility to their words on peace. They fail to point out specific stages corresponding to such down-to-earth steps toward peace as may be possible from time to time. Most of all we have to work on concrete projects for peace.

Our Christian commitment is, therefore, solicited on two fronts: that of *responsibility* towards the possible forms of peace and that of *prophecy* of that definitive peace which we expect as a gift of God and which is already foreshadowed in the increasingly complete forms of peace we are building up on earth.

September 2
Educating Consciences for the Journey Towards Peace

Can anyone continue to be indifferent in the face of the renewal of the arms race and the increasingly terrifying and costly armaments? We must not get used to a paradoxical and, frankly, to an unbearable state of things. While the greater part of humanity is short of what is necessary for a human life worthy of the name, and while a considerable number of people literally die of hunger, larger and larger financial resources are committed to manufacturing instruments of death which we sincerely hope will never be used.

The Second Vatican Council denounced the injustice not only of the eventual use of such arms but even of their manufacture and stockpiling. "Therefore we declare once again: the arms race is one of the greatest curses on the human race and the harm it inflicts on the poor is more than can be endured. Moreover there is every reason to fear that if it continues it will bring forth those lethal disasters which are already in preparation" (*Gaudium et Spes*, No. 81).

It would certainly be gullible to think that there are simple solutions to complicated problems. Yet it is possible to suggest viewpoints and, better still, to recall the necessary conditions to make them a reality. The hope is to have human coexistence so structured that conflicts between opposing parties can be peacefully resolved by recourse to decisions of higher authority analogous to what for some time has been happening internally in individual states.

A necessary condition for that purpose is a more firmly based and universally accepted ethical and cultural foundation. We need an authentic humanism, a culture founded on absolute values and capable of promoting peaceful coexistence and of rousing enthusiasm for reconciliation and for the ideal of unity between peoples. It is tragically true to say that humanity today has reached heights of scientific and technological competence but is still in its infancy so far as development of morality and wisdom is concerned.

There is no other remedy for the ominous possibilities of this imbalance. And so we have to accelerate the growth of the collective conscience through an increased commitment to the education of individual consciences.

September 3
"Help Carry One Another's Burdens" (Gal 6:2)

Each of us should be able to appreciate the burden of others. Each one ought to empathize with and understand the conditions in which others often find themselves. Nobody should withdraw from the duty of solidarity and sharing with those who are most tried. But, above all, each one should give to the maximum, according to professional circumstances, a generous and practical contribution to the solution of problems which are really everybody's and which cannot be solved in isolation.

All those taking part in public debates, in trade union or workers' meetings, should always be open to serene discussion, should know how to grasp the needs and train of thought of others and never neglect a careful evaluation of the data to be taken into consideration. They should, finally, be able to agree on practical solutions taking into account all legitimate interests involved but principally safeguarding the interests of the poorest, of those who have no voice. It is the duty of believers to be everywhere the impassioned and intelligent voice of all those people.

Actually, favoring solidarity in no way means failing in efficiency or in the rules of a healthy economy but means recognizing the common good in every phase of each individual decision-making process. This is supplemented by the conviction that every decision, especially in the economic, social and political fields, in one way or another involves human beings with their problems, their yearnings and their dignity which has to be universally respected and promoted.

Favoring solidarity is a duty which in the first place concerns Christian communities internally. They must personally live experiences of charity and service in imitation of the primitive Church as testified by the Acts of the Apostles.

People involved in a crisis and sometimes paying a big price for it live within the boundaries of every single parish. We have, for example, young people looking for work, families in extremely precarious and financially insecure situations, who may well lack even essentials, old people feeling marginalized before their time and the handicapped feeling that they are locked out.

These situations have psychological and moral repercussions and consequences which leave a mark on individual and family life. These people need community support and, to some extent, they have a right to it. It would, in any case, be a serious fault if our communities were not aware of these people's existence and did not feel united to them. Sometimes urgent financial aid may be absolutely indispensable but a profound comprehension will always be required to enable us to share in their problems in a practical, common search for a solution.

Nor should we neglect the duty of each member of the parish community to conduct a searching, personal examination regarding lifestyle, attitudes and eventual co-responsibilities for a situation which raises questions for all of us.

The Life of Jesus Shows Us the Meaning of Work

"The interior effort of the human spirit, guided by faith, hope and charity, is needed to give work the meaning which it has in the eyes of God" (*Laborem Exercens*, No. 24). In the final analysis this meaning is revealed to us in the life of Jesus.

As a human being Who — though the practical details of His human existence were exactly like our own — is also the Only Begotten Son, the Eternal Word of the Father, the first and incomprehensible reason for the communion between God and humankind, Christ is the meaning, the hope and the truth of human life.

The fact that work had a place in Jesus' life and such an important and lasting place, shows that it is also a stage from which we must move if we are to understand the message of Jesus of Nazareth; it is a piece of that mosaic making up the Gospel. At the same time it is an experience whose meaning is fully understood because we begin with the reality of Jesus Christ.

The original plan of God is shown in its fullness in Jesus. In Him, work appears as a "fundamental dimension of human existence on earth." When human beings work they "reflect the very action of the Creator of the Universe," and each person becomes fully his or her self as the image of God to the extent that they put into effect "dominion over the visible world" (cf. *Laborem Exercens*, No. 4). Through the action of transforming this visible world, people experience their character as a "gift" and recognize their relationship of dependence on God and the reciprocal dependence on other people as traits which define their essential identity.

Jesus' Resurrection and the expectation of eschatological completion reveal that human salvation and its full actualization — though requiring the total commitment of human freedom — remains a gift of God, a work of His gratuitous love to be accepted in faith and hope. And, as the Second Vatican Council told us: ". . . the expectancy of a new earth should spur us on for it is here that the body of a new human family grows, foreshadowing in some way the age which is to come" (*Gaudium et Spes*, No. 39).

But it is still true that the Kingdom of God is not a human work. Work, too, belongs to the order of penultimate realities. It does not tell us everything about the meaning of human existence. And so human work, too, not only calls for rest every "seventh day" but must leave an interior space in which human beings — as they increasingly grow towards what, by the will of God, they should be — prepare for that "rest" which the Lord reserves for His servants and friends.

September 5
Reflections and Warnings on the Crisis in the World of Work

Faced with social tensions which risk getting more complicated to the point of producing feelings of exasperation or, worse, skeptical and distrustful attitudes, the Church plays its part in the way proper to it. Beginning from its reflection on the word of God and from prayer, it promotes solidarity in behavior and action not only with those who suffer but also with all those who act efficaciously to overcome the crisis and fight against its causes.

We are aware of the fact that the crisis affects pretty

nearly everyone. In the first place it affects those who are financially and socially weaker and who have no guarantees or protection. But it also extends to "people on whom weighs the grave responsibility of decisions destined to have wide social repercussions." And so each one is stimulated to evaluate the burden of others. Those who take part in public debates, in trade union or workers' meetings, are to be helped to become aware of problems, to evaluate data objectively and to be able to agree on practical solutions. Waste and luxury are no longer acceptable in the lifestyles of those who are barely even aware of the meaning of the crisis we are going through.

Those who organize the labor black market, which all too often is superficially tolerated, in reality hinder other more efficacious reforms in the organization of work itself. The person who evades taxes must ask themself serious questions and become convinced that this is not the way to work for the solution of problems about whose gravity we all complain.

In addition, it seems to us especially necessary to have input from the reflection and study of those who have the task of following the evolution of the economic situation: universities, research institutes, the study departments of the various trade union organizations, political parties and organs of government.

We sincerely hope that this commitment does not fail to take into consideration the stimulus which is offered on this point by the Church's social magisterium.

The current commitment towards those who are victims of the failures of the system to guarantee dignified and stable work to all, will be joined to trade union and group commitments and to political and professional efforts. Each one should act so that one's social group is not turned into a corporation preoccupied merely to defend its own interests.

September 6
The Role of Christian Workers in the Unemployment Crisis

I think that the role of Christian workers, whatever their particular relationship, close or not, to the trade union world, is to attentively discern and to demonstrate liberty and creativity in analyzing the current historical phase of the trade union movement. Certainly it is a phase requiring the ability to review ideological and social basics, to review structures and strategies and above all to review objectives and relationships with other social forces.

It is not an easy task. But it is still urgently needed because the trade union as an expression of solidarity between workers and as an exemplar of justice and humanity in the work organization, cannot fail itself nor can it leave the new proletariat to its fate. So Christian workers must commit themselves to a serious reflection, aimed at creating a climate of fundamental serenity, a climate marked by constructive relationships. Christian workers must give witness of reconciliation in the fruitful sense of the word, of creativity and of a search for formulae fit to interpret and service the cause of the one working.

Christian workers must contribute to free the air of ideologies which do not support the cause of justice and of human advancement. This involves taking into serious consideration, for example, the measures necessary to encourage the development of work and especially of work for young people. It involves accepting, if required, the renunciation of closed trades in favor of those who have no protection. It means also promoting trade union action which will give evidence in its suggestions of a profound change of mentality and of approach.

Such a change cannot but emerge from true conversion of the heart guided and supported by an ethical and spiritual vision which is hard on oneself but open and generous towards others.

In this special moment we cannot fail to think a great deal of trade union representatives, of those who have responsible positions in the trade union movement and especially of those who have fought and are fighting in the trade union itself. We are close to those who in trade unions have found opportunities to testify to their faith and Christian solidarity and we hope that they may always be able to draw from reflection and prayer the force and clarity of judgment required today.

September 7
Work and Christian Communities

Every day we hear news of new dismissals and of record-breaking payments to the unemployed. Our communities cannot remain aloof from these problem situations. Actually, many workers who are also our people are living through the drama of these social processes.

We are thinking, for example, of the many, many older workers who have contributed with fatigue and sometimes with damage to their health, to the progress of our industrial society and who now seem to be discriminated against and compelled to pay the price of this social crisis. This is often true especially of them.

The Christian community, animated and oriented by the Gospel, cannot dispense itself from its duty of solidarity and justice. Sometimes, actually, the Christian community itself is not free of a certain "hardness of heart" when it fails to face up to these problems and reduces its pastoral programs to more gratifying stages and sectors.

On the contrary, the Christian community located in this time and in this bit of history called "the crisis of industrial society," is invited to be in harmony with that situation, weaving together Word and history so as to bring the Good News to today's people. We are not talking about naive illusions about approaching the masses, but of learning to put ourselves in the biblical logic of "preaching at Nineveh" like the prophet Jonah and of finding the correct place of service in a society which has the right and the desire to be evangelized — not to talk of the need.

I would indicate four practical courses of action to channel the commitment of every local Christian community.

1. Communicating faith in the family, in groups, in the areas of community commitment. We have the duty of speaking out, of "preaching from the rooftops." Sufficient listening and contemplation so as to assimilate a substantial message which we will communicate is taken for granted. And it requires that we find a language understandable by the people.

2. Having the ability to express — in the light of the Word, of the social magisterium and in dialogue with other people of good will — a critical judgment on the most significant aspects of this time of ours, with courage and with constructive intent, going beyond purely

economical criteria and bringing attention back again to the moral component of the problem. This is a way to work for hope for everyone and in particular for many isolated categories of workers.

3. The witness of practical action based on the principle of "beginning with the poorest." Christian communities should ask themselves

— who, in reality, are "the poorest" in the context of their social makeup;

— what causes have provoked this situation of crisis of divisions, of failure to share, or of marginalization;

— what style of pastoral acceptance should characterize their choices.

4. Prepare more lively and willing lay people through an adequate formation.

September 8
The Joy of Having a Mother

No authentic text of Sacred Scripture tells us directly of Mary's nativity. This very ancient Feast is born of the Church's own filial love for its mother. It marks the beginning of the liturgical year in the Eastern Church and for our Church in Milan it marks, together with the patronal Feast of the Cathedral, the beginning of the pastoral year.

Thus the whole Eastern and Western Church lovingly celebrates this solemnity just as children celebrate their mother's birthday, even though they may have no exact idea of the circumstances and conditions of her birth and infancy. One might say that when we celebrate our mother's birthday, we are not drawing attention to a particular circumstance but to the fact that she is our mother, to the wonder of the fact that there is a mother and that there is *this* mother through whom the divine design became real for us.

This is why the Church exults with joy at the thought that it has a mother and that it has *this* mother. As the Scripture texts tell us, Mary is the one who made Jesus part of a people. From Abraham through David and through the long genealogy of Jesus' ancestors, she made Him part of a people, of a tribe and in the context of a real little place in Israel (Bethlehem). She placed Him in a specific set of surroundings. She made God human, so to speak, and incarnated Him in time.

The divine design (which, according to the Letter of St. Paul to the Romans, is expressed in five great "transcendental" stages — awareness, predestination, call, justification and glorification — which cover everyone destined to share in the design) becomes a detailed and precise reality, assumes a local color and geography. It becomes part of a certain culture and is expressed within precise historical limits.

We might say that, through Mary, the divine design passes from the abstract to the concrete.

September 9
God's Gratuitous Gift

It may seem that there is no need of the genealogy in the first chapter of Matthew's Gospel (1:1-16) just to prove that the Messiah comes from Abraham and David. But through this long series of names, we are reminded of the whole ancient Israelite tradition. It is a story of great and glorious ancestors with celebrated names such as David, Solomon, Jacob and Isaac. It is also a wretched, painful and humiliating story with names of failed kings and queens. It is simultaneously glorious and miserable. And Jesus is associated with it.

The Messiah and our salvation come from a great story and from a simple and humble one. We ask ourselves how this might help us grasp the meaning of the Feast of the Nativity of Mary which we are commemorating.

What is it here that we are celebrating? What is Mary's personal and free gesture? We are not celebrating today any particular action on the part of Mary but are considering her passivity, her being generated, her birth in the love of God and in the love of her parents with the simplicity which has nothing and receives everything.

The birth of Mary is a totally gratuitous event. It is a pure and radical act of receiving. This infant, this little girl called Mary, does not accomplish any personal work but is simply destined to be the object of the work of God. From this point on, all of Mary's actions will have her personal, courageous and definitive commitments, their own origin and consistency.

The birth of the Madonna prefigures in a meaningful way the approach Mary will consciously cultivate for her entire life: her total dependence on God's action, on His initiative and on His love. "Behold the handmaid of the Lord. Be it done to me as you say." Only God is great. The life of Mary, seen from this vantage point of her birth, appears to us as the triumph of God's free initiative, of what the Scripture calls the divine "hesed" — a nearly untranslatable Hebrew word meaning the initiative of tenderness, of compassion and of love through which

352   SEPTEMBER

God bends down over men and women and in pure love calls them to a mysterious alliance with Him.

September 10
Guidelines for Christian Commitment Today: Reconciliation

We must be alert to the challenges of history today. Let me sum up my guidelines in four words which, while they refer to the needs of society today, seem to me to be in harmony with the direction proposed by the Italian Church: reconciliation, marginalization, institution and education.

Reconciliation is a need of today's society which is full of energy, riches, potential and unresolved tensions but which has no unified image of humanity to prevent these riches from becoming dissipated and turned against humanity itself. Besides, this lack of a patrimony of human values produces incurable divisions and conflicts which unfortunately have always existed among people. If there is some common ground, one can always use this to overcome division. If, however, common points of reference are missing, opposing viewpoints risk running wild and contrasts cannot be resolved.

Our society needs people of peace and dialogue. We have to agree once more on some essential values: human dignity, human life and liberty, family relationships, human work. If statements of principle are to become increasingly evident and effective rather than useless discourses, these values will have to be factually lived, defended and cultivated through a series of moral commitments, through a search for the real good of humanity and through the abandonment of every form of egoism and exploitation of others. These values, born in the conscience and in the ethical life of each person, should become a common way of thinking, should become social custom and civil law. And, as this work of reconciliation has to do with victory over egoisms and exploitation, one sees its connection with the Christian Gospel which announces the real, efficacious victory of God's pardon over mankind's sin.

September 11
Guidelines for Christian Commitment Today: To the Marginalized

Reconciliation must be particularly attentive to those who are more likely to be overlooked, marginalized and abandoned. This explains our commitment against the different forms of marginalization, ranging from those which are an inevitable concomitant of human life to those which are typical of our own society. It becomes an urgent Christian duty to help each individual communicate with others and find — or rediscover — a place in society.

Reconciliation and commitment to the *marginalized* must also find its expression in public policy. Each human life is bound up with the lives of others in society and depends on the organisms and institutions which regulate social living. When diffidence, separation or contradiction between private life and public institution becomes hardened, social life is threatened. A lay commitment typical of our times might be to promote an intense social initiative born of freedom, of free association and of core

354

communities. At the same time it should question public institutions, get them to intervene, offer them concrete examples of scholastic, educative, cultural and rehabilitative initiatives which may be further extended and consolidated.

These few remarks lead us to think that such a commitment cannot be amateurish. We need educative action in the family and in the community. Christian institutions which have a meaningful experience of lay commitment should offer families and parishes, those places, instruments and stimulating programs where young people can be trained in forms of lay commitment in proportion to the enormous needs of today's society. These are increasingly capable of channeling the marvelous energies of generosity, missionary zeal and voluntary dedication found in young people.

September 12
Attention To Our Handicapped

Our commitment to making each person's life more and more human on the basis of its absolute dignity deriving directly from God, leads us to talk of those brothers and sisters of ours who encounter special problems in cultivating the physical, psychical and social qualities of their lives.

To them and first of all, Christian faith says to seek the Kingdom of God with intensity and joy.

The difficulties they endure in their physical and emotional life do not distance them from the Kingdom. Indeed, they are its privileged recipients. They are its closest and most loved children. They are those poor, those meek ones, those who weep, for whom the

Beatitudes proclaimed by Jesus have a particular value.

A Christian community, truly and profoundly open to the Kingdom of God, must cultivate these consoling certainties within itself and must proclaim them with its behavior. This means, first of all, trying to grasp in the light of faith, the meaning that fatigue, handicaps and suffering have on the way to the Kingdom.

It also means to translate, to show forth, to actualize, the call of the handicapped to the Kingdom by rediscovering their place in the Church, by recognizing their charisms and by renewing our pastoral action to make it truly take into account the needs and riches of these brothers and sisters of ours.

It means making a place for them in our churches and meeting places — including a physical place — by facilitating their access through technical means. This calls for intelligence and creativity.

But can these facilities ever be better utilized than for the service and joy of these brothers and sisters of ours?

I would like to remind you today of our commitment to improve our neighbor's quality of life. Because we believe in the Kingdom of God we have to commit ourselves to showing the ''signs'' of the Kingdom. Because we believe that the life of every brother and sister has the dignity of being loved by God, we must honor this dignity, cultivating if possible all those characteristics and gifts which allow each person to live a serene, free and dignified life.

I would like to add that these efforts towards socialization, rehabilitation, and human communication, by which we continue to improve the quality of life for each of our brothers and sisters, will be all the more effective the more they are founded on a deep faith in the Kingdom.

It is this faith which, on the one hand, offers an indisputable and peremptory motivation to all efforts favoring the handicapped while, on the other hand, helping us not be discouraged by the occasionally insurmountable limits experienced in our efforts towards socialization, rehabilitation and communication. It is this faith in the Kingdom which raises up great Christian vocations, guaranteeing that free, courageous and inspired human service without which laws, institutions and social work for the handicapped risk being ineffective.

I want to mention in particular the vocation of the Christian family and of special consecration.

A family which avoids introspection (as if it were itself an absolute value) but sees itself as a sacrament, an image, a sign of the Kingdom is able to give its daily life that openness, that availability and that creativity which find the appropriate solutions even to the most difficult cases.

I want to encourage families with handicapped children to be united among themselves and with other generous and willing families so as to find intelligent and prophetic solutions for many cases which otherwise would become unsolvable.

And then, as a support for the family, other helps are needed, and those who have received from God the call to leave aside family life so as to witness prophetically to the values of the Kingdom, have a particular predisposition for this.

September 13
The Drama of the Mentally Ill

We come up again, in a dramatic way, against the problem of the presence in our midst of mentally ill people and of their care and treatment. For some time and from different directions, especially from suffering families, the bishop has come to hear complaints and appeals for a more responsible, objective and concrete consideration of the grave situation in which these brethren of ours find themselves.

The gradual transformation of psychiatric care in our day and age suffers on the one hand from serious delays and defects hindering the correct application of the valid and innovative outlines inspiring it, and, on the other hand, throws light on some of its controversial and debatable aspects. And so the process is concluded by unloading on families the crushing burden of difficult situations which, in the long run, are unbearable.

A common commitment is urgently needed to tackle with clarity and decisiveness problems which touch so deeply the human dignity of many people and the serenity of many unfortunate families. A society cannot be called truly modern and civilized if it fails to create the possibilities for a correct application of therapeutic, caring and rehabilitative work in a way which may be hard but not impractical.

We are not talking of going backwards towards out-of-date and no longer acceptable solutions. But neither can we get bogged down in ideological schemes, forgetting the living reality of actual suffering people. Rather, we need an effort on the part of all of those responsible to apply themselves creatively. As soon as possible we must provide all the support and medical care structures in the area foreseen by the reform. And, at the same time, we need to rethink courageously anything which has shown itself, on the basis of experience, to be contradictory or inefficient, and we need to work together to find more adequate solutions.

The decisive criterion for every choice must be that of attention to the sick person and of co-responsible family participation, suitably guided and supported. We must also have unity between the total social body and its institutions with a view to obtaining the greatest and most useful social integration.

I address a warm appeal to all those responsible for administrative and health structures to keep these delicate problems at the center of their concerns and I ask them to appreciate and encourage the existing reflections and projects.

But especially I ask the Christians of our community to have an attitude of more shared and factual attention to the drama of many families living in our midst, so that through their dedication, their friendship and their ability simultaneously to suffer and to hope, the mystery of the healing and consoling Jesus may become increasingly and concretely present among today's people.

September 14
The Cross: Mystery of Reconciliation

When the subject of reconciliation comes up, we immediately feel questions and opposition both within ourselves and from outside us. But what does to be reconciled mean? Why be reconciled and with whom? The reconciliation of whom?

That is why we contemplate Jesus' cross and ask Him to help us understand what reconciliation between people and God means. In his Letter to the Romans, St. Paul writes: ''We were reconciled to God by the death of His Son'' (5:10). And yet, even if we try to clarify with these words the meaning of reconciliation and its relationship to the death and Resurrection of Jesus, we still ask ourselves: why is there reconciliation in this death, in this cross, in this torture of the Son of God?

Guided by Scripture and contemplating the cross, we have to learn to see with the eyes of faith in the crucified Jesus, the obedient Son, the Son of God, true God and true man, who makes real in this situation a very distinctive relationship of obedience to the God of the patriarchs Who is His Father.

In the mystery of His passion and death, Jesus lives an obedience to God with a trust and an abandon which does not fail no matter what contradiction He meets on the part of those who are not His Father. All may be against Him and yet He goes straight ahead in fidelity to His mission.

The attitude characterizing the figure of the Crucified One is real, filial obedience right to the end in an abandonment of self to the Father in carrying out the mission received. And so we are taught how to fulfill ourselves as people before God, how to enter into Jesus' death and Resurrection, to be fully reconciled to God and so to become sowers of peace and reconciliation.

That is the clear, exacting and cutting message born from the cross of Jesus with regard to reconciliation: not easy-going agreements, not patching up flawed relationships at any cost, not closing our eyes to human failings, not ignoring the past, but rather deepening our understanding of the death of Jesus through the mystery of His obedience and fidelity to His Father.

September 15
Jesus' Words in His Passion and Our Reconciliation

Contemplating Jesus crucified in His role as obedient Son of the Father, we can get some help, too, from some words of His pronounced during His terrible passion.

"Father, everything is possible for You. Take this cup away from me. But let it be as You, not I, would have it" (Mk 14:36). These are the words Jesus pronounced in Gethsemane as He really began His passion and they express the prayer of obedience even before the radical risk of death. Jesus trembles, suffers loneliness, sweats blood, feels fear and repugnance, lives an extremely real and painful experience but still entrusts Himself totally to His Father. "Let it be as You, not I, would have it." In this mystery of obedience, of which we catch a glimpse but do not grasp in its very depths, we have an insight into what it means to be Son of God, to entrust oneself to Him and to bring mankind with oneself on the path of reconciliation with the Father.

There are also some words of Jesus on the cross which repeat the same theme and show us the identical radical approach of the Son of God's obedience before His Father. The first word is directly related to reconciliation at the human and social level: "Father, forgive them; they do not know what they are doing" (Lk 23:34). It is not an easy-going attitude, condoning, condescending or closing one's eyes before an irreparable evil. On the contrary, it is the attitude of the Son Who lives in communion with the Father's mercy and Who expresses His pardon as a colloquy and a prayer with the Father to Whom He has entrusted Himself with His own life and the life of His brothers and sisters, including those who have made a mistake and have harassed Him.

It would be interesting to reflect some more on the final word of Jesus, that one which appears to contradict trust and hope and which Luke does not mention, perhaps considering it too difficult to be understood. We read it in Matthew 27:46 and in Mark 14:34: "My God, my God, why have You deserted me?" We have here all the drama of what Jesus is going through on the cross. It is a disconcerting struggle between life and death, between light and darkness, between hope and desperation, between reconciliation and the wall of hatred. Jesus lives this struggle and carries it on to the last bodily spasm.

"My God, my God, why have You deserted me?" We know that these are the words with which Psalm 21 begins, the psalm of the Just One who fails to understand the meaning of what is happening to him and complains to God: from what I can see it would appear that You are no longer with me, that You are no longer on my side.

This prayer of the psalm which Jesus makes His own is an affectionate lament, not a contestation of God. It is a lament within the context of a trust which admits one's inability to understand what is happening. All possibilities have failed, the individual is trapped and there is no way out. So he prays: "My God, my God, why have you deserted me?" It is a new way, though more dramatic and mysterious, to make us feel the closeness Jesus, as a Son, has with the Father. This nearness, however is crossed by a wall, by the solidarity of Jesus with the sinner, by Jesus sharing in the situation of someone who, in his or her sin, feels far from God.

September 16
"Today You Will Be With Me"

Similarly, the words Jesus spoke to the thief on His right: ''This day you will be with Me in Paradise'' (Lk 23:43) refer us to a human mystery of reconciliation and begin, consistently, from His great abandonment and unlimited trust in His Father. Jesus is certain that He will drink the new wine in the Kingdom of His Father. He is certain to enter into the Father's Kingdom. And this hopeful attitude allows Him to involve a condemned man, an outcast of society, and make him part of His dedication.

Just as the Father has prepared a Kingdom for Him, so the Son prepares one for His own and the first among these is a criminal. Jesus reconciles him with the Father not with an easy pardon, not closing His eyes on the criminal's transgressions, but rather absorbing them into the power of His salvific and merciful love.

Reading about the Crucified One and contemplating Him, shows us Jesus' filial trust, hope and mercy. All of these are attitudes in which He involves people, beginning from those closest to Him and expresses the power of reconciliation in the immediate actuation of what His death on the cross implies and not just in symbol or generic promise.

September 17
Education For Old Age

The Third, and so-called Golden, Age is really a serious point of human existence. We are confronted with a most fundamental problem in human life, one which was unforgettably stated by Qoheleth in the final chapter of his Book of Ecclesiastes where he says: "Remember your Creator in the days of your youth, before evil days come and the years approach when you say, 'These give me no pleasure' " (12:1). The serious situation of growing old is expressed very strongly in this biblical text. The experience involved is not the same as just years passing by, but it rather consists in the drama which each of us lives or will live because of weakening physical and psychical energies due to the multiplication of impediments and ailments which lead to a situation of profound suffering which is often difficult to share with others.

From a certain point of view, this drama cannot be resolved unless we begin with the human person. There is no health care — the Swedish type, for example — which will impede the sense of desperation common to the elderly. A human being, on the contrary, is called to be reborn internally through those perennial and definitive values which allow one to overcome the repugnance and suffering deriving from the failure of temporal values. Nobody escapes this — apart from those who die young.

For this reason, we must insist on the only basic and infallible solution. And by this we mean the ability to rethink one's life, seeing the commitments and values of a permanent and definitive character as more important than things which fail whether we like it or not. We know well that companionship or abundance of wealth cannot replace fundamental solutions. In fact, it is noteworthy that there are not many cases of old people's suicides due to lack of financial resources. For the most part the motives leading to the drama of suicide are the inability to express oneself, not because there is nobody around but because company becomes distasteful and unbearable or

364

because one feels that they are a burden to others.

And so, correctly, we face up to the power of this human trial by an approach which is adequate as far as our own interior energy goes.

Together with what so far has been classified as basic, we can usefully find a place for what can be done externally, to support and comfort financially and through friendship, people's reassessment of their situation. They must be helped to understand that they can rehabilitate themselves although, inevitably, losing some ability in terms of efficiency. Values of knowledge and wisdom are permanent. Interior life is without end. When these perspectives of conscience have been recovered, we have to say that everything else that can be done for the benefit of the daily life of the elderly is to be seen as necessary and a duty. Indeed, it is one of the fundamental duties of the Christian community. An education as to how to live this Golden Age well must begin early in life. We are talking about training people about their biological limits and so about the prevalence of certain values and the diminution of others.

This education may lead to acquiring an awareness matured in wisdom and in one's way of acting towards others, largely because one changes one's personal way of behaving. Only in the context of such an education do provisions for the old cease to be condescending and become the sign of an all-embracing attention, full of love and realism and capable of speaking about fundamentals. We are well aware that these basics are often avoided because nobody wants to go to the heart of the question. As a result, the individual in question is not satisfied and he or she complains a great deal. Actually, the complaints of the elderly mean that the person's fundamental drama has not been understood even if there are repeated complaints about problems of method and form.

We must have the courage to help people in substantial terms and this is extremely difficult. Harsh words are no use, but neither are unrealistic ones. We must find, between these extremes, the opportunity for a word suggested by charity touching delicately on the crucial point and helping the person involved to breathe more easily because he or she feels understood in an almost incommunicable drama. This drama is like that of Jesus in Gethsemane, placed decisively, as He was, face to face with the formidable coordinates of His destiny.

September 18
Honor Your Father and Your Mother

The Bible exhorts us in these words: "My son, support your father in his old age, do not grieve him during his life. Even if his mind should fail, show him sympathy; do not despise him in your health and strength, for kindness to a father shall not be forgotten" (Ec 3:12-14).

And so the Bible challenges our society, and us in particular, to put first among our preoccupations attention, respect and service to the elderly — above all to the sick, to those who cannot help themselves and to the saddest cases, those who are alone. This service is the expression of a commandment as old as society itself. And when this commandment is observed, society is healthy, whereas a society which abandons its elderly is decadent.

This is the invitation coming to us from our own local traditions and, still more, from the very revelation of

God which shows one's duty towards one's father and mother especially when they are old and the duty of society as a whole towards those who are abandoned or alone.

This service — we know it very well — implies many problems: problems which become all the more grave the more complex society becomes and the more this service becomes technically exact but also more troublesome and inhumane, sometimes exposing individuals to unnecessary red tape and suffering. I know that there are many reasons for not resolving these difficulties more quickly, ranging from finances to organization as well as to other, broader reasons which more directly touch general political realities.

In a way, it is normal that this should happen in our society, that these difficulties should arise and that they should also cause hard problems every day. This is because pain, physical and moral sufferings and sometimes delusions and frustrations are concentrated in later years. Often we may also have the most painful evil: the danger of a loss of hope. And this requires particular qualities of dedication, of love and of help and so causes considerable weariness as one works to keep this hope from failing.

But in all of this the fundamental needs and interests of the old must prevail, beyond all the problems, conflicts and difficulties, and this in an extensive and marked way. No personal interest, no personal or group problem can override the principal purpose: the interests of the elderly, love for them and care for them. All other realities relating to this center acquire a sense of reasonableness, value and gravity to the extent that they reveal realistic goals as well as the means for attaining them.

May the Lord assist us so that all that our society does to help the elderly may truly better their health and well-being, both moral and spiritual. May it comfort them in their loneliness so that we may be spared the biblical judgment: "Cursed be the one who forgets his father and mother." Rather may we come to enjoy the biblical blessing: "Honor your father and mother that you may have long life in the land the Lord has given you."

September 19
Towards Prophetic Volunteer Work

I should like to offer some specific points for our reflection in this regard. First of all, we must pay constant attention to real needs. There is a danger that some initiatives which were started to deal with certain necessities may gradually tend to feed on themselves and to self-preservation instead of being open to new necessities and to self-transformation and modification. An open, frank dialogue between volunteer workers will always help them face up to real needs.

In addition, we have to take great care of the formation through which volunteer workers acquire the fundamental motivations, the personal attitudes, and the operational capacities which can stand up to fatigue and delusion and make the one concerned flexible and versatile in discovering the latest needs.

Christian faith and charity offer an exceptional formative basis. Nor should we fear the risk of rigidity. A person who has learned to know human nature deeply in the light of faith and to love it in the perspective of charity, knows how to appreciate all forms of honest commitment to people and also how to collaborate with people of differing religious and cultural backgrounds. Such a person is able to be diplomatically serene in a pluralistic society in the name of those fundamental human values which acquire a greater light in the vision of faith though they are also found in every honest and open heart.

Cultivating basic attitudes of personal dedication, of self-giving and of creativity, the volunteer worker finds inspiration in those prophetic vocations which the Spirit raises up in the Christian community and which urge some people to the total gift of their life in the service of the Lord and of their brethren.

The beneficial multiplication of various forms of voluntary service in the Christian community should not become an alternative to the great vocational choices. Indeed, it should lead to those choices and at the same time receive new energy and new impulse from them.

September 20
The Christian Community and the Volunteer Worker

The prophetic liveliness of voluntary service is also dependent on the Christian community's way of looking at things. Here again I will confine myself to some examples:

a) We have to cultivate in our communities a new awareness of the place the service of charity has in the overall pastoral action. This awareness leads to an appreciation of the volunteer's prophetic action and also gives the volunteer continuous and clear Christian motives while at the same time generating a "volunteer sensitivity" in whoever is not formally committed to an official volunteer service but who can, and must, always be a "volunteer" in their normal daily life and activity.

b) Dioceses and parishes through the mobilization of their members and through suitable organizational instruments must put themselves in a position of being able to discover the real needs of the people living in their territory.

Some needs can be attended to by the communities themselves. Other, more complicated ones, should be brought to the attention of better-equipped groups. Others still, not already being handled by existing initiatives, will require the response of pioneering methods. In this way, Christian communities will help the various types of volunteer work avoid dealing with imaginary needs or casual ones while concentrating on the more urgent real cases.

c) The diocese and parishes must also give the volunteer worker the formation methods and the structures for a constructive linkage, i.e. volunteers must compare notes, must come together in groups and must have at least a minimum of organization. ''Caritas'' — at the national, diocesan and parochial levels — could be a valuable point of reference for formation and linkage.

d) Finally, Christian communities can evaluate the role of volunteers in their educative and vocational task. Even though volunteer work embraces all ages, it is evidently of particular interest to youth with its greater availability, psychologically and age wise.

As they guide young people in their vocational choices, Christian communities can find in every type of volunteer work — but especially in that organized in view of social service — an exceptional pedagogical instrument which, while meeting real society needs, trains young people to enter life in a generous and responsible way.

Some phenomena which are becoming more of a

370   SEPTEMBER

reality, such as the increased requests to be allowed to do public service or the proposal for a year of volunteer work open one's heart to hope. We must begin with these practical examples so as to find many new ways of inviting young people to develop a "volunteer" mentality in their outlook and in practical life, rather than to be forced into some kind of youth work or reduced to a state of sterile pessimism. This may prove to be the true redemption and the liberation of the contemporary situation of our restless youth.

September 21
Absence From God

Chapter Three of Genesis offers us a biblical extract featuring a concise dialogue between God and mankind, a dialogue which reveals the confusion, the darkness and the shame of human sin. The Lord speaks four times, and His first three comments are specific questions: "Where are you?" "Who told you that you are naked?" "What have you done?" These three peremptory questions are followed by a tremendous prophecy, showing a state of enmity and of division at the heart of human experience and of history.

The people involved reply three times to God's four words, in a timid, uncertain, reticent and partially untrue way. Adam says: "I was afraid," afraid of God. And he thus admits to a falsified relationship with God in Whom he is no longer able to see the Father, the Merciful One, and Whose countenance he no longer discerns.

Then he adds, accusing Eve: "The woman You gave me, whom You put beside me, gave me the fruit from the tree and I ate it." Here he admits his irresponsible relationship with the woman, with his life companion, off-loading on her the guilt which was pricking his own conscience.

For her part, the woman replies out of fear and in a state of confusion: "The serpent deceived me." Eve admits an irresponsible relationship with herself, with her personal guilt, with the clarity of her responsibility.

The sum of the three replies underlines the division, the darkness, the tendency to shift the blame from one to the other, the fear, the uncertainty which human beings suffer when in the state of sin, in the state of being far from God.

In the three timid, confused and deceptive replies which mankind gives to God, we find that, really, the only adequate response we might have expected on this occasion is missing: that reply which has to struggle to come to human lips because we have lost sight of the face of God. It is the simple reply of David: "(I have) sinned against none other than You . . . my God. Create a clean heart in me; put into me a new and constant spirit" (Ps 50).

September 22
Reconciliation is Difficult, Still God Reconciles Us

Is a real reconciliation between peoples possible today? Are we not over-supplied with words on these issues? Appeals for peace are repeated unceasingly. Sometimes it is difficult to vary our language and so we run the risk of making ourselves ridiculous, as if all that is needed to make something happen is big words! There is even a Gospel parable which confirms this. It is the

Parable of the Prodigal Son which we normally explain as a parable about reconciliation.

The young man in the story, who left his father's house for a distant land and unknown future where he wasted all his goods, returns and is embraced by his father. This is undoubtedly one of the most beautiful pictures in all of literature about reconciliation. But often we forget to comment on the lines immediately following: peace between the father and the prodigal son has caused new divisions in the family because the other son was so angered by it. We don't have any idea how successfully the great banquet — which was prepared with so much care and joy — turned out. In this parable, the father was unable to avoid creating a new family disagreement through his reconciling action. And for this reason I see this as a striking example of just how difficult these themes are.

But at this point the biblical word gets to us. And powerfully! It is the Apostle's exhortation: "Be reconciled to God" (2 Cor 5:20). If we read this in the context of the guilty and unsettling feeling which all those words inviting us to reunion and reconciliation cause us, then the words of St. Paul about perfect peace — something which we are unable to establish even among people of the same faith — strike us as paradoxical.

We have to accept the paradoxical power of this word, though! Why does Paul not say: be reconciled to one another, love one another, be perfect brothers to one another, instead of "Be reconciled to God"? It seems perfectly clear to me that the paradoxical quality of this expression lies in the fact that, going beyond our fatigue and the near impossibility of finding lasting forms of reconciliation, it proclaims the necessity and the primacy of being reconciled to God.

Saving Love

"Joseph wept at the message they sent to him" (Gn 50:17). This scene describes the peak of commotion. *Why* did Joseph burst out weeping? Joseph is the beloved son of Jacob, envied by his brothers, betrayed and condemned to death, then sold to the slave merchants and subsequently taken to Egypt. But Joseph accepts with open arms the brothers who had done him so much harm.

"I am a big-hearted man," Joseph said, "able to pardon and not bear grudges. And you are the people who must believe in my ability to pardon." However a doubt arises, which questions Joseph's reply. The brothers do not believe that Joseph has pardoned them. They do not entirely trust him. They do not believe that someone can truly and totally pardon when so much harm has been done to that person. For this reason they become uneasy as soon as their father dies, are afraid and want to make Joseph believe that their father said: "Pardon the crime of your brothers and their sin." Joseph weeps because he feels misunderstood, because his brothers do not believe him and do not trust him.

Our feelings towards Jesus are similar. Every time we feel lazy and depressed we have the impression that God Himself cannot count on us any longer! We have disappointed Him and we think that, through our fault, our relationship with Him is irreparably broken. Instinctively, we form an idea of Jesus as a person who understands us but who eventually gets tired of us just as we get tired of ourselves.

This means that we do not know the Lord, do not trust Him, have not grasped Who He is. If we did, we would be, as the Genesis story allows us to see, full of consolation and joy: "He reassured them with words that touched their hearts" (Gn 50:21). To understand Who the Lord is, to succeed in making a true act of awareness of Him, means feeling that we are appreciated by Him for what we are and also valued for what we can become. And so this twofold awareness is extremely important: that I may know myself and that I may know God and be aware that I am known by Him. It is the root of everything. When this awareness is flawed, what happened to Joseph's brothers happens to us: we are gripped by fear and awe, by suspicions and anxiety. We suspect Jesus, we suspect others and we suspect the Church.

September 24
Reconciliation Should Be Proposed To All

There cannot be lasting social and political peace and reconciliation which is also stable and universal if there is not conversion of the heart.

And, from the other point of view, there is no true, authentic conversion of heart without social and political repercussions. Thus the reality and duty proper to the Church and the universal repercussions of this reality are clear.

Here we have many things the Holy Spirit invites us to do. I will point out at least some of them.

I am thinking of the community of ex drug addicts. I am thinking most of all of the prisoners. I am speaking of prisoners rather than of prisons, so as to draw attention to people, an attention whose final purpose must be reconciliation and the complete assumption of one's role in society once more.

We can also use the word rehabilitation or, in Christian language, conversion. But the final goal is full reconciliation beginning from the consideration of personal dignity.

Reconciliation should be proposed to all and to all the forms of wrong-doing from the commonplace forms to those of terrorism. It should be proposed to the repentant and to the disenfranchised. It should be proposed to each of the powers involved in this complicated and dramatic reality, until we come to the innocent ones (and there are such!), to the depressed, to those who are degraded by an overly long detention prior to trial and incarceration.

Naturally, the field is extremely large and our interest has to begin from a Eucharistic point of view and from a glance at the model of society which is born of the Eucharist. It will then take its place in the thrust of all realities linked to the struggle against forms of wrong-doing and crime, against the roots of this wrong-doing and crime, roots often hidden like subtle leeches or like an invisible, corroding society cancer: all the forms of grave social and collective evil — abortion, drugs, drug-pushing, mafia, etc.

We have no prerogative and we do not want to boast any privilege: we have merely the firm desire to serve humanity to the very end.

September 25
Reconciliation Is Gradual

Reconciliation is a journey, not just an arrival, a perfect state. Thus we cannot say that we have not got there yet and that we will never arrive. What is important is to take steps, and take another step, and take the step we can take here and now.

I believe it is extremely important to understand this ongoing aspect of our journey to reconciliation, of the penitential journey, of the Christian journey. In any case, this is the obvious aspect of the whole Church structure in all the economy of revealed truth. We have it before our eyes and it is told to us every day. However, our laziness to listen and to understand — ''Are your minds closed? Have you eyes that do not see, ears that do not hear?'' (Mk 8:18) — do not allow us to grasp it sufficiently. And so we continue to theorize about Christian realities — reconciliation included — and fix them forever in a near-perfect state. This is why we hear complaints that we cannot become perfect and that we are always at the same stage. The discussion becomes just empty talk because it never gets us where we would like to be, neither as a family, nor as a parish, nor as a civil entity nor as an international society.

What does the fact that Advent, Lent, Easter and Pentecost repeat themselves every year tell us? It tells us that the incessant human journey is always ongoing, that it never ends, that it constantly has to begin again as if we had gone nowhere yet and that it never stops. And so, a little at a time, the journey is seen as a part of the history of individual existences and of individual communities. Even when these undergo crises and upheavals, the journey continues without cessation till the end.

September 26
The Good News of Reconciliation

The penitential journey consists in increasing acceptance of the Gospel of pardon, the good news that the mercy of God in the Passover sacrifice of Jesus destroys our sin and gives us a new heart.

The acceptance of this Gospel generates in us a far-sighted spiritual condition. We acquire a vivid and concrete awareness of sin. We are able to grasp how injustice is rooted in our heart and reaches out into our social behavior which, in turn, reinforces the roots of oppression and arrogance and makes them more powerful in us.

The certainty that the mercy of God destroys sin helps us find and courageously cover all the roads leading in the opposite direction to the destruction of egoism and its roots and ramifications.

When we examine things from a complementary point of view we can note that overcoming social divisions and struggles certainly calls for analytical instruments and political ways of acting. But it calls also for something more profound: for a broad and wise vision of human life. This vision will endeavor to link external evils with their internal roots and will help to set the analysis of the evils against the background of the sincere search for mankind's true and total benefit. Especially, it will convince people that definitive victory over evil requires that purely human efforts, necessary and obligatory though they may be, should open themselves to the redeeming action of the One Who is the Father of everyone.

In brief, we can say that human aspirations and commitments to overcome divisions and struggles seek a place to clarify and consolidate themselves. And the Gospel of pardon, accepted and preached by the Church is this very place given us by the mercy of God, going beyond any aspiration or commitment of ours and remaining at the same time its foundation.

378

The Church, a Reconciled Society

There is a reconciled society and this reference, this point of contact, does not exist only in Utopia but in some way is the experience of history.

The Church is in no way immune from divisions and sufferings. And yet it has the experience of a society now reconciled, endowed with good will and with a feeling of mutual belonging, going beyond tribal attachments, beyond attachments of blood, of culture, of race and of religion and producing a variety which has never before existed in Church history. Never more than at present has the Church been diversified not only in individual members but even in its top leaders. In other words, the fact that we have in the Catholic Church more than fifty percent of the bishops coming from the southern hemisphere constitutes a new equilibrium, a new awareness that the southern hemisphere, from the point of view of numbers and Church leaders, has the upper hand.

Let us try to think about what this fact means. It is certainly an enriching phenomenon but at the same time a very risky one. What is the implication of the growth of self-awareness in the various local churches, of their personal self-awareness, of the power of their traditions, of the riches of their customs, of the relevance of their literature, sagas and oral legends?

It involves the risk that the required great and rapid culture and language differentiation may swiftly lead to considerable misunderstanding and to mutual inability to comprehend each other. This was in medieval times the drama between the Eastern and Western Churches. As they no longer understood each other's language, eventually they separated. From these misunderstandings and oppositions, hardened theological positions emerged which corroded even more fundamental elements of agreement on a common faith and a common discipline.

At present there is certainly a great risk in the tensions between the different cultures in today's Church and it will continue to be increasingly so because at the present time the unity of Western culture, dominated as it was by the Church, is disappearing. Certain references to Church history in recent centuries which appear part of tradition to us are in no way obvious or evident to those who come from a different background.

And so a Church in these circumstances could come to the point of reciprocal lack of trust and of division unless the human beings involved speak to each other, listen to each other, try to communicate with each other without letting a long time elapse.

From this comes the practical secret of reconciliation and that is the constant effort to be together, to speak and listen to each other, to seek continually a new and better understanding of what the other has said.

This vision becomes the practical and comforting one of a society which is reconciled and is continually trying to become reconciled and to lay the foundations for mutual understanding among people, among groups and among mentalities, cultures and positions which are potentially sources of conflict.

September 28
Nominal and Practicing Catholics: A Journey of Reconciliation

It is important for many people to take some steps to enable them to grasp the reality of the Church as a reality of love and service, not as a competitor for power, not as a reality from which one must in some way defend oneself as if it were the tax people. The Church is not an extraneous reality. It is a friendly one, at our service. It is a reality which certainly makes mistakes in its people and in its institutions but which, taken overall, is animated by a will to serve people.

This very simple fact, when properly grasped, is something we must wish for ourselves and it is something with which we must work. It is a fact that requires a conversion on the part of nominal Catholics to ensure that they understand that, to accept Jesus Christ, means accepting Him as He has come to us. And that means with His apostles, His Church and His historic reality. That is how Jesus came: as a bodily reality, as a life which became a family, as a life which became the ''great hall'' of the Gospel where we meet each other; it is not merely an interior, personal factor but a community one.

Nominal Catholics must come to sense that one cannot accept the historical, bodily Christ or the historical life of Jesus of Nazareth, without accepting the Eucharistic body or the ecclesial body which are His real continuation, forming a single entity with Him.

This fact requires that practicing Catholics have more and more as a factor in their lives the spirit of the washing of the feet, not as a simple Holy Thursday function but as a reality of service. I decided to put the scene of the washing of the feet in the handle of my pastoral staff to ensure that the episode would be a continual reminder for me.

Actually, the washing of the feet is a daily reality which expresses the love, humility and service of Christ giving His life for His own; of a Church which must imitate Jesus and which must be this reality of love and service for the true good of people, for the promotion of every interior and human facet of the social atmosphere, of the great ethical values, of the great and profound social common denominators which only an institution such as the Church can promote with international credibility. It can promote all this with international credibility because of its experience of peace among so many different realities and of its ability to dialogue even in the midst of all the difficulties which it, too, experiences.

September 29
The Dynamism of the Sacrament of Reconciliation

Reconciliation is a reality forming part of a dynamism equal to that of the Gospels and it is important to find this in the Sacrament of Penance.

Many times the penitent hesitates because he or she feels largely unchanged. The self-image which in the Sacrament of Reconciliation one returns to view every week or every month is so stereotyped that it proves annoying. Actually, the penitent perceives life merely in terms of some exterior coordinates and does not see into the very depths of a personal dynamism, a personal journey and personal desires, and so is unable to see any progress. Thus there is no interest in taking steps towards progress. The penance received in the Sacrament is repetitious: three 'Hail Mary's which have been said so many times that they produce no effect or change. Penance does not become an action, a gesture, a journey helping one towards a step ahead.

It can be frustrating for the priest, too, to find himself dealing with continually identical situations, perhaps with situations which appear to be blocked or motionless. On the other hand, think of the priest's joy when he sees that things are moving, that the situation is coming alive and that the individual concerned really has work to do and is doing everything possible.

We have to believe that it is possible to reach at least that richness of vitality which is required of every individual and of every community. We have to walk without tiring, walking in love and entrusting ourselves to God Who will bring us to Himself, Who will save us, Who will meet our fragility halfway because it is He Who drives our inner dynamism, accepts it lovingly on the outside and pardons us continually.

The dynamism of reconciliation is a dynamism repeated not with tired resignation but because there is a ray of light for me and for the other and through this pardon we shall take a step ahead and be more authentic and true.

September 30
Penitential Colloquy

What do I mean by penitential colloquy? I mean a dialogue with a person representing the Church to me, and in practice with a priest. In the dialogue I try to live the event of reconciliation in a broader way than that of the short confession in which I simply list my failings.

Let me try to describe how this happens. If possible, it is better to begin the colloquy with some reading from Scripture, a Psalm for example. After that follows a three-fold process which I call in brief: *confessio laudis* (confession of praise), *confessio vitae* (confession of one's life), and *confessio fidei* (confession of faith). The first means to begin this penitential colloquy by replying to the question: since my last confession what are the things for which I feel I must particularly thank and praise God? Those things where I feel that God has been particularly close to me, in which I felt His help and His presence? Underline these things, beginning with this expression of thanks and praise which puts life in the proper context and perspective.

Next follows the confession proper. Evidently I go along with what was taught us when we learned how to confess our sins, that is, to examine one's conscience following the ten commandments or some other such scheme. But for those who have more time at their disposal I would suggest that they also ask themselves this question: since my last confession, what is it that, before God especially, I would like not to have happened? What is a burden to me? Rather than being concerned about compiling a list of sins — which might be the case if we were dealing with very serious and specific matters, though then these will surface spontaneously — we are talking here about reviewing the situations through which we have lived and which weigh on us, which we would like not to have happened and which, for this reason, we put before God to have them forgiven, to be purified of them.

In this way, we truly put ourselves under the spotlight as we feel ourselves to be. What would I want not to have happened? What is my principal burden now before God? What would I want God to take away from me? In this way it is easier to become aware of the individual involved in constantly changing situations and with a sinful reality not always easy to document.

Finally, there is the confession of faith which is the immediate preparation to receive God's pardon. It is a

384

proclamation before the Lord: "Lord, I know my weakness but I know that You are strong. I believe in Your power over my life, in Your ability to save me just as I am now. I entrust my sinfulness to You, risking everything. I put it in Your hands and I am no longer afraid." In a word: we have to live the experience of salvation as an experience of trust, of joy, as the moment when God enters our life and gives us the Good News: "Go in peace. I have taken on the weight of your sins, of your sinfulness, of your burden, of your fatigue, of your lack of faith, of your interior sufferings, of your sorrows. I have taken them all on myself. I have burdened Myself with them so as to make you free."

OCTOBER

October 1
Jesus, The Definitive Word

"The Word was with God and the Word was God.
. . . The Word was made flesh; He lived among us" (Jn
1:1, 14).

Jesus' actions and His discourses, His behavior
towards other people, His miracles, His way of entrusting
Himself to the mystery of His Father, His courageous
freedom, His comparisons with personages of the Old
Testament, the demands He makes on His disciples, His
far-seeing gaze penetrating deep into the future, lead us to
affirm that God was present in Him in an exceptional
way. Not only is God present in Him, but God is one with
Him. In Him God not only communicated with mankind
but He communicated Himself: "It pleased God in His
goodness and wisdom to reveal Himself" (*Dei Verbum*,
No. 2). What we could neither expect nor demand was
mysteriously fulfilled in Jesus by a magnanimous divine
decision. This Man of Nazareth Who takes His place in
the ongoing story of humanity and speaks human words
is, in the mysterious depths of His being, one with God.

And so He is the full and definitive Word. He is the
totally fulfilled human being. Every other human person
and every other human word are truly human if they
hearken back to Him and begin with Him. This means
that the life of Jesus, from His Incarnation to the Paschal

effusion of the Spirit, is the definitive Word of God. In it God tells us Who He really is. He is communication of life. He is love. He is Trinity. And it also says what God wishes to be for us: He wishes to be our loving Father, our accepting and saving ally, our friend Who shares our human condition to the point of death, so as to make us sharers in His divinity.

October 2
The Word Crosses Human Life

We come to the Bible bringing with us the dignity and the burden of our freedom, of our restless searching, of our spiritual involvement, of our spasms of courage and hope and of our real but precarious conquests in the various sectors of human experience. We have an insight, constantly dimmed and denied but which constantly re-surfaces, that we are the astonished, fragile and unworthy guardians of the incomprehensible mysteries of God. We have a sense that we are ourselves a sign, a cipher, a word of God in a way that God alone can clarify, determine and free from all ambiguity and distortion. We perceive that we can be fully ourselves only by transcending ourselves in an attitude of confident abandon and humble adoration of One Who is infinitely above us. Thus this very insight in which our various human experiences find their culmination is the spiritual condition which the Word of God simultaneously presumes and supports.

As we proceed in our contemplation of the Word of God, we come to understand in sacred history the mystery of the will of God concerning human history. As we come up against an infinite variety of human situations enlightened and saved by the Word of God, as we immerse ourselves particularly in meditation on the life of Jesus, we meet the pure and authentic form of human life which God Himself proposed as a luminous self-revelation.

And so we return to our everyday commitments with a new light of hope and new resolve: to witness, through the practical example of our conduct, to the victorious energy of the Word of God protecting our freedom from the illusion of self-sufficiency, from ambiguous desires, flamboyant arrogance and hopeless desperation.

October 3
Word and Church

The Bible is situated within the Church. It contains the Word which stirs up faith and calls the Church together. In turn, the faith of the Church accepts the Word, gives it resonance and consistency in time, guards it very carefully and faithfully hands it on. The Church interprets the Bible with authority through that variety of functions and ministries which Jesus Himself instituted and which the Holy Spirit animates internally with His gifts. Church tradition is the practical area within which Sacred Scripture receives its definitive shape and form. In this tradition Scripture finds the characteristics which set it apart from other non-inspired writings and meets the living memory of apostolic witness which is an authoritative source of interpretation and a guide to practical living. So the study of Sacred Scripture, while it calls forth the intense application of one's personal energies, equally requires a cordial and active harmony with the faith of the whole Church.

This point must first be heard as a call to agreement with the authoritative directives of the Magisterium. In fact "the task of giving an authentic interpretation of the Word of God, whether in its written form or in the form of Tradition, has been entrusted to the living teaching office of the Church alone. Its authority in this matter is exercised in the name of Jesus Christ" (*Dei Verbum*, No. 10).

To this we must also add an invitation to a felicitous convergence of the competencies, charisms and intuitions of all believers. "There is a growth in insight into the words and realities that are being passed on. This comes about in various ways. It comes through the contemplation and study of believers who ponder these things in their hearts (Lk 2:19, 51). It comes from the intimate sense of spiritual realities which they experience. And it comes from the preaching of those who have received, along with their right of succession in the episcopate, the sure charism of truth" (*Dei Verbum*, No. 8).

Many potential insights in Sacred Scripture which would be a valuable message of hope for today's world remain unexplored and unproductive because a great part of our Christian people is inert and silent, either from indifference or from lack of preparation as far as the sacred text is concerned.

October 4
Word and Liturgy

There is a "place" where the saving Word resounds with exceptional efficacy and that is in the sacred liturgy. The liturgy is really an uninterrupted dialogue between the Word and human beings who are called to re-echo it.

In reality, the sacred liturgy is the saving meeting place between the Father in heaven Who comes to speak lovingly with His children. It is the colloquy between the Groom, the Lord Jesus, and His beloved Bride, the Church, sharing in the eternal song of praise which the Incarnate Word has introduced into this earthly exile of ours (cf. *Sacrosanctum Concilium*, No. 83).

Thus the sacred liturgy nourishes itself abundantly at the table of the Word of God. It takes its readings from the Bible, sings the psalms and finds its inspiration in Scripture when composing hymns, prayers, acclamations and invocations. In its practical development it shows forth a dialogical structure expressing the very life of the Church. Just as in the Old Testament the assembly of Yahweh is called first of all to listen to God speaking: "Today, listen to His voice" (Is 94:4), so the liturgical assembly, the true People of God, comes together principally to listen to the Word, Christ the Lord, to unite itself to Him and be guided by His Spirit in praising and supplicating the Father.

It appears clear in the sacred liturgy that the person to whom the Word is addressed is not an isolated individual but the redeemed people called together. It is clear that its living voice is not that of a human being proclaiming the Word to himself, but is the Church's Magisterium which, through the various ministers, announces it to the assembly. And its natural result is transforming sacramental energy and the palpitating life of the Spirit in human hearts.

So the Word of Scripture, when it is proclaimed in the celebration of the liturgy, constitutes one form of the real, mysterious and indefectible immanence of Christ among His own as Vatican II teaches: "He is present in His Word since it is He Himself Who speaks when the

Holy Scriptures are read in church'' (*Sacrosanctum Concilium*, No. 7).

When God speaks, He solicits a response. We respond to God speaking and reminding us of the events of our salvation and of the mystery of His love for us whenever we celebrate the Eucharist.

October 5
The Word: A Mutual Gift

The Word asks that we allow it to become a constant part of our own words and life. Through some progressive steps it wants its presence in us to be manifested.

First of all, it humbly asks to become a ''mutual gift'' among us! Communion must be made concrete in communication. We must share the Word of God with one another (Col 3:16). With the Word and in the Word we are mutually edified as we share the respective reactions and responses which have been stirred up in us by the Spirit. We may even criticize and correct one another. Authentic fraternal correction is a profoundly evangelical reality. Each of us is responsible for the other. Each of us is a humble listener to the Word and needs mutual communication in faith.

Only along this road do we come to construct community in communion. The community is born as a reality in which we believe, in which we give witness to our faith and from which we go forth with a missionary spirit: ''It was from you that the Word of God started to spread'' (1 Th 1:8), and ''You yourselves are our letter'' (2 Cor 3:2).

As they get used to this kind of more intense communication, our communities will acquire skill in interpreting different human situations more efficaciously in the light of the Word. Faced with urgent questions from the world of work, from the new circumstances in which the family lives, from the restlessness of young people and of women — to cite just a few meaningful cases — our communities find themselves mute and hampered because they are not accustomed to a constant review of these situations in which reference to the Word of God is interwoven in all its complexity and truth. Only from this point of view does the Word reveal its ability to be "Truth," that is, to give a profound meaning and integral salvation to a human situation.

October 6
The Word in the Family

If the family could only gather together around the Word of God either by going over again what was proclaimed at Mass on Sunday or by reading the Bible directly and systematically, it would find an inexhaustible source of valuable messages for family life itself, for the events which family members go through in the different stages of life and for things happening in the world today. If this were to happen, facts and situations would no longer enter the family in a rough and sometimes dangerous form, but would be passed through the filter of the wisdom and serenity of God's Word.

Consider the warning of Christian wisdom which shines forth from that page of Manzoni's *The Betrothed* in which the good tailor of an unspecified town reminds his family gathered at table of the sermon given by Cardinal Federigo during one of his pastoral visits. For his children he comments on the words of the Archbishop and it is really the memory of those words inviting people to share in the suffering of others which produces the action of almsgiving in the simple and moving sense of making the poverty of others one's own. The tailor sends one of his little girls with some food to a widow's house nearby. The word the Archbishop spoke came alive and was made effective through the mediation of family dialogue.

October 7
The Word: A Buried Treasure

The primacy of the Word must be lived. At present this is not so. Our life cannot even vaguely be described as nourished or ruled by the Word. Even in doing good we are guided by some sound habits and by some common sense principles. We take our cues from a traditional content of religious beliefs and received moral norms. In our better moments we feel more strongly that God is something for us and that Jesus represents an ideal and a help. But, apart from this, we usually feel very little, indeed, of how the Word of God might become our true support and comfort, how it might enlighten us about the "true God," Whose manifestations could fill our heart with joy. Rarely do we experience how the Jesus of the Gospels, known through listening to and meditating on the Bible, can really become "good news" for us individually, here and now in this particular time of our history; how He can help me, for example, see in a new and exalting perspective my place and my responsibility in society; how He can really turn upside down the sad and narrow-minded idea I had formed about myself and my destiny.

Sunday Mass often goes over our heads without filling our hearts and changing our life. We keep feeling that the Word of God and the daily news make up two separate worlds. Our life could be filled with light by a prolonged and attentive contact with the Word. But instead we pass it by because we are resigned to live in darkness and are too lazy to do anything about it. Why don't we shake ourselves out of this lethargy and get down to making the treasure we possess productive?

October 8
The Word: Light of Hope

When sorrow knocks at the doors of our life, when we are swept up in suffering and in the mourning of people close to us, when we are stricken by social tragedies, then we become keenly aware of the impotence of human words. An instinctive sense of decency moves us to keep silence in the presence of the suffering one, though we testify to our solidarity by a discreet and active presence. But does impotence strike the Word of God, too? Is there not in the Word of God a real light of hope of which we should be witnesses without rhetoric or affectation, but with humility and simplicity? Shouldn't the very fact that, when He gave us His Word, God assured us of His presence in every moment of our life, set us off on a journey of consolation and commitment?

Or is it true that we are not interested in God and are more interested in the good things we demand of Him? We should grasp that God, while He is indeed the source of the goods which are the object of our short-term desires, is, however, greater than they are and can prepare goods for us going far beyond our expectations. Instead, the goods we desire and have planned for ourselves are sometimes of more interest to us than God is and the good things He has prepared. This explains our lack of confidence in or even our refusal of God, when we do not have those gifts of life, of health, of personal, family and social serenity which we desire. These are certainly important and we should humbly request them of God, without, however, making the granting of our request for them a condition for believing in Him.

In moments of sorrow the Word of God can illuminate our life as a real reminder of what is essential: God is speaking; God is near; God is faithful. This ought to be enough for us.

Because it is the Word of God, the Bible becomes a consoling viaticum for every moment of life, even apart from the content it offers us. But the content, too, kindles rays of hope. The example of believers who have entrusted themselves to God and above all the example of Jesus Who remains faithful to the Father until death, fuel in us a profound sense of God Who is greater than the good things we desire.

In addition, the Word of God shows us that, while some things are not granted us or are painfully taken away, other more profound goods are revealed: courage, a deeper human solidarity, a humbler sense of our fragility, a greater vigilance over our superficial desires and a more faithful dedication to duty, over and above short-term gratifications. Finally, the Word of God kindles hope in us in those mysterious but real and wonderful goods which the Father is preparing in the new world for those who, united to Jesus, His Son, have totally entrusted themselves to His love.

396

October 9
The New People of God

The proclamation of the "Beatitudes" opens the first of the five great discourses of Jesus on which the Gospel of St. Matthew is built. These discourses which re-echo the ones Moses addressed to the people of the Old Covenant, describe for us the characteristics of the *new* People of God.

It is a people made up of the poor and meek, of lovers of justice and peace, of those who weep and who are persecuted. It is a people made up of those who seek God and trust in Him with a poor and humble heart. It is a people who have no importance or prestige so that in their lack of wisdom and power the wisdom and the power of God may be more clearly revealed.

To understand these characteristics more fully, we have to link them up with the central theme of Jesus' preaching and messianic action, that is, the Kingdom, the good and paternal lordship of God Who is present in Jesus. God bends down mercifully over humanity, the slave of evil, of sin and of death and enables it to pass from the sorrowful condition of a servant to the joyous condition of a freed, reconciled and beloved child.

The Kingdom becomes, for the disciple of Christ, the ultimate value, the absolute good, the definitive goal towards which all one's existence is polarized. The disciple is converted and believes, changes his or her mentality and stops seeing possessions as the measure of true good while concurring with humility and courage in that project of life and liberty which the Father reveals a little at a time in the words and actions of Jesus.

This, however, does not mean the elimination and down-grading of other goods which are the object of human desires: life, friendship, health, clothing, housing and food.

When He performs His miracles and commits His disciples to concern themselves about the hungry, the naked, the stranger, the sick and those in prison, Jesus teaches us that these goods, too, have a meaning. They are the *signs* of the Kingdom. All else are simply provisional goods through which the Kingdom is manifested. They are gifts to be received from the hands of God and to be shared with one's brethren while waiting for those mysterious and definitive goods which the Father is preparing for a renewed world.

Material goods are not something absolute to which our heart can be greedily attached, nor should we war with other people over them or place our hope in them. As far as they are concerned, the disciple of Jesus maintains a poor, pure and detached heart, ready for renunciation and privation in an attitude of meekness, of endurance and of peace.

October 10
"Happy Are Those Who Mourn . . ."

Let us reflect a moment on the second Beatitude: "Happy are those who mourn, for they shall be comforted" (Mt 5:5). Some Bibles talk of "mourners" but an ecumenical translation of the Bible talks about "those who are sad." A parallel passage from Luke reads: "Happy are you who weep now" (Lk 6:21).

In this passage we are confronted with a subject which we would rather avoid: mourning and sadness. Both refer to situations which ought not be. It is better not to speak of them. We would rather pretend they didn't exist.

And yet the men and women of this world who mourn and are sad are very numerous indeed. Besides, if Jesus spoke of mourning and sadness as a blessing, a beatitude, and if the Church today proposes this approach to us as a characteristic of the Saints on earth, it is important that we should give some attention to it, thus better understanding what our Lord means by this expression.

Let's begin with the dictionary. I have already quoted two possible translations of the Greek text, one which says "to mourn" and the other which talks of being "sad." The Greek word refers more directly to mourning, to that deep interior sorrow which breaks one's heart after the loss of a loved one and which is expressed externally by weeping and lamentation.

The meaning of the word is then extended to all situations which cause pain and sadness because they have about them something incomprehensible and humanly unacceptable.

Who are these mourners, these persons who are sad? What interior situation determines their state of mind?

Take a look at Jesus weeping over His city, or for His friend Lazarus who has just died. This weeping is born of a dramatic interior contrast. The person whose self-expression is tears is one who lives torn by the contrast between the desire and the interior vision of the Kingdom of God; between *its* fullness of life and peace and the contrasting vision of death all around. We are not dealing here with a simple, negative emotion over the loss of something dear to us. We are dealing with a rending contrast between the supreme good of God and the gift of His friendship and the unbearable situations of wretchedness and death born of the refusal of God's love.

The affliction proclaimed as a Beatitude flows from a contemplative gaze turned towards the infinite mystery of God and at the same time from an awareness of the human condition, full of love, tenderness and compassion.

For this reason, it is an attitude proper to the Saints, those people who have looked with realism and with love on humanity with their gaze purified and rendered compassionate by the vision of God. And so we understand that sanctity is in no way an avoidance of the human condition. And still less is it a getting lost in dreams.

Sanctity is the ability to grasp, with a pure gaze, our human drama, our human suffering and the contradictions inherent in our historical human condition.

October 11
". . . They Shall Be Comforted"

The Gospel does not confine itself to helping us grasp the reality of the affliction of the Saints and of the Church's sorrow. It tells us also that the afflicted will be consoled.

The Word of God assures us that God Himself will be the comforter. He is the One Who wipes away every tear from the face of suffering humanity and this statement at first sight seems incredible. Often we would be satisfied with human consolation, to be embraced and comforted by a friendly person. The Scripture, however, repeats many times that God, God Himself, the God-with-us, our Emmanuel, will wipe away every tear from our eyes (Is 25:8) and that God will console us as a mother consoles her child (Is 66:13).

Saints have experienced this mysterious communion with the God of the Covenant and of Life, with the God of Peace Who made their eyes turn to His coming Kingdom and led them to live, even in this life, the beginning of the definitive peace of that Kingdom. They became Saints because they knew how to accept in their hearts the afflictions of all who work for peace. Compassionate and afflicted while they were on earth, they are now overflowing with divine consolation in Paradise.

In a moment in which world peace is subject to so many threats and dangers, we feel that the Saints whom we contemplate in heaven and, by reflection, in good people on earth, have a potentiality for pacification and reconciliation which is the hope of humanity. The Saints invite us: "Share in our sufferings and do not be afraid to open your heart and be afflicted by the evils of the world. You will share in the peace of God and will be workers for that peace."

October 12
Jesus and the Crowds

I would like to underline here a characteristic aspect of the Gospel excerpt from Luke which narrates the multiplication of the loaves (Lk 9:11-17) and which responds to the question: *who are the beneficiaries* of the miracle of the multiplication of the loaves which Jesus brings about?

It is the crowd, the people, the multitude of those who were there, the five thousand.

And re-reading the Gospel with a careful eye, we can see in almost every verse this vision of the immense crowd listening to the words of Jesus, this crowd pleading for aid, this crowd lost in a lonely place without anything to eat as evening comes on. And the crowd is welcomed by Jesus. He is concerned about their needs. He has it divide in groups of about fifty, thus organizing them in manageable seatings as one would for a banquet — the sign of fellowship and communion.

The entire episode is pervaded, therefore, by the importance of the crowd, of the multitude, of the people who surround Jesus. We could also review other Gospel pages and note how often there is reference in them to crowds, to the tens of thousands thronging to see Jesus, seeking Him out, pressing to be near Him as they listen to His words, running after Him, going before Him when He moves onto the lake, awaiting Him when He arrives on the other shore. Truly distinctive and characteristic is the significance of the masses, of the throngs of people, in all the excerpts which treat of the ministry of Jesus.

We immediately grasp the difference in the context of the reality of those times. Jesus feels perfectly at ease in the midst of the multitude. He is not afraid of the crowd but rather accepts it, dialogues with it, listens to it, allows Himself to be surrounded by it and nearly trampled on by it. He is concerned about its support and even about its material well-being. Above all, He nourishes it, heals it, educates it. Jesus' attitude is a goad for us. All too often, actually, we stick the label of "mass civilization" on our society and make that label stand for "anonymous or amorphous group," unorganized, violent, unruly. We especially stress that the "masses" are foreign to us and that we are loath to associate with them, as if the masses could not accept a humanizing message born in the human heart before they are "born again" of the very words of Scripture.

Jesus does not consider as time wasted the dedication of His days to His people. He believes that an education of the human heart is possible, an education which will turn the masses into a people known for its fraternal spirit and communion.

October 13
The Faith Journey of the Man Born Blind

St. John the Evangelist (in Chapter Nine of his Gospel) underlines the ability of the blind man to walk and not give up, to go to the extreme in order to meet Jesus. In this passage John began with an episode about a miraculous healing and — through a well-balanced composition of scenes and dialogue — he made it into a paradigm, an example, a model of the faith journey through which human beings encounter the Lord.

In the background are a small group of Jews and Pharisees. They stay the same and do not change. They already know everything about God and don't let themselves be aroused by the mysterious signs by which God is manifesting Himself. They judge Jesus to be a sinner because He doesn't correspond to the idea they had formed of God and of His Messiah, His Anointed One. They are the very ones who think they see and know everything and they end up by not seeing the very glory of God present in Jesus and in His works.

On the other hand, the blind man is ready to be renewed. His physical transformation is absorbed and eclipsed by his greater faith transformation. Perhaps moved by his bodily need, he comes to an awareness of other poverties. He seeks something or rather Someone to fill his life and make him whole again. He is ready to leave behind old concepts so as to open himself to something new. He is also ready to be laughed at and pushed aside, so long as he can have a share in that newness of life which God has kindled in his heart even before He enlightened his bodily eyes.

The Gospel outlines an admirable growth in this passage. First, the blind man recognized that Jesus is the one who helped him. Then he sees Him as a prophet sent by God. Finally, he accepts Him and adores Him as Messiah and Savior.

October 14
The Three Groans: The Groan of Creation

In the superb text of Romans 8:18-27, the Apostle explains what we might call the "doctrine of the three groans." What is a groan? It is a repressed shout, something having to do with a certain type of suffering. There is an inner desire to shout but the air is, as we might say, blocked, and only a part of the shout emerges.

This is the characteristic of the groan: a shout with a violent cause but a limited expression.

And so what are the groans Paul speaks of in his Letter to the Romans?

The first one is the groan of all creation: "The whole of creation is eagerly awaiting for God to reveal His sons. . . . From the beginning till now the entire creation as we know it has been groaning in one great act of giving birth" (Rm 8:19-22).

It is a grandiose picture, describing the dynamism of human history. Human history is a continuous groan like enormous labor pains.

In the Greek, the precise word means "groan with." The whole world groans together, as if in the throes of great labor pains. Humanity, history and creation reach out to something different and desire it immensely, yearning intensely for it. This cry for freedom, which is at the heart of the world, does not however succeed in expressing itself clearly and, for all its depth, only a groan results.

Note the beauty of the expression: "From the beginning till now the entire creation as we know it has been groaning in one great act of giving birth." So it is a moment in which life is ready to manifest itself through pain and suffering. All of us know that the figure of birth pangs which make ready the emergence of new life can grip the imagination and give meaning to a person's life even in the most anguished of circumstances.

Humanity today finds itself in a situation similar to that which confronted the people of Israel when they were slaves to the Pharaoh in Egypt. We are slaves, though, of nonsense, of fads, of stupidity. Slaves are those who ask themselves what on earth life is good for, what meaning their grief and fatigue could possibly have. Slaves are those who live thoughtlessly and without purpose, or who pass rapidly from thoughtlessness to desolation, anger and frustration.

The groan expresses the need for a meaning, the will to understand the deep significance of things. And so humanity groans because it desires at any price to be freed of emptiness, from its slavery to idols (drugs, lust, various forms of violence, hunger, abortion, exploitation, manipulation and greed).

And the Christian, as a Christian, is called to perceive the groan of creation and to listen carefully to it, because it does not often express itself loudly. It must be grasped somewhat as a night nurse might sense the groan of a sick person who has lost the strength to shout.

The Three Groans: Ours and that of the Spirit in Us

"We ourselves, who have the first fruits of the Spirit, groan inwardly as we wait eagerly for our adoption as sons, the redemption of our bodies" (Rm 8:23, NEB).

Although we have the first fruits of the Spirit — indeed, for the very reason that we have already had some taste of what it means to be saved from nonsense, from frustration and from vanity — we ourselves as Christians groan because we know that our salvation is not yet complete. Our groans are our deepest and truest desires tending towards liberation, tending (the Apostle says) to becoming fully what we are. We are children of God and yet we often live in this state of ignorance, in limited awareness, in laziness and in mediocrity. We are wrapped up in our weaknesses and our ignorance. We would like to see ourselves as children so that we could truly speak to God as our Father, to a "You" Who loves us and saves us ". . . and Who redeems our bodies," as St. Paul adds.

We desire to be set free from the weight of our carnality so as to live our bodily condition as a gift. Pope John Paul II has said many fine things about bodiliness as a symbol, as a spousal sign. But is anyone able to live these things in reality? And so we groan as we feel the weight of our carnality. We are fatigued, tempted, sensuous, obtuse, unable — forgetful of ourselves — to put ourselves truly at the service of others.

These groans which close in on us are important because they are the sign that the Spirit is within us, lives in us, leads us to reach out towards something we do not yet have but which gives a meaning to our long and difficult journey. "The Spirit, too, helps us in our weakness . . . (and) expresses our plea in a way that could never be put into words" (Rm 8:26).

To a certain extent our groans can be expressed, and we have tried to say something about their content. However, it is impossible for us to be explicit about the groans of the Spirit crying out in us and guiding us in prayer. But when we do succeed in grasping this voice of the Spirit, our groans, too, will be purified and made perfect.

We ought to get to the point of perceiving the groans of creation and of our people, united with the inexpressible groans of the Spirit. They may be very loud or very soft but fundamentally they can be summed up, as Paul leads us to understand, in the word "Father" which we are able to say by this very power of the Spirit with increasing truth, peace, abandon, tenderness and confidence.

October 16
The Canticle of Fidelity

The last page of the Canticle of Canticles or Song of Songs might well be entitled: The Canticle of Fidelity. It begins with an invocation which the loved one addresses to her beloved: "Set me like a seal on your heart, like a seal on your arm." The seal — especially if we relate it to a person — is *an indelible sign of belonging*. When it is put on the heart and not just on a paper document, it shows that the belonging is total, that it has to do with the very core of the individual.

Why is there a request to be like a seal on the heart of Christ, indelibly impressed on Him? So that the bond may be unbreakable! In the Canticle the unbreakable nature of love is expressed with some extremely significant examples.

"*Because love is as strong as death.*" Love possesses an irresistible power which nothing can stop, just as nothing can resist death. "Neither death nor life, no angel, prince, nothing that exists, not any power . . . can ever come between us and the love of God made visible in Christ Jesus our Lord" (Rm 8:38-39).

Because love is *tenacious*, "jealousy is as relentless as Sheol." This means that love becomes a need that the loved one should not be distracted or taken up by other desires. This power of love, which can become jealousy, is tenacious. As the years pass, the changing circumstances pass but love persists stronger than ever.

"The flash of it is a flash of fire, a flame of Yahweh Himself." Tongues of fire embrace the universe and rise up from earth towards heaven.

Love makes things glow. Love burns. Its flames divide and are passed on. It warms and gives light. Nothing can suffocate it if it takes its spark from the love of God: "Love no flood can quench, no torrents drown." His love is a love so great that not even floods, rains or deluges can extinguish its flames.

Nothing can separate two human beings loving each other with a love willed by God. Nothing can separate the sincere love between the soul and Jesus.

"Were a man to offer all the wealth of his house to buy love, contempt is all he would purchase." It is the Canticle's final example to express the incomparable nature of love. It is a precious pearl which cannot be seen as equal to any other value, which cannot and must not be bartered away.

October 17
Welcoming Silence

In the beginning there was the Word. And if our redemption started to become a reality when the Word of God dwelt amongst us, it is clear that there must be silence on our part at the beginning of our personal salvation history, a silence which listens, accepts and allows itself to be brought to life again. Certainly words of gratitude, of adoration and of supplication must be our response to the Word which manifests itself. But first there is always silence.

We may even say that the ability to live with some interior silence is a sign of the true believer and detaches the believer from the world of incredulity.

The person who, following the dictates of the dominant culture, has expelled from his mind the living God Who, alone, fills every space, cannot bear silence. He sees himself living on the edge of nothingness and silence in a terrifying kind of vacuum. Any noise is more pleasing, no matter how dull and annoying. Any word, even the most tasteless, is freedom from a nightmare. Anything is preferable to being put unmercifully — when every voice is stilled — before the horror of nothingness. Any idle talk, any complaint, any shriek, is welcome if in some way and for some time it succeeds in distracting one's mind from the fearful awareness of the empty universe.

The "new" person to whom faith has given a penetrating glance to perceive beyond the scene and to whom charity has given a heart capable of loving the Invisible, knows that a vacuum does not exist and that nothingness is eternally conquered by divine infinity. He knows that the universe is populated with joyous creatures, that he is a spectator and that in some way he shares in the cosmic exultation reverberating with the mystery of light, of love and happiness which is given reality by the inexhaustible life of the Triune God.

And so, like the Lord Jesus Who at dawn used to go alone to the mountain top (Mk 1:35; Lk 4:42; 6:12; 9:28), the new man yearns to have some personal space immune from every alienating din where it is possible to listen carefully and perceive something of the eternal feast and of the Father's voice.

But let me make myself clear. The "old" man who fears silence and the "new" man generally live together in each of us though in different proportions. Each of us is externally assailed by hordes of words, sounds and noises which deafen our day and fill our night. Each of us is interiorly seduced by worldly chit-chat which distracts us and wastes our energies with a thousand futilities.

In this cacophony the new man in us must struggle to ensure in the heaven of his soul that prodigy of "a silence in heaven for about half an hour." Let it be a true silence, filled with the Presence of God, resounding with His Word, reaching out to listen and open to communion.

October 18
Living Experience

When His disciples saw Jesus returning, happy and relaxed, from His prayer they asked Him: "Lord, teach us to pray'' (Lk 11:1). Jesus is the true teacher of prayer and we sit near His disciples and listen to His word.

The experience of prayer is principally linked to the ability to be silent within ourselves, to the attempt to isolate ourselves from city noises and distractions so as to rediscover the echo of God's voice.

Let's take what happened at Bethany in the house of Martha and Mary for an example. An unexpected visit by Jesus with His disciples has upset Martha who begins to prepare something for them to eat. Instead, Mary, at the Master's feet, listens to His every word. Jesus replies to the protests of her busy sister: ''Martha, Martha, you worry and fret about so many things, and yet few are needed, indeed only one. It is Mary who has chosen the better part'' (Lk 10:41-42).

To daily dedicate a time to prayer is to choose, as Mary did, the one thing necessary. It means that we have grasped that meeting God is the most important and meaningful news of each day of ours. We read in the Bible that God would speak to Moses, the guide of the Israelites, ''face to face'' (Ex 33:11). What a wonderful thing it is for us, too, in our prayer to feel this kind of intimacy, this breathing of the Lord, the sound of His footsteps in our garden.

We shall learn to pray when we learn to contemplate the depth of things with an unbiased eye. Only the one who has the courage to ''waste'' time in prayer has the possibility of also penetrating the mystery of the Divine Presence with his or her gaze. When this happens, amazement melts into joy and, as in the psalm, our lips can barely murmur: ''Yahweh, our Lord, how great Your name throughout the earth'' (Ps 8:8). To praise is the immediate response springing from our heart when we give ourselves to contemplating the greatness of God.

To pray does not mean cutting oneself off from the world. It is not an evasion of one's daily responsibilities. As we praise the Lord and thank Him, a very practical question arises in our hearts: What does God want from us? From me? What does He want from our family, from our parish community?

Here prayer becomes acceptance of the role the Lord has entrusted to us as parents or as children, to me as bishop, to the priests as pastors, to the religious as consecrated people, to the laity as builders of the earthly city.

In the Garden of Olives Jesus prayed: "Father . . . let Your will be done, not mine" (Lk 22:42). Dialogue with God increases our availability to put aside limited interests so as to enter into the ways of God and go to our neighbor's aid.

October 19
Prayer and the Awareness of Reality

Considered in its deep nature and in its origin, prayer is not an activity extrinsically juxtaposed to people, but gushes forth from within one's very being, exudes and flows from each one's core reality.

We could say that prayer is in some way the very essence of humans who put themselves transparently in the light of God, recognize who they are and, as they recognize themselves, recognize the greatness of God, His holiness, His love, His merciful will. In a word, they recognize all the divine reality and the divine design for salvation as they have been revealed by the crucified and risen Lord.

Before it is a word, before it is a formulated thought,

prayer is a perception of reality which immediately flowers in praise, adoration, thanksgiving and in a demand for mercy from Him Who is the source of all being. From this global, synthetic and spiritually concrete experience, the following fundamental points emerge in their appropriate place:

— the perception of the vanity of things cut off from God's project which turns into a plea that we ourselves may be saved from the seduction of meaninglessness and emptiness;

— the perception of the Presence of Him Who is fullness and is never absent or far away wherever anything else truly exists;

— the perception of the living Christ in Whom all these divine projects are summed up and personalized — "Where Christ is, there is the Kingdom," as St. Ambrose said — and this is the foundation of our recognition and confirmation of what really constitutes our relationship of communion with Him Who is both Lord and Savior;

— the perception, in Christ, of the will of the Father as an absolute norm of life and thus our prayer is no longer an attempt to bend the divine will to ours but is the continually renewed attempt to conform our will to the will of the Father (Mt 6:10; 26:39-42);

— the perception of the reality of the Spirit, source of all ecclesial life, Who prays in us (Rm 8:19-27), and so prayer becomes a yearning to emerge from solitude and from the closed condition of individualism and a request to open ourselves more and more to the Kingdom of God, the Church, established in hearts and among people;

— the perception of the cross as a victory over the evil in us and outside us which makes prayer a way of contesting sin, injustice, "the world" and a nostalgia for the heavenly Jerusalem where everything is holy.

October 20
The Prayer of the Whole Christ

God, Who speaks to us repeatedly, listens to our reply in the Liturgy of the Hours and even suggests the very words with which we respond.

The whole of creation which has its head in Jesus crucified and risen and His body in all those who are vitally connected to Him, replies to its Creator, measuring its praise and its cry for mercy, one might say, on the very breathing of the universe, on the passage of time and on the perennial and continually renewed coming and going of light.

Every being in some way is linked to this cosmic prayer which is raised to God especially in the two key moments of sunset and early morning. "What sensitive person would not be ashamed to conclude the day without reciting the psalms, seeing that the smallest birds accompany the beginning of the day and of the night with an habitual act of piety and a sweet song" (St. Ambrose, *Hexaemeron*, V. 12, 36).

"Invited by so much grace given to the Church and by such great rewards promised to piety, let us anticipate the rising sun. Let us go to meet its dawn before it says, 'Here I am!' The Son of justice desires to be awaited and looks for our anticipation of Him" (*In Psalmum 118*, 19, 30).

Vatican Council II reminded us of the singular dignity and value of this prayer: "Therefore, when this wonderful song of praise is correctly celebrated by priests and others deputed to it by the Church, or by the faithful praying together with a priest in the approved form, then it is truly the voice of the Bride herself addressing her Bridegroom. It is the very prayer which Christ Himself

414   OCTOBER

together with His Body addresses to the Father'' (*Sacrosanctum Concilium*, No. 84).

October 21
Meeting the Lord in Recollection

When you want to meet the Lord ''go to your private room and, when you have shut your door, pray to your Father Who is in that secret place, and your Father Who sees all that is done in secret will reward you'' (Mt 6:6).

With these very simple words Jesus teaches us a method: the secret of recollection. Many times we have the experience that if we want to live moments of true prayer a certain atmosphere is required. We have to retire to our room, go apart, not speak to others and not listen; in a word, be recollected. This term has a profound psychological significance because it underlines the fact that often our energies are dispersed. We speak, we listen, we laugh, we move about and are distracted by a thousand things.

Oriental spirituality — apart from the Christian tradition — has examined deeply the subject of recollection. The image which orientals normally use to express it is the image of the tiger or panther which draws itself up in deep concentration to gather together all its strength before hurling itself on its prey.

To encounter God we have to gather up all our strength and become concentrated. We must remove ourselves from externals so to speak. Actually, concentration implies having a single center. If we succeed in putting ourselves before the Lord in this condition an incredible capacity is released in us. Even to ourselves we appear to be different and to have a lucidity and a clarity never before experienced. We understand better the question: "Who am I?"

October 22
Prayer Reveals Christ To Us

If through prayer and contemplative silence we truly confront ourselves and confront God Who lives in our most profound depths, we understand how everything in us tends towards charity and how an intimate relationship with God in prayer reveals that charity to us.

I use the word "charity" although I know that it may be misunderstood. Many people, hearing this word, think immediately of an action, a service, assistance or help to one's neighbor. Charity includes all this but goes much further. It has to do with the whole attitude of human beings who are made for love and can fulfill themselves only in self-giving. Going out of oneself and out of one's egoistic or private interests in this way, offering one's life (and not just some isolated act) for others, each of us feels that the image of God Who is love (1 Jn 4:8) and Who manifests Himself to us in unconditional dedication is being formed within.

This reality is so deep and mysterious that it takes a lot of time to even begin to understand. As long as we have not grasped it we shall not be able, however, to understand ourselves. And the life of other men and women in this world will likewise remain an enigma.

Silent and deeply personal prayer puts us face to face with the truth about ourselves and the Truth which is God. The truth about ourselves is that we have been made to

416   OCTOBER

love and we need to be loved (*Redemptor Hominis*, No. 10). The truth about God is that God is love, a mysterious and exacting love but at the same time a most tender and merciful love. This love with which God embraces us is the key to our life, the secret of our every action. We are called to act out of love, to spend our life willingly for our brothers and sisters, to allow our creativity to express itself and to exercise our intelligence for the service of others (1 Jn 4:7-21).

October 23
Prayer is the Exercise of Charity

The desire to be practical and to engage in dialogue in the exercise of charity leads me to read again Chapter Twenty-five of the Gospel of St. Matthew. The some-times complicated word of Scripture here is very simple, basic and to the point.

The Last Judgment is described. It will have as its sole criterion the practical exercise of charity. Someone has spoken of this as a "secular" Gospel because there are no references in it to faith, to prayer or to worship. The just do not even know that, in the needy ones, they have helped the Lord Himself: "Lord, when did we see You hungry and feed You, or thirsty and give You to drink? When did we see You a stranger and make You welcome; naked and clothe You; sick or in prison and go to see You?" (Mt 25:37-39).

What counts here seems to be the purely material gesture of help for the hungry, the thirsty, the stranger, the naked, the sick and those in prison. To understand this excerpt we have to see in it the overall teaching dealing with the activity of Christian life. Matthew wrote his Gospel for a community which was tempted by empty words, by superficial enthusiasms, but without committing itself seriously to works of charity. This explains the invitation not to be satisfied with saying: "Lord, Lord," but actually to do the will of God and put into practice the word of the Lord. The excerpt about the Last Judgment has to be read from this realistic, concrete, practical point of view.

From this point of view there is no opposition between works of charity and the practice of worship. If what truly counts is intense realism in exercising charity, try to imagine the strong urge towards practical charity which the believer receives from a life of sincerely practiced worship. When a Christian, explicitly professing faith and celebrating liturgical actions, becomes aware of the immense love of Christ for him or her and for everyone, that Christian cannot remain indifferent. He, too, wishes to spend himself totally for others.

This desire, inspired by faith, harmonizes with other spontaneous or reflex desires which we experience regarding the problems of our neighbors. Their needs move us. Their poverty urges us to deprive ourselves of something so as to help them. The wrongs and injustices they undergo arouse our displeasure and indignation and our condemnation for the one inflicting the injustice. They lead us to strive against violence and to commit ourselves, so as to renew society profoundly.

Motives suggested by faith and those coming from our natural sentiments reinforce each other mutually and lead us to a more and more realistic and constant activity.

October 24
The Prayer of Faith

Different levels of prayer coexist in the Christian, and need to be explicitly cultivated especially in certain circumstances and by people called to particular missions. These are the prayer of faith, the evangelical prayer and the apostolic prayer.

The term "prayer of faith" is found in the Letter of James (3:15), where he speaks of a prayer of faith which, if said over the sick person, will save him or her. I would like to extend the term to all those prayers which ask for a grace and which form the majority of the prayers said by the faithful. Prayers of faith fill the nooks and crannies of our shrines. All the candles which are lit in churches throughout the world are fruits of faith. The prayer of faith is that which seeks a particular grace but presupposes faith.

Jesus asks whoever wants to be healed: "Do you believe?" We are not talking about belief in God in general, but of a conscious faith that a good and provident God can come to our assistance in a difficult situation. The prayer of faith involves asking grace for oneself, for a sick person, for our work, for peace in the family, for the health of the children, etc. It is a very beautiful prayer because it takes for granted a particular power God has to help *now* in this moment.

October 25
The Evangelical Prayer

From the very common and simple prayer of faith we distinguish what I call the "evangelical prayer." We might also call it "catechumenal prayer," "baptismal prayer," or — according to circumstances — "penitential prayer." The object of this prayer is not this or that grace but salvation itself, the heart of the Gospel. It asks for Gospel salvation. Compared to other prayers, it is more universal because it presumes that one has understood that the goods of this world are important but only in relation to the ultimate good which is human salvation and reconciliation with God. When we speak of human salvation and reconciliation with God we are talking of being freed from sin and able to conduct a life of faith and hope on a daily basis. An example of evangelical prayer is that of the publican who, standing at the back of the temple, strikes his breast and says, "O God, be merciful to me, a sinner" (Lk 18:13).

It is also called penitential or baptismal prayer because it is the prayer the adult catechumen must say when requesting Baptism: "What do you ask?" "Faith, grace and eternal life." The request is for the totality of the evangelical good: pardon. To say this prayer sincerely one must understand that one does not live by bread alone, by health, by work or by family peace. Underneath and beyond and over all these things, one lives by the grace of God.

We have to train others and train ourselves to say the evangelical prayer in all its ramifications. It can be expressed in its central exclamation: "O God, be merciful to me, a sinner."

October 26
Apostolic Prayer

What distinguishes apostolic prayer from evangelical prayer? A very simple example is the "Our Father," the prayer taught to the Twelve in their role as disciples: not just as individuals to be converted but as persons already co-responsible for the community. For the most part, evangelical prayer is said in the singular: "O God, be merciful to *me*, a sinner." The "Our Father" is in the plural and takes for granted one's awareness of a "we," of a people, of co-responsibility, of solidarity, linking each of us to the other. It asks for goods which are the salvation of this people, not individual goods. It takes for granted that those who say this prayer have taken on themselves problems at the level of the Kingdom of God: "*Your* will be done, *Your* Kingdom come." Even the very remission of sins is no longer an individual but a community commitment: "as we forgive those who have offended us." Behind this there is the whole problem of reconciliation within the community, of the reconstitution of unity through pardon. The "Our Father" is already moving in the realm of apostolic prayer.

We have another simple example of apostolic prayer in Acts 4:24-30. It is closely connected to the effusion of the Holy Spirit on Pentecost. It is something which manifests itself after an individual's Pentecostal experience when the person is already a mature adult in the faith and has become aware of his or her responsibility for the community. It is a prayer which contemplates the action of God in history: "Master, it is You Who made heaven and earth and sea . . . You it is Who said through the Holy Spirit. . . ." It goes on to speak of Jesus' work: ". . . in this very city, Herod and Pontius Pilate made an alliance with the pagan nations . . . against Your holy servant, Jesus, Whom You anointed." Then it asks for fundamental benefits for the community and for the salvation of the world: "And now, Lord, take note of their threats and help Your servants to proclaim Your message with all boldness, by stretching out Your hand to heal and to work miracles and marvels through the name of Your holy servant, Jesus.'' The prayer does not ask that *my* healing should take place, but that healings should take place *so that* the name of the Lord may be glorified. The perspective is that of the Kingdom of God understood as a whole.

October 27
The Prayer of Meditation and Contemplation

Meditation is the exercise which begins from a prayerful reading of Scripture and reflects on the different values of the text. Thus it has the characteristic of multiplicity: thoughts, reflections, and resolutions. It is absolutely necessary to practice it. Indeed it is already a great grace of God because, through the power of the Holy Spirit, it stirs up whoever practices it to attitudes of charity, truth, justice, chastity, pardon, mercy, joy, patience, long-suffering and foresight.

Meditation is indispensable to arrive at a mature spiritual personality. But if we were to see it as an end in itself, we would run the risk of losing ourselves, forgetting its unifying character.

It is contemplation which unifies our various meditative exercises. *Contemplation* consists in looking at the Lord Jesus, Center and Synthesis of all the world, as God. To look at Him, to be satisfied with Him beyond any thought, to nourish ourselves on His person, to allow ourselves to be attracted by Him and to see the Father's face in Him is what contemplation is all about.

Contemplation is a pure gift of God and, clearly, it cannot be produced by our own efforts. If we pretend to have it with our own devices and without having preceded it with the work of meditation, we make a mistake. We have to humbly make the journey, beginning from the reading of the sacred text and passing through meditation which a little at a time becomes easier, opening us to the gifts of the Spirit. At a certain point we shall arrive at that spiritual moment in which our gaze is unified in the Crucifix, contemplates it, adores it and listens in silence for the voice of God.

Nobody should presume to have arrived at one point or another of the journey and each one must understand, with the help of a spiritual director, one's own personal stage. Naturally, God retains the sovereign liberty of introducing a soul into contemplation, making it skip over the ordinary stages.

I repeat, however, that it would be dangerous to want to get to contemplation while overlooking the reading of Scripture and meditation. It is very important to nourish oneself abundantly with many "words of God" so as to be able with truth and humility to contemplate, when the Lord wishes, the Word present in all the "words of God" and behind them.

October 28
The Theme of Unity in the Priestly Prayer (Jn 17)

While conversing with His Father, Jesus questions Himself. And it is in the light of this familiar colloquy of Jesus with His Father that the *object* of prayer is mentioned. It is a word here translated in different ways — "one thing only," "one thing," "unity." Actually, in Greek, it is one little word of two letters (e'n) and means "one," "unique," "a unity," "something mysterious." The Greek word is neuter and can be applied to many realities. It is a mysterious allusion to something which the believer may not so much seek to describe but rather, as happens for all realities in the Johannine Gospel, must seek out through contemplation, through a taste for the presence of these things.

We may, however, refer to some other Johannine images. For example, in Chapter Ten, John speaks about the perspective of "one fold" and of "one shepherd." The image helps us to understand something about this "one" which is at the end of Jesus' prayer. "One fold and one shepherd" refer to all the people, to a multitude of persons, to humanity reunited under the guidance of Christ.

Another word of John which does not include this term but which is very close to it in meaning is the image of the vine. The vine is only one. However, it has many branches. From this point the image can proceed to the expression "one body" which occasionally is found in Paul and which can be read behind this word of Jesus.

The "unity" for which Jesus prays is a mysterious reality and yet important enough to have been at the center of His work. In Chapter Eleven, John speaks of the Lord when His death was imminent and says that according to the words of the High Priest: ". . . Jesus was to die for the nations . . . to gather together *in unity* the scattered children of God" (Jn 11:51-52). This unity, therefore, is not only the object of the prayer of Jesus to His Father, but is also the supreme purpose of Jesus' death, indeed the purpose of His entire life which terminates in His sacrificial death.

October 29
"Father, That They May Be One In Us!"

What is this unity for which Jesus prays? What is the real object of His prayer? That His disciples may be one, that they may be united, that they may become one people. Whenever we hear these words, we think of peaceful and harmonious co-existence and we are concerned when such is not always the case among us, when we find occasional tensions and quarrels.

The prayer of Jesus is actually much deeper, though, than that. It does not in reality say, "that all may be one," and leave it at that. But rather it says, "that they may be one *in us*, as You, Father are in Me and I in You." It is not a unity born of understanding, goodwill, dialogue, group dynamics or endless discussion. It is born of the power of Trinitarian love which, when accepted by Christians, makes them one with Jesus *as* Jesus is one with the Father: "Me in them and You in Me, so may they be wholly one." This is equivalent to being perfect in unity: *to all be in Christ*.

This is the unity which is the object of Jesus' prayer. He does not tell us to reach it with our own powers. He prays: "Father, as the last request of My life, place them in this unity! Put them into this unity so that the world may believe." The meaning is not obvious here either. He doesn't seem to mean: the world sees that we are united and, as a result, believes. But rather: the world sees that our unity is the reflection of the Father's glory in Christ. And so it believes that the Father has sent His Son. It is the Son, not us, Who is revealed. Unity in Him, being one with Him, means being like Him, being where He is, living His life, reproducing in the world His likeness and attitudes.

"As You Are In Me and I In You"

There is a completely clear and unequivocal explanation of this unity: it reflects the way Christ is in the Father and with the Father. So it is not something with which we can draw easy parallels, examples of unity, of gregariousness, of agreement, such as we see in real life. We are talking here about the very mysterious unity of Christ with His Father.

It's not easy for us to grasp what the unity of the Son with His Father means. If, however, we think of other words of Jesus we can grasp this at least: the unity of the Son with His Father is not simply a mutual, pacific and intense co-existence in a reciprocal dwelling. It is a unity expressed in an ongoing dedication and in the fact that those involved are committed to each other. It is a unity whose sign, fruit and instrumentality, is love making a gift of life, the unity of love which makes the other more important than I am.

Evidently, we should not get alarmed here, because even if we have nostalgia and a desire for this unity we know it cannot become a reality through some human program, or a series of arguments or round-table conferences! It is the unity poured out in us by the Holy Spirit, putting us in a state of loving dedication to Christ and with Him to our neighbor. It is a unity yet to be achieved, something for which we want to prepare ourselves by listening, and by opening our hands and hearts to the gift of the Spirit Who, by the power of Jesus' prayer, comes to give us this unity.

And this unity is, after all, symbolized and made concrete in the historical Church. It is the human family. It is the unity of the human race and of all peoples. It is the unity which is a shadow of the reflection in the Kingdom of God of that perfect Kingdom towards which all social, economic and political realities tend. It is the unity *Gaudium et Spes* speaks a great deal about in its final chapter where it describes the action of the Church for the cause of unity.

October 31
"I Say To All of You . . . "

To all of you *young people*, I say: "Grow in your ability to pray!" Try to be aware that the Father loves you and has a plan for each of you for salvation and happiness. Try always to meet Jesus in the fullness of faith. Jesus is the Son Who makes us sons of God, to Whose imitation we are called, by Whose death and Resurrection we are saved and made free from the shackles of sin, and Who is always waiting for us in Eucharistic silence.

Let the Holy Spirit work in you, He Who within you makes the resemblance with the Son grow according to the Father's plan. Feel yourselves in communion with the whole Church.

Be open to the action of God so as to make His will a reality in your life. Ask for this ability, call out for it in the words of Jesus: "Your Kingdom come, Your will be done." Make yourselves available, offering yourselves to the Father in union with Jesus Who offers Himself for us in the Eucharistic mystery.

To you *young people*, I say: "Live the serene joy of your life as children of God." Live in fraternal friendship with everyone. Be faithful to your daily commitments to prayer, even at the cost of sacrifices. Be ready to pray in your families too. Try to get to know the Lord better and better. Ask Him every day for the grace you need to discover your vocation.

To all of you who are young, I say: "Love the silence of prayer which is 'full of the resounding Presence of the Word.' Be ready to listen to the Lord and open to Him in true communion." In reflection with God seek to find your way of being committed to your brothers and sisters in service. Seek the solution of human problems, big and small, in the light of the Word which reveals itself to you in Christ. Find the strength you need to make serene decisions regarding your life in an encounter with Jesus Who makes Himself our food and our offering. Become models for the modern world. Teach it how a person today, in striving to achieve concrete success, can find equilibrium in a continuous ongoing relationship with God.

NOVEMBER

The Saints and Christ

The Council (*Lumen Gentium*, No. 50) reminds us that every intercession on the part of the Saints depends on Christ and is linked to Him, the sole mediator between God and man. Thus our weakness is greatly helped by their fraternal concern. They intercede for us together with Christ in virtue of His power as mediator which is unique to Him to Whom they are intimately bound in virtue of their sanctity and their total gift of self. As regards the power of the example of the Saints, it is related to their unsullied union with Christ by which God, in them, ''vividly manifests to mankind His presence and His countenance.'' He Himself ''speaks to us in them and shows us the proof of His Kingdom.'' The Saints, the Council goes on to say, ''are a visible sign of the presence of the Kingdom of God in our midst.'' But they are also ''God's word,'' a help in interpreting and understanding the Word of God in Christ.

Thus the Saints tell us what living the Word of God in our day means. They are ''witnesses to the truth of the Gospel,'' a decisive, vigorous and, if necessary, polemical affirmation of Gospel truth.

Actually, for the Saints there are no half-measures. They do not have moments of uncertainty. They are a necessary, though polemical affirmation because they also give witness to God's truth in contrast to what seems to be a common mentality in acting and thinking in the world today. It is the culture of the Beatitudes which the Gospel tells us is that way of living and being which manifests the presence of the Kingdom and appears to us to be so opposed to many commonplace aspects of daily life.

November 2
Death and Life

"It is in regard to death that man's condition is most shrouded in doubt" (*Gaudium et Spes*, No. 18). With these grave words the Second Vatican Council describes the anxiety and poverty of humanity before the mystery of death. And we are called to approach this mystery not as an abstract reality but as something which has caused painful breaks in our human nature and in each of our lives. Let us remember our departed dear ones who have entered into eternal life.

Names, persons, faces and kind words come back to our minds, filling them with the memory of days past in their company, of places animated by their wonderful and loving presence. The great Saints, too, lived through the agony of these separations. St. Augustine describes this in words which bear the imprint of the suffering he endured at the death of his mother. He tells us: "As I closed her eyes an immense sadness pressed heavily on my heart and became a flood of tears. But what was it then," he asks himself, "which hurt me so terribly within if not the raw wound caused by the sudden breakup of our sweet and dear life together to which we had grown so accustomed?'' If the Saints can feel such separations so deeply that their hearts break, can things be any different for each of us? How can we fail to feel pain as we relive these moments of sorrow and separation?

At the same time, the great Saints also show us the way which has been opened before us when confronted with the mystery of death. It is the way of Christ's Passover, Christ Who by His death has destroyed our death and by His Resurrection has given us the gift of life. So we remember our departed ones not only in the sadness of separation but also in the gladness of Christ's Resurrection, because it is in Him that our dead live and will live forever. They are with us now and live in our presence. We sense them to be united with us in our prayer. They speak to us in Jesus' words and bring us the consolation of the Lord.

November 3
A "Culture of Holiness"

More than ever today the world needs a "culture of holiness." When the Council underlined the universal call to holiness, to a certain extent it said something new. It said that "all Christians in any state or walk of life are called to the fullness of Christian life and to the perfection of love." It is this generation of holiness which the Council desires: a holiness which, so to speak, one can find in the streets, on the buses, in the subway, in the factory and office, in the family. It is a holiness which leaves the church to enter the reality of everyday life. It will necessarily be a quiet holiness, an unacclaimed one. But it will be a luminous and transparent one, letting us sense the face of Christ from Whom the glory of God radiates. Through the discreet, humble but decisive and courageous presence of this holy generation, the prodigy of the salt of the earth will be renewed, a spirit capable of conserving life and the hope for life in a world which feels itself inevitably moving towards death.

The Council also says that "by this holiness, a more human manner of life is fostered in earthly society." If we think of the life of the Saints with whom we are most familiar, we see them exactly as the Gospel describes them: poor in spirit, meek, thirsting for justice, merciful, pure of heart, persecuted for the Gospel's sake. And for this very reason all of them are workers for peace.

Did Francis of Assisi, Catherine of Siena, Ambrose, Charles Borromeo, Vincent de Paul, not shape the history of the time in which they lived? Did they not cause the sense and the search for true peace to spring up around them? Did they not renew the world with their charity?

November 4
A Crucified and Donated Life: St. Charles Borromeo

What did St. Charles do? He took a risk. He gave his life. While the plague was devouring his city, he threw himself at this scourge, not isolating himself from the plague stricken like a hired hand but like a good shepherd, remaining in their midst without fear of death. This is simply a sample of a thousand other things which he did, a sign of his tireless gift of himself to his own people.

He left us no autobiography, no spiritual writing telling us of his secret, of his inner life, of his prayer. As a witness to the intensity of his prayer we have a few pictures showing him in ecstasy and in tears while he venerated the Crucifix. Apart from these, his swiftness in comprehending the significance of the Madonna's tears at the Shrine of Rho was a confirmation of the faith he lived. He moved in an atmosphere of intense awareness not only of the wounds on the living flesh of his city devastated by the plague but also of the same wounds in the side of Christ, of Christ's sufferings and sorrows. God is not recognized as God nor loved by lazy Christians who are deaf to the Word.

If St. Charles lived his secret inner life in an inexhaustible capacity for praise and suffering (which are the two aspects of human prayer as the psalms tell us), it was probably suffering which primarily manifested itself exteriorly.

St. Charles was a man of prayer, of tears, of penance understood not as an heroic work but as a mysterious and impassioned sharing in the sufferings of Christ and in Christ's entry into the depths of the world's sin, finding there the absurdity of refusing God and living the shock of this until His heart almost broke and His soul was sundered.

St. Charles is one of those great witnesses who penetrated to the very depths of this mystery, who drank the last drops of this bitter chalice and so were capable of a lucid understanding of their own age, its events and its history.

November 5
Saints Are Happy People

What astonishes us in this excerpt from Matthew (5:3-11) is that the proclamation of happiness in several of these Beatitudes has nothing to do with fundamental options (as could be the case for "do not kill," "do not steal," "honor your father and your mother") but rather with situations and attitudes which are not commonly linked to happiness and well-being.

Indeed, the Beatitudes which most impress us are not those which, in a certain sense, are obvious (blessed are the peacemakers, blessed are the single-hearted), but are rather those expressed by striking contrasts: blessed are the poor, the mourning, the hungry.

So a mysterious anthropological reversal is hidden behind the Beatitudes, consisting in passing from *having* to *being* — indeed, from being to giving, from having for oneself to being for others. Understanding the dynamics of this fundamental bridge for human beings we reach the secret of God which is also the secret of being human: to give oneself, to exist for others.

The Saints are happy people. They are people who have found their true center, have accomplished their conversion from having to being, and from being to giving. For this reason they were happy and are happy. As we celebrate their feasts we are invited to share, in faith, their experience of joy and happiness.

A contemporary critic, commenting on a new edition of an ancient and famous *Lives of the Saints* (including Anthony, Ambrose and Augustine) says that the first characteristic that one notes in these lives is a form of great and almost hilarious felicity, of serene and total abandon, of absolute and complete trust in the plans which God's hands have fashioned for their lives. Sanctity — the only way to conquer the sadness of the world — is not presented to us as an impossible dream but as a realistic goal to which we have all been called through Baptism.

Sanctity is our vocation. It is a call which concerns each one of us as the Second Vatican Council said: "There is, therefore, one Chosen People of God . . . there is a common dignity among the members deriving from their rebirth in Christ, a common grace as children of God, a common vocation to perfection."

November 6
Our Friends

The Saints call forth other Saints. What brought about St. Augustine's conversion was the reading of the life of St. Anthony written by St. Athanasius. Eleven centuries later, Teresa of Avila will read the *Confessions of St. Augustine* and will write: "When I read the words that Augustine heard in the garden, I thought the Lord was addressing them to me, so great an emotion did I feel in my heart." And Teresa's life took the turn which brought her to sanctity. Four centuries later, Edith Stein, the Jewish convert turned Carmelite nun who was executed in Auschwitz (and who was beatified by Pope John Paul II in the Spring of 1987), became a Catholic after reading the life of St. Teresa, left her academic career in the University and entered Carmel.

Saints inspire sanctity in others and each of us must find inspiration in their lives. Thus we come to a simple and at the same time a very practical conclusion: let us begin again to read the *Lives of the Saints*. There are plenty of them written today in a healthily critical spirit, keeping in mind the historical context and the fatiguing journey of these brothers and sisters of ours. There are many fascinating and interesting autobiographies, lives of the Saints told by themselves, from the most famous of these such as Augustine, Teresa of Avila, and Therese of Lisieux to others who have lived closer to our own day and age.

In the Book of Revelation, St. John describes the immense multitude of God's witnesses. They are our fellow travellers. The love they have for us assures us that they are never far from us, ever interceding on our behalf. Perfectly united to Christ, they are also united to all those who are in heaven. We can become their friends. Between us a relationship of pleasant and enlightening comradeship can be established. Indeed, while we can experience a warm friendship with someone still on earth, we still come up against our limits and inability to love as we would like. In our friendship with the Saints we are already able to experience ineffable and perfect communion with them in God and the peace of the divine presence, a peace without misunderstandings. To a certain extent, we can already begin to possess on earth that joy and happiness which is our eternal destiny.

November 7
Jesus Has Something To Say About Death

The Church has always spoken about death. It is a word, however, which carries with it a number of graduated shades of meaning which must be borne in mind if what we say is to be appropriate for the person to whom that word is addressed. For example, at times a Christian's comment on death — because it is complex — may even appear contradictory to an outsider. Wisdom says: ''Death was not God's doing . . . He created all to be" (Ws 1:13-14), and St. Paul makes this statement: "Death came through one man." It is the quintessential enemy: ". . . the last of the enemies to be destroyed is death" (1 Cor 15:21-26).

But Sacred Scripture teaches us something else as well: that there is such a thing as a "good death," a death like a baptism from which life is reborn. This is the death of Jesus and He goes to meet it detecting in it a necessity and a purpose: "He had always loved those who were His own in the world, but now He showed how perfect His love was" (Jn 13:1). And the expression which Jesus uses to speak about His own death is repeated every day in the liturgy: "This is My body which will be given up for you." Jesus speaks of His own death and through His words He dissolves its bitterness and ameliorates its cruelty.

He addresses a sober, quiet word commemorating His death, in patience and without hurry. It is a word which was probably understood only very imperfectly by those sitting around Him when He uttered it. And yet it was not forgotten, but rather guarded jealously in the expectation that later days would reveal the fullness of its meaning and its promise. Those days continue up to now.

As Christians we celebrate the action over the bread and wine "in memory" of Jesus. In this way we seek to understand His testament and we look in the New Testament for a word and a hope for our own death as well. This is the true task which the prospect of death offers our liberty: to find the word and the hope which give death a meaning and allow us not to rebel against it in vain as if we were dealing with something totally meaningless.

This is the real "happy death" to which each one has a right.

November 8
Communicating With Our Departed Ones

It is possible to communicate with the dead. They *know us* and, though now in heaven with God, they know the world they have left. Most of all, they know its relationship to God and to His eternal plans which they now can contemplate. And so, from God, they know our affairs and our problems and speak about them among themselves and with God.

They not only know us. *They are near us.* It is true that they have left the world to live where the glorious bodies of Jesus and Mary are — that is, outside and beyond this universe and all its space. But they still intervene in the world and are near us with their prayers, with the power of their love, with the inspirations they offer us, with the examples they remind us of, with the effects of their intercession.

They haven't lost the affection they had for their loved ones, for us, for me, for you. They keep it in heaven, transfigured by a glory never to be abolished.

The expression of St. Therese of Lisieux, ''I want to spend my heaven doing good on earth,'' doesn't only apply to this saintly Carmelite. It also applies to all those whom we piously believe have been received into the mercy of God.

Parents, relatives, close friends, all speak to God about us and present our intentions and our problems to Him. They certainly keep in heaven their intentions and affections and their interest in the things that really matter in this life, the things which also interest us, which they left us as a heritage and in which they educated us. They pray for us so that these interests, intentions and values may mature in us and reach that perfection which will

438   NOVEMBER

allow us to one day enjoy the face of God with them as they do.

There is another way in which the deceased are present which I would like to emphasize. They are close to every tabernacle in which the Eucharist is kept and to every altar on which it is celebrated. The Risen Lord is in the Eucharist as is the power of His Resurrection. With the Risen Jesus all the Saints are present, all those who have died in the Lord. They are present adoring and loving Jesus and also loving us who are gathered around the Lord in the Holy Eucharist. In a special way those are present who love us most, who are dear to us and who adore Jesus with us.

It is true that there is, and there remains, a terrible veil between the visible and the invisible worlds. But it is equally true that love is stronger than death and that the love of the Risen Christ fills the heart and the life of our beloved dead. The same love, or charity, which is in us, is also in them although in them it exists in all its fullness. And, beginning from this very fullness, they reach out to us and we, too, are joined to them in love and prayer.

On the other hand, we could not contact them and we would risk getting involved with phantasms, the fruit of hysteria and false credulity if we presumed to communicate with them in extraordinary ways which have nothing to do with faith and are not founded on prayer. We can sympathize with the desire that some — tried by sorrow following the loss of someone dear to them — might have to get in touch with that departed soul. But superstitious means are not the way to do so and are of no use.

In faith, in prayer, and in the Eucharist we have the means, the place and the setting for a real, loving communication with the dead.

Man, The Image of God

What is the basis of our personal dignity, the dignity of each and every person? To the eyes of faith, it is the creation of human beings in the image of God. This creation, told in Genesis, constitutes the biblical foundation of the dignity of the person and the root of his or her rights and duties.

So let us briefly reflect on the words of Scripture: "Let us make man in our own image" (Gn 1:26). Right at the start let me say that the more precise translation is: "Let us make *mankind* in our own image." In Hebrew, *Adam* (man) is a special, concrete and collective noun. And so here we must read the creation not only of the first human being but of humankind, of people. And this has to be emphasized: it is not just the first human being, or the one who has not yet sinned, who is worthy of respect. Each and every human being, every individual, is created by God in His image.

The story continues: ". . . in the likeness of ourselves, and let them be masters of the fish of the sea, the birds of heaven, the cattle . . . God created mankind in the image of Himself, in the image of God He created him, male and female He created them" (Gn 1:26-27).

What is, properly speaking, the image of God in humankind? Evidently it cannot be limited to a human quality nor to a human function and not even to a human way of acting.

Human beings are the image of God in their nature, in their very being. Later the Bible will use another expression to clarify the concept of image when it will reveal that human beings are called to be children of God, that they have the power — as St. John says — to become the children of God. They have this power to the extent that they are desired, created, loved and now saved by God in Jesus.

Their value is one produced by God, Creator and Savior. The supreme dignity of the human person lies in that person's very being and in his or her inalienable vocation. It is born of a special intervention on the part of God, their first and principal cause. It manifests itself in our participation in the sovereignty of the Creator over all things. It is expressed in our capacity for relationships, for awareness, for dialogue and for love of God. It is, in other words, born from the fact that God always loves this living human being, dialogues with him or her, calls him or her into communion with Himself and truly makes that individual His child.

November 10
A Threatened Dignity

Human dignity, as Genesis (Ch. 3) again teaches us, is always a dramatic and threatened dignity. It is not a pacific gift, not something given as the tranquil beginning of an inevitably harmonious development. From the very start it is marked by, and exists in the context of, a struggle, an enmity: "I will make you enemies of each other, you and the woman, your offspring and her offspring." The bloody conflicts we are living through and which fill our hearts with dismay, remind us that the basic reality of mankind is marked by an implacable conflict, that peace and tranquility are the end of a process and are a conquest, the fruit of a profound education of the human heart.

Mary Immaculate is placed in our midst as a sign of the beginning of this new world, of the regaining of peace and of the meaning and dignity of life.

Human dignity is always threatened by untruth. Eve says, responding to her Questioner: "The serpent tempted me." There is a continuous untruth which tries to seduce human dignity and get it confused with quality of life. It tempts us to desperation as we attempt to succeed in our efforts. The desperation expressed in so many realities of modern existence is often hidden by a pathetic veil but is not for this reason less dramatic. The sufferings human beings endure are also understandable as a struggle against evil, as a clear distinction, a clear opposition to everything which continually tries, from our infancy, to mar our human existence.

Mary Immaculate is placed in our midst as a sign of victory and hope, as the one to whom we must look in this struggle against everything tending to oppress or trample on human dignity.

The dignity of human life has to be defended against incessant attacks of desperation which are found especially in the most fragile moments of that life: at its beginning and at its end.

Mary addresses a message to each of us, to each of you. It is the message of a strong, tenacious struggle, with the arms of truth and of justice, so that life may be defended in every moment and in every instant; so that all temptations to terror and to violence may be continually and strongly opposed by the search for truth, for justice and for love; so that everyone, looking at Mary, may become aware of their own personal dignity and may feel, as she does and along with her, supremely loved by God.

Sinful Humanity: The Starting Point for God's Action

In what way do the people of today bear the presence of the God of glory? How are they the image of God — those individuals who find themselves downcast and discouraged through their own fault or that of circumstances? If we are to give a correct and illusion-free response we must take into account the following:

Certain promoters of human justice see the "sinner" as a stubborn, unredeemable brute, someone to be punished. Period. I use the biblical word "sinner" for the one who is often called "delinquent" both because of its actual meaning of "one who deviates or skids" and also because it is a definition of humanity in which all of us recognize ourselves.

It is true that each of us may experience an instinctive and primal sense of rejection when confronted with people who have, for example, killed, who are salespersons of death, who use violence against innocent people, who have robbed an older person. How are we going to be able to see in those individuals the sacred image of divinity? Evil has stained and disfigured and lacerated them.

But it is here that we are called to a more correct understanding of the scriptural message and not simply to an initial, optimistic, facile acceptance of it. Actually, the sinful human being, "deviant and delinquent," is the protagonist of the human drama narrated in the Bible. Time and time again and in the smallest detail the impiety and injustice of this individual is described in its pages: from Adam to David, from Solomon to Herod to Pilate.

There is no crime committed by human beings which is not described in the Bible, and described not as a final, irreparable stage of human degradation but as a starting point for God's rehabilitative action.

This is so because God "does not desire the death of the sinner but that he be converted and live." In reality, Christ took our human nature so as to be totally like us, so as to become a compassionate and trustworthy high priest (Heb 2:17). Christ experienced temptation as we do, so as to be able to come to the aid of those who are tempted (Heb 2:18). He can pity our infirmities. He can feel just compassion for those in ignorance and error.

And Jesus said openly and often in the Gospel that He came into the world not for the just but for sinners, not for the healthy but for the sick and those needing a doctor. He said that He had come to seek out and save the lost (Mt 9:12-13; Lk 19:10; 1 Tm 1:15). Finally, Jesus founded His Church to be a mother and a refuge for sinners.

November 12
Close To Everyone, Equal To All

The first thing that, as Christians, we have to do to put ourselves close to sinful and fragile human beings who have yielded to the temptations of the Evil One, is to feel ourselves bound to reform our own life, to begin by regaining in full our dignity as children saved by the mercy of God, because it is this which renews us in the mission of mercy to which we are called.

We cannot presume to be just, as the Pharisee in the parable did (Lk 18:9). We must recognize ourselves as sinners. Looking into our heart we shall easily discover inclinations to evil, to every evil. We shall see that we are immersed in many miseries and infidelities and we shall see our deviations, our transgressions of the law, the beam in our own eye. The desire for all evils lies factually within us.

Many Catholics go to confession and then say they have nothing to confess because they have not stolen anything or killed anyone! But it is very easy to kill filial, fraternal or married love. One can extinguish the smouldering wick and create a night of death for one's neighbor. One can poison that neighbor's existence and bring him or her to desperation even without using arsenic, if one makes life in the community impossible and infernal.

Certainly one can steal millions by swindling and robbing but one can equally, with slander, calumny, rumors and insinuations, steal a good name, the honor and the innocence of one's neighbor, all of which have more value than money. One can rob another of his or her hope of remaking their life, of finding acceptance at home, of love, a job, the pardon of the Lord! To all of us Jesus says, "If there is one of you who has not sinned, let him be the first to throw a stone . . ." (Jn 8:7).

Aware of our own sins, we can then take our stance with the rest of this sinful world. Our fraternity is founded in creation and is present by the power of the vocation of Jesus. We should feel ourselves equal to all people in a profound way, walking together with our shackled brothers and sisters, covering the same road as they, just as Jesus always did.

November 13
The Logic of the Incarnation

We have to live in the logic of the mystery of the Incarnation, which is to be "with" and to be "in." I know that I am asking a great deal. But it was the request God made of Jesus: to be "with" and to be "in." It is what we desire to live in the liturgy of the mystery of Christmas, Easter and the Eucharist.

"For our sake, God made the sinless one into sin" (2 Cor 5:21). With these few words Paul sums up all the depth of the mystery of the cross and at the same time the divine dimension of the reality of redemption.

We are called to believe in these words and not to make two worlds: one by *speaking* of these things and another *acting* as if they did not really exist or as if only worldly realities existed to be maintained, so as not to create too many external difficulties.

Jesus is the Lamb of God who takes away the sin of the world. On the cross He made himself "sin" in our place. He bore our sins in His body on the wood of the cross, and became "accursed" for us (Gal 3:13).

We, too, have to bear our daily cross and the cross of our brothers and sisters. Certainly, many sacrifice themselves for the sins of others. I think, at this moment, of those unjustly condemned. I think of those — and they are numerous — who after a long time of imprisonment without being charged see themselves freed. I think of those — and I know them because they write me about their spiritual journey — who accept pain and make a real interior voyage of prayer, study and listening to the Word of God. I am thinking of Christians, priests and bishops condemned to prison and to hard labor for their faith.

How do we have to *be* to make human dignity live again?

When a person suffers, it doesn't matter any more whether he or she is innocent or guilty, that individual is always worthy of human compassion. We must draw near to them, understand them, raise them up by our

446   NOVEMBER

words, our actions, our fellowship. It is the duty of every Christian to take care of a brother or sister who is in need.

November 14
The Person: In the Gospel and In Society Today

No matter how the society in which we live every day may be judged from the social and political point of view, it is certainly subject to the rough arrogance of materialism, especially its consumerism, its search for immediate enjoyment, its worries about life, its anxiety about quality, its fascination with power and with mass movements. It is concerned with numbers and with "having" over "being." It is intolerant of waiting, of needing to be patient and of having to build things up attentively. It wants to have everything and to have it immediately.

These are the thousand and one things we sense around us in people's daily lives, people who tend in one way or another to forms of depersonalization. Maybe what most characterizes our times is this very decline in respect for the person. There is no respect for other people as evidenced in terrorism and in all the forms of attack on one's neighbor and on the tranquility of social life. Nor is there any respect for one's own person. Drugs, which amount to self-destruction for the sake of an immediate thrill and a short-term excitement are the most extreme manifestation of this. It is out of this terrible phenomenon of drugs that many of our society's problems emerge and explode. Between terrorism and drugs, I would also put the abortion mentality as a form of contempt for the person and for the vocation to motherhood.

The Gospel message is radically opposed to this way

of living and thinking. The Gospel underlines the value of a single person, of a single individual, the good news of Jesus in particular. In their comment on the first verses of Chapter Eighteen in St. Matthew and of Chapter Fifteen in St. Luke (the three parables about mercy) exegetes have noted that one of the characteristics of these two excerpts is the importance of the individual in the ecclesial community and the importance of each one in the mercy of God. Chapter Eighteen of St. Matthew begins with Jesus putting a child in the midst of His listeners.

Respect for the person, attention to the person is the sign by which one identifies the ecclesial community.

November 15
Man: The Sign of the Absent God

We are not totally identified with life, joy, love and the light of truth. These goods are present in us but are also at a distance. We go looking for them as absent goods, driven by those partial forms of their presence in us.

When we fail to recognize this presence/absence of life, of truth and of love and pretend that we ourselves are life, truth and love in a total and exhaustive way, we deceive ourselves and our words produce death, untruth and discord. At this point we should give a more exact name to life, to truth and to love or we will not be able to travel down those arduous paths leading us more deeply into the mystery of reality.

Suffice it to say that, through an intuition which is always present at the heart of the human experience and which must also assume the progress of a rigorous reflective discussion, human intelligence can understand that the fullness of life, of truth and of love are to be found in a reality which — though making itself present in human beings — is beyond them and is called God.

And so we find ourselves as the presence of an absent God, as a sign of Him, as an expression through which He manifests Himself though He is the inexpressible. In this sense, we as human beings are the word of God. And in human speech this radical human characteristic comes to light.

Thus the word and the being of humans are creative but only to the extent that — in an attitude of expectation, availability and fidelity — they obey what God says to them. What God can say to people, with what intensity, with what communicative power, cannot be anticipated, determined or decided by a human being. The only proper anticipation, the sole decision, is that of silence full of expectation, of respect and of obedience.

November 16
Illness, Liberty, Obedience

The only way in which illness can be embraced and lived — and not simply tolerated as a dead time in human existence — would be a way allowing us to recognize a meaning in it, a positive sign for the spirit's journey, even though one's members are paralyzed in the suffering and humiliation of the flesh.

It is certainly possible to recognize this sort of meaning in sickness but only on condition that the meaning of human life is likewise reexamined. Recognizing that human freedom is nourished by — and especially by —

what is suffered, requires first of all a recognition that every human freedom begins under the sign of obedience.

When a man learns to go beyond a possessive and self-sufficient vision of earthly goods, then he also learns to believe and to hope even when they disappear. The loss of one's health does not lead to the discouraging conclusion that life is now impossible or not worth living, but rather leads one to invoke and hope for a health or a salvation which arrives when one has finally joined his idle hands in prayer.

The disappearance of the possibility of saying a clear and explicit word, of all easy and untrammeled communication, does not lead to desperate and lonely resignation but rather leads to the thought of, and the search for, that more perfect and mysterious communion to which every human word aspired without ever succeeding in reaching it.

The inability to communicate which is shown painfully and incontrovertibly in relationships with suffering people, is present and latent in every human communication. To be able in faith and hope to challenge this incommunicability when it shows itself in extremely painful forms is an indispensable condition if one is also to believe in the very imperfect communication which takes place in ordinary human relationships and in the ordinary moments of life.

We are not our own master, nor are we the master of our words and works, our destiny and our life. In this light, it is understandable that we can never arrange our own death, can never conclude that enough is enough, that there is no sense in remaining here to suffer or that there is no sense in someone else's remaining here to suffer. Those who reserve such a judgment to themselves are really proclaiming their desperation.

The extreme suffering of terminal illness is the human experience in which, mysteriously, one finds supreme liberty: the freedom of faith and not that of works.

November 17
Individual Conscience and Justice

We have to guarantee and revive the conditions which enable the individual conscience to mature in its ability to notice the meaning and value of living, of "justice." Under what conditions can the individual conscience mature in this ability? Briefly, we can sum them up in three: memory, contemplation and relationship.

We have to recover our ability to recall, to keep the *memory* of our roots. To pretend to begin continually from the beginning would be really inconclusive and exasperating besides being presumptuous.

We have to recover and develop a *contemplative* approach to make us able to understand and accept the demands of reality contained, for example, in the most basic experiences of human existence: birth, love, family, suffering, work, festivity and death. These invitations to growth are suffocated today by the increasingly artificial character of our way of life.

We must especially recover the possibility of an immediate — and thus more transparent — *relationship* among people. The exasperating pragmatism of relationships in our society today is an obstacle to seeing one's neighbor's humanity because it is hidden by the role in which he or she is confined.

There is no problem in recognizing the linkage

between these three needs, a linkage made urgent by the current socio-cultural situation and the dynamism of Christian experience. It is born of the memory of the events worked by God in human history, a memory which has its climax in the Eucharist. It is developed in the progressive acceptance and understanding of the Word become flesh which is contemplated in assiduous meditation on Sacred Scripture and assimilated in the Eucharistic bread. It is expressed in a fraternal closeness animated by the one Spirit.

We are not talking about exploiting faith for some ulterior purpose, no matter how worthy, such as moral education or cultural and civil progress. We are rather talking of throwing light on the deep and objective connection between the different stages, aspects and experiences of human existence. It is a unity in which the faith option does not appear as a simple, juxtapositioned accessory — and, therefore, a valid alternative — but rather constitutes the last horizon in which all the rest is located, interpreted and oriented.

November 18
Jesus Encounters Every Person

In the Gospel according to St. John (20:11-18), the Risen One is presented to us in the simple familiarity of an encounter, of a personal encounter from which the most basic sentiments and emotions flow.

We are faced with a very simple reality, rich in feeling and emotion: a woman's weeping for the death of a Person Who had been of great importance in her life and to Whom she felt she owed the new, luminous, orientation of her existence. In fact, as soon as she recognized Him, she calls Him "Master" --the One Who had taught her how to live.

We are dealing here with noble and elevated sentiments but still in that field which, with a justifiably critical accent, we should feel tempted to call "the private sphere." What has this "private sphere" — the personal feelings of Mary of Magdala, whom we barely know — to do with the great cosmic event of the Resurrection which changes world history?

One of Jesus' words enlightens our effort at replying. Jesus asks her: "Who are you looking for?" It is still a personal sort of question dealing with the direct relationship between a human being and another person even if this person is more than human.

Then there is the other word of Jesus which He uses to give a name to this woman: "Jesus said to her, 'Mary.' " Being called by name like this reveals to the woman the mystery of the Resurrection. In her weeping, in her sadness, in her lack of hope, she hears herself called by name and with love by the One Who was dead and now lives, is before her and calls her. From this moment onwards Mary of Magdala has a deep understanding, and a totally reversed one, of reality; she has a new way of seeing and comprehending things. Her eyes and heart are opened.

At the same time she is shown the cosmic, universal and permanent meaning of this message. Jesus says, "I am ascending to My Father and to your Father, to My God and to your God." As a human being like us, Jesus brings to the sphere of God His reality as a human being, our reality as human beings, poor, weeping, sad and searching. With Jesus we are brought into a new reality as children of God, brothers of Jesus Christ and brothers and sisters of one another. All our world, our affairs, the realities of our life, work and family, the apartment where we live, our working tools, our school commitments, all this is raised up with us towards this sphere of life illuminated by God's gift. In Jesus we are His children.

This Gospel excerpt, in which the glory of the Risen One enters into us through the reply to our most profound and personal emotions, reminds us that the mystery of the person is always an essential point of reference where we are talking of life, of faith and of the most profound realities. And even where great interests are in question and very grave problems (think of the grave problems of work, of world hunger, of violence, of the defense of unborn life), a profound attention to the person, to the individual, to his or her dramas and desires, is, and always will be, necessary.

November 19
Abraham's Journey

Vocation means the authoritative proposal of a goal, of a journey to reach liberty. Vocation is Jesus' word: "Come, follow me. Come, I will make you a fisher of men." This proposal which Jesus makes to each of us offers the practical possibility of leaving our personal limits, fears and uncertainties and constitutes a formidable stimulus for a journey of true liberation.

Let us now try to check the definition through the excerpt from the Letter to the Hebrews where it speaks of Abraham and Moses.

Who was Abraham before his call, before his vocation?

As far as we can know anything about him or understand him, he was a shepherd, an unambitious individual without great prospects, who liked a quiet life and was tied to and conditioned by a comfortable milieu — we might call it consumeristic. He was somewhat refined and liked to enjoy life.

Abraham lived in that situation and his rather narrow life, though it was not evil, was certainly undemanding. Then, at a certain point, God calls him.

The Letter to the Hebrews tells us: "It was by faith that Abraham obeyed the call" (Heb 11:8).

God calls him and, calling him, He tears him up by the roots: "(He) obeyed the call to set out for a country that was the inheritance given him." God calls him to a new existence, to become a father of peoples, and Abraham believes, takes a chance, frees himself from all about him and sets out: "He set out without knowing where he was going." This mysterious and wonderful phrase moves me every time I read it. It brings me back about twenty-five years to a time when I found myself faced with a very important decision. For days on end I meditated on this verse of the Letter to the Hebrews: "He set out without knowing where he was going." Those were decisive words for me, confronted with a choice which was meaningful for all the rest of my life: a decisive faith choice and a reply to a call through which I accepted Abraham's journey into freedom.

November 20
Moses' Journey

In the Letter to the Hebrews Moses is briefly defined as "the son of Pharaoh's daughter." Although he is the son of Hebrews, Moses comes to be considered as the son of Pharaoh's daughter through a twist of fate recounted in the book of Exodus, and thus he is educated as a dignitary.

St. Ambrose, however, commenting on what happened at the Egyptian court, underlines that Moses was a dignitary but was also the slave of the court and of a paganism which penetrated the very marrow of his bones. He was the slave of a society which lived on the riches of a few and on the poverty and wretchedness of many.

That was Moses' slavery: the slavery of a dignitary of his day.

Moses, called by God into the desert, accepted a new journey into freedom, came out from the situation in which he was, freed himself from what was a privilege but also a heavy kind of bondage, so as to move in the direction of truth and justice. The Letter to the Hebrews says that he "chose to be ill-treated in company with God's people rather than to enjoy for a time the pleasures of sin" (Heb 11:24-26).

Abraham had accepted the call and had left his country. Moses accepts the call, leaves a situation of bondage and accepts the "opprobrium of the Christ, the Anointed." This mysterious expression, meaning that Moses accepted the "opprobrium of Christ" many centuries before Jesus did, is taken from a psalm and actually does not refer to Jesus' opprobrium but to that of the Chosen, Messianic, people.

Moses preferred poverty and the maltreated social state of the Messianic people to the pomp and privileges of the court of Pharaoh. He preferred to be poor with the poor and he began a journey of freedom with his poor people.

Being With Jesus

The Lord asks us to assume the active role of those who know how to speak the word of Jesus, to the role of being with Jesus, of being on His side.

Actively taking our place with Jesus means, first of all, being able to repeat His words. Perhaps we think that for Him it was easy to say, "Your sins are forgiven," because He was the Son of God. In reality, Jesus suffered deeply, paid a personal price, endured long nights and hours of prayer so as to appropriate the divine power to forgive sins and enable it to operate.

Although He had it already within Himself, we know from the Gospel that, when faced with the dramatic moment when He pronounced divine words of salvation (think, for example, of the Lazarus story), Jesus was moved to tears (Jn 11:35).

As far as Peter is concerned, it is easy to imagine how he felt himself tremble when he said those words to the cripple; how he must have felt himself shaking as he said words which could have made him look ridiculous before everyone! How do you say to a paralytic, "Get up and walk," without coming close to being ridiculous?

Inspired by the Holy Spirit, though, Peter entered courageously into this situation, put himself in Jesus' shoes and decided to participate in His holy work. This meant taking an active role and putting himself on the line for Jesus.

Entering into an active role means accepting the power of the Lord Who wants to produce by my hands, gestures of salvation, love, mercy, truth and friendship. It means accepting the power of my call to be like Jesus and like Peter, accepting the commitment to save others, to bring the saving word, to pronounce not just words of exterior comfort but words having in themselves the power of the Holy Spirit for that type, kind and method of salvation which the Lord has prepared in my vocation.

November 22
Evangelical Virginity

By Christian virginity we mean total dedication to the Lord, we mean sitting at His feet.

In his First Letter to the Corinthians, the Apostle says: "Brothers, this is what I mean: our time is growing short. Those who have wives should live as though they had none, and those who mourn should live as though they had nothing to mourn for; those who are enjoying life should live as though they had nothing to laugh about; those whose life is buying things should live as though they had nothing of their own; and those who have to deal with the world should not become engrossed in it. I say this because the world as we know it is passing away.

"I would like to see you free from all worry. An unmarried man can devote himself to the Lord's affairs; all he need worry about is pleasing the Lord" (7:29-32).

Christian virginity is not merely celibacy but a renunciation of matrimony — in this case we could define it as "not belonging to anybody" — so as to be of service to everybody. It is, rather, a *spousal virginity*, a "being with the Lord." A difficult problem now surfaces: is there any point in talking of *espousal* in relation to virginity, or is this not a language leading to anthropological and social complications? I believe we must never use words at random for these definitions and we must explain their exact meaning.

What does espousal mean? To avoid defining it simply in relation to sexuality and to the body and rather in relation to the person, we say that espousal means "to define oneself in relationship to another," to have an awareness of oneself only in relationship to someone else.

So defined, it raises profound questions about the mystery of the person and even foreshadows the mystery of the most Holy Trinity. Actually, the Father is He Who is in relation to the Son. The Son is He Who is in relation to the Father and the Spirit is the One in relation to the Father and to the Son.

This mystery of the spousal gift can enter intimately to become part of the very mystery of a person, defining that individual and providing the horizon of his or her life.

And so Christian virginity means seeing oneself not as someone existing just for oneself but in relation to Christ in virtue of a reciprocal gratuitous action. In this way Christian virginity enters into the most intimate part of the life of the person and surrounds it.

All this, among other things, brings us back to an historical-biblical reality: Jesus desired gratuitously to define Himself in relationship to a people and desired that a people, by grace, choice and love, should define itself in relation to God. This is the mystery of the Covenant whose fundamental formula is: "I am your God and you are My people." This is the same as saying: "I am yours and you are Mine." Frequently, in fact, the Covenant is expressed in Scripture with spousal symbols: think of the Canticle of Canticles, of the book of the prophet Hosea, of those parables of Jesus about the Kingdom which mention weddings.

It is not easy "to say" these things. When we say them we merely touch them superficially in the twofold sense that we barely skim the surface and that we risk destroying their petals and perfume. It is contemplation as a gift of God which allows us to enter into an intuition of the mystery of espousal which defines consecrated virginity and then becomes the source of interior discipline and of rigor in thoughts, actions, words and gestures.

November 23
Leave and Receive

"Leave everything, everything you love, your house, your boat, and receive in exchange a new dwelling, a new house . . . become able to build for each other a house which is hospitable, a sign of hope." These words confront us with a paradox. Leaving everything so as to belong solely in faith, to that unique, singular and unpredictable Person Who is Jesus Christ, becomes for us the beginning of a new life in the world, of a mission to people capable of creating and motivating new forms of acceptance and hospitality.

Let us pause for a moment before this paradox. We have to reject a twofold temptation as we face it. On the one hand, the temptation to approach the two extremes of the paradox simply and superficially without understanding its profound logic (leave everything on the one hand; be able to accept everything on the other); on the other hand, the temptation to allow the tension to grow weaker, reducing the radicality of our belonging to Jesus Christ or evading the need of accepting others.

And so, what does faith ask of us, that faith we have professed together? It asks us to choose, to accept this evangelical paradox rigorously, to understand its riches and truth and to make its needs realities.

At this point some personal questions arise:

how shall we be able to understand its riches and truth?

in what areas of experience will we be able to emphasize this paradox and make it a reality?

To begin with, take passionately to heart and do not cease to praise God for the mystery of the living human person. It is this praise of God for the mystery of life which gives so much warmth to the writings of Paul VI in his so-called "Thought of Death" which is really a "Thought of Life." Find the ability in yourself to discover life and the human person as realities open to the Absolute and help your friends and followers with kindness.

Let us always have, and grow in, the availability to accept goodness, truth, joy, love and life itself from God. These things, part of our words and actions, are open to the next life and towards that communication with God and among ourselves which satisfy our every desire.

November 24
The Various Christian Vocations

Inexhaustible are the depths of the heart of God and the cross of Christ and they can be present in Christian life in continually new, different and complementary ways. Each one receives a different call to serve the world through a different way of imitating the heart of God and the cross of Christ. And so, from a single root, come different calls and vocations.

There is the way of total dedication to the mystery of intercession and of suffering, of silence and of contemplation in a programmed distance from concrete, worldly occupations so as to assure for the world the thing it most urgently needs: the nearness of God.

There is the way — true and legitimate because it derives from the same source — of complete dedication to the Church's evangelizing mission through the acceptance of the duties connected with pastoral ministry. This vocation normally involves renunciation of direct tasks in the professional and properly political fields, with the object of giving to the world a particularly effective image of Jesus the Good Shepherd Who offers all His life for His flock.

There is the way — and this, too, stems from the cross and the heart of Christ — of a more direct involvement in daily worldly realities, in economic and social events and in political power so as to free them from every false and sinful use and to make them serve the true good of people according to the plan of God.

The Holy Spirit raises up discernment and Christian vocations, and a Christian vocation means to understand oneself fully, understand freedom, history, one's own tasks and the life of people in the light of Christ. Christian vocation is obedience to this light. It means telling others that only this light is the full truth for people.

November 25
Who Am I?

The Gospel of Luke (7:11-17), narrating the resurrection of the son of the widow of Naim, quotes three expressions of Jesus at verse 14: "Young man, I tell you to get up." Scripture never says things for the sake of saying them. And if it uses three expressions it is because it intends to express three things and wants to go deep into an aspect of Jesus' relationship with us.

"Young man." This term indicates a young man like all others; son of a weeping widow, member of a community, part of a people. Jesus takes him in his actual setting and draws near him in his social and cultural context.

"I tell you." Having taken him in the generality of his social, cultural, familiar and affective milieu, Jesus now speaks to him in his absolute individuality: "I tell *you*." "Get up." When this word resounds in the New Testament it is a peal of heralding a resurrection. It means, "You are alive; there is a new life for you!" New possibilities are opening before you in this totally new life.

The three expressions which Jesus utters help us reply to the question: Who am I? I am first of all a distinctive part of a family and social group. Each of us here is a child of our parents, part of a religious, cultural and human group. As such, each of us is the object of the love of God Who calls us into history.

"You, O Lord, are the One Who has loved me, Who has sought me in this family, in relation to these parents, brothers, sisters, relatives and friends — all people who share the immediate experience of my existence. You wanted me and You love me in my school, and in my cultural and societal relationships." Within the total picture of these relationships there is, nevertheless, a personal and unrepeatable word: "I tell *you*." And nobody else. We are requested to become aware of the singularity of our history so as to understand who we are.

Our personal life is so unique that God desired it for Himself and did not make it depend on anybody else.

This is the absolute dignity of my person: the fact that God wants me for Himself. And so He is concerned with the individuality of my life and of my journey, even if to me it appears to be poor, modest and rather uninteresting.

God has in mind and in His hands my history as a highly individual story which He does not want to exchange for anybody else's. He does not want to barter us for anybody because our value is definitive and irrevocable.

God has compromised Himself for my personal history. Maybe we think too little of this truth. We do not attach much importance to ourselves and yet here we find the very source of our personal dignity. The root, the origin, of our being with others, of our forming community, of our creativity, resides in this expression: "I tell you!" It is vital to grasp in prayer, even for a single instant, the beauty of, "I tell you!" "Lord, do You really mean me?" "Yes, I really mean you." "Lord, do You really mean that You Who are so great and limitless, You Who have created the universe, Who always have lived and always will live . . . You say these words to me?" "Yes, I say them to you and for you." We should never cease to be amazed by this truth! And we could then understand that young paralyzed man who on his deathbed exclaimed, "Thank You, my God, for all You did for me!" He had grasped that his life was made for him and was an act of love.

Then in prayer we should try to hear said to us the order: "Get up! Arise!" "O Father, You said this to me when You gave me life and created my soul; You repeated it with love at the moment of my Baptism." Indeed this is, for each of us, our baptismal command: "Arise!" Live the life of Christ, a new life. Show the world its potential. Who am I? I am the one who has been called in this special way by God.

November 26
Who Are You?

How does the Lord reveal Himself to us? First of all in His Word. You are the Word of God. Understanding the Word of God well is the same as understanding who I am, as understanding that sometimes I am happy and other times, on the contrary, I am sad, I suffer and am disturbed.

The Word is a "You" which explains me and I must learn to read it in Scripture praying: "Lord, You have made me and this Word is the One which created me at the beginning." I begin to listen in silence. I reflect. I respond. I supplicate. Prayer must always be a reply to this "You," to the Word.

You are also the Church. I understand myself when I trust in Jesus Who is in the Church, Who becomes Church. And so I must listen to what the Church proposes and follow it.

But I must also learn to see the Lord Who speaks to me and reveals His greatness in every creature and in every work of His. The whole of life must be unified in dialogue with Jesus, in prayer, in listening to the Word, in relationship with the Church, in cultural concerns, in attention to others, in listening to society.

If the Lord is the One Who saves me and teaches me the truth about myself, if I have accepted that He is to be the "You" of my life, then every value is reclaimed.

Situations and external or internal cultural conditions will change and tomorrow other things will be done, different from those of today. But the fundamental meaning of existence is to have understood Who the Lord is for me and in relation to me. His Word remains even when everything changes and passes away. His Word is an unshakable rock.

When Peter said to Jesus: "You are the Christ, the Son of the living God," he also discovered himself. And actually Jesus responded: "I tell you, you are Peter." When we have thoroughly understood this fundamental dialogue, we have understood many other things and we can become witnesses to that "You" we have learned to know and which has given us an awareness of our being.

"O Mary, you were able to make of your life a continuous and uninterrupted dialogue with the Lord. Grant that we may continue to know Him as the truth of our existence and to be able to manifest Him in joy and serenity every day of our lives."

November 27
Constructive Communication

In his Letter to the Ephesians, Paul writes from prison and we are impressed and moved to admiration by the contrast between his situation as a prisoner, limited in possibilities of self-expression, and the universality of his message, the impassioned power of the universal proclamation to pagans.

"I have been entrusted with this special grace . . . proclaiming to the pagans the infinite treasure of Christ" (Ep 3:8).

This proclamation is then offered to all the world: ". . . explaining how the mystery is to be dispensed. Through all the ages this has been kept hidden in God." The message which, as Dante would say, "joins heaven and earth," is offered so that the comprehensive wisdom of God may be shown forth. And so from the depths of a prison, from a situation of limitation and suffering, the power of a universal proclamation is born, a power that lights up the whole world.

As I reread this excerpt, I was especially impressed by the presence of verbs dealing with "proclamation," "illumination" which burst forth from the heart of St. Paul. He speaks about "proclaiming" (in Greek the word means "evangelizing") the riches of Christ. He speaks of "enlightening" the eyes of all with the hidden mystery. He speaks of "manifesting" God's truth.

To evangelize, to proclaim, to make shine out, to illuminate, to manifest, to make known: we read in these verbs the expression of a constructive communication, of a striking communication, of an enlightening communication which proclaims, which broadens our horizons, which brightens the eyes of the one receiving it, because it comes from a heart having a project and a universal point of reference.

And so we can ask ourselves a question: Is every communication automatically constructive?

By the term "communication" we usually indicate something positive as is proper to the root word "communion," "put in common." We put riches, gifts, talents, affections, passions and enthusiasms in common. There is a communication which expresses merely the vulgarity or meanness of the speaker: public blasphemy, for example, and especially where there is no possibility of reply or rebuttal.

However, the most frequent case may be when communication spreads sadness, bitterness or skepticism. I am not saying that these sentiments are not equally constructive of human life, but if they become the sole way in which we exercise our commitment to communicate, all that results is bitterness and resignation.

The constructive communication St. Paul speaks about is that which always keeps a basis, a horizon, an ideal of a constructive kind even when for the love of truth one must share news which is neither beautiful nor good.

November 28
Communication and Culture

Is it possible to communicate among people?

Sometimes this question is asked at the cultural level, about different cultures and languages which move along on parallel tracks or even clash without an attempt at mutual understanding. More dramatically, perhaps, the question is asked within the context of daily reality: is interpersonal communication really possible between members of the same family? Is it possible to avoid those group and ideological conflicts which may even degenerate into violence, covering the streets with blood?

We have an ungovernable need of true, authentic, interpersonal communication among us. We need to learn the art of this all over again, to rediscover its roots which are found in the heart and in the basic need of the human person. Beginning from these profound values of our being — distinct from that of having, doing and controlling — it becomes possible to open the channels of communication between people again.

No man is an island, nobody is able perfectly to divide what is his from what belongs to others, what he is himself from what others are.

First of all, each one depends on immediate others: mother, father, brothers, sisters, educators and friends.

But, even beyond these relationships and with them as a background, there is the community and human society at large, linked by multiple bonds such as tradition, land, civil setting, common language, ideals, values and models of behavior commonly recognized as normative.

At the ultimate root of such bonds lies deep human identity, human "nature" as willed by the Creator Himself.

But human "nature" does not come to self-awareness, either in the individual or in society, unless through a history dense with relationships which in their totality give its outline to human "culture." "Culture," because of its intrinsic quality, has a history and a gradual development made up of progress and also of relapses, of memory and of creative intuitions, of forgetfulness and of renewed understanding of the past.

The individual can, and certainly must, take up knowingly an attitude of critical distance, and of active contribution, with regard to common culture. And yet one arrives at such an autonomous discernment on the basis of an education and an apprenticeship which are themselves debtors to the common culture of the age.

November 29
Giving a Voice to Every Person

The texture of contemporary life which at first glance appears so lively and dynamic, hides in its folds many human stories marked by suffering, forced inertia, neglect and loneliness. Think what it means, for example, that in this very city, according to statistics, one person in seven lives alone.

We must have the courage to engage in dialogue with these situations, because what makes them especially painful is not simply the burden of suffering which is part of them but the fact that the burden can become inhuman, not known or shared, not made part of the channels of human communication.

I am thinking of many old people who to their straitened economic condition must add the more subtle anguish of loneliness. I am thinking of many sick people who, side by side with the providential intensification of medical assistance, see a corresponding decline in human sharing in their affairs. I am thinking of families who are barely able to take their place in the social context and are crushed by the excessive weight of economic, psychological and educational burdens. I am thinking of many outcasts and social rejects who have become so through traumatic disappointments following upon false hopes proposed by our affluent and self-centered civilization.

At this moment I should like to give each one of these a voice, to become the voice of the one who has no voice. I would like to repeat to this immense and silent crowd the liberating word of Jesus, ''Ephphatha! Be opened! Speak!'' The reactivation of communication with these brethren does not just constitute a duty because of the seriousness and urgency with which their human situation questions us, but becomes also a species of challenge which must be courageously accepted. The impact which these borderline cases have on us becomes a benchmark, a checkpoint, a prophetic incentive for every other form of communication. Actually, even in a single individual unjustly excluded from communication — as St. Ambrose says — "the communion of all humanity is interrupted and human nature and the community of Holy Church are profaned."

November 30
The Christian Way of Communicating

The example of Christian communities must be prophetic and stimulating. For this purpose it is not sufficient to launch new initiatives or defend the institutions of former times. The service offered must be adequate at a technical-professional level and it must be interiorly animated by the unmistakable style of charity.

This is the style Jesus taught us in the parable of the Good Samaritan: to approach every human being with the same disinterested and unconditional purity of the love of God; to accept each person simply because that person is a human being; to become a neighbor to everyone, leaving aside the extraneous factors of culture, race, mental/emotional qualities and religious beliefs; to anticipate desires and always to discover new needs about which nobody has yet thought; to give preference to the one who is most rejected; to confer dignity and value on the one who has least rank and abilities.

To recognize everyone as a child of God, inundated with the mysterious gifts of grace, allows us to accept every suffering person as a brother or sister who gives and receives according to the wonderful laws of the Communion of Saints.

Communion in Christ is the unexpected, transcendent seal on the various forms of human communication. It is the inexhaustible source of increasingly new forms of communication. It is the exacting paradigm in which the Christian community must measure and renew its own behavior where ways of acceptance are involved and as far as catechesis, liturgical life and the evaluation of charisms are concerned.

Communion in Christ is the source of unity and the guarantee of beneficial diversity. Because of this "there are no more distinctions between Jew and Greek, slave and free, male and female, but all of you are one in Christ Jesus" (Gal 3:28). But at the same time ". . . all of you in union with Christ form one body . . . our gifts differ according to the gifts given us."

DECEMBER

December 1
Our Fears and the Great Light

"The people that walked in darkness has seen a great light; on those who live in a land of deep shadow, a light has shone" (Is 9:1).

In this manner the prophet Isaiah presents the mystery of the appearance of the grace of God among people. In this manner the Church today presents the mystery which is the Nativity: a light in the darkness, light shining upon a gloomy earth.

And the Gospel, too, describing the appearance of the angels to the shepherds says: "The glory of the Lord shone around them" (Lk 2:9).

These words — "light among the shadows," "a light shining on a dark earth" — stir up the image of many realities. The prophet, speaking to the people of his time, was dealing with the salvation God would show in the pitiful situation of that people who appeared to be without a future or whose future was filled only by phantoms of war and death. The liturgy, proclaiming these words for all people, is talking about God's light shining in the darkness of sin, shining into the state of ignorance in which people find themselves and which hinders them from knowing God, from knowing themselves and from knowing their future.

If we were to say, in a still more relevant way, what

these darknesses mean and what we mean by a state of ignorance at the present moment, we could characterize them as a situation of diffidence and lack of faith.

Behind the words which Scripture uses to define the state of the "sin of mankind" are many feelings forming part of our daily experience: the fear one person has of another; the fears of the city; the fear of being mugged and assaulted; the fear that someone smarter than we may get to know our business, enter into our affairs and turn them upside down. And then, from an even broader perspective, there is fear of the future, associated, for some, with fear of living and for others with the fear of giving life.

This diffidence constituting our situation of ignorance can reach the point of expressing itself as fear of God, that fear which Adam was the first to feel after his sin, the fear of a God Who rebukes us, Who casts our egoism and sin in our face.

In this atmosphere of diffidence and of generalized fear making us doubt the good faith of everything and of everyone, suddenly, the great light appears. The Letter of the Apostle Paul to Titus puts it differently: "God's grace has been revealed and it has made salvation possible for the whole human race." We have experienced that merciful, benevolent and gratuitous approach with which God has first loved us.

December 2
The Way of Trust

Faced with the world's diffidence and with the reciprocal fear which might overcome us and spoil all our human relationships, God makes us have trust. He comes to meet us and shows us so much trust that He puts in our hands His infant Son.

An infant is a human being who believes in total trust: who entrusts itself completely, abandons itself, believes, does not know what diffidence is. God places His infant Son in our hands as an example of this confidence, of this abandon, of this trust. He trusts us to the extent of making a gift to us of what is most dear to Him: His defenseless Son.

And so God chooses the road of dialogue and trust to heal the hearts of diffident and fearful people. Jesus does not come with power but with amiability. He comes to make the benevolent, sweet and patient mercy of His Father available to us. And so He teaches us, as the Letter to Titus says: "to give up everything that does not lead to God and our worldly ambitions" (2:12). This means that Jesus comes to teach us a trusting relationship among ourselves and to have us put aside or behind us, all those relationships which risk becoming fearful, aggressive, defensive or offensive as we try to anticipate an attack from someone else. Those things which the Apostle called worldly desires are: a contest for the one who can most skillfully swindle the neighbor, who can take most advantage of another. It is a contest founded on egoism or on the fear that the other will take advantage of us first. In the name of God, Jesus comes to teach a different approach, the merciful approach, the approach of "*pietas*," the trusting relationship between the Son and the Father, opening our hearts and making us ready for mutual trust.

December 3
A Living Witness: John the Baptist

The Advent liturgy presents us — and continues to do so — with the figure of the precursor.

In the excerpt from Matthew (17:12) the mission of John the Baptist is highlighted through a comparison with Elijah and his return.

To a certain extent, Jesus accepts the popular concept — current in His day — about Elijah's return, a concept based on the writings of the prophet Malachi and of Ben Sirach.

He accepts it but makes no clarifications. First, Jesus says that Elijah has already returned and it is in the Baptist that this popular belief has come true.

Secondly, Jesus understood that the way the Baptist had been killed was but a foretaste of what the Son of Man would suffer: ". . . Elijah has come already and they did not recognize him but treated him as they pleased; and the Son of Man will suffer similarly at their hands.'' From this Gospel excerpt we can deduce that the mission of the Baptist, of the precursor, is not just a proclamation in words but a witness incarnated in his life. It is an imitation of Jesus and a sharing in His destiny of suffering.

And each of us, called according to God's will to prepare the way for the coming Lord, must take inspiration from this witness in word, facts and life. So we need a life spent in charity, beginning from the Eucharist we celebrate, which makes us truly precursors of Christ and able in some way to prepare for His coming into people's hearts and into the different expressions of social life even into its most difficult and inconvenient expressions.

December 4
Serenity and Availability

The prophet Samuel arrives in Bethlehem, calls Jesse's family and says to Jesse: "I want to make a sacrifice." Later he lets the whole city know what he wants. He makes Jesse and his sons prepare for the rite and invites them to the ceremony. Let us read the excerpt from the First Book of Samuel, Chapter Sixteen, beginning from verse 6:

"When they arrived, he caught sight of Eliab and thought, 'Surely Yahweh's anointed one stands there before him.' But Yahweh said to Samuel, 'Take no notice of his appearance or his height for I have rejected him; God does not see as man sees; man looks at appearances but Yahweh looks at the heart.' Jesse then called Abinadab and presented him to Samuel, who said, 'Yahweh has not chosen this one either.' Jesse then presented Shammah, but Samuel said, 'Yahweh has not chosen this one either.' Jesse presented his seven sons to Samuel but Samuel said to Jesse, 'Yahweh has not chosen these.' He then asked Jesse, 'Are these all the sons you have?' He answered, 'There is still one left, the youngest; he is out looking after the sheep.' Then Samuel said to Jesse, 'Send for him; we will not sit down to eat till he comes.' Jesse had him sent for, a boy of fresh complexion, with fine eyes and pleasant bearing. Yahweh said, 'Come, anoint him, for this is the one.' At this Samuel took the horn of oil and anointed him where he stood with his brothers; and the spirit of Yahweh seized on David and stayed with him from that day on. As for Samuel, he rose and went to Ramah" (1 S 16:6-15).

I draw two conclusions from this excerpt.

First of all, David does not become proud. What do I

mean? Certainly he had been told, though he was not in Bethlehem, that a great prophet had arrived in the city. David knew he had gone to his house and that he had begun to call his brothers one after the other. We might think that David would have been envious and irritated: "Why did they not call me? Who do they think I am? They despise me because I am the youngest. They won't even let me see the prophet! They are having a good time and they leave me alone in the country looking after the sheep . . ." On the contrary, from the story we see that David did not give himself airs, has no pretensions and does what he is asked to do, saying; "The Lord will look after me." David is not an egoist. He is not quarrelsome or worried about himself. He lives simply and knows how to find the will of God day by day wherever he is.

And so he keeps calm and continues with his duty even if he has heard what is happening back home.

Although he knows his personal worth, David is a serene young man because he is able to live his daily life, entrusting himself to God. He is like Jesus of Nazareth, growing each day in wisdom, age and grace, in divine peace and in expectation of the moment God would point out to him.

This characteristic of David is paralleled by another one: he does not draw back. The same energy with which he lived his simple day becomes the will to accept a position which makes him superior to his older brothers. Faced with a most serious responsibility, he accepts it as a gift of the Spirit. "The Spirit of the Lord came to rest on David." He well knows that he is the youngest and is convinced that he cannot presume anything. However when the Spirit of the Lord is given to him, he receives it with total trust.

The question for us is: Who am I compared to

478

David? Who am I? Do I not run the risk of getting irritated, of getting worried when I feel I have been left aside? Do I become proud and harden my attitude when I am not central to the situation?

"Lord, help me enter into that peace which consists in having put my life in Your hands."

December 5
Ambrose, Bearer of Hope

It would be fine to enter into the heart of Ambrose to understand how he lived his mission as a disciple of Christ and as a shepherd, through what interior moments and what trials, lights and shadows his life passed. We cannot learn much from his writings because — unlike St. Augustine — he did not write a book of Confessions. But St. Augustine personally knew him and was later able to reflect on this knowledge. He helps us penetrate a little way into the heart of this holy bishop.

Augustine in a passage from his *Confessions* (Bk. IV, Ch. 30) writes: "I thought Ambrose was a happy man in the eyes of his people because he was honored by being such an outstanding person. I was unable, however, to know — nor could I experience — what sort of hope he was the bearer of, what struggle he had been called upon to undergo against the temptations of his high position, what comfort he experienced in adversity and what savory joys he tasted in his heart as he consumed in silence the bread of Your Word." Augustine distinguishes two aspects in Ambrose: an exterior one of a man honored in relation to the society surrounding him, and an interior and secret one full of a hope incomprehensible even to Augustine.

Of what hope was Ambrose the bearer? Jesus says: "I am the Good Shepherd. I know My own and My own know Me, just as the Father knows Me and I know the Father." The relation Jesus has with His own is not a simple relationship born of an immediate knowledge lived day by day and growing through encounters and conversations, but is a knowledge growing from the awareness Jesus has of the Father — an awareness rooted in the infinite fullness of the love and mercy of God. Jesus contemplated His plan of action towards His own as He contemplated the love of the Father. And Ambrose brought to his relationship with the diocese, to his daily encounters, a hope that came to him from the contemplation of the love of the Father and of the Father's project for his community.

This is the great grace we have to ask for all of us. You must ask it for me, as your bishop. And I ask it for each of you having responsibility, in the family, at work, in social, civil or public life. Each person has some responsibilities, some daily relationships of which an account must be rendered before God. And so an interior vision is needed, a hope which cannot be won by looking around and calculating circumstances and possibilities but can only be grasped — as the Scriptures say of Moses — if we are people who walk as if they saw the Invisible, looking upwards to the Father's merciful design for us, for our society, for this diocese, for our family, for the milieu of the people entrusted to our care.

From this upward gaze we can draw the consequences and directions for our daily behavior.

December 6
Struggle and Comfort for Ambrose

Augustine then asks himself what struggle Ambrose was called on to tackle. Occasionally, Ambrose speaks of this, referring to himself or to others in similar circumstances. For example, in a letter written in 379 he says to a confrere who had just been consecrated a bishop: "Keep your hand on the rudder of faith so that the violent storms of this world will not disturb your course. The sea is truly great and limitless but do not be afraid." If he wrote like this, Ambrose must have already contemplated the great and limitless sea of the society in which he lived, of the persons entrusted to him, and must have felt fear and a sense of his inadequacy in the face of that immense reality. But in this struggle for faith, he must also have heard the word of Jesus to His apostles upset by the stormy sea: "It is I. Do not be afraid." We, too, may be gripped by fear and upsets and have to bear interior struggles when we find ourselves face to face with difficult and worrying circumstances. It is then that we experience all the truth of our weakness and poverty. But, looking around us, through the violent storms of this world, we can hear the word of the Lord reassuring us, giving us courage and asking for trust.

"And," Augustine continues, "what comfort he experienced in adversities." Certainly, Ambrose was comforted by many external circumstances: by people who followed and helped him, by the goodness of those around him, by the assistance he received from many. But he experienced internal comfort even more. He writes, actually, in a letter to a confrere: "There is a river which overflows on your saints like a torrent. Anyone who has received from the fullness of this river, raise his voice, gather the water of Christ, that water which praises the Lord.'' These words refer among other things to the writings of St. John who speaks of the inner spring which, through the gift of the Spirit, gushes up in the heart of every Christian. By the grace of God, we have around us many reasons for comfort, for support, for help. But the fundamental comfort we possess internally, in our interior and contemplative dimension, in that reality of ours in which spring up the waters of the Spirit praising the Lord in spite of everything — praising and blessing the Lord in prosperity, in joy, in success, in adversity, in sorrow and in suffering.

December 7
The Savory Bread of the Word According to Ambrose

Augustine concludes: ''What savory joys he tasted in his heart as he consumed in silence the bread of Your Word.'' Ambrose filtered all his daily comfort through the pages of Scripture. For him the Bible was not just a book that one reads every now and then to draw an occasional inspiration from it. It was the book from which he drew every day and every moment reasons of hope and comfort for his life. It was truly, as he himself declares, ''a sea which hides in itself concealed meaning and the depth of prophetic enigmas.'' For each of us Sacred Scripture should become the book in which we daily seek hope, light for the future, and the solution of our deepest problems. But, above all, Ambrose found in Scripture the fundamental Word summing up all the others: Jesus, the merciful Savior Who has come close to us. In an explanation of the Gospel of Luke he, in fact, writes: ''The Lord became everything for you. For the suffering of your body, He became weak with the weak; He made Himself all things to everybody, poor with the poor, rich with the rich, weeping for those who weep, hungry for those who go hungry, thirsty for those who suffer thirst, lavish for those who have an abundance of everything.'' There is no human situation to which the Lord does not come close. And in the Bible it is possible to find, for any situation of ours whatever, the nearness of Jesus Who made Himself like us to give us comfort and clarity of life. He is in prison with the wretched, weeps with Mary, is at table with the apostles, thirsts with the Samaritan woman and is hungry in the desert. Christ is our life in all of its aspects and He has something to say to every facet of it.

And so we conclude with one of the most profound of Ambrose's hymns: ''To You, O Christ, I hymn the depths of my heart. May our ringing voice sing for You. May our undivided love, love You and our austere spirit find You.''

December 8
Mary, a Sign of Benediction

In this liturgical feast of the Madonna, let us listen to a truly impressive page of Scripture. It impressed me because, for the first time in the Bible, there is in it the word ''accursed.'' ''Be accursed beyond all cattle, all wild beasts'' (Gn 3:14).

The malediction of the serpent is a symbol of the malediction of all those things which ruin people. It impressed me because I thought of how many other times the word ''accursed'' has been repeated since, of how many times maledictions have been hurled in the world by one group against another, of how many times we have come to curse ourselves and even curse God.

Beginning from the account Scripture gives us, the sorrowful sign of sin and sadness entered the world and, so to speak, it persecutes us.

Maybe we do not always get to the stage of pronouncing that word, but many personal events — events around us and events in society — go wrong. We do not want them and they move us to rebellion.

We rebel against ourselves because we are not always what we would like to be. We rebel against others whom we consider the cause of what is wrong with us. We rebel against God, too, because we are unable to understand how much He loves us.

And so it is a terrible word which reproduces itself in human history as sin reproduces itself. Sin is the true cause of all the unhappiness, all the sadness, all the wars, and of all those things which in reality are the curse of humanity.

But the Gospel brings us the memory of a word contrary to malediction: ''Of all women, you are the most blessed'' (Lk 1:42). Said to the Madonna, this word is a symbol of the best in us.

We are not called to curse ourselves and others. We are really called to bless God, to bless life, to bless the future. The Madonna is the symbol of all this. She is the symbol of all those things we would like to be. She is the symbol of what we would like the world to be, of what we would like others to be and of what we would like society to be.

And so, as we pray to the Madonna today, we are praying with the best of ourselves, with everything that is good in us. We pray that this good may spread. We pray that what is in us, and is perhaps only a faint light, may become greater. We pray that what in us is a gleam of serenity, may grow.

We may wish that the Madonna might enter into our life with her benediction so that we can truthfully say: "You are blessed, O Mary, among all women! Make me share in your blessing. Grant that I may feel how much there is in me which can become part of your benediction."

December 9
Signs of Salvation For All People

God gives Himself to the world through signs and wonders. "In the beginning was the Word," not human searching and not our efforts to go to Him. In the beginning there is God Who makes Himself known through visible signs, accessible to the human mind and heart and to human searching. When a person reaches the fullness of self-consciousness, he need not demand on a specific occasion what to do or to say, but rather and principally what God says, what He says to me, what He manifests through the signs of His will. Human beings are hearers of the word of God and they fulfill themselves and their life by putting themselves totally in a listening attitude to the word of God manifested by Jesus.

Paul, in his Letter to the Ephesians (2:11-13) says that the Gentiles — the pagans, the non-Jews, those who were not children of the promise and so could be seen as secondary with respect to the divine promises — are called to share fully in the same inheritance as the children of God.

Every human being, without any exception, is the object of the divine salvation initiative. We can draw a practical reflection from this and express it with a question: Do I have, do we have, brothers of the first and second degree?

How do we see those who do not belong to our nation, who do not speak our dialect or language and who are nonetheless in our midst?

Do we see them as foreigners or as children of a call identical to ours, destined to share in the same heritage, mentioned with equal rank in the same testament of God and with the same love?

Should we presume to avoid war if we cannot avoid the estrangement dividing us one from the other and if we do not adopt this universal ecumenical spirit, catholic in the full sense of the word, which concerns all those called to the single reality which makes us children of the same human family?

December 10
Searching For Truth

We are all seeking truth, and so am I. We desire truth. We look for it, ask for it, want it at every moment of our life. And if I had to explain this search I would explain it, at least in my case, principally as a desire for authenticity.

Before the Lord I want to be authentic and that means that I want a correspondence between my words and my actions, a correspondence between promises and the execution of promises, a correspondence between what through the grace of God we want to be, what we seek to be and what we force ourselves to be in daily life.

We desire the truth. We desire authenticity. We desire that in our words, our gestures and our actions, all we say and do should correspond to what the Lord inspires us to be.

Let there be no rejection, no distance, no difference between what we feel and what we live. And so let us search together for authenticity. Let us desire it. Let us want it in friendly and fraternal relationships, in daily contacts among ourselves. And let us seek this truth with particular characteristics, characteristics which sum up some images I find in John's Gospel.

I seek, O Lord, a truth which springs like water, is simple as bread, clear as light and powerful as life.

December 11
A Truth Which Is . . .

I seek a truth which springs up like water; a truth I do not always have to be given by others; a truth for which I do not always have to seek external models but which rises from my innermost self; a truth which is continually renewed in me and in each of us just as the water of the fountain is continually renewed, continually new and continually reliable.

I seek a truth which is simple as bread; a truth which can be touched, can be seen, which does not deceive, which is uncomplicated, is not difficult and which, like bread, can be broken, divided and distributed to others. I seek a truth to be looked in the face, touched, considered and spread around in a simple way; not a truth one is forced continually to question, to ask what it means, but a truth which itself — like bread — tells us its substance, its ability to nourish, its reality as something concrete and immediate.

I seek a truth clear as light; a truth without darkness, without subterfuge, hiding places, hindrances or reticences; a truth to enlighten my journey and to enlighten also the journeys of others.

I seek a truth as powerful as life; a truth always able to renew itself, never tired of itself; a truth which incessantly raises us up from weariness, from lack of confidence, from lazy slouching; a truth which continually comes to life in us, a truth powerful as life and powerful above any other reality.

December 12
"I Am The Truth"

This observation, however, goes hand in hand with another one. I refer to a phrase of Romano Guardini quoted in the *Catechism of the Young*: *Not By Bread Alone*, a phrase which says: "Truth is weak, a very small thing can hide it and the most stupid of people can wound it." Truth is weak.

It is weak in itself because a slight thing can hide and wound it.

It is weak in us because our fragility continually questions it. It is so easy to dirty a fountain — just throw a handful of earth into it.

It is so easy to take bread and make it look commonplace, throwing it away on the road.

It is so easy to close one's eyes and not see the light.

It is so easy, unfortunately, it is so tragically easy, to suppress life. A little is sufficient, a gesture is enough, a moment of hate. It is enough to have a gun in your hand, a syringe, just a very few things that can suppress life.

Truth is fragile.

It is fragile as water is fragile. As it passes through the earth, each of us can trample on it.

It is fragile as bread thrown away.

It is as fragile as the light which need not be seen, as life which can be wounded and snuffed out.

It is not only fragile in itself but because it is put into fragile hands, it is put — as St. Paul says — into vessels of clay. And that means us.

It is fragile because it may, at any time, be broken, smashed, trampled on, forgotten or betrayed.

And so a spontaneous prayer comes to our lips: "Who will give us this spring of water which will never fail? Who will give us the simple bread of daily nourishment which we can feed on every day and which we can break for our brothers and sisters? Who will give us this clarity, like the clarity of light before which we do not close our eyes? Who will give us the power of life?" And see that the Lord responds and says: "I am the Living Water. I am the Bread of Life. I am the Light. I am the Resurrection and the Life. I am the living, unfailing water which slakes every thirst. I am the water springing up to eternal life. I am the bread of life and whoever eats it will not die. I am the light shining in the darkness which the darkness cannot overcome. I am the Resurrection and the Life. Whoever believes in Me, even if dead, will live and whoever lives and believes in Me will have eternal life."

December 13
"Lord, You Are My Truth"

The word of Jesus becomes for me and for all both a prayer and a profession of faith.

"Lord, I desire this living water. I believe, Lord, that You are this source of living water for me and for each of us. I believe, Lord, that You will never fail us, that even when we feel alone, lost, abandoned, thirsty as a desert, and when the journey appears too long for us, You, O Lord, will not abandon us. As a living fountain, You will refresh us at every instant of our journey.

"You, O Lord, are my bread. Without You I cannot live. Without You I wouldn't know where to go. Without You I wouldn't know what to do and what to say. Lord, You are my nourishment. You are the power giving me the grace to break this daily nourishment for others, too, for all those who ask me for it and in particular for this church. All of us will be nourishment for this church, for all churches and for the whole Kingdom of God. We, too, shall be the bread of the Lord, given away and even broken, chewed, made into a host of humility, if the Lord wishes."

December 14
"Lord, You Are My Light"

Lord, You are my light. Without You I walk in the darkness. Without You I cannot even take a step. Without You I do not know where I am going. I am a blind man leading another blind person. If You open my eyes, Lord, I shall see Your light and my feet will walk on the way of life. Lord, if You enlighten me, I will be able to enlighten others. You will make us the light of the world.

"I have placed you as a light to the ends of the world." You say these words to us, Lord, and we accept them because they are Your saving words.

Lord, You are my life, and without You life is not really living. With You, Lord, we see not only things but life and indeed the Source of life. Lord, You are the life even of those who are dead. You are the life even of those who have been killed. You, Lord, will be our life even in death. Lord, with You life is already in us forever. You are for us a fountain springing up to eternal life.

Lord, You are my truth. You are the truth of mankind. You, Father of Christ, have become my truth and in the Spirit each day You are truth in me. And You are the first, Lord, to make me human and to give me this truth. If You fail, if You go far away, I am not even human but a species of derelict, a species of shipwreck seeking salvation and not finding it, someone near death.

Lord, Your grace, Your truth, Your light, make me human. They are my grace, my truth and my light.

December 15
"Lord, We Ask You . . ."

We ask You this, Lord. All together we make our profession of faith before the whole community, before the whole Church and before the assembly of Saints, before the assembly of the celestial Jerusalem.

We ask You, Lord, that You make of us, too, water springing up for others, bread broken for our brothers and sisters, light for those who walk in darkness, life for those who grope in the shadows of death.

Lord, be the life of the world.
Together we shall approach You.
We shall bear Your cross.
We shall taste communion with Your
Resurrection.
Together with You we shall walk towards the
heavenly Jerusalem,
towards the Father.
All of us shall form the city of God,
the holy people,
the redeemed people,
which sings to God the eternal hymn
to God, Father, Son and Holy Spirit. Amen.

December 16
Awaiting the Coming of Jesus

St. Paul teaches the Thessalonian church how to live ''for the coming of our Lord Jesus Christ'' (1 Th 5:14-19). The Apostle does not chill the hearts of those young Christians who greatly felt the absence of the Christ they were expecting but opens them to the action of the Spirit as he preaches continuity and constancy (''always'' — ''incessantly'' — ''in everything'') and exhorts them to discern their actual situation: ''Never try to suppress the Spirit or treat the gift of prophecy with contempt; think before you do anything — hold on to what is good. . . .'' Faith is life and thus is a movement within fidelity.

So we must humbly and constantly keep on searching, attentive to questions and to objections, open to the practical aspects of people's daily life, the life of lay people immersed in the ambiguity and conditioning effect of the world, in their family, in their scholastic and professional lives plus the real relationships making them up. This is the life which has to be reached by the proclamation and so lead the listener to discern the real-life aspect which the Kingdom of God takes for him.

Christ is not a figure from the past but is risen, living this moment. The Kingdom of God is already here sacramentally and we are committed to building up the Body of Christ as we await its glorious coming. The Church is prophetic, tending totally towards its complete fulfillment. Tradition itself is not static but is integrated in the ongoing Church just as every person bears past experiences.

Each person must feel invited to enter into a great, ongoing story, where one who wants to can work to keep it moving ahead according to the program of Christ, together with His Spirit and with all those brothers and sisters who are with him now and those who went before him and those who will come after. All of these are alive because God is not a God of the dead but of the living.

December 17
Hope and Expectation

Hope and expectation: without these two virtues it is impossible to live in trust among ourselves because, all too often, this trust can be betrayed. All of us have had bitter experiences, tending to close our hearts. Only a great hope can open them, that hope which the Church continually reminds us of: Jesus will show Himself, Jesus will fill our life. We live in this expectation, in this reaching out towards a loved and desired future good, towards the manifestation of the fullness of the life of God in us.

If it is lacking, if it languishes, then an attitude of trust and of benevolence will be almost impossible because daily circumstances tend to destroy it in us. The lack of this expectation, of this hope, can be truly one of the great tragedies of our time.

If we get bogged down in the present only and yearn to enjoy it to the maximum, or if we get bitter because the present disgusts us and is unsatisfying; if we lack this vision of the future, this hope of the manifestation of the glory of God — shown now in the amiability of Jesus and which one day will be manifested in the fullness of the Kingdom — we can neither be the salt of the earth or the ferment of yeast in the dough. We shall be fatally led astray by daily experience, joyful when something goes well but sad and pained as soon as something fails to respond to our immediate expectations.

Jesus teaches us to live in expectation of the blessed hope, in expectation of the manifestation of the glory of our great God and Savior, Jesus Christ.

We await Your return. We await Your glorious manifestation. We proclaim it every time we celebrate the Eucharist.

Contemplating Jesus' crib, contemplating the amiability of God Who conquers our diffidence and fears, we also contemplate the greatness of the hope awaiting us.

Let us talk freely and openly about this hope, of future life, of the fullness of life in God, of the glory God is reserving for each of us and of which He gives the pledge in the presence of Jesus in the Eucharist. May this vision of hope illuminate our everyday journey.

December 18
Christian Hope

What hope is the Christian community called to proclaim as a monument capable of promoting a new mode of being?

First of all, we have to recall that hope has to do with something not yet possessed and not seen. Hope has to do with the future. It has to do with a desired and expected goal. So Christian hope has to do with the Kingdom of God in its fullness, with the future city — the one the Hebrew Bible calls "shalom" (peace understood in its totality) — the possession and sharing of every true good communally among people and among people and God, the perfect communion of God with the human race and of people among themselves.

This Christian hope is a gift of God. It is not earthly hope. It is not produced by us and in this sense it is a hope for everyone: for the healthy and for the sick, for the living and for the dead. Nobody is ruled out of Christian hope because it is founded in God Who never deceives us.

This hope is the terminus towards which the person of faith walks. This hope is Jesus Christ in the totality of His Mystical Body become real in its fullness. Moses kept his eyes fixed on this hope when he walked at the head of his people, as surely as if he had seen the Invisible.

It is the hope of Abraham who lived serenely among trials because — as the Scripture says — he expected a city not made with human hands but one whose Builder and Architect was God Himself.

On the other hand, hope understood in this way has also an earthly value in the sense that it strongly influences the construction of the world. If it did not have a correspondence in history it would not be human hope.

The vision of the goal given by God becomes then a stimulus and a model in the work of building up a human world which will have, as far as possible, the characteristics of this terminus towards which the Christian tends.

What are these characteristics?

They are the characteristics which are also frequently accepted and promoted by modern movements — apart from any confessional or religious context: justice, liberty, fraternity, peace, human rights and the consequent struggle with marginalization, hunger, unemployment and all the realities disfiguring the ideal image of the human city built in imitation of its perfect goal: the Kingdom of God.

December 19
Light Shines in the Darkness: The Darkness

If a word could give us some understanding of what is going to happen in our midst, perhaps it would be the word of John's Gospel: ". . . a light that shines in the dark, a light that darkness could not overpower" (1:5).

We are talking about darkness, about night and about light. We appear to see before us the Christmas scene where only the cave is illuminated by a tiny light and all around is darkness.

The darkness is everything in the world which is confusion, lack of meaning, self-sufficiency. It embraces all attempts to build one's life but beginning only from oneself, attempts at self-organization within our own poor and limited efforts. These attempts often lead to

496   DECEMBER

bitterness and desperation or at least to resignation as we see the many things we cannot do or reach. The darkness is in us and outside us: lack of reasons for hoping and for living. We drag ourselves along from day to day hoping for something better but it never comes. We try to distract ourselves with little, everyday, things but never reflect deeply on what gives meaning to our life.

This confusion is often very widespread. It is in each of us and it is amplified in society, in many surrounding realities and in many absurd things which should not happen, be they near us or far away.

And for this reason we feel deeply the suffering of the darkness of this world.

December 20
Light Shines in the Darkness: The Light

The light shines in this darkness. Certainly, this light is not a big one, but everyone knows that where there is a thick darkness even a tiny flame can be enough to ease our fear. All that is needed is a moment, a flash of light, to help us hope and to ensure that this darkness be not any more an irrevocable destiny but a reality in which we can live and walk.

This light shining in the darkness is not a chance happening but a personal and living power tearing us away from confusion and from nonsense to give direction, an ability to walk, move and see where we are going.

The light shining in the darkness is not an abstraction, a generic truth, or a simple exhortation to love each other. It is a living and personal reality. It is Jesus Christ,

Son of Mary and Son of God. For the first time, Mary the mother of Jesus understood everything perfectly and grasped that her life has suddenly acquired a completely new meaning, that the life of humanity was to be renewed in that Infant lying in the straw before her.

The Gospel tells us that this light has not been extinguished by darkness. Once it has been lit in the world, within us, in a family, in a society, there is no power on earth that can put it out. Darkness has no power over this indestructible light.

This light burning within us and which each of us is now invited to feel again internally, is the certainty that in Jesus Christ God loves this world of ours, this society of ours, and this city at this time.

In spite of everything, in spite of every darkness and every fear, we are loved by God in Jesus and we can give a true and constructive meaning to our life.

December 21
Christmas Is A Word For Us

The Christmas scene which we contemplate in the crib is wordless. We see Mary, the mother, the Infant and Joseph. Nobody speaks. It is a happening taking place in silence. And, even when the shepherds which the Gospel speaks about go to visit Mary, Joseph and the Child, there is no record of any word they exchanged, or any expression of emotion, of any verbal participation, of what they felt within themselves. It is a scene unfolding in silence but which, however, is three times called "word" in the excerpt from St. Luke. Indeed, this Greek expression in the original is so difficult to render that our version has given it three times with three different translations.

The text we have tells us that the shepherds said among themselves: "Let us go to Bethlehem and see this thing that has happened." But the original text says: ". . . and see this *word.*" We are told that the shepherds, returning, "related the word that they had been told about Him." It is interesting to note that the shepherds do not speak about what they have seen but about "the *word.*" It is also said that Mary for her part "treasured all these things in her heart" but the Greek text says: "Mary treasured all these *words.*" And so this event is presented to us as a word to see, a word to proclaim or speak about, and a word to meditate on and keep close to our hearts. Christmas is a word, an event which speaks, a fact having meaning. And its meaning should be interpreted and understood beyond what we may see or what our sentiments vaguely remember as we reflect on past impressions. Christmas speaks to us.

December 22
Christmas Is A Word of God

Christmas is a Word of God for us just as it was for the shepherds, for Mary and for Joseph. It is a Word of God for us who, like the shepherds, are expecting an event in the night; for us who, like Mary, want to rejoice over the birth of a Child; for us who, like Joseph, seek perhaps a house to live in for ourselves but cannot find one in which to begin a new family.

The word of Christmas cannot be quickly grasped or summed up, because Christmas is a beginning and it is impossible to understand its meaning fully unless in the light of Jesus' total life. His birth is the birth of the One Who, through His life, death and Resurrection, speaks to us the saving Word of God for humanity and the irrevocable judgment of God on humanity — a judgment of love. This Child Who begins to weep, and get excited and Who then begins to smile, is the Word Who was with God in the beginning. In Him, each of us is supremely loved by God, forgiven, accepted, interiorly regenerated.

Jesus in His mercy towards the sick, in His attention to the poor, in His predilection for outsiders and sinners, and for the rejects of society, in His ability to love His disciples and to die for them, shows that it is not true that everything is lost for humanity, that for tomorrow there is only skepticism and fear. He shows that death, loneliness and desperation are conquered by the person who accepts this Child, by the person accepting this Word — as the shepherds do — by the person repeating it joyfully to all those who approach him or her.

December 23
Joy, Liberty and Peace

The last word on human beings is that they are loved and that they are free and able to go forward to better things, to begin all over again with the Infant Jesus, to become as little children, to recover their experience of life and take up again the rebuilding of society.

This word of hope lies behind all the good wishes we exchange and is the truth of all the gifts we give each other. Even beneath our irritability, our quarrels, our inability to get organized during the week after Christmas, beneath the divisions which sometimes happen over little things, there is the immense desire to communicate, to love, to be understood and to be loved. The Child coming among us is the sign that God has opened the door for us towards this life-giving journey.

And so, even we, like the shepherds, say, "We want to see this word at first hand. We want to tell others what has been told to us about this Infant. We want, like Mary, to meditate and keep these things in our hearts so that they may not end up being just a passing impression but a flame lit in us which for the whole year, no matter what our other duties, will accompany us with the promise of joy, liberty and peace.

December 24
The Infant Jesus Is The Messiah

Jesus is the Christ, the Messiah promised by God, the God Who comes into our history, Who shares our human condition to make us sharers in His life and grace.

This is the Good News which the Christian community proclaims to all the people God loves.

In this sense we can say that Christmas is a late feast. At the beginning the Church first grasped the mystery of being saved and redeemed. It received Christ as Savior at Easter. It is the mystery we celebrate in every Eucharist, the mystery of redemption.

From that point on, the primitive Church enlarged its reflection regarding its roots, towards the beginnings of Jesus' "epiphanies." It began to contemplate His hidden years, the mystery of His birth. It found out that even in Jesus' first manifestations of Himself, those ways of being through which Jesus — as the Anointed One of

God — would give us salvation, shone like pearls hidden in the shade.

At His birth, the humility of Jesus appeared, His choice of poverty, the glory of the only Son of the Father: obedient, available, listening to the Father.

The Gospel account then takes up this profession of faith in Christ the Savior and Lord and, from Easter onwards, makes it grow until the moment when Jesus makes His entry into our history.

This first Christmas message, as the Christian community had handed it down to us from the beginning, sounds like an invitation not to cut anything from the story of Jesus' birth to make it express our human sentiments, even very beautiful ones: sentiments of poetry, of life, of struggle against poverty.

Beyond these things we are invited to approach the birth of Jesus with humility, allowing it to speak to us of something beyond ourselves, of messengers from on high, of a Lord, of a Messiah.

December 25
Jesus, A Gift For Us

The Church feels itself touched by this birth of the Son of God and here and now it expresses the power of His birth. As a mother sings because a child has been born to her, as a brother sings because there is a new sister in the house, as a bride sings for the bridegroom, as a woman sings for the man who fills her life, so the Church sings for Christ Who fills every human life with fullness.

The Church sings this night about the birth of the Son of God Who is our life, Who changes our existence,

Who touches the individual moments of our experience, because He takes on Himself sin, sadness, desires and hopes.

A story tells us that one day Jesus returned visibly to earth. It was Christmas time and many children had come together for the Feast. Jesus came into their midst. They recognized and acclaimed Him. Then one of them began to ask what gift He had brought. A little at a time all the children began to ask Him where were His gifts. Jesus did not reply but opened His arms to them.

Finally, a boy said: "You see? He brought us nothing. It's true what my father says, 'Religion has no purpose.' It gives us nothing, no gifts." But another boy replied: "When Jesus extends His arms, He means to say that He is bringing Himself. He is the Gift! He is the One Who gives Himself to us as a brother, as a Son of God, to make all of us sons of God like Him." And it is for this reason that the birth of Jesus is an event which touches each of us and touches our problems to help us see them with a new heart. We could remember some of these grave problems: violence, war, kidnapping, drugs, unemployment. All these problems have a common denominator: the laceration of human flesh, human suffering.

Jesus is among us to heal lacerated human flesh, to make it truly human. Jesus is in us to enable us to live these things humanly and with dignity, to open our hearts and our intelligence. We have to set out on our journey to Bethlehem to recognize this great happening which is in our midst.

December 26
God Reverses Appearances

God reverses appearances. We should reflect on the importance of this simple commentary: "God has upset human appearances; He has overturned them." Things seem to go in a certain way leading to diffidence, defeatism, lack of courage and a feeling of uselessness. We must not stop here. God is able to reverse our life situation just as He reversed the situation, the human judgment on Jesus' life. Note the importance of this principle if we apply it to many pages of the Gospel of Luke: "How happy are you who are poor . . . Happy are you when people hate you . . . When they drive you out, abuse you and denounce your name as criminal . . . Happy are you who weep." The Lord comes to reverse human appearances, to overturn unjust realities and suffering and to create a new possibility of existence with the things which apparently crush us. He comes to give us the space of a new world in these realities whose consideration would appear to us to be suffocating and revolting. He comes to create inside me, beginning from me, from my community, a reversal of values and so give a new hope to my existence.

All this can be expressed in many forms. I am aware that I am extremely distant from the reality of the kerygma when I say the things I am saying but I would just like to invite each person to enter into this reality and then to learn how to express it in a very personal kind of way. The upsetting intervention of the power of God Who raised Jesus up gives us new hope of arranging human life differently. In that very thing which now appears difficult, our resurrection, our passing to ways and experiences of unhoped-for life, can be immediately revealed by the power of God.

God Is Present

In his Letter to Titus, St. Paul says, ". . . the kindness and love of God our Savior for mankind were *revealed*" (3:4); then he adds that God does not offer salvation in virtue of the works of justice that we do.

Actually all people before God need salvation and nobody can boast of works. I, too, a bishop, need to be saved by God. Priests need to be saved by God, to be forgiven by God. All Christians need pardon and salvation.

Each of us is pardoned and embraced by the love of God.

St. Paul adds that we are "justified by the grace of God." And God Who in His goodness looks down on us, bends down over us, over me, pardons me, saves me and gives me the power of salvation. Each one of us must repeat today: this salvation of God is for me personally.

The Lord is near each of us. He opens His arms to accept us and says: "I am here for you, for your life. I am here to give you a hand, to help you, because I want you to be happy. I want you to have dignity and I want you to be free." Let us accept this Presence of the Lord with love and faith.

Jesus, Gospel of Joy

A reality very dear to me is expressed in the Gospel: "I have told you this that My own joy may be in you and that your joy may be complete." The purpose of the Gospel is to fill our hearts with joy.

When, on occasion, I hear talk of the demands of the Gospel and of the need to observe them, I think that we are blowing things out of all proportion because the Gospel is first of all joy, opening, certainty that we are loved beyond what we can imagine or hope. And so the Gospel offers the hope of giving to our life, no matter how humble, poor and hidden, a meaning of love and of service. It offers the hope that we can make something good of our life, something for others and for all those who wait to receive the manifestation of this gift.

Christian joy is openness to our possibilities. It is breath and enthusiasm. From this derives, evidently, all the rigor of evangelical observance. Because we are much loved by God, we feel ourselves urged to love others greatly: *Caritas Christi urget nos* ("The charity of Christ urges us on") and places in us a need which becomes a lifestyle, a commitment, a morality, a Christian tradition exacting in its manifestations but always, continually, rekindled by this evangelical joy.

On the other hand, when we fix our gaze on Christian moral demands, separating them from evangelical joy, they appear heavy and difficult. It becomes hard to explain to ourselves to what extent the Gospel leads us to love. And we end by putting on our shoulders a weight which not even we could bear if the great brazier of the Gospel were not burning within us.

For this reason I believe that the way of moral observance has its degrees. Only gradually do we succeed in grasping the detailed needs of Christian life, of the Christian lifestyle. We can come to understand it, a little at a time, as the Gospel becomes clear to us and we finally grasp the immensity of the love of God manifested in the crucified Christ.

Faced with the discovery of the love of God, one can

506

understand a life spent for others in an exacting rigor of service, of renunciation which in itself inspires fear and remains otherwise humanly inexplicable.

December 29
The Road of Hope

The Gospel tells us that the journey of the Magi is marked by a star. This star is the sign of hope in the world, a sign which all can see without becoming blinded. All see the stars, but not all set out on a journey, not all open their eyes and ears to interpret their meaning. The stars are all about us and they are luminous but we must have a heart able to understand them and to understand the road they indicate.

Many are the signs which Jesus gave us of His divine mission: His miracles, His death and Resurrection, the preaching of the Church, the truth of the Spirit, the presence of the Spirit of God in today's Church.

All the signs of opening and of grace showing us the right road in the world up to our time are signs of hope: the great generosity of many people, the great faith of the relatives of victims of violence, a profound and noble faith, full of openness towards the power of God in spite of the suffering of the present moment.

All these are signs of hope which each one sees from a personal vantage point and which are multiplied. Each of us is called to find them in our personal life.

And so the Magi set out following the signs along a road which — as the Gospel text says — is not always easy and obvious but has obscure and uncertain moments. Thus we have to ask for directions from others because we ourselves are no longer able to continue.

It is the tiring, difficult but wonderful journey of human beings seeking hope. It is the journey of humanity to God.

December 30
Jesus: Negative Sign of Contradiction

Two power lines run through the Gospel text of Matthew (2:1-13).

The first is the line of opposition. It confronts us with two contrasting ways of acting with respect to our search for truth.

The second is a line of progression. It leads directly towards the manifestation of truth.

In the first case, the line of opposition, we are faced with a series of contrasts concerning people, milieux, attitudes and situations.

We see the Magi on the one hand, and on the other we see Herod. Between them they are opposed, just as the sincere search for truth is opposed to a hypocritical resistance to truth.

On the one hand we see Bethlehem, a modest little country town; on the other we see Jerusalem, the city proud of itself and of its power.

On the one hand we see the simplicity and joy of the Magi, a joy which eventually becomes extraordinary and uncontainable. "The sight of the star filled them with delight." On the other hand, we see disturbance, suspicion, Herod's anxiety and the anxiety of the whole city.

At the center of this series of opposites we find Jesus — a simple and defenseless Child.

And among the many questions raised by this

picture of opposites, one emerges today with special importance.

Why is it that not only Herod, who feared for his royal power, but the whole city seems frightened and disturbed by this child? Did that city not groan under Herod's tyranny? Should it not have looked with hope to a new state of things? And why do the people themselves of that period seem to become accomplices of that laziness and resignation if they read Scripture correctly? None of them is concerned about going with the Magi to seek the Infant.

Can we not read in all this a painful fact of every age? And that is the power of passivity and incoherence induced by the dominant power. Even the Hebrews in Egypt, groaning under the burden of Pharaoh, did not bother to take the risk of shaking off the yoke which, though suppressing them had got them so used to a sort of comfortable life that they felt no need of taking any risks or enduring any fatigue for liberty.

We might ask from this point on profound and burning questions for our times too. What today can be called, in our world and milieu, a dominant power capable of putting people asleep or of distracting them from seeking the truth — that truth which is also the indispensable nourishment of human life?

If we had to point out in our case a dominant power of opinion and custom analogous to Herod's, we would probably not mention names of well-known people or clearly defined forces. We might more probably quote the phrase of Erich Fromm: "There is a specter moving about among us, but only a few see it clearly. We are not dealing with the phantasms of the past. This is something new: a completely mechanized society whose purpose is the maximum material production and the maximum consumption.'' This new, dominant power of our time, a deceitful accomplice of not a few slaughters of the innocent, certainly has other names but in every case it is linked to that type of life-organization, of culture and of the economy which all of us bear in one way or in another and which has, as a common denominator, a purely material view of existence. It kills every search, cancels every deep enthusiasm, is nourished by ephemeral sensations, discourages sacrifice and saving, laughs at gratuitous giving and at fidelity, encourages violence and abuse of power. It connives with every suppression of life which appears to be homogeneous with the cult of private interests and knows how to cloak itself with an appearance of piety.

December 31
Jesus: Positive Sign of Contradiction

How different and how much more consoling, on the other hand, is the picture born of contemplation of the ascending and progressing power line which the Gospel text also shows us. We are dealing with a human journey towards the truth and with the stages of this journey. The text speaks of the arrival of the Magi, of their enquiries, of a moment of uncertainty and doubt, then of their leaving, seeing, being joyful, entering the house, prostrating themselves and adoring.

It is a long process in which there is a human journey and a journey towards truth. This journey has a tension founded on unselfishness. No self-interest moves the Magi to seek the new-born Messiah. Nothing can explain their wearying journey, their sacrifices, unless the inborn

510   DECEMBER

taste for truth, and the mysterious and splendid attraction exercised on the heart of a well-disposed person by the appearance of a decisive certainty in human history.

The journey toward truth is not simple. It suffers various crises. It is expressed in various stages and successive moments, none of which denies the preceding one but goes deeper into it and faces up again to the essential question, almost as if one were always somehow not far from the beginning.

The question the Magi ask at Jerusalem — "Where is the King of the Jews?" — is the same one they asked themselves at the beginning of their journey though now they are just a short distance from their goal. But the nature of this search is such that human beings come close to it while still maintaining their basic tension in searching and in again facing up to new difficulties.

It is only in this way that one can explain, for example, a phrase written by Bonhoeffer from prison when he had long since admitted his belief in Christ and had suffered for Him and was going to die for Him. He wrote: "The problem which will not leave me in peace is to know who Christ is." There is an anxiety in the search which moves the one who has already found something towards new insights into the mystery and causes one to arrive at that "fullness of delight" which explodes when the Magi finally see the star again.

Stampa **t.s.g.** ARTI GRAFICHE - via Mazzini 8 - Tel. (0141) 54.286-54.702 - 14100 ASTI